Good Intentions Gone Awry

15 14 13 12 11 10 09 08 07 06   5 4 3 2 1

Printed in Canada on ancient-forest-free paper (100% post-consumer recycled) that is processed chlorine- and acid-free, with vegetable-based inks.

Library and Archives Canada Cataloguing in Publication

Hare, Jan, 1965-
  Good intentions gone awry : Emma Crosby and the Methodist mission on the Northwest Coast / Jan Hare and Jean Barman.

Includes bibliographical references and index.
ISBN-13: 978-0-7748-1270-2 (bound); 978-0-7748-1271-9 (pbk.)
ISBN-10: 0-7748-1270-2 (bound); 0-7748-1271-0 (pbk.)

  1. Crosby, Emma, 1849-1926 – Correspondence. 2. Crosby, Thomas, 1840-1914. 3. Methodist Church – Missions–British Columbia – Port Simpson – History. 4. Tsimshian Indians – Missions – British Columbia – History. 5. Missionaries' spouses – Canada–Biography. I. Barman, Jean, 1939- II. Title.

BV2813.C76H37 2006   266'.792092   C2006-902976-8

Canadä

UBC Press gratefully acknowledges the financial support for our publishing program of the Government of Canada through the Book Publishing Industry Development Program (BPIDP), and of the Canada Council for the Arts, and the British Columbia Arts Council.

This book has been published with the help of a grant from the Canadian Federation for the Humanities and Social Sciences, through the Aid to Scholarly Publications Programme, using funds provided by the Social Sciences and Humanities Research Council of Canada, and with the help of the K.D. Srivastava Fund.

UBC Press
The University of British Columbia
2029 West Mall
Vancouver, BC V6T 1Z2
604-822-5959 / Fax: 604-822-6083
www.ubcpress.ca

Jan Hare and Jean Barman

Good Intentions Gone Awry

Emma Crosby and the Methodist Mission
on the Northwest Coast

UBCPress · Vancouver · Toronto

In memory of Helen Hager,
for her appreciation of women's lives past, present, and future

Contents

Illustrations

FOLLOWING PAGE 102

Acknowledgments

Many people have made this book possible. Our greatest debt is to Helen and Louise Hager for deciding that Emma Crosby's letters deserve to be in the public domain. Having decided to donate the letters to the University of British Columbia Library's Special Collections Division, they asked us to tell the story of, respectively, their grandmother and great-grandmother. Helen and Louise Hager have encouraged us at every step along the way.

We are grateful to the Tsimshian of the Fort Simpson area, where the Crosbys had their mission, for keeping their history alive and making it accessible to outsiders like ourselves in various forms. Caroline Dudoward has been an invaluable support to us.

Brenda Peterson and George Brandak accepted the letters, photographs, and other Crosby family records into the University of British Columbia Library's Special Collections Division and generously arranged copies for us. Bob Stewart gave enthusiastic support at the United Church Archives at the Vancouver School of Theology. Margaret Houghton, archivist at the Hamilton Public Library, helped us to find out about Wesleyan Female College. Susan Neylan and Robert Galois shared their understandings of the Northwest Coast with us, Maureen Atkinson and Howard Aldous, their insights on Odille Quintal Morison. Sheila McManus and Chris Hanna provided valuable research assistance in Toronto and Victoria. Louise Soga meticulously transcribed Emma Crosby's penmanship, and Joanne Hlina proofread the typed copies. A SSHRC UBC Large Grant provided funding. Jean Wilson of UBC Press encouraged us at every step along the way. We owe special thanks to Atticus Hare and Roderick Barman for their patience.

Crosby Family Chronology

	BORN	DIED
THOMAS CROSBY	July 12, 1840 Pickering, Yorkshire, England	January 13, 1914 Vancouver, BC
EMMA JANE DOUSE CROSBY	April 17, 1849 Coburg, Ontario	August 11, 1926 Sidney, BC
JESSIE ASH-SHE-GEMK CROSBY HARRIS	December 23, 1874 Fort Simpson, BC	November 2, 1946 Vancouver, BC
GRACE ELIZA CROSBY	September 10, 1876 Fort Simpson, BC	June 21, 1970 Vancouver, BC
IDA MARY "POLLY" CROSBY	May 21, 1878 Fort Simpson, BC	November 20, 1879 Fort Simpson, BC
GERTRUDE LOUISE CROSBY	May 12, 1880 Fort Simpson, BC	August 23, 1901 Vancouver, BC
ANNIE WINIFRED CROSBY	March 29, 1882 Ontario	June 15, 1885 Fort Simpson, BC
MABEL CAROLINE "WINNIE" CROSBY	February 17, 1884 Port Simpson, BC	June 8, 1885 Fort Simpson, BC
EMMA JANE CROSBY	November 8, 1886 Port Simpson, BC	December 8, 1886 Fort Simpson, BC
THOMAS HAROLD CROSBY	March 7, 1888 Port Simpson	July 16, 1965 Vancouver, BC

Fort Simpson's Early Women Teachers and Missionaries

CAROLINE KNOTT

Born c. 1843, England
October 1876–October 1879: teacher at Fort Simpson day school
October 1879: married Charles Tate (born 1852, England),
    who was ordained in 1879, missionary Fraser Valley

SUSANNA LAWRENCE

From Toronto
March 1880–November 1882: teacher at Fort Simpson day school
November 1882: became a missionary to Kitimaat in her own right

KATE HENDRY

Born c. 1841, Brantford, Ontario
Earliest acknowledged woman missionary
July 1882–September 1885: matron at Fort Simpson
September 1885: married Edward Nicholas (born c. 1847, England),
    who was a teacher and missionary in Bella Coola

MARY ANN GREEN

Born c. 1863, England; sister to Alfred E. Green
?–August 1886: Teacher at Greenville, Nass
August 1886: married George Hopkins (born 1862, Chicago),
    who was a missionary in the Queen Charlottes

AGNES KNIGHT

Born c. 1857, Ontario
September 1885–March 1890: matron at Fort Simpson
March 1890: married Robert Walker (born c. 1865, Ontario),
    who was a teacher

Sara Hart

Born c. 1868, New Brunswick
March 1888–August 1894: assistant matron/matron at Fort Simpson
August 1894: married John C. Spencer (born 1859, Ontario),
    who was ordained in 1893 and was a missionary in Kispiox

Margaret Hargrave

Born c. 1872, England
September 1889–August 1890: teacher at Fort Simpson day school
August 1890: married William Henry Pierce (born 1856, Fort Rupert), who
    was ordained in 1886 and was a missionary in the Fort Simpson area

Kate Ross

Born in Toronto
July 1890–September 1891: assistant matron at Fort Simpson

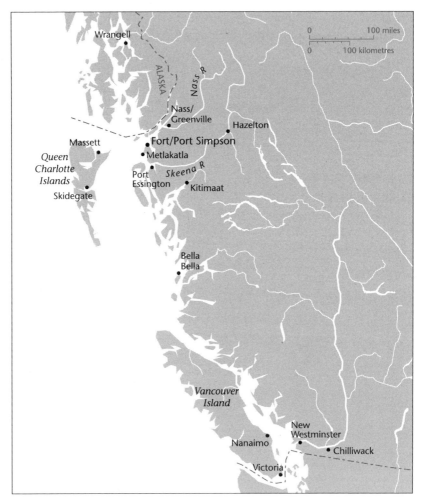

British Columbia in the late 1800s

Introduction

Emma Crosby's letters to her mother, so lovingly kept across the generations, are at the heart of this volume. Emma's correspondence begins just prior to her meeting the missionary suitor who would become her husband. The exchange of letters between mother and daughter continued from Emma's departure from Ontario in the spring of 1874 for the British Columbia north coast until 1881, when her mother died. The deaths of her mother and then of her father five years later slowed Emma's letters to her family to a trickle. To fill in her later years as a missionary wife on the north coast, we have added some of the public letters Emma wrote to Methodist missionary groups.[1]

Born in Ontario, the daughter of a Methodist minister, Emma Douse was early on immersed in her father's faith. Her training at Hamilton's Wesleyan Female College, an institution offering higher learning for women in literature and the classics, broadened Emma's social and intellectual horizons. She became a teacher, a craft that would see her through a lifetime. It is little wonder that Emma would find a place in the missionary realm. In her husband Thomas Crosby's words, "through the years that followed [her marriage in 1874, she] bore as important a part in the work in the far north as the missionary himself."[2]

A dutiful daughter, Emma maintained a close relationship with her family. She kept ties through written correspondence with her mother, sharing day-to-day events together with her hopes and aspirations. In one of the earliest letters that survives, dated February 18, 1874, she solicited her mother: "Would it grieve you very much – would you be willing to let me go to British Columbia, not exactly as a missionary on my own responsibility, but to be a help and a comfort, if possible, to a noble man who has been there working for years by himself."[3] While her mother expressed ambivalence, Emma embraced the marriage proposal. Two months later this young Ontarian teacher wed Thomas Crosby, already a dozen years in British Columbia, and headed west to spend the next quarter century as a missionary wife on the north coast.

Gender attitudes at the time prevented a woman from being a full-fledged missionary in her own right. She could assist, either as a wife or a single woman in some helping capacity, but she was not considered capable of preaching the word of God or offering the rites of baptism and marriage that marked stages in the life cycle. Missionary work was men's work, most often examined from their perspective, which doubly denied the nature and extent of women's involvement. Emma assumed the "feminine" work of the mission, which involved teaching at the school, caring for young Aboriginal girls, and creating and participating in social activities aimed at improving the missionary spirit.

Historian Dana Robert makes the important point that people expected more of missionary wives than they did of their husbands: "The missionary men were supposed to devote themselves single-mindedly to disseminating the Gospel in preached or written form. The missionary women were expected both to assist their husbands in the primary mission responsibility of spreading the Gospel and to evangelize the women, teaching them of Christ, enlightening their minds, raising their characters, and challenging their social customs."[4] Emma not only complemented her husband's work but also, out of necessity, transcended the gender divisions, ensuring that duties otherwise carried out by her husband were kept up in his many absences. Her varying degrees of participation in the mission demonstrate how the functions of a missionary wife went well beyond those of a "companion in the wilderness."[5]

Yet, it is Thomas Crosby who remains at the forefront in accounts of the missionary work he and Emma carried out on the Northwest Coast. He quickly acquired and maintained a reputation as a leader in the missionary enterprise among the Aboriginal peoples of British Columbia and Alaska. His long career spanned the time period when, as summed up by religious historian David Marshall, "the 'evangelization of the world in this generation' was thought to be within reach," and "mission work was regarded as the ultimate act of dedication to the cause of Christianity."[6] The two books in which Thomas dramatized his missionary adventures bolstered his reputation. His death in 1914 brought an outpouring of emotion. His was "a noble life, who like his Master, so loved God's Indian children that he gave his all for their upliftment."[7] Subsequent writers with religious interests and affiliations have followed suit in lauding Thomas Crosby. In conjunction with the anniversary of Confederation, the British Columbia Centennial Committee initiated verbal portraits of "Founders of B.C." and included Thomas among them. The culminating lines described how "his service, far from civilized comforts or medical aid, cost the lives of three of his children – but it won the hearts of the native people to his religion."[8] Clarence

Bolt's biography describes Thomas Crosby as "the most famous Methodist missionary in British Columbia, if not all of Canada."[9]

But Thomas Crosby's story, told either by him or by others, provides only a partial view of the missionary enterprise and its impact on Aboriginal groups on the Northwest Coast. A larger picture emerges when we account for women like Emma, who shaped the gendered practices of conversion attempts, and also for the Aboriginal people who as much guided this process as they were co-opted by it.

Following their marriage in 1874 Thomas and Emma Crosby headed to Fort Simpson near present-day Prince Rupert, where they lived among the Tsimshian people, whose territory stretches between the Nass (formerly spelled Naas) and Skeena Rivers. Intending to preach the Gospel and to teach the arts of civilization, the Crosbys were seemingly unaware that their invitation to go there rested on an extremely complex set of circumstances operating among the Tsimshian and the already established competing presence of Anglican missionary William Duncan. Aboriginal-missionary alliances served a range of purposes for groups in the area, where status, wealth, territories, and trade relationships marked their living traditions. Prominent local families, like the Dudowards, sought missionaries' practical skills and newcomer knowledge as a means of helping their people to accommodate to the dramatic changes occurring all around them. Missionaries relied on particular Aboriginal persons, often those of mixed-race ancestry born of fur traders' unions with local Aboriginal women, to ease the transition into the area and to gain the confidence of the local people. Alignment with high-ranking families of Tsimshian descent served to validate the Crosbys' presence. The reciprocal relationship that developed between the Tsimshian and the Crosbys was significant to the success of the mission and, though not always stated explicitly, coloured Emma's correspondence with her family through her years at Fort Simpson.

Emma was deeply invested in this relationship, which was maintained through written text, and she reminded her mother, "You must try and not give up writing, for, you know, you are my most reliable correspondent." And, in another instance, "Thank you, dear Mother, for being so faithful a correspondent. It is a comfort to be sure at least of a letter from you."[10] Her missives were a lifeline and provided one of the only means through which she could make known the motivations that informed her roles as mother and missionary wife.

Though these letters capture Emma's private thoughts and remain immediate to her experiences, she had at every point to make considered decisions about what to share with her mother and others. While her personal letters assured her parent of her safety in this far-off wilderness, she also took liberties to claim for herself a greater role in the enterprise than she would have done publicly. If always very aware of her role as missionary wife, Emma was also her own person.

Transforming the gender relations of the Tsimshian formed the core of her duties. Embedded in the text of her correspondence, as with that of other missionary wives and women, was the need to raise up Indian women from their supposed despair so as to make them good Christians capable of managing marriage and family based on Victorian models.

From the time of her arrival in Fort Simpson, later renamed Port Simpson, Emma extended her presence into the community, whether visiting in the homes of local families or teaching school and attending services at the home of the Dudowards while the newcomers' own home was being built. Her husband's conversion conquests resulted in increasing absences, positioning Emma as a maternal authority, which gives her reporting all the more credibility. While Thomas was away, often for extended periods of time, Emma organized mission activities, the only exceptions being rites of passage and Sunday service. It is clear that Emma found the loneliness difficult at times, but she accepted the responsibility to maintain the mission in stride, along with her duties to her children. It was to her mother that she revealed the true extent and nature of her work in Fort Simpson.

Giving birth to eight children, four of whom she buried on the Northwest Coast, Emma could not help but seek assistance from young Aboriginal girls. The challenges of keeping up the mission home and caring for her young children made these girls necessary. As a mother, she could model – in her home and in full view of the community – the expected roles for a Christian home. As Dana Robert explains, "the missionary contribution of the missionary wife was not merely to teach doctrine, but to model a particular lifestyle and piety."[11] The Crosbys' home offered great opportunities to exert influence, enabling Emma to train Aboriginal girls to maintain a home and family life based on newcomer ways. Aboriginal girls came to the Crosby home either on their parents' request or simply because no other choices were available for their care. Recalling the arrival of a "young half-breed girl, the daughter of a man in charge of the H.B. Co.'s store," Emma explained to her mother that the young girl's father wanted "her to have the advantages of better training than would be possible for her there."[12] As her husband Thomas described, "they would come, one after another, and ask the Missionary's wife for her protection; and thus one and another and another were taken into the house."[13] Emma accepted without question the need to protect the Aboriginal girls who came to her home.

In public representations of mission life, Emma was less assuming about the extent of her involvement in the day-to-day operations of the mission but no less modest about her good intentions towards the Tsimshian people and, particularly, the young Aboriginal girls who came into her care. She had no choice but to take the offensive. Common among missions was the need for financial support from "home" societies. Both Thomas and Emma penned Methodist missionary reports that juxtaposed their accomplishments with the vast amount of work that remained to be funded. Like most colonizers, they found it difficult to conceive that Aboriginal persons might eventually become good Christians in their own right, and this reinforced the need for a continued missionary presence.

In part because she was writing to comfort a mother about a daughter so far away, Emma's letters only hint at the Aboriginal contribution to the mission. Women like Kate Dudoward and the others whom Emma and Thomas engaged come across principally as model converts: exemplars of what it was possible to achieve so long as support was forthcoming. Aboriginal women's entrance into the mission fold was seen by missionaries more as a consequence of conversion than as a means by which these women negotiated changes in their own lives. Missionaries and their wives did not appreciate how, in the words of historian Susan Neylan, the "mission environment provided Native women with new opportunities to exercise power and influence, opportunities that were challenged or restricted in other social milieus" or how it fulfilled an "important social function for higher-ranking women, by providing a new venue in which they could receive public acknowledgement and sanction of rank and power."[14] By following up the glimpses in Emma's letters, we can discern the critical role played by Aboriginal and Aboriginal mixed-race intermediaries. It was the women in the community, and those whom Emma cared for in her home, who made possible her expanded role in the mission, propping up the position of authority that she gained at Fort Simpson.

The young Aboriginal women incorporated into Emma's daily round so that they would be able to understand what it was like to partake in a civilized home responded to her in ways Emma had not anticipated. Their companionship during Thomas's numerous, and sometimes lengthy, absences; their maintenance of the home; and their oversight of the Crosby children resulted in a mutual exchange of protection that facilitated Emma's greater role in the missionary enterprise – a role that without them may not have been possible. When Emma took notice of this escalating exchange, she set in motion events that would remove the girls from the Crosby home and place them within the formal institutionalized care that formed the core of the residential school system, which was then coming into existence for Aboriginal children across Canada. There were also pragmatic reasons to form the girls' home. The number of girls coming under Emma's care grew, increasing her sense of responsibility towards them. So after careful consideration she reported, "we decided to build an addition to the Mission-house which should serve as a 'Home' for the girls, and could be under our closer supervision, but entirely separate from our own family."[15] With these new living arrangements Emma could reconcile her good intentions to care for these young women with her primary concern for her own family. As a well-educated woman, Emma could convince those with whom she corresponded that her decisions were consistent with missionary aims informed by a colonial agenda that, in all aspects of life, set Aboriginals apart from newcomers.

The necessary funds for the girls' home were raised in Ontario, where Emma could depend on her family and friends, prominent in Methodist circles, to support her efforts. A native of Hamilton, where the Woman's Missionary Society (WMS) originated, Emma was successful in representing the mission and the much-needed work that remained to be done on the Northwest Coast. Fundraising gathered momentum, and the girls' home was built in 1880. The next year the WMS made a formal commitment of support, allocating a salary for a matron. The Crosby Girls' Home was intent on instilling Christian values and behaviour, which these girls might then replicate in their own homes, thereby reproducing the Victorian order. Still at close range, Emma could continue to act upon her good intentions by keeping the WMS apprised of the home's needs and accomplishments.

About Emma's good intentions, there can be no doubt. It is also the case that by the time she left the Northwest Coast of British Columbia with her husband in 1897, her good intentions had gone dreadfully awry. The girls' home, a mainstay of the Crosby mission, grew in its capacity to take in girls and to transform the mission order within gendered spheres. While spiritual and moral direction remained the home's goal, the means of achieving that end changed dramatically. The protection afforded to the girls transformed into confinement, with rules and structures dominating the operations of the home. Girls came under surveillance and were admonished to adhere to strict obedience so as to save them from what they might become should they return to their families and communities without a suitable marriage partner. Confinement was intended to prepare them, through example, to be subservient to the men who would become their husbands. Women might no longer be sold, as missionaries were convinced occurred up until the time of their arrival on the Northwest Coast, but they were still treated as commodities. In his memoir Emma's husband gloried over the Aboriginal women "who married into Indian homes in the different villages and, by their industry and cleanly habits in caring for their homes and children, showed the marvelous civilizing influence such work as ours may exert on whole communities."[16] Another shift in the school came when, in 1891, its administration was turned over to the Woman's Missionary Society, which purchased two acres at Port Simpson for a new building. The girls' confinement turned to incarceration.

We have tended to focus on the missionaries themselves as being responsible for the subordination of Aboriginal people. Emma's good intentions cannot be disentangled from those of her husband. Emma's letters reveal that the gender assumptions of the time determined that Thomas's actions and Aboriginal peoples' responses to them would have an enormous impact on what she was able to do or not do. At the same time, as a number of scholars, almost all of them female, have recently shown, women were no less complicit than were men in this colonial attempt to subordinate indigenous peoples around the world to the political, economic, religious, and cultural goals of newcomers. Most of the critical attention paid to missionary wives relates to the first half of the nineteenth century and to New England women.[17] Dana Robert explains how, during the second half of the century, another option opened up: "A phalanx of unmarried women built upon the efforts of the missionary wives and carried out works of education, medicine, and evangelism."[18] It is this shift, and its meaning, that has principally interested scholars.[19] It is almost as if missionary wives were worth examining only until something better, something closer to the male model of missionization, came along.

Emma Crosby's letters bear witness to the contribution of missionary wives. They help us to understand mission work as something more complex than simple tales of conversion on the part of men and women invested in Christianity. Multiple participants shaped the missionary enterprise, each of them acting on their own motivations, with consequences that no one would have anticipated.

Good Intentions Gone Awry

I

Courtship and Marriage

From her earliest years, Emma Jane Douse was aware of the missionary enterprise. She came out of a strong Methodist tradition, one nurtured in Ontario and in industrializing Hamilton. Her father had every opportunity to impress upon his daughter the Methodist doctrines that formed his faith and that lay the foundation for hers. Higher education gave Emma the training and skills that defined women's roles in the mission, making her a credible missionary companion. The connections she acquired from her family's social position and those she fostered on her own supported her transition to missionary wife. Though excited by missionary ideals, she was, at the same time, unprepared for the isolated north coast of a faraway province – a province that was almost wholly a frontier, much of it still largely occupied by Aboriginal peoples.

By the time Emma was born on April 17, 1849, in the Ontario town of Coburg, about thirty-five miles east of Toronto on Lake Ontario, her father was well established as a Methodist minister. His career paralleled, and reflected, the growth of Wesleyan Methodism in Canada. The denomination emphasized subjective personal experience over adherence to dogma. As summed up in one interpretation, "the supreme challenge was an experience positive, conscious, and thrilling, of the joy of Salvation and victory over Sin ... of the conscious living experiences of salvation from sin, [as] not only a right and a privilege, but a necessity." Once a "note of certainty" was obtained within oneself through an individual act of conversion, a second obligation kicked in, and that was to witness, to give "testimony before others of what God has done for my soul."[1] Such witnessing found its expression in evangelical campaigns, or camp meetings, intended to convert in quantity, and in the obligation to go wherever potential converts were to be had on what were termed circuits.

The missionary impulse at the heart of Methodism was responsible for John Douse's emigration to Canada. Born in humble circumstances in the northern English town of Hull in 1802, Douse was converted at the age of eighteen and five years later began witnessing and preaching as far afield as Leeds and Sheffield. In his early thirties he was taken "on trial" as one of a "band of English missionaries sent out to assist the Wesleyan Methodist Church in Canada."[2] He was posted near Brantford to, as he wrote at the time, "the six nations of Indians on this [Grand] River, the chief of which is the Mohawk, a very shrewd and haughty people, looking with contempt on the other Indians."[3]

The descriptions Douse sent back to England were also very likely the stories with which he regaled the young Emma. "Religion has done great things for them ... while most of the unconverted are miserably wretched, and lost in drunkenness and poverty." Douse became ever more convinced of the necessity of Aboriginal conversion.

> Methodism has affected a great change in the morals and habits of several among this degraded people ... I am forcibly struck with the differences ... The pagans are so degraded, by immorality, drunkenness and vice, they make no improvements comparatively, but live chiefly by hunting and fishing ... Christianity has done great things for them in relation to this, as well as, another life. You may soon find out the Xn [Christian] Indians. They are cleaner in their persons and dress; have better houses, and far more cleared land.[4]

John Douse's origins in no way hampered his rise within the Church; indeed, his modest beginnings typified Methodism's ethos and appeal. The "brusque manners" and "rough exterior" that others associated with him gave him a greater affinity with ordinary people – both Aboriginal and non-Aboriginal – than had he been born a gentleman.[5] Douse did so well as a missionary that he was ordained after just a year in Canada. Three years later, in 1838, he was received fully in the Wesleyan Methodist Church of Canada, which gave him the freedom to marry. The same year he wed Eliza Milner, a dozen years his junior and very likely a sweetheart from home who had waited for him to make good.[6] Rev. Douse took up the first of a number of positions that, over the next three decades, took him across much of southern Ontario.[7] He was clearly an ambitious man, and perhaps for that reason so fully sloughed off his origins that, when he visited Yorkshire later in life, he discovered that one brother "had been dead nearly ten years" and that another had recently died. He was told his deceased brother "often expressed his wonder at not hearing from me" or knowing where he had gone. In a long letter written to his wife Eliza in Canada, he reflected: "I never expected to see England again. There is something oppressive & melancholy in the thought & feeling under such circumstances, yet I long for home & shall be content to live & die in Canada - should the Lord restore me to you."[8]

Emma Douse's earliest memories were of the village of Barrie on Lake Simcoe, whence her father rode a circuit in the early to mid-1850s and, as was the practice for Methodist ministers, served as local school superintendent.[9] Emmie, as she was known within the family, accepted from a young age the notion that a preacher, first her father and later her husband, would travel to his parishioners rather than expecting them to come to him.[10] Chapels were locally maintained in anticipation of a preacher's periodic visits. Methodists "went to meeting," both to Sunday services, where they were exhorted, and to smaller ones during the week, where they were encouraged to give public witness to their religious experience. From time to time they might also attend outdoor camp meetings that were intended to revive religious fervor. A teacher living at the edge of Barrie wrote in his diary on a September Sunday in 1854:

> We went to meeting this forenoon. Mr. Douse preached a most excellent sermon. I think it was the best that has ever been preached in our (Victoria) chapel. Text Amos 4th chapter, 12th verse. We had a lovefeast and sacrament was administered after public preaching. A good number told their religious experience in lovefeast. I spoke; it was hard work but blessed be God, he enabled me to do it.[11]

Emma, together with her sisters Eliza, Annie, and Susie and her brother George, grew up in a family that took its religious faith very seriously.[12] Their father was not just any father; he was the Rev. John Douse, author in 1853 of the first register of Wesleyan Methodist ministers across Canada.[13] During Emma's childhood, respect for him grew across Methodist Ontario.[14] As his obituary later put it, "he occupied prominent positions, such as Toronto, Hamilton, Belleville, Kingston, London, and Guelph, and was for a number of years Chairman of the Districts in which he resided."[15] His reputation assured Emma a place in prominent social circles associated with Methodism and afforded her the opportunity for higher education.

No Ontarian community had a more formative effect on Emma than did the bustling commercial city of Hamilton. In 1863-64 her sixteen-year-old sister Annie spent a year at Wesleyan Female College, and Emma followed three years later at about the same age. Incorporated in 1861 through the efforts of Methodist ministers and Hamilton businessmen, Wesleyan Female College was intended to offer women advanced learning. While not universities, such collegiate institutions went beyond the secondary level. At Wesleyan Female College it was possible to earn a Mistress of English Literature (MEL) or Mistress of Liberal Arts (MLA) degree, the former by far the more popular, the latter emphasizing the classics.[16] The college's name harked back to 1854, when various Methodist groups in Canada united to form the Wesleyans; this group lasted until 1874, at which time yet another union created the Methodist Church of Canada.

Hamilton took special pride in Wesleyan Female College, which opened when the city was vying with Toronto for commercial supremacy on the northwestern shore of Lake Ontario. Hamilton's population, mostly British-born, climbed to 25,000 by 1871. Historian Michael Katz describes how the same entrepreneurship that backed the Wesleyan Female College was responsible for impressive civic buildings and fine private residences, a city hospital, planked sidewalks and macadamized streets, gas lighting, public waterworks, and a rail line.[17] Hamilton was becoming industrialized, with over 80 percent of its 1871 workforce employed in establishments consisting of ten or more people. Hamilton sported several foundries, three sewing machine factories, and a variety of clothing manufacturers. A business elite, among which could be found the college's backers, set itself apart from ordinary Hamiltonians, who earned from one dollar a day as

Wesleyan Female College, which Emma attended during the late 1860s

unskilled labourers to $2.50 a day as skilled labourers. Organized sports and recreation proliferated, as did voluntary associations. Historian John Weaver describes how crime and punishment in Hamilton became professionalized, as befitted a city on the cusp of modernity.[18]

Wesleyan Female College both reflected and facilitated these larger changes. Housed in an elegant 150-room former downtown hotel, the college attracted girls not just from Hamilton but also from across small-town Ontario and the northeastern United States. At the time Emma Douse arrived in 1866, it enrolled some two hundred day girls and boarders and sported a faculty of fourteen, who offered the entire range of intellectual pursuits considered suitable for young women. As well as taking classes 9-12 and 2-4, all students were instructed in penmanship, composition, vocal music, exercise, and could, if they wished, also draw, paint, and learn to wax fruit and flowers. Whatever the activity, they were taught "self-control, obedience to *principles*, and a conscientious regard for the right." The principles at the heart of Wesleyan Female College were, despite the name, not explicitly Methodist but general for the time. "Truthfulness in opposition to pretence in anything, patriotism, love of home, devotion to parents, simplicity, inartificiality, avoidance of *heartlessness* and *display*." For most students, this was enough. As did Emma's older sister Annie, they pursued a general course of studies and left with a certificate attesting to their attendance.

Not Emma Douse. She went where few students had gone before, and that was to pursue a demanding MLA degree. In her first year Emma studied Virgil in the original Latin as well as Latin prose composition, Racine in French together with French composition, English classical literature, logic, trigonometry, astronomy, and chemistry. The next year she followed up with Horace's odes and satires in Latin, advanced French reading and composition, more English classics and composition, mental and moral philosophy, and geology. Emma likely also participated in the Library Society, a select group of advanced students who composed papers that were read "at stated periods before the students." In the spring of 1868 Emma Douse was awarded an MLA, joining fourteen others who gained less rigorous MEL degrees. Emma then got a job as a school teacher. A nephew half a dozen years her junior recalled Emma "as a most beloved young aunt, full of fun, [but] when you were a teacher at that school & when you looked very much down upon little boys – I didn't like you quite so well then."[19]

Emma honed her skills and two years later, in the fall of 1870, returned to Wesleyan Female College as a faculty member. Its enrolment was approaching 250 students, and Emma was hired into the "academic" stream, intended for girls who "do not propose to graduate through the College." She was one of three instructors of a range of courses encompassing geography, grammar and orthography, composition and penmanship, arithmetic and algebra, natural history and philosophy, and bookkeeping. For the next three and a half years, Emma's life revolved around the college, its alumnae association (she served a year as its secretary), and the social life to be found with her five male and sixteen female fellow faculty. All but one of the latter was, like her, seemingly settled into a single life.

It was the urbanity of Hamilton and the rarified atmosphere of the Wesleyan Female College that the twenty-five-year-old Emma Douse exchanged for a mission life. Women and men of strong religious conviction did not question, at this point in time, that the missionary enterprise was the highest calling. For a generation and more, men and women caught up in the colonializing enterprise had rushed to convert indigenous peoples. The heroic tales that came back to missionary societies, and that were necessary to secure funds to continue the cause, heightened the appeal of missions. Written accounts from faraway lands made their way into mission records, gave nuance to church sermons, and were the talk of mission social circles that gave generously towards such work. Women who either took interest or became caught up in the cause through their voluntary work had more limited options for participation than did their male counterparts. A woman could marry and become a missionary's helpmate, or, as was only just becoming possible, single women might be accepted for the mission field so long as they did not interfere with the "real" work of missions but restricted themselves to women and children.

Fundamental differences separated missionary wives from women missionaries. Women missionaries gave up one life for another and received a salary for doing so, whereas missionary wives layered one life on another. Conversely, women missionaries retained the option to return to their previous lives, whereas missionary wives were in for the long term. They were expected to maintain the way of life identified with wives – indeed, they were to become its exemplars for the indigenous peoples in whose midst they succored husband and children. At the same time, by virtue of their gender they became caught up in the missionary activities viewed as women's work; namely, the care and conversion of indigenous children and women. This difference helps to explain "the relative 'invisibility' of missionary wives," to borrow historian Deborah Kirkwood's phrase.[20] Their contributions, and its printed record, have for the most part been subsumed within those of their husbands.

Most women imbued with missionary zeal saw marriage to a male missionary as the most practical means of realizing their vocation. They were assisted in their goal by the conviction within the enterprise that, for male missionaries to do their job most effectively, they needed to be married. Wives were considered essential to modelling appropriate behaviour to their indigenous counterparts and, at the same time, to ensuring that men did not, for any reason, become emotionally involved with their female converts. Emma Douse's upbringing, her access to Methodist social circles, and her advanced education made her a "suitable companion of the wilderness," to use Hilary Carey's phrase.[21]

The series of events that caused Jane Douse and Thomas Crosby to light on each other in January 1874 began to unfold a dozen years earlier. By the time they met, he had already demonstrated his passion for the mission enterprise that would enfold Emma in its embrace. Born in Yorkshire, England, in 1840, Thomas, he later recalled, "went to work at ten years old, so had little chance for school." Fourth of fourteen children, he emigrated with his family at the age of sixteen to Woodstock, about thirty miles west of Hamilton. He described how, "while working as a tanner during the day, he spent a good part of his nights in study" and was, as one account put it, "practically self-educated."[22] At the age of twenty-one Thomas underwent religious conversion after attending a camp meeting. He later described the process in classic Methodist terms: "Two weeks of terrible struggle followed this awakening. At last, one evening, while on my knees, the answer came, and I was enabled to believe that God, for Christ's sake, had pardoned all my sins ... My happiness was so great I felt constrained to give it out to others."[23]

A year later, in 1862, Thomas's new-found religious zeal took him to British Columbia at the height of the gold rush which had erupted there four years earlier. Previous to the discovery of gold, the future Canadian province was under the loose oversight of the Hudson's Bay Company, whose interest in furs ensured that it would pay little attention to colonization. Anglican and Roman Catholic missionaries tended to the traders and to their children, born mainly to local Aboriginal women. It was the gold rush that caused the first Methodist missionaries to be dispatched from Ontario, arriving in British Columbia in early 1859. Thomas headed off in response to an appeal in the Methodist *Christian Guardian* "urging the importance of Christian young men coming out to the West to labor for the salvation of souls." As he explained, "I felt it was my duty to go, and further that I feared if I disobeyed the voice of God I would lose my soul."[24]

For young men of modest circumstances caught in the tedium of everyday, such as Thomas Crosby, mission work offered status and respect not otherwise attainable. Perhaps his religious motivations were further sparked by the freedom of action and adventure that religious belief made possible. Lent the money for the trip, he spent his first eleven months doing whatever work he could find – rough carpentry, bush clearing, road work – to repay the loan. While still doing this, Thomas began to make his mark. At the first Sunday prayer meeting he attended in Victoria he shouted "Amen" and "Hallelujah" so enthusiastically that older members cocked their eyebrows at "that young fellow in homespun, who has the audacity to come in here and make such a noise."[25]

Taken under the wing of one of the early missionaries, young Thomas was invited to teach school in the Vancouver Island coal mining community of Nanaimo, whose population was made up of newcomers and Aboriginal people in roughly equal numbers. Teaching himself the local language, Thomas, in the Methodist tradition that holds that ordination is not necessary to spreading the word of God, also preached and held prayer meetings. Assisted by Aboriginal people he built among them a little church and mission house in the hope of encouraging a model village mimicking newcomer ways of life. A colleague recalled Thomas's self-discipline, how he would rise at four o'clock in the morning so as to spend two hours in prayer and devotions before breakfast. During the day he would stop wherever he found two or three people, attracting attention by breaking into a gospel song tending towards the simple and rhythmic, followed by some preaching. He was never satisfied to stay in one place for any length of time and later recalled making "trips from Nanaimo to Yale in a dugout, a distance of three hundred and forty miles."[26]

By 1868 Thomas had determined on a missionary life. He became a probationer for the ministry with responsibility for "Indian tribes." His preaching, sometimes outdoors in the long-standing Methodist tradition of camp meetings, gave the basis for religious revivals that enhanced his reputation. He travelled extensively, claiming "an average of two thousand miles annually in all kinds of weather, risking life and limb in order to bring to the Indian enlightenment and Christianity."[27] In 1869 Thomas was transferred to the Fraser Valley on the nearby mainland and, two years later, ordained in Victoria by the visiting president of the Canadian Conference headquartered in Toronto in what was the first such event held in British Columbia. His record of service was considered a sufficient qualification in lieu of systematic instruction in theology. Very significantly, ordination gave the right to marry.

The newly ordained preacher was granted leave to visit Ontario, a trip that made it possible for him both to raise funds and to get his private life in order. Thomas needed a wife as a role model for the indigenous persons whose conversion he sought, as a helpmate to assist with the tedium of everyday life, and as a protection against rumours of his being in too close proximity to female parishioners. The last was particularly important, given the stories dogging his Anglican missionary counterpart, Englishman William Duncan, on the British Columbia north coast. A single man, Duncan kept in his mission house at Metlakatla a number of adolescent Aboriginal girls to whom he was bringing the Christian message. When one of them, Elizabeth Ryan, married his missionary assistant, Irishman Robert Cunningham, Duncan turfed the pair out in an action that may have been revealing of his own desires. The captain of a Royal Navy gunboat that visited Metlakatla at the time of Cunningham's marriage in 1864 was aware of the rumours swirling around Duncan. "No white man or Indian has dared to breathe a taint on his name" for having "young women living alone with him in his house ... at the most critical ages," but it was, all the same, "a task that few young men would care to undertake" and one "not the best appreciated by the public."[28] The moral was that missionaries were better safely wed.

The need to return with a wife became critical once Thomas learned he was to go into direct combat with the irascible William Duncan. As scholar Terrence Craig discovered in reading through Canadian missionary biographies and autobiographies, "hasty, institutionally-arranged marriages" were commonplace. "Callow young men were fitted out with brides selected for their suitability to the missionary life, much as the rest of their kit was provided for them. Divine guidance was invoked for these matches, and who would be so presumptuous as to resist once the sponsoring bodies made their decision?"[29]

Emma Douse represented in her person as well as her firmly Methodist upbringing the ideal attributes of a missionary wife. Her granddaughter recollected her as "a small person, a gentle, kind type of person."[30] Emma was, friends from Wesleyan Female College later recalled, "a lady of cultured mind and retiring disposition."[31] Among her single friends there were Carrie Robertson in the Preparatory Department, French instructor Marie Séguin, and Marietta Stinson in the Academic Department. Emma may have been particularly close to Marietta Stinson, who obtained her MEL degree the same year Emma got her MLA. Also in the Academic Department with Emma was (Mrs.) Mary Wright, who, like the others, had been there as long as she had. Robert Steele Ambrose had been music director since the time Emma was a student, and his daughter Eleanor had been his assistant from the time Emma was hired. Also enmeshed in college social life were Methodist minister Rev. William Stephenson and his wife. At the helm of Wesleyan Female College since 1868 was Samuel Dwight Rice, a medical doctor and Methodist minister who had been the main force behind its foundation.

Emma's friendships at the college existed alongside a strong commitment to her family, which was scattered across Ontario. Rev. Douse retired in 1872. He and his wife Eliza and son George, five years Emma's junior, were undecided as to where to settle down. Emma's three sisters were married and so were subsumed within their husband's identities. Susie had become "Mrs. George P. McKay" and lived at Lefroy, north of Toronto on the south shore of Lake Simcoe not far from Barrie, where the Douse daughters spent part of their childhood. Annie was now "Mrs. Henry Hough" of Coburg; and Eliza was "Mrs. George Brown," living in Castleton just north of Coburg, where her husband was the local Methodist minister.

In a tradition of correspondence that Emma developed and sustained over time, we get our first glimpse of her in the fall of 1873. She was beginning her fourth year teaching at Wesleyan Female College.

W.F. College
Hamilton, Sept. 24th 1873

My dear Mother,

You will think it strange or Susie may perhaps that I have not written you promptly on this interesting occasion [of the birth of Susie's child] but there were so many things I wanted to say when I did write – so it appeared to me that I thought it best to wait till I had time to say them all. I do not know that there is anything very particular either but I did not want to write in a hurry and forget anything. I have not very much time now, after all, but I will postpone no further. I promised Miss Robertson to go to the John H. service this evening and it is not very far from the time. Well to begin, I wish Susie very much joy with her daughter – and trust she – the baby – may do honor to the illustrious family to which she is so favored as to belong – and especially I hope Susie is getting on well. Let me know as soon as possible, please, how she is, and things are generally. I want to hear from you soon, too, for another reason – of course I did not allow myself to be deceived by George's hint at twins – but Miss Ambrose firmly maintains that it must be there were two arrivals and as an oyster supper depends on it I am anxious to know the truth as soon as I can. Miss A. *says* she requires a certificate signed by the nurse and doctor, but perhaps your word of honor would be enough. I want some oysters very much only if I should have to give them I would be in no hurry. I suppose Papa is back by this time so I need say nothing of his visit to Hamilton. Annie and Harry H. came up by boat on Monday, and spent the afternoon and night here – leaving the next morning for London. Annie took dinner with me and they both were in college for tea and then we went to hear Newman Hall in the evening. It rained very heavily but the lecture rewarded us for braving it. Annie and Harry were well and in good spirits. They return tomorrow, spend tomorrow night in Hamilton, and take the boat for Cobourg Friday morning.

I was to have spent tomorrow evening at Mrs. Stephenson's but I cannot now. I called there the other day. Miss Baldwin of Ottawa is visiting them. It was to see her chiefly I went. I heard from Eliza lately – they were well.

My valise turned up all right so I am no longer in destitution. Papa was saying that Auntie had offered to take you to board. Would you like that? I suppose you could not go anywhere else now in Barrie if you wished to do so, and I dare say you would be very comfortable. I am sure you must wish yourself settled somewhere, and Papa even more. Could you not arrange things there and then go back to Lefroy if necessary? It would be very nice for Susie to have you so near and I am certain Auntie would glory in having you with her. You have plenty to occupy you now – I doubt not. The children will depend chiefly upon you, I suppose. How do they take to the little stranger? I would write to Susie tonight but I really have not time. Give her my best love and the same to all. Write just as soon as you can, dear Mother, to,

> Your affectionate daughter,
> Emma

The first, fateful encounter between Emma Douse and Thomas Crosby grew out of his other task while in Ontario, apart from finding a wife, which was to raise money for the missionary cause. With the blessing of the Toronto Conference, which had authority over western Canada, including British Columbia, he and fellow missionary Egerton Ryerson Young travelled together to solicit support. The two turned up at Wesleyan Female College to plead their cause in late January 1874.

Hamilton Feb. 9th, 1874

My dear Mother,

It seems so long since I wrote to you that I will not let tonight pass without a letter to you however short it may be. It is late and I am very tired, so it will not likely amount to much. I got your letter in due time, and heard from Susie that you and Auntie were going down to Lefroy. Susie must have had a hard time with only a little girl [to help her]. I have heard from Annie and Eliza too lately. Eliza was to be in Cobourg tonight for the Miss[ionary]. meeting & to stay a few days. Annie was not very well when she wrote. It seems too bad that Eliza's best friends should be leaving Castleton – they will miss them so much. Our Miss. meetings were two weeks ago – both the returned missionaries were here & the meetings were really very interesting & quite enthusiastic. You have not heard either of them have you? They were in the college one afternoon & addressed the school. I spent an evening at Mr. [William Eli] Sanford's lately very pleasantly – the last few weeks have been so busy I have not known what to do. We have a good deal of sewing on hand in a Dorcas Society we have in the college and that does not leave some of us much time – my incentive has been more useful within the last few weeks than ever before. We have good sleighing now – I have had several good drives but not since the last snow came. I am glad to hear of your cloak – I should think it would be quite pretty.

A new term begins this week and quite a number of new students are coming in so the school promises to be very full. I wish I could write more but must not. Let me know when you go to Susie's. Do write soon. Love to Auntie & Sallie & with much for yourself & my father.

> Believe me, dear Mother,
> Yours affectionately
> Emma

At the time Emma and Thomas first caught sight of each other, she was in her mid-twenties, he almost a decade older. Thomas personified everything a missionary was meant to be, as Emma would have been aware from her involvement with missionary activities at the college. A man who met Thomas about the same time recalled, forty years later, how "I was much impressed by his manliness, his strength, his unselfishness, and his devotion to his work."[32] Thomas Crosby was a missionary's missionary.

Emma Douse's way of life at the Wesleyan Female College and in urbane Hamilton was, at the same time, not of Thomas's experience. He was "lacking in the culture that colleges give," recalled the preacher who first befriended him in Victoria. "No matter where he was the decorum of any gathering was liable to be gloriously punctuated by irrepressible 'Amens' and 'Hallelujahs.'" A longtime acquaintance described him as "honest, bluff, breezy, big-hearted." He was, one view has it, "possessed of a remarkable voice and a commanding and magnetic personality."[33] Thomas Crosby knew what he wanted, and it was now Emma Jane Douse.

The courtship between the two was helped along by intermediaries. William Eli Sanford, at whose home Emma spent a pleasant evening, was a prominent Hamilton manufacturer. He was president of the Wesleyan Female College's board of directors and very interested in mission work in British Columbia. An earlier visit to Victoria had impelled him to contribute $500 a year towards missionary work in its "China Town."[34] Sanford was likely not troubled by the couple's differences in background. The missionary rhetoric associated with Thomas gave him a status overshadowing his lack of personal attributes. His humble origins and brash exterior were not so very different from those of Emma's father, a similarity she likely also observed. Both men were driven, as was Sanford, to save what they perceived to be "heathen" souls – a goal in which Emma shared.

Not only that, but also, as Thomas later put it, "the Macedonian cry, 'Come over and help us,' comes from Fort Simpson, where I am recommended by the District Meeting to go and start a new Mission."[35] The notice of his new posting on the British Columbia north coast hurried events along, so Thomas recalled in his memoir. "When we learned that instead of returning to my loved field among the Ankonenums [in the Fraser Valley] we were appointed to the remote work at Fort Simpson, on the borders of Alaska, six hundred miles away from civilization, she offered no objections, but, like a true, devoted follower of Christ, said she was ready to go."[36]

Emma had every encouragement to acquiesce to Thomas's needs and desires. The letter she wrote her mother in mid-February, a little over a week after describing her first encounter with Thomas, indicates that she had already made up her mind.

Hamilton Feb. 18th 1874

My dear Mother,

You will not be expecting a letter from me again so soon, but I have something particular to write about today and I do not think I ought to postpone doing so any longer. I put off writing the last thinking I might be prepared to say what I am going to say now – but I did not feel as though I could mention it then. I fancy I hear you say just here – "O! My! What a girl she is – in some trouble again I suppose." I do not think it is going to be my <u>trouble</u> – I hope not but really, Mother dear, I do feel badly to have to say anything to you about it – but you must know – and the sooner, perhaps, the better. Now, dear Mother, it is just this I want to ask you & my father – would it grieve you very much – would you be willing to let me go to British Columbia, not exactly as a missionary on my own responsibility, but to be a help and a comfort, if possible, to a noble man who has been there working for years by himself. You know who it is I mean – I wish you had seen him yourself and heard him speak – but you remember what Eliza said about him, and I believe your confidence in him would be as strong as mine if you did know him. I know it would be a very serious undertaking to go there – a great deal both for ourselves and others, might – would depend upon it, and yet the conviction grows upon me that I might be both happy & useful – perhaps more so there than anywhere else. Only one view of it troubles me and that is in reference to yourself & my father. If you were to be less happy for the want of what I might give if I were with you – then I do not think I could feel sure it would be right for me to go. I have not given my promise yet and shall not do so until I hear from you. Let me know, Mother dear, just how you feel about it as soon as you can. Of course there would not be much time for preparation, perhaps not longer than till May and it would be, likely, a good many years before I could come back even for a visit. You will think, perhaps, Mamma that I have been very hasty – I saw Mr. Crosby for the first time four weeks ago next Monday but things are no less safe, although hasty, when they rest, as I firmly believe this does, with higher wisdom than our own. We have met a number of times, last evening we spent together in the college here, and have talked about it as fully as could be. Do not think either that I am carried away by the romance of the thing – I would not go one step if I believed that to be what influenced me. I have thought calmly about it, and while my own feelings prompt me to go, I do not trust to them alone, and whether I go or stay I shall take all to be well. I wish I could talk to you about it – but I think you will understand the matter. Let this be, at least for the present, between ourselves alone. I have not said a word on the subject to the girls so, please, do not mention it to them or anyone else. I expect Mr. C. here next Thursday. If I could have some word from you before then I should be very glad, but take your own time about answering.

I believe we should love each other and you know that would make up for so many wants in other ways. Now, Mother dear, forgive me if I give you trouble and anxiety, and with much love to yourself and my father,

> Believe me
> Your affectionate daughter
> Emma

Emma needed her mother's approval in order to go ahead. Eliza Douse's letters to her daughter do not survive, but the tone of Emma's next letter suggests a certain degree of reticence on her mother's part. At the same time, the Douses had no alternative but to permit their daughter to follow what they must have believed was God's will for her.

Hamilton Feb. 27th 1874

My dear Mother,

I cannot tell you how glad I was to get your letter Wednesday evening – thank you very, very much for writing so promptly. I know it is hard for you and there seems to be so little time to think about it and get used to the idea. I could wish that this were different – but I feel sure that all will be right, however it may seem now – I believe firmly that a blessing will rest upon my life, and I do hope you and my father will feel that there is nothing to fear. I shall be taken care of wherever I am.

Then I think, dear Mamma, that you have an exaggerated idea of the privations to be undergone, if so you like to call them. I shall likely have a comfortable enough home and all that is necessary to my happiness. Mr. Crosby was here last night and, dear Mamma, we settled it then – it was not wrong, was it? You know the time is so short and it was not right for either of us to leave it

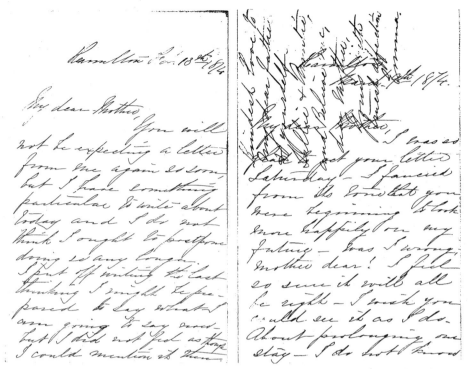

Two samples of Emma's letters, dated February 18, 1874 (left), and March 9, 1874 (right)

undecided. Till the early part of May will likely be the longest we can stay, though it is just possible we may remain till after [the Methodist Church's annual] Conference. I told Dr. Rice about it today. He spoke very kindly indeed, without discouraging it at all and promises to relieve me as soon as it is possible to do so. I shall need all the time I can get for preparation. I should like to be with you in two or three weeks if I could.

Tell Auntie about it if you think best. I do not want it talked about any more than is necessary but I do not suppose it would be possible to keep it a secret. Mr. Crosby sends kind regards & will see you as soon as he can. Write again soon. With truest love to yourself and my father.

> Believe me, dear Mother,
> Ever your affectionate daughter
> Emma

The public announcement of Emma Jane Douse's engagement was made at Centenary Church in Hamilton at a meeting where Thomas Crosby made his usual pitch for financial support. The announcement was itself part of the missionary phenomenon. While the collection was being taken following Thomas's appeal, fervent missionary supporter William Eli Sanford told the assembled throng that, as soon as a thousand dollars was subscribed towards Fort Simpson, he would reveal an important secret. Having secured the goal, he announced that "a young lady in that corner is going out with the missionary."[37] An observer recalled his words: "Miss Douse, one of the teachers in the Ladies College, who is down at the corner with the college girls, is my secret. She is going to marry Mr. Crosby and go with him to his far-off field in Northern British Columbia."[38] The excitement was so great, the story goes, the money just kept pouring in.

Hamilton
March 9th 1874

My dear Mother,

I was so glad to get your letter Saturday. I fancied from its tone that you were beginning to look more happily on my future – was I wrong, mother dear! I feel so sure it will all be right. I wish you could see it as I do. About prolonging our stay – I do not know that it would be best even could it be done, which is doubtful. I would not urge it myself. I will explain why when I see you. There is a lady here already who is to take my work – and tomorrow will be my last day in the school.

It will be well for me, I think to remain ten days longer in the college. I want time to say good-bye to everyone – and to give out some dress-making – that grey silk might as well be made up, I suppose and I want to get a black one. I can get it at wholesale price and both had better be made here. I shall keep myself supplied with work as long as I am here. I scarcely see how everything is to be got ready but mean to manage it somehow or other. I wrote to Susie to know if George could meet me in Toronto so that I could get there pretty much all I want. Will you let me know Mamma, what you think I will want most, and what resources I may expect to have to draw upon, if I get knives & forks or anything of that kind. I might get them in Toronto – better than elsewhere. Thank Auntie & Sallie for their kind offer of help. I think I shall make most of my preparations in Barrie. Will you write immediately, Mamma, please, and let me know what you think about all these things.

Kindest love to my dear father & yourself, Sallie & Auntie, and Believe me, dear Mother,

Yours with truest affection
Emma

Events now proceeded at a breakneck pace. A very efficient Emma took charge. Her family became her helpmates rather than the other way around, as it had been previously.

Hamilton
March 11th 1874

My dear Mother,

I am troubling you again – I write on business this morning. The time promises now to be very short before we leave for the west. Mr. C. was here last night – and it is almost certain the 1st May will be the latest – no time must be lost. I want to get dress-making done here – and my time is altogether my own now so that I can sew all day. So I think it will be best to stay here till the end of next week. I shall take that grey silk today to be made & also a black lustre – as to the black silk I hope I shall be able to get it. It would be so useful for years perhaps – but I shall wait till I know how much I shall have to draw upon – then I shall need a travelling dress & some dark prints & perhaps winceys.[39] These last can be made in Barrie.

I wish very much, Mamma if it will not give you too much trouble you would begin at once to get house-linen ready for me. Get some woman to do this sewing for you. You know, Mamma, I should like to take as many things with me as possible. Everything will be so expensive there as well as difficult to get where we shall likely be. Sheets, pillow cases &c. – the more the better. I should like them too, Mamma, quite as nice as though I were going to live in Ontario, all the comfort & refinement of my life, I suppose, I mean that kind of comfort will be in my own home, & I do not mean to be careless or slip-shod in my own house. And, Mamma, I am a great beggar – but could you send me twenty or thirty dollars this week to keep me going. I have not been paid up yet. Write, please the day you get this, and with much love,

Believe me, dear Mother
Yours affectionately
Emma

Having given their consent, the Douses did all they could to make the marriage happen in the fashion desired by their only still unwed daughter. In turn, Emma continued to cajole them into providing the whole-hearted acceptance she so much wanted them to give.

Hamilton
March 13th 1874

My dear Mother,

I was so glad to get your letter this morning. Many thanks for all the trouble
you are taking and to my father for the money – it was more than I expected
or shall need before I get home. Dear Mamma, I do wish quite as much as you
that I was with you. But, besides the dress making I have to have some den-
tistry finished next week which will keep me over Tuesday and if I wait till
Saturday Miss [Marie] Séguin & Miss [Marietta] Stinson will come to Toronto
with me – so I think I will fix that as the day of my leaving. Mr. C may come up
with me. I am not sure – if not then very soon after. I dare say it is not worth
while for [brother-in-law] George McKay to meet me in T. I think I will stop
at Lefroy on my way up, if you can be there. I want to see you and my father as
soon as ever I can. We can talk things over then at length – it will be a good
deal of expense to take much with us – but for all but large heavy things less
than the difference of the price, here & there. It is very kind of Papa to place so
much at my disposal as he has – it will be ample for all I want. I do not like to
think of taking your things Mamma for fear you should want them again. I
think this is all I need say about these things now – I don't feel like writing
business today.

Dear Mamma, I do hope you and my father are feeling quite reconciled and
happy about my future. I am so sure it will all be right, and can trust for all I
shall need. You can trust for me too – can you not, Mother dear? I wish you
would write to Georgie about it. This morning I had a letter from him. He
feels very bitterly about it and speaks of my grieving you & my father. Surely
you do not feel that my going is wrong – only that I think would really grieve
you.

Love to Auntie & Sally. With dearest affection for yourself and my dear
father,
dear Mother, I am,
Yours as ever,
Emma

Miss [Carrie] Robertson sends love

The enthusiasm Emma hoped would come her way from her family may have
been tempered even among her friends. A third of a century later, Maria Orme
Allen, a classmate who taught literary criticism when Emma was on staff,
recalled how a mutual acquaintance, whose husband was on the college's board

of directors, "said with great chagrin – 'Emma Douse is buried! How could her friends consent!'" She remembered Emma as being, at the time, "a lovely girl consecrated to Christ and His Cause."[40]

Emma took any criticism, implied or overt, in stride. A nephew who knew Emma well over the years recalled her outlook as she was "about to leave ... for Port Simpson." According to her sister Eliza's son Henry: "You weren't a tiny bit afraid. None of John Douse's offspring have ever had any fear. There must have been something in the blood of us, Aunt, that we derived from the great old man, my grandfather."[41]

Emma Douse married Thomas Crosby in the home of her sister Annie and brother-in-law Henry Hough in Coburg on April 30, 1874. Thomas gave his address on the marriage registry as Fort Simpson; Emma, harking back to her childhood, gave hers as the "Town of Barrie," in Simcoe County, Ontario.[42] Her father assisted at the ceremony, which was witnessed by her brother-in-law Henry Hough and sister Eliza Brown.

The next phase in Emma's life began with her journey west. The Canadian Pacific Railway linking Ontario to British Columbia would not be completed for another dozen years. The newlyweds travelled by train across the central United States.

Waukegan [Illinois] May 9th 1874

My dear Mother,

It is rather late but I write a few lines. You and father will be looking for some word from us and then I want to write for my own satisfaction also. I do trust you are feeling happy and cheerful as many, many times I have thought of you both and hoped and prayed that you might be kept in peace. Our way hitherto has been prosperous. We have much – very much – to be thankful for. Mrs. Sanford met us at the station in H[amilton]. and we went with her for dinner. Mr. S. was away then down to the college. Every one was so kind and very cheery that it was not at all so trying as we had thought. Ever so many of them came to the depot with us. Mrs. S. gave me a doz. silver tea spoons, the last of my many gifts. We came on to Ingersoll [where Thomas Crosby's parents lived] Thursday evening – it was late when we reached our destination and the next day was a busy one. I was sorry we could not have more time there. Then we took the train for Chicago – and came through, reaching Waukegan this morning about eleven. Uncle & aunt came to meet us – they are very kind. We had a row on the pond this evening. Mr. C. preaches tomorrow morning. The minister met us at this station with uncle. Do not feel anxious Mother dear about me. I have been kept in such quiet trust that the excitement & fatigue

have not affected me much & I feel really quite well. Love to Auntie & Sallie
and believe me dear Mother of the fondest affection of,

>   Your daughter.
>   Emma

We leave Monday morning likely between seven and eight to catch the
western train in Chicago. My thoughts are with you both. Love to my dear
father. E.

Sunday night

                                        May 10th

My Dear Mrs. Douse, Emma says I may write a word on the back of her letter.
We have so far had a very happy and prosperous journey. And my dear Emma
has been so happy and well amidst it all that I feel God has truly been with us
to sustain us. We had a very happy day today. Uncle and all have made it so
pleasant for us. I preached twice today and God was with us. We leave for the
West tomorrow morning (D.V.), and will write you again soon. Love to Father
and Aunt & Sally & all.

>   Yours affectionately
>   T. Crosby

   Through her letters, Emma did what she could to reconcile her family to the
lengthening distance between them. They also gave her an opportunity to name
Thomas on paper as "my husband." She sometimes termed him "Mr. C.," which,
in the style of the day, would become, increasingly, "Mr. Crosby."

                                        Union Pacific Railroad
                                        Nebraska May 12th 1874

My dear Mother,

I am going to send you a few lines today though they can only be written with
a pencil. Our way still has been pleasant and prosperous. I was really sorry we
could not remain longer at Waukegan. Uncle and Belle & Louise came to the
train with us yesterday morning. Uncle expressed his good will by giving his
niece twenty dollars. The girls talk seriously about coming out to Fort
S[impson]. The weather has been all that could be desired – it rained enough
last night to lay the dust. The country we have passed through is pleasant,

mostly prairie. Several fine towns and numerous villages. We spent about an hour and a half in Omaha this morning – such crowds of travelers, quantities of luggage, the time was all occupied in getting them arranged. We brought quite a reinforcement of provisions from Waukegan. My husband tells me I am to say that I stand the journey better than he does. I do bravely according to his opinion. It is very easy when I have nothing to do but be made comfortable & have some one to think of everything for me. I have slept splendidly, better than he has done. He took a cold & has had a slight sore throat since yesterday. I have seen since leaving Omaha a new sight to me – prairie grass on fire – no very extensive burning however. The train by which we meant to send this has just passed so I will have to keep it till tomorrow.

Pine Bluffs (75 miles from Omaha) – Wednesday near noon. Since I wrote yesterday we have passed over boundless plains & this morning have been in a hilly region but still no trees but a few stunted pines. Mr. C.'s throat still troubles him some. I am well. The further I get away from you all at home the more my heart goes out towards you – but there is one Lord over all. If you have not written before you receive this – and if you have – please do write immediately again. We shall likely reach Victoria by the twenty-fifth. Love to all from us both, especially to my father & yourself

> dear Mother,
> Emma

The first stage of Emma's trip west concluded with her arrival in San Francisco. The break in the journey gave her the opportunity to describe recent events as well as the train trip west in as much descriptive detail as she could muster. While her husband got a reduced fare by virtue of being a minister, Emma had to pay the full price. Her concern to make her mother comfortable with her marriage is evident in her long, newsy letter.

San Francisco
May 18th 1874

My dear, dear Mother,

The first thing this Monday morning after breakfast, of course, and a few other necessary things, must be a good long letter to yourself & my father. There is nothing to tell so far, I am thankful to say. That's good news. All along our journey we have been taken care of and blessed. Scarcely a cause of annoyance ever has there been – the wrong trunk was taken to Waukegan but that was only a trifle and we were delayed some on Saturday morning so that it was ten o'clock at night before we reached San Francisco, but that I could not grieve over as it brought us by daylight through some of the finest scenery I suppose there is on earth. We have indeed every reason for gratitude and to feel that the hand of the Lord has been upon us for good. To be sure the long days on the train were sometimes rather trying – especially when the route afforded nothing very interesting – and a few times, I confess, I fell to thinking more about you all at home and what I had left than was good for me – but my good husband was always ready and had a word in season that suited exactly, so I would soon get back to the light again. I shall need a great deal of help every day, I know – help from on high and help from my husband but neither, I believe, will ever be wanting so long as I look for what I need. Do not feel anxious about me Mother dear. My God will supply all my needs, and I trust that the future may bring cause of rejoicing to all of us. It would be as well, perhaps, for me to begin the history of our journey with what occurred just after we left you, as the letters I have sent were so short, and then there will be less likelihood of my omitting anything I want to tell you. Our parting was so hurried that morning – and yet perhaps it was as well for us both that it should be so. I know, I think, Mother dear, all you would feel, and you, I believe, know my heart towards you and my father – always you must be first among those I love in my thoughts and prayers. But to begin – we reached Toronto in good time. Mr. C. had some business to attend to and I thought I would rather go with him to some places than remain alone. So I went up to Mr. Brown's – there I was left a few minutes and had a little talk with Mr. Hunter (S.J.) who happened to be there. We had then just time to take a lunch at the depot before leaving for Hamilton. On our way there we had the company of Mr. Lewis of St. Catharines. Mrs. Sanford I think I told you met us at the station – Mr. S. was away – and with her we went for dinner. Miss Robertson had come up to meet us. Mrs. S. was very kind indeed. After dinner T.C. had to go to the depot to see after the freight there and Miss R. & I proceeded to the college. My husband joined us after a while. There the teachers were all gathered in Mrs. Wright's room and all were so cheerful and so cordial, it was not trying at all as I had thought, and it seemed so good to have Marie [Séguin] sitting at my feet again and Mollie [Stinson] & Ellie [Ambrose] and all the rest about me. We four got away for just a few minutes talk together, but the time was not long and I wanted to see all as much as possible. Dr. Rice was there. There was no opportunity of seeing the students – nor, perhaps, would it have been best to have met them all again. Ever so many of the teachers came to the depot to see us off and I shall not soon forget how they stood there on the platform so cheery and kind, till the train moved off and the last good-bye was said. Mr. and Mrs. Clarkson were on the train on their way home. We had a little talk

with them and a kind farewell. At Woodstock twenty or thirty friends of Mr.
C.'s had come to say good-bye. Ten minutes of hand-shaking and we were off
again. Mary C. and her father were at Ingersoll to meet us, and we drove at
once to their home. I was tired then – and the next morning there were letters
to write and so much to be done. I could not really become acquainted with
the family as I should have liked to have done. Mary is really a fine, good girl.
She was so busy all that morning. Nothing seemed too much for her to do –
and then in the afternoon she and her father and two younger sisters drove to
Ingersoll with us. There I found two sisters of Miss Robertson's and one of our
old students wanting to see me at Mr. C's sister's house. We had tea and took
the train. Then for the first time I really felt that we had parted with all whom
we had most cared for. Passing London three friends of Mr. C's were at the
train – among them one of the Abbots.

Our trunks were not even opened at Detroit. I told you, I think, a good
deal about our visit to Waukegan. We went round the pond. I took a turn at
rowing to prepare me for future canoe paddling and we walked through the
woods and inspected the stock &c. Uncle and all were just as kind as they
could be. We have their sympathy I know, and prayers, I believe, will go up
from Waukegan for us through our being there and my husband's preaching
on the Sabbath.

Mr. Muir [?] of the G.W.R. kindly left a pass in Toronto for us both from
Detroit to Chicago and from Chicago to Omaha. Mr. C. got half fare for himself – that was all the reduction allowed us on any part of the route. Leaving
Chicago there was nothing of particular interest, only as we went westward
through Iowa the orchards we found in full bloom and vegetation more advanced than eastward. We reached Omaha Tuesday morning. There was an
hour's bustle and hurry, such numbers of passengers and immigrant families
with their huge provision baskets and bags – and yet the arrangements for
checking and securing tickets and berths and so on on these American railways
is so perfect that really travelling is made as safe and comfortable as it seems
possible to make it. I should have mentioned perhaps the prairie fires we saw
east of Omaha. They were a novelty to me and one at night was a fine sight –
though none of them were on a very large scale. A day's journey from Omaha
through a monotonous country, over vast plains – a village here and there and
large herds of cattle on the prairies. Wednesday morning found us on high
ground – crossing a broad plateau skirted with a line of hills on all sides and
snow capped peaks in the distance – grass and stunted bushes about the only
vegetation, huge piles of rocks rising abruptly from the plateau. Wednesday we
passed Sherman station the highest point on the road. The air was cool and
bracing with a strong wind. In some places snow still remained on the ground.
We passed through several snow sheds also.

Thursday afternoon the really grand scenery began, passing Castle Rock [Colorado] through what are called Echo and Weber canyons. There the rocks in all kinds of grotesque forms of towers and columns and all imaginable shapes tower away above us, sometimes rising perpendicularly with the track just at their base – here and there a deep awful looking gorge and perhaps just the other side of the track a series of rolling hills – their tall sloping sides covered with grass. The Devil's gate was one particular point of interest – a stream of water rushing along at the foot of an immense pile of rocks. Then we came to Ogden, Utah where there was another change of car. I had spent nearly all the afternoon on the platform of the car where it was rather windy and cold so I found myself quite tired by tea time, at which time we found ourselves at Ogden [Utah]. There we had tea and then on we went past Salt Lake, a pretty lake as we saw it in the evening sun, bordered on the opposite shore by a long line of hills.

Friday we traversed a barren desert like country with scarcely any vegetation but sage brush with hills of course still to bound the view. By evening however we reached Humboldt, an eating station – where by means of irrigation and cultivation there has been produced a fertile – a very fertile spot in a desert. The greenest of grass, fine little trees and well cultivated fields with a fountain before the station house are refreshing and pleasant after such a dusty, monotonous route. As to dust however we had much less of it than I expected – even in that famous alkali region we suffered very little.

So Friday passed on then Saturday – and what it brought us to I do not know how to describe. Such grand scenery I had scarcely pictured to myself. We crossed the Sierra Nevada, mountains winding round their sides or piercing them on tunnels after a most wonderful fashion. At one place the road wound round from one mountain side to another opposite – till the two lines were almost parallel and we were turned nearly round. One scene was very beautiful, Donner Lake [in the Sierra Nevada Mountains] – a clear sparkling depth of water lying down between high sloping mountains covered with snow that glistened in the sunshine, tall pine and spruce trees growing up their sides to the very summit. Just beyond that was a valley where the morning mist had gathered giving such a softness to the view as it was intensely delightful to look at. I wish I could describe all this as it should be described. Here the snow was even then six or eight feet in depth in some places – and we entered a long line of snow sheds and tunnels, between twenty and thirty miles in length. This hid from us much fine scenery of course, but here and there when there would be an opening in the side of the shed we would catch just a glimpse of some deep sloping valley with the shadows of the dark pines thrown across the sparkling snow. We stopped for breakfast right here among the mountains where the snow lay, I suppose, eight feet in depth. Here as you may suppose it was quite wintry and a warm shawl was a comfort. But we were on our way to a much warmer climate and on we sped till the snow disappeared except as we saw it on distant summits, as it could be seen from pretty much every point of our route through California. But now the air grew mild and we came to lovely hill sides and valleys beautifully green. Here was Cape Horn. I do wish I could give you an idea of the view we had. Fancy a tall almost perpendicular mountain – some fifty feet from the summit is a shelf encircling it round which the train sweeps. Down below us, almost straight down, rolls a view. Way before us stretches a long valley on either side of which rises a line of high hills, their sides clothed with the richest verdure. The guide book says that at this point – rounding Cape Horn – "Timid ladies shouldn't" &c., but I enjoyed it too much to feel any fear whatever. Very soon now we found the wild flowers in profusion all along the way – and passed the scenes of mining operations – tracing the water courses caused along the sides of the mountains and from one mountain side to another in flumes – and a most beautiful country these miners have to live in. Beautiful bouquets of roses & all kinds of flowers were brought to the stations now as we passed and strawberries and oranges in abundance. The course lay through what seemed to me one lovely garden. Most beautiful effects – nature & landscape gardening – clumps of trees of various kinds and most charming little works and grassy glens where the flowers bloomed in endless number & variety. It was very warm by this time – by noon – so different from the morning among the snows. We reached Sacramento City about three. The hay and grain were being harvested here in the valley and the pears were formed on the trees and the flowers were lovely. We passed some beautiful gardens. It grew cool again towards evening – about ten when we reached San Francisco. The railroad does not run into the city. We crossed the bay on a ferry boat – but as soon as could be expected we found ourselves safe at the Russ house.

I have said nothing about any people we met on the train. Well there are no particular celebrities to be detailed upon – those we had most to say to were a lady & gentleman of San Francisco who came through from Chicago – fair samples of Americans with more money than they were born to. He, by his own story had been a California miner and now, I believe has a music store. He gave us his address & requested us to call at his store, having learned of our destination, and estimated that he would be happy to give me some songs for my use in our distant home. The lady was on her way home from a European tour bringing a few foreign airs with her – but was very kind and invited me to call upon her. However that could not be very well. Americans certainly are very friendly with each other and really seem to enjoy themselves anywhere. One young girl who came from Omaha to within a few miles of San Francisco kissed me good-bye though I had not even learned her name. I did not go out yesterday morning – but my dear Thomas went to one of the

M[ethodist].E[piscopal]. churches, and speaking to the minister after the service was pressed into work for the evening in a church whose minister was absent somewhere. The people showed quite a little sympathy with us – a number came to be introduced to me – and more took pains to speak to Mr. Crosby – one gentleman slipping a half eagle into his hand for his wife.

Today has been spent quietly. I have not been out except for a walk this afternoon. Tomorrow we intend going about the city more. The boat leaves Wednesday morning so we shall probably reach Victoria by Tuesday some time. So you see, Mother dear, by all this that a kind Providence has been with us so far and we have reason to thank God and take courage. I do hope that we may be always faithful to our work and successful in it. There will be a good deal for me to overcome, I know. My own feelings and prejudices may have to be sacrificed – but I believe the power I trust in is stronger than my own nature which has to be overcome. Pray for us – I know you will, both of you – that we may be useful and happy. May the Lord take care of you and us, and bless us abundantly. I have written to you, Mother at greater length than I shall be able to do to the girls. If you think it worth while you might send this letter to them to read – and to Georgie. Perhaps I have said more than I need have done but I wanted you to know what our journey had been like. I trust I shall find a letter from you in Victoria if not when we arrive there, soon after. I shall look so anxiously for letters and to know that everything is going on happily and well with you will be such a comfort to me. Remember, dear Mother, I am in the hands of God. He has given me a good kind husband in whom I know I may trust for all any human friend can give. I might not say this so plainly if you were to have the opportunity of seeing it for yourself, as you would if we were to be with you. And I believe so long as I am true to myself and my husband and to God and the work he has given me, my life must have a sufficient blessing resting upon it. My dear Thomas has written to you too – so you will have his view of things as well as mine. I sent a postal card to Georgie and one to each of the girls on Friday and shall try to write to them all again before we leave on Wednesday. Give my kindest love to Auntie and Sallie and Mr. H. also – and let me assure both you, dear Mother, and my father, that you both have the fondest love of

Your affectionate daughter,
Emma Crosby

Thomas Crosby had promised his in-laws he would write them about their departing daughter's welfare and, while in San Francisco awaiting the boat that would take them north to Victoria, penned his first separate letter to Eliza Douse.

It would be one of the few he wrote, in part certainly because he never really got to know her or his father-in-law as individuals.

San Francisco Cal.
May 18th 1874

My Dear Mrs. Douse

According to promise I take the first opportunity of writing a few lines to you.

We have had a most happy & prosperous journey so far and nothing to in any way to make us feel that darkness was in the way, indeed it has been all light. Of course we shall never forget the parting. I would not wish to forget those hours at Castleton, Coburg & most of all at Lefroy and yet how God sustained us amidst it all. And the kind counsel of dear Father the night he left the station did me so much good. And the very great kindness of dear Mr. & Mrs. [George] McKay to the last, was a great blessing indeed. All seem to cause thankfulness to the giver of all good for such friends at <u>such</u> a time and then at Hamilton the dear friends were so kind. And of course I felt it very trying to part with my dear Father and Mother but with them also the Good by passed off more happily than I expected indeed our Heavenly Father seemed to be ordering every step of our journey. And although it is hard to part yet we have done it all for Christ sake, and in it I believe we shall all be blessed and in leaving Ingersoll Frid. evening the time was mostly spent in thought & prayer and many a God bless them went up to heaven for our friends while doubtless they were praying for us. At Waukegan we had such a pleasant time all were so kind and it was such a pleasant place to stay over and rest before starting on such a journey. I need not tell you much about the journey (for Emma has promised to write it all) suffice to say upon the whole it was pleasant a little dusty and as I had a cold, my dear wife stood it better than I did for I never saw any body could sleep better and as a general thing she eat well <u>for her</u> and as you know she does not tell all she feels yet I think for the most part she has been happy. And I think she always will be. I have so much confidence in her judgment that I am sure she will be a great blessing to me. And this I can rejoice in that blessing the Wise Man speaks of as from the Lord. <u>A good</u> wife. We leave on Wed. for Vict. and I must close for perhaps I have said enough in this strain for the present. Will write you and if there is a dark side you shall have it. Love to Father & Aunty and all accept the same from

Your Affectionate
Son T. Crosby.

By the time Emma described her trip north from San Francisco to British Columbia to her younger brother Georgie, she was already looking ahead. She no sooner arrived than she was enveloped by the province's Methodist hierarchy. In 1867 the Toronto Conference, which had charge of the then British colony, dispatched west a longtime Ontario minister, Rev. Amos Russ, to take charge of the Pandora Street Church in Victoria. There was also, it should be noted, a second Amos Russ, a young Haida who had turned to Methodism in Victoria several years earlier, had been given the Methodist minister's name and taken under his wing. The Russes whom the newlyweds encountered near San Francisco were likely Rev. Russ's relatives.

When Rev. Russ was transferred to New Westminster in 1871, the Toronto Conference appointed William Pollard as his successor. Already a senior minister, Rev. Pollard had charge of the Pandora Street church for three years, whereupon he would move to its New Westminster counterpart for two more. Rev. Pollard had a personal interest in Fort Simpson, which grew out of his visit there in February 1874 at the invitation of local Tsimshian converts. It was this trip that led to the Methodist Church's decision to open a mission there under Thomas Crosby. Two of Rev. Pollard's children met the Crosbys on their arrival in Victoria. His unmarried daughter Annie taught Sunday school and held classes in English for Aboriginal and Chinese people in Victoria. The Pollards' daughter Jessie was about to give birth at the time of the Crosbys' arrival. Her husband, Rev. Joseph Hall, had come west from Coburg as a student minister in 1871. He first served in Barkerville and had just been posted to Nanaimo. Thomas Trounce, whom the Crosbys also met in Victoria, was a local architect celebrated for his "material service to the Church in this Province."[43]

Chilliwhack May 29th 1874[44]

My dear Georgie,

However it may appear to you all at home, to me it seems that the difficulty of finding time and opportunity to write is quite a trial. I have wanted so much to write to you all but so much going about have we had and so much visiting that it has been impossible to get as many letters off as I wished. Then another difficulty is that when I do sit down to write there is so much to be told that even one letter takes quite a time. I have thought so much about you all and hope and pray so earnestly that every blessing may be yours – I feel that we have been kept from so much possible evil that I cannot but be glad & thankful – our way has been so bright and happy all through. The long effusion I sent our mother may perhaps find its way to you – I have trusted to that for you all and written the girls scarcely a word of anything that occurred before we reached

San Fran. I cannot do better perhaps than begin there and give you a sketch of our experience since. There are not many wonderful things to be seen in San Fr. excepting what was there before the city was dreamed of – the bay bordered by hills – the sea beyond and the situation of [the] city which is built upon steep, steep hills are all very fine – we had a good view of it one morning and sat down in a quiet place on the top of an eminence (is that a correct expression?) and feasted upon the view and the fresh sea air. The gardens were radiant with the loveliest flowers – roses – fuchsias Egyptian lilies – ivy &c – all growing in the open air & in full bloom. We were nearly four days coming from San Fr. to Victoria – we had smooth weather mostly but were not either of us spared the delights of sea-sickness, nevertheless – for the first day we neither of us could sit up much but after a while we recovered and enjoyed the rest of the way very much – some of our fellow-passengers were very agreeable people – one gentleman – a young man from Brantford who was coming to Victoria to enter a bank we had a good deal of talk with. Sunday morning brought us to Victoria – which is really a beautifully situated place – we are in about seven – Miss [Annie] Pollard & her brother met us and soon we were established in the parsonage. I went to church twice and all attended the Indian school in the afternoon. These poor people not only in Victoria but all through where we have been seem so delighted to see their old friend the missionary back – it really does one good – and they take my hand & talk away in their own language – or in English if they can to give me also a welcome. We had only two days in Victoria but were out for tea both evenings & saw a good many people – Tuesday morning we left to come up the Fraser – it is really a beautiful river, with the low-lying fertile lands along its shores – and the mountains barren, wooded – snow capped – in endless variety rising beyond – then in some places the river lies just at the foot of great ranges of hills – it really is a grand country, this – the scenery is a delight to me – but then the society is rough, of course. Still there are some nice people and I think I could be happy if my home was here. We reached Sumas [in the Fraser Valley] Wednesday noon – having spent Tuesday night in New Westminster – and remained till yesterday at the Chilliwhack parsonage about a mile from the landing – We are now staying where Mr Crosby used to board – now while I write he is busy packing his books and other things to take with us. You will likely see Annie's letter so I need tell you none of my fresh attempts at riding. I came over here – two or three miles – by the same mode of travelling yesterday on such a slow old horse – my good husband won't trust me with a very spirited one – and under an umbrella – it was raining heavily. I should soon, I believe, be very fond of riding. We mean to leave again for Victoria Monday – unless, indeed, arrangements can be made to stay over a camp meeting that begins next week – everyone is crying out against our leaving before that – and for the sake of the Indians who will be much disappointed I am really sorry we cannot remain. Now Georgie, as Annie will likely give you her letter to read – perhaps I need write no more. I feel rather tired this evening, though quite well. Thomas sends his kindest love to you. Let us hear from you soon dear. May your life be bright & useful.

> With fondest affection, Believe me,
>   As ever yours,
>   Emma

By the time Emma got around to writing her mother from British Columbia, she had already had her first encounter with Aboriginal people.

Chilliwhack, June 8th 1874

My dear dear Mother,

Our wanderings have brought us to a camp meeting – it is to close this afternoon. I seize a few minutes now – writing on the bed at that as breakfast is going on – so as to send this by the boat this afternoon. We have been here since Wednesday tenting with Mrs. Evans a widow with whom Mr. Crosby used to board & we spent two or three days since we came up here. There has been a good deal of rain but the tent has been dry and comfortable and the meetings have been very good indeed. You know my good husband is a great camp meeting man. We did not mean to remain for it when we came but everyone was so urgent that we should stay & the Indians seemed so much in need of their old friend that Mr. Crosby felt he could not leave them without the opportunity which the camp meeting gave him of seeing a large number of them together. It does me good to see how fond these poor people all are of him and how much good he can do them, and to me they give a very warm welcome. I have been at their meetings mostly and go through their tents sometimes with Mr. Crosby. I do not attempt much Indian of course. How do you do?, and good-night are about all my stock – the latter is very difficult to say. They always laugh when Mr. C. will have me try it. When I want to speak to them in the meetings or anywhere else Thomas interprets for me. I have to shake hands with them all generally two or three times a day and when I come across a baby that looks a little cleaner than the rest I kiss it sometimes. There were four marriages among them yesterday. Four children were baptized Sunday before last and some more are to be today.

We were to have left for Fort Simpson last week only for our staying here. I hope, Mother dear, you have seen the letter I sent Susie as I cannot write as much now as I did then. I have been trying to write to you for ever so long, but we have been scarcely two days together in the same place and it has been very difficult to write at all. We reached Victoria the 24th May. Stayed there two days then Tuesday morning left to come up the Fraser. Spent the first night in New Westminster then the next morning came on to Sumas & Chilliwhack neighbouring settlements. I wish I could tell you all I want to about the last three weeks. Everyone has been extremely kind. All are so glad to see Thomas back and for his sake welcome me. I have really enjoyed myself very much. We have been going about from one place to another, of course, so I visit as many as possible. There are no carriages, you know, and only one buggy in the neighbourhood – no roads for them – so canoeing and riding on horseback are our only modes of conveyance. Canoeing I delight in, that is if the canoe is nice and clean and there is a good Indian mat made of rushes to sit on. My good husband always has a nice place fixed for me and it is just grand to be paddled down – or up – a stream with the rose bushes in full bloom all along the edge dipping in the water or the trees hanging over, for the water is everywhere very high. Some parts of the country are overflowed. Then the mountains – but O I must not begin about them. As to riding – my husband says I will soon be quite a jockey. I will write again & tell you more about these things. We mean to go to New Westminster Friday – likely shall spend Sunday there – then on to Victoria. I scarcely know when we go to Fort S., likely in a couple of weeks. I suppose my father is at conference now. Do write soon. Love to Auntie & Sallie. Much for yourself dear Mother and my father from,

> Your affectionate
> Emma

The length of time between Emma's letters home was irregular. It was another two and a half weeks before she again wrote home. By then she had gotten to know the Methodist hierarchy in Victoria and was anticipating her new home on the north coast.

> Victoria, B.C.
> June 25th 1874

My dear Mother,

It may be a good while before I have another chance of sending you a letter so I had better write today. Tomorrow morning, five A.M. the "Otter" is announced to leave for the North to have, all being well, the Fort S. missionary and his wife on board her. If she leaves so early we shall likely sleep on board ship. Then we begin in earnest – but we are both hopeful and happy. I shall be the only lady passenger of course – it is chiefly miners on their way to the gold fields on the Stickeen river who go on this route – however, the Captain, I believe, is very agreeable – he is a H[udson's]. B[ay]. officer and we will likely be very comfortable.

We remained a few days after the camp meeting at Chilliwhack. We received so much kindness there, as indeed we have wherever we have been, that I really felt quite attached to both the place and the people. Over sixty dollars was collected and presented to Mr. Crosby before we left the camp meeting. Then there is a farmer there who says he promised that whenever Thomas married he would give Mrs. C. a cow, and declares his readiness now to send it to Fort S. any time or if we cannot keep one there to send butter instead. I got to be quite in love with riding. Did I tell you about a little horse Thomas has there, a fine spirited horse but quite gentle? I had one splendid ride on him. If there was any use for a horse and any way of keeping on[e] at Fort S. we would have this but I scarcely think there will be enough use for him to make it worth while. Thomas wants to take him up for me to ride if he can but I don't suppose I should have much time for that.

We spent a week at New Westminster on our way down the Fraser, making our home at the Parsonage with Mr. and Mrs. Russ. They were so very kind. Mrs. R. was as affectionate with me as a sister could be. Offered even to take care of us in case of illness if I would go to her and I know she would do it in a kind Christian spirit. We remained longer than we had intended there. Thomas was completely tired out and it was a good place to rest. I think I know pretty nearly all the Methodists of the place now – besides some others. One lady there had a large box of bottled fruit put up for us before we left.

We reached Victoria again Saturday afternoon last. As a little Hall had been added to the family at the Parsonage a week before, we could not stay there of course, so we are guests of a Mr. Trounce. The house is a very handsome one with a beautiful garden. The family are somewhat peculiar. There are no children – just four elderly people, two sisters and their husbands. They are painfully particular in their house keeping. Mrs. T. makes it a point to see that no soiled boots enter. Did you clean your boots? is an inquiry frequently addressed to visitors. She always says just what she thinks regardless alike of politeness and other people's feelings. "Get off that chair, no one is allowed to sit there but me" were almost the first words she addressed to Thomas after we came. Fortunately she does not mind one's laughing – it has been impossible for me to keep my gravity sometimes. Temperance is a hobby with her. Her husband I like very much indeed, they are all as kind as they can be to us. A lot of fruit – preserved – is being put up for us to take to our new home. So you see I shall have quite a lot of fruit to begin with. They say too that wild fruit is very plentiful there so I hope we shall get on nicely.

Miss Pollard and Mrs. Hall, too, the other day gave me for a wedding present, I suppose, a silver gravy ladle, a couple of knife rests and two napkin rings – all very pretty. We have been very busy this week, Thomas especially, arranging plans for the future, and buying furniture &c. It is mostly through now, though. We have all we need to make us comfortable and make the house pleasant except one or two things we may have to send down for again – wait till we get settled then I will, all being well, give you a full description. The freight we had such a time packing arrived last week, apparently in excellent condition, and will go on with us. I do not know yet how long it may be before we are in our own house. It may be we shall use one of the Company's till spring next if we can be comfortable – and the church be built first. Or if the house is put up first as I hope it will be, we shall likely stay in the meantime in a couple of rooms in the [Hudson's Bay] Fort. For a few days it is likely we will stay with the family of the H.B. officer in charge. We are taking up a few groceries with us – baking powder &c. Indeed as a grocer here wishes to present us with ten dollars we may take it all out in groceries. Almost everything, they say, we can get at the Fort.

So you see, Mother dear, that thus far our way has been blessed, and we have every reason to feel encouraged. I did not get your letters till Saturday. They had some of them been waiting some time. There was one from Annie too. It seemed so good to hear from you. I hope we shall have more today. There will likely be a mail in and perhaps we shall have no other for a month. Our address will be Fort Simpson. The mail is sent on from the office here. I suppose Papa is back from the Conference by this time. I am anxious to hear some news from it – and more anxious to know what your plans are for the coming year.

Love to Auntie and Sallie, I will write to both of them as soon as I can. And now, Mother, do not feel uneasy about me. I am taken good care of and have been well. It is wonderful to me how quiet and trustful I have been kept. "Not unto us" be the praise. Thomas would write again now but he really has so much to do it is impossible. He joins me in truest love to yourself and my father. Write often, dear Mother, and pray for,

Your affectionate daughter,
Emma

Through her letters Emma sought to assure her family that her decision to join the missionary ranks as a dutiful wife was more than just a romantic inclination. Her decision was pragmatic and part of a larger agenda: the civilizing and conversion of Aboriginal people. Thomas followed suit, echoing the sentiments of his wife to her parents and validating the important role she was playing in accompanying him west. The journey acquainted Emma with the supporters of her husband's efforts, who adorned her with gifts that would help make a comfortable life for the couple. Given that Emma's first child was born two months premature, just before Christmas, she must have been pregnant by the time she arrived in British Columbia. While Emma would continue to report on her new acquaintances, a more dynamic set of relationships soon took precedence.

2

Arrival at Fort Simpson

Emma Crosby's likely first view of Fort Simpson was caught by an arrival a decade and a half later: "Ft. Simpson was a beautiful site then, the Fort nestling on sister harbours, with rolling hills in the background ... In the foreground was Rose Island 'Loo-lamish' (Indian), part of the Indian reserve. The Fort buildings were enclosed by a high log stockade ... The buildings were of logs and comprised a store, family dwelling and three staff houses and a powder magazine."[1] An arrival eight years before the Crosbys was struck by how "the Hudson's Bay establishment was a true old fort, a large square enclosed by a solid stockade twenty-two feet high with huge gates in the centre or side facing the sea, at each corner was a bastion loopholed for musketry."[2] Looking out from the post over the sheltered harbour, the view was impressive, especially at sunset, "the sun dropping into the sea, like a great red ball, leaving a path of crimson and gold, and the full moon rising in the background, shedding new tints on the harbour of gold and the darker blues of the Alaskan hills."[3] Emma's eldest daughter later described how "the harbor commands a magnificent view westward over an immense expanse of the Pacific."[4]

The minute Emma stepped on land at her new home, she was enmeshed in ways of life that went back to time immemorial. This was Tsimshian territory, which extended from the Nass and Skeena Rivers south to the rivers and islands of the Douglas Channel. The term "Tsimshian" was, and is, the most common name used for the culturally related Aboriginal peoples inhabiting northwest British Columbia, and it derives from *ts'm* – "those inside" and *ksiaan* – "the Skeena." According to anthropologist Margaret Seguin Anderson, Tsimshian territory was bounded by the Tlingit and Athapaskan groups to the north, the Carrier to the east, the northern Kwakiutl groups to the south, and the Haida of the Queen Charlotte Islands to the west.[5]

The Tsimshian travelled seasonally in families or clans, moving from fishing sites in spring and summer to hunting territories in the fall. With the arrival of colder weather, attention shifted from economic activities and food preservation to ceremonial practices, and the Tshimsian gathered in winter towns. The principal social event was the potlatch, at which witnessing and gift giving affirmed changes in the life cycle. Matrilineal kinship ties, social classes, and "houses" determined a hierarchical order fundamental to Tsimshian society.[6]

Fort Simpson, known to the Tsimshian as Lax Kw'alaams, or the place of the wild roses, is located about 600 miles north of Victoria on the south bank of the mouth of the Nass River on the tip of a peninsula extending north from the mouth of the Skeena River. About fifteen miles to the northwest lies the Alaska panhandle. The former Russian America, today's state of Alaska, had been purchased by the United States from Russia in 1867. Metlakatla, where Anglican missionary William Duncan ruled supreme, lies equal distance to the south on the western edge of the peninsula facing Chatham Sound.

The Hudson's Bay Company (HBC) trading post that gave Fort Simpson its name, and Emma her first, temporary home, harked back to 1831 when it was Fort Nass. In 1834, having already been renamed Fort Simpson, the post was moved to its current location. Maritime traders had travelled up the coast to collect furs since the late eighteenth century. Concern over the extension of Russian influence southward from Russian America encouraged the HBC to establish itself as far north as possible. Its doing so was facilitated by Tsimshian chief Legaic, whose daughter was married to HBC trader John Kennedy, and who offered them the Fort Simpson site.

The post's establishment attracted Tsimshian to the vicinity on a seasonal basis. The HBC post was surrounded by the houses of the Tsimshian peoples, both in its immediate vicinity and on Rose Island, which was reachable by foot at low tide. Thomas Crosby described Fort Simpson's changing role:

> It was formerly an old camping-ground of the Tsimpshean people while on their way from the Skeena and Old Metlakatalah, where they resided originally, to the Nass River for oolachan fishing. The Hudson's Bay Company established their fort here about 1835, and soon great crowds of Indians gathered around the post and built a large village of between two and three thousand people. It became not only an important trading-post but also a distributing point to other places inland and on the coast.[7]

An arrival in the mid-1860s evoked "the large Indian houses with huge Totem Poles in front of them, the Indian men and women promenading in their bright colored blankets their faces touched up with vermillion (like unto their white

FORT SIMPSON FROM THE BEACH. E.T. 1868

ENTRANCE FORT SIMPSON. E.T. 1868

INTERIOR OF FORT SIMPSON. E.T. 1868

Fort Simpson as Emma saw it for the first time in 1874

FROM EMIL TEICHMANN, *A JOURNEY TO ALASKA IN THE YEAR 1868: BEING A DIARY OF THE LATE EMIL TEICHMANN* (NEW YORK: ARGOSY-ANTIQUARIAN, 1963, ORIG. 1925), 105-7

sisters) and the men following suit, the beach lined with their splendid canoes, some sixty feet long."[8]

Keeping to their seasonal round, the Tsimshian were almost all away from Fort Simpson between early spring and late autumn. During their return in the winter months related groups lived together in large houses. The Crosbys' oldest daughter, Jessie, recalled these houses from her childhood:

Totem poles at Fort Simpson about the time Emma arrived

PHOTOGRAPHED BY RICHARD MAYNARD, GEOLOGICAL SURVEY OF CANADA, LIBRARY AND ARCHIVES CANADA, C-066430

The old fashioned houses were very large and low roofed, built out of slabs hewn from logs and the roof of each was a hole through which the smoke might escape from a fire built in a square cut in the ground floor which served the purpose of a fire place. These houses had no windows or openings through which light might enter but through this one hole in the roof, and often three or four families lived together in one house.[9]

Even though the HBC never went beyond being a business, having no reason to transform Tsimshian culture, many decades of encounter acquainted the Tsimshian with newcomer ways. The more profound impact came with missionaries, who were intent on reforming both Tsimshian spirituality and Tsimshian lifestyles to accord with Christian doctrine and Christian notions of what constituted a "civilized" way of life. On the west coast of Vancouver Island, a Spanish voyage in the late 1700s brought the first Roman Catholic missionaries, whose presence there and further up the coast was brief. Priests returned in the 1840s, effecting little change on Aboriginal lifestyles and beliefs, but successfully initiating contact in areas of the fur trade. With more permanent settlements, the stability of missions increased, as did their influence. Missionaries came with what might be termed, from their perspective, good intentions, although their priorities certainly did not match those of Aboriginal peoples.

It may also be the case, as some scholars have suggested, that the Tsimshian found within Christianity a certain continuity with their own social and spiritual foundations. Neylan compares fundamental concepts of Tsimshian spirituality with evangelical Christian doctrine, arguing that the Tsimshian were predisposed towards certain aspects of Protestantism not because they were "new" but because they were familiar: "Given that material and spiritual worlds were not separate in Tsimshian cosmology, it is certain that Christianity was not received for its religious messages alone. Likewise, status derived from those who demonstrated initiative and leadership in the Christian church signified more than merely religious authority." For the Tsimshian, Christianity provided "access to not only the spiritual power of Euro-Canadian culture but economic, political, and social links as well."[10] Christianity was a new source of power, allowing some Tsimshian to circumvent traditional modes of acquiring status and power.

Anglican missionary William Duncan of the Church Missionary Society was the first to begin missionary work at the trading post of Fort Simpson. Historical geographer Robert Galois describes Duncan's arrival in 1857: "At first, Duncan must have been something of a mystery – a White man, a resident of the fort, but his relationship to the HBC unclear. Moreover, the newcomer confirmed his difference from company men by seeking instruction in the Tsimshian language and information about Tsimshian society."[11] Duncan remained there until

1862, when he moved to nearby Metlakatla to establish a new missionary community in response to what he perceived to be increasingly negative newcomer influence and because he believed that Tsimshian turning to Anglicanism had to give up their "old ways."

Duncan's presence created new opportunities for some Tsimshian at Fort Simpson. Most notable was the relationship between him and a Tsimshian man named Arthur Wellington Clah, known also as Damaks. In his extensive analysis of Clah's diaries, Galois suggests that Clah acted as Duncan's language teacher and intermediary with the wider Tsimshian society in order to improve his English and in order to learn to read and write: "Writing and literacy were probably viewed by Tsimshian as part of the material and spiritual 'powers' accessible to the white world. To Clah, more familiar than most Tsimshian with the workings of the fort, the acquisition of literacy may have represented a form of initiation into these broader 'powers.'"[12] Missionaries brought to their new locales "a new pressure of very intense literacy. Individually and as a group they were daily readers, writers, and reverers of books." Writing about the literate practices among missions in Oregon, Albert Furtwangler suggests that other forms of power and influence, including material goods and new economies, came into play before the direct teaching of Christianity and literacy, and they make it impossible to disentangle the power or appeal of white religion from other Euro-American cultural influences."[13] The association with Duncan eventually led Clah towards Christianity and made possible new social and spiritual opportunities for Clah, who remained at Fort Simpson following Duncan's departure to Metlakatla. In her discussion of the politics of religion at Fort Simpson, Peggy Brock reminds us of the fundamental differences in perspective: "Duncan and his successor at Fort Simpson, the Methodist Thomas Crosby, were typical nineteenth-century missionaries who believed that conversion occurred only when Christian beliefs and demeanor replaced pre-existing religious beliefs and moral codes. In Clah's world, this dichotomy did not exist."[14]

Just as Clah aligned himself with Duncan to raise his own status among his Tsimshian relations, so other factions pursued other associations as a means of competing for their own power bases. The sequence of events that brought the Crosbys to Simpson harked back half a decade. While in Victoria prior to his marriage, Thomas encountered Tsimshian and other Aboriginal people from along the Northwest Coast, men and women who had long migrated seasonally to trade. A fellow missionary remembered how it was "a mission to the Indians, held in a vacated saloon, on the corner of Fisgard and Government streets, which was the spiritual birthplace of the Port Simpson Mission."[15] Among those taking up Methodism were several hybrid children of fur traders and Aboriginal mothers searching for an intermediate space for themselves that might reconcile and empower their two inheritances. Included in their number were Alfred Dudoward and his wife Katherine, or Catherine, Holmes.

The Dudowards would become the Crosbys' principal support during their quarter century at Fort Simpson. Alfred Dudoward's father was Felix Dudoaire, or Dudoire, his mother a Tsimshian woman.[16] A butcher's son from Quebec, Dudouaire joined the HBC in 1840 at the age of twenty-four and spent most of his time at Fort Simpson, where he worked as a tailor.[17] Alfred's mother Diex, or Deiks, was a chief's daughter of the house of Legaic who fled to Fort Simpson, and hence to Dudouaire's arms, to keep from being married off to a man twice her age.[18] Born about 1849, Alfred was enrolled in the school Duncan opened in October 1857 and was still there three years later, possibly to the time of his father's death.[19] While young Alfred was at school, his surname was anglicized to Dudoward. Alfred then spent some time in Victoria, where his widowed mother worked as a domestic before marrying a Scots customs officer. During this time period the Dudowards broke with Duncan, who accused Alfred of having been "engrossed in heathenish customs and [having taken] a lead in a canni-bal party there."[20] In 1871 Duncan, acting in his capacity as justice of the peace, fined Alfred twenty blankets for selling liquor and obstructing justice, promis-ing to return them if Alfred behaved for a specified period of time.[21]

Alfred Dudoward's wife Kate was, like himself, of mixed race. According to Tsimshian tradition, as told by a man who lived and worked among them, in about 1853 a newcomer named Holmes, possibly a ship's captain, took the daugh-ter of the local Tsimshian chief into Fort Simpson, where they had a child named Katherine. Kate's father thereafter disappeared from view and her mother took her to Victoria, where she got work as a domestic servant. The Tsimshian ver-sion of the story has Kate's maternal grandfather dying at Fort Simpson and her mother being elected chief, whereupon a delegation travelled to Victoria to bring her home. Kate's mother is said to have left her young daughter in the care of nuns before heading home by canoe; unfortunately, she was killed on the journey in an attack by southern peoples. The records for Catholic St. Ann's Academy in Victoria indicate that Kate Holmes was enrolled there at the be-ginning of September 1865, aged twelve, and that she left briefly and then re-turned at the end of September 1867, aged fourteen.[22] The Tsimshian version of events has young Kate Holmes then being brought back north to assume chiefly duties and, in 1871, wedding Alfred Dudoward, who was of similar chiefly descent. A missionary at the time described the young couple when they mar-ried in 1871: "Dudoward is a half-bred, was born at Fort Simpson, speaks good English, and is a chief. His wife is also a half-cast, she was educated at the con-vent in this city [Victoria]. She is a good English scholar, and quite capable of teaching."[23]

According to Thomas Crosby, writing in retrospect, Alfred Dudoward's mother, Diex, was converted to Methodism in the fall of 1872, being baptized with the name of Elizabeth. "She was a woman of commanding appearance and of great force of character, and exerted a powerful influence over her people ... She was the means of leading into the light quite a number of her own people who were wandering in sin on the streets of Victoria." Among those whom Methodism appealed to were her son Alfred, her daughter-in-law Kate, and many other Tsimshian who, on returning north as professing Christians, "began to sing and pray and repeated the Gospel stories as best they could."[24] These spiritual leaders organized their own Sunday school and prayer meetings. Kate and Alfred put their literacy skills to good use by opening a day school attracting over 200 children. Recognizing the value of having their own missionary, Alfred and Kate Dudoward wrote a letter to that effect to the Methodist hierarchy in Victoria during the winter of 1873-74.

Alfred Dudoward's mother Diex (or Deiks)

BC ARCHIVES, ZZ-95324

With Duncan firmly ensconced at Metlakatla, a denominational alternative at Fort Simpson would open up possibilities for Tsimshian and others who, like the Dudowards, opted to remain there. To the extent that traditional ways had broken down, opportunities existed for newcomers and persons in between cultures to acquire influence. At the same time, by encouraging a competing mission so close to Duncan's little fiefdom, they ensured his enmity – both towards Tsimshian who persisted in preferring Fort Simpson to Metlakatla and towards whoever happened to be the newcomer.

As Methodist head in British Columbia, Rev. William Pollard took the letter of invitation seriously. Following a personal visit to Fort Simpson in February 1874, he dispatched Charles Montgomery Tate north on an interim basis until Crosby returned from Ontario. Tate had arrived in British Columbia from the north of England in 1870 as an eighteen-year-old hoping to get rich by finding gold; however, through contact with Thomas, he was soon caught up in the missionary enterprise and took on the Nanaimo school. Arriving at Fort Simpson in April 1874, Tate taught and preached in anticipation of Thomas's arrival a few months later.

Thomas and Emma reached Fort Simpson on the last day of June 1874. A day later, Emma described their trip north and their welcome to their new home in a long letter to her mother. Since mid-century, when the HBC brought out the 120-foot *Otter* from England to supplement its venerable *Beaver*, Fort Simpson had had a regular means of transport and supply.[25] Travelling every month or so north from Victoria during the spring, summer, and fall, the steamer moved a handful of passengers as well as freight up and down the coast.

At the time the Crosbys took their first trip on the *Otter*, it was also carrying miners headed to Wrangell in Alaska. Wrangell, or Fort Wrangell, was located on the Stikine River at the site of the former HBC post of Fort Stikine, which had been vacated when the United States purchased Alaska in 1867. Wrangell, where the Americans stationed a small garrison of soldiers, was the entryway to a gold rush that had begun a couple of years earlier at Dease Lake in the Cassiar region of northern British Columbia.[26]

Fort Simpson, B.C.
July 1ˢᵗ 1874

My dear Mother,

This the first letter I have dated from this much thought of and talked of place I address to you. We arrived yesterday morning. I will tell you all I can of the journey and the appearance of the village. Early Saturday morning we left Victoria – one day later than we had expected. Our craft – a H.B. Company's boat

is not fitted up for a passenger boat – however we had a state room below
decks which was fitted up as comfortably as could be. The only trouble being
that it was lighted and aired by a port-hole which could be opened only when
the water was very smooth. We were made very comfortable on the whole. Of
course I was the only lady passenger. There were some forty miners on board
going beyond Fort S. to the Stickeen mines and a number of Indians, both
men and women.

The miners were mostly a rough lot of men but not at all disagreeable to us.
Our way lay chiefly among rocky mountainous islands rising abruptly from the
water's edge – and in very quick water. In one place though, crossing Queen
Charlotte's Sound it was quite rough and I had a touch of sickness. It rained
most of Monday but we managed to be on deck a good deal. Then Tuesday
(yesterday) morning came and found us between seven and eight opposite
Fort Simpson. The boat was not to come in to the Fort till her return from
Fort Wrangle, a days journey further on, so our choice was to either go ashore
with a few of our things in a canoe or lose three days by going on with the
"Otter" and returning. We preferred the former plan. The Captain had secured
a fine large canoe – so with four Indians, two men and two women bound for
Fort S. who paddled, a trunk and a number of smaller pieces of baggage – we
transshipped some eight or ten miles from the Fort. The morning was fine, the
sea pretty smooth, the scenery very fine – islands and points of land thickly
wooded and hilly. The village itself is at the head of a bay, built partly on what
is an island at high tide and partly the main land. The Indians have built a rude
bridge between the two which they use at high water. When within about two
miles of the village we came across a canoe full of the Indians returning from
some expedition. They having learned who we were wished us to stay behind
somewhere while they went on to tell the news. So we landed on a beautiful
little beach where the shells & mosses & sea-weed would have delighted Auntie
and waited a while – then re-embarked.

In the mean time the tidings had been given and by the time we came
within hearing we were greeted by cheers from the Indians who were out in
hundreds. Flags were flying and guns were fired as we approached. The landing
place was crowded with men, women & children. Mr. [Charles] Morrison the
H.B. officer stationed here and Mr. Tate who has been teaching the school
were down to meet us. We came up at once to the Fort where we were very
hospitably received. This Mr. Morrison is very agreeable and gentlemanly, and
very friendly to our mission. His wife is a half-breed, but a sweet pretty little
woman, very quiet. She was educated to some extent at that English Church
Mission near by [at Metlakatla] and is really a nice ladylike woman. There is
one child, a little girl, thirteen months old. As to their way of living it is half
aristocratic, half uncivilized, everything seems to be left to Indian servants

who are not very methodical, the meals vary a good deal in their time and are not cooked exactly according to our ideas of excellence in that art, but an Indian boy waits on the table, and everything is served in order. The house is very large and well-built – but old fashioned, of course. We have a bed-room that has been made quite comfortable for us, and really are quite nicely accommodated, notwithstanding the bread is without salt and the potatoes always cold. The salmon is nice – so is the venison. Until the Otter returns day after tomorrow we are to remain here – then we shall have our things and go into one of the company's houses (there are a number of buildings within the enclosure) containing three rooms, which is being fixed up and cleaned for us. It is not unlikely we shall remain here over the winter. It was Thomas' intention to build the house immediately but the people seem impatient to have the church and both cannot be put up before the cold weather comes on. There is a great deal of rain during the fall and winter, but no very intense cold. There was a meeting held this afternoon [at "Chief Scow-gate's house on the [Rose] island," at which "the Indians crowded in from all parts of the village"] and Crosby talked through interpreter Alfred [Dudoward][27] to talk about the church, and see what the Indians would do themselves towards it. They had the idea in their minds that somehow it was to be built altogether for them, but their new missionary talked them out of that and succeeded in arousing quite a little enthusiasm so that there was subscribed in money and blankets, a musket and a coat – the sum of about five hundred dollars just at the meeting, a result which quite surprised Mr. Morrison and Mr. Tate. Several gave ten dollars each, and one man gave eleven blankets worth two dollars a piece. It was amusing as they grew interested to see them. They would go off to their houses and return with their blankets to hand over to the missionary – and even the little children in response to Thomas' urging were brought up to the table with their subscriptions. A plan of the church brought from Victoria was put up on the wall to interest them. There was a religious service, a kind of fellow-ship meeting last night also, at which some four hundred were present. There is a very good site for the mission buildings and also for the Indians' houses on a rising ground just beyond the company's limits. The idea is to build the church, school house and mission house here, and the Indians say many of them that then they will pull down their present houses and build there. This however, of course, cannot be accomplished all at once. The village is said to number over eight hundred. Many of them are away now fishing. They have large houses – several families living in each house. I have not been in many of them yet, but for Indians' houses they seem to be nicely kept. They dress well too – the women in gay shawls and prints with handkerchiefs tied over their heads, and the men many of them in black suits – still there are some who are very dirty and degraded. About two hundred have been attending the school. The teacher [Charles Tate] who has been here is to return at once to Nanaimo. I scarcely know what we can do until another teacher comes. However there are two half-breeds, a man & his wife [Alfred and Kate Dudoward] who have been helping to teach and might do for a while with a little oversight. The school is held in their house – and the services in the chief's house. A pulpit has been put up in it and it does quite well for the present. The soil is good so that we can have as much garden as we like. Grain will not ripen nor all kinds of fruit but Mr. Morrison has currants, goose-berries and rasp-berries doing well and cranberries and other kinds of wild fruit are abundant. There is plenty of wild hay to be had so we can keep our cow. There will be no difficulty in getting vegetables, potatoes are kept in the company's store. Fish is plentiful also venison &c. and sometimes we may get beef from the Otter when she comes up, so you see, Mother, we are not likely to want for anything. Indeed we feel that we ought to be very thankful for the opportunity there seems to be to do good among these people. I do hope we may be a blessing to them.

It will be such a comfort too, to have our own house and by ourselves though it be in three rooms. I can have any help with the house work that I want. There is a boy here [possibly Amos Russ] who lived with Mrs. Russ a while. My good husband proposes engaging him but I would as soon depend on myself except for the heavy work, indeed I feel quite impatient to begin house keeping. We shall not put down any carpets nor can we use many of the things we have while in this little house – the Indians here make a kind of mats with thin pieces of bark woven together which will do nicely. I intend sending this by the Otter as she goes down, and as I cannot probably write to the girls before the next boat likely a month hence, I think I will trouble you to send this round. If I have time tomorrow I will write to Georgie but I may not be able to do so. I would like to write more but this will give you some idea of our surroundings. I am so glad that the situation is so fine. It is a beautiful prospect we are likely to have from our house and to me that is no small thing.

Know, Mother dear, I shall look anxiously for letters by the next boat. You will not have forgotten as I know. Love to my father Auntie & Sallie & all and much for yourself from Thomas who will write as soon as he can get time, and from dear Mother,

Your affectionate,
Emma

The "mission house," or residence, that Thomas intended to erect at Fort Simpson was intended to be "a small cottage," whereas the church would accommodate some 600 persons.[28] The church's architect was the same Thomas Trounce with whom the Crosbys stayed in Victoria. He drew the plans as his "subscription to the mission."[29] The Tsimshian would contribute about $1,400 in total, mostly as HBC trade blankets, towards the church. As well, they provided much of the labour overseen by an experienced carpenter. In July 1874 the Methodist newsletter explained that "Bro. Crosby is getting out all the heavy lumber by Indian labor, but the greater part of the sawed will have to be sent from Victoria."[30]

The remainder of the church's cost was raised through the Methodist Mission Board. The faithful, who were being cajoled to contribute, were comforted by references to denominational rivalry, which was commonplace during these years. "It will cost considerable to start this Mission, but it is by far the largest we have in the Dominion: it is much larger than Mr. Duncan at Metlahkatlah."[31] The church was intended, as Thomas would later explain, to attract Aboriginal people in a visual as well as a religious sense, its spire rising over a hundred feet into the sky. Duncan was just finishing building his church at Metlakatla and Thomas was determined that his would be superior.

As Thomas turned his main attention to the two structures, Emma must have realized just how alone she was in this far-off wilderness. No other person in Fort Simpson shared both her gender and her race.[32] At this point in time persons of paler pigment, termed "white" in the parlance of the day, had no doubts whatsoever of their innate superiority to persons of darker skin tones. Indeed, nothing troubled missionaries more, at the very core of their being, than whether or not the latter could in fact ever become truly Christian. Writing a couple of years later, the Indian commissioner for British Columbia explained the situation in which Emma found herself. "With the exception of the Missionaries I believe there is not one white family within four hundred miles of the Fort. There are only two white men at the Fort, Mr. Morrison, who is the Agent for the Company, and a German, who is <u>his</u> servant."[33] A few years later a count put, apart from Thomas and the head of the trading post, a dozen other male newcomers at Fort Simpson.[34]

Except for Emma, all women at Fort Simpson were either Aboriginal or mixed-race, the offspring of newcomer men and Aboriginal women. From the perspective of women like Emma, they embodied a double complexity. Their Aboriginality made them suspect, but so did their paternity. For a newcomer man to consort with an Aboriginal woman was to demonstrate a weakness of character that would be passed down to their children, who were thereby doubly contaminated by the accident of birth.

The race mixture Emma encountered at Fort Simpson was a complex phenomenon with a long history, going back to the first contacts between newcomers and Aboriginal people. Since the HBC post's foundation in the early 1830s men who arrived with the fur trade cohabited with local women, an arrangement that brought benefits to both sides. Hired on renewable contracts, some of them opted to remain at Fort Simpson for long time periods with their wives and families. A Royal Navy officer reported, based on conversations with Duncan, that when the missionary arrived in October 1857, "he found eighteen men assembled – one Scotch, one English, three Sandwich Islanders [indigenous Hawaiians], and thirteen French Canadians, each having an Indian woman living with him ... There were also seven children, and he was told there were some half-breed children scattered about the camp, who, if he pleased, might be received in the Fort for instruction." It was for that reason, according to an account written five years later, that Duncan almost immediately "opened school with but five half-breed boys belonging to the Fort as pupils, the eldest not five years old," and a week later began another for their fathers.[35] Among their number were young Alfred Dudoward and his father Felix, who used the opportunity to acquire basic literacy by enrolling in the night school Duncan held in the evenings. Katherine Holmes was also a student there, Kate so reminding Duncan sometime after being taken to Victoria by her mother: "I can never forget how kind you were to me when I was a little girl at Fort Simpson when I was at your school. Perhaps you do not remember me, now."[36] In little more than a year Duncan had some 140 Aboriginal and mixed-race children and 120 adults on the school's rolls.[37]

The head of the HBC trading post, Charles E. Morison, Thomas recalled as a "kind English gentleman."[38] Lured to British Columbia in 1862 by the gold rush, the brash seventeen-year-old London merchant's son soon headed north to help lay a telegraph line to Asia. The project was aborted when a competitor got there first; Morison was then hired on by the HBC and moved between its northern posts. In 1870 he took over Fort Simpson from Robert Cunningham, who struck out on his own as a trader after a short stint with the HBC following his break with Duncan over his marriage. During Morison's travels between posts, he gained a deep appreciation for the local women who made their lives in the fur trade. "Truly those Hudson's Bay Ladies were the kindest women on earth ... they were in fact and deed glorious women, good wives, good mothers and kindness itself to all around them." Given that "it was very lonely in that big house at night," Morison not unexpectedly searched out a woman he termed "the best of girls, who has been my true wife and helpmate for forty seven years." Charles Morison, age twenty-six, and Odille Quintal, age seventeen, each signed with a sure hand at their marriage in an Anglican ceremony at Metlakatla on August 10, 1872.[39]

Morison's wife Odille, three or four years Emma's junior, was Elizabeth Cunningham's niece. She and her brother Peter, or Pierre, were the children of

Odille Quintal Morison, c. 1880

PHOTOGRAPHED BY HANNAH MAYNARD,
COURTESY OF HOWARD ALDOUS

François Dubois Quintal and of a local Tsimshian woman named Mary who was the midwife at Fort Simpson and Duncan's first teacher in the Tsimshian language. Born in Quebec in about 1810, Quintal signed on with the HBC in 1832 and spent almost all his time at Fort Simpson until his death in 1862. Peter Quintal would become active in the Methodist church at Simpson. Despite his being Roman Catholic, Odille's father was among the first to take advantage of William Duncan's arrival for both himself and his two children. As did his HBC contemporary Felix Dudouaire, François Quintal enrolled at Duncan's night school at Simpson when it opened in October 1857. He was described in the register as being able to read a few words of English. Quintal dispatched his two children to the day school alongside Dudouaire's son Alfred: Pierre began in October 1857, aged four and a half, and Odille began the next January, aged just two and a half.[40] Odille later taught school at Metlakatla. At the time Emma got to know Charles and Odille Morison they had a daughter named Dolly.

Also giving the Crosbys assistance on their arrival at Fort Simpson was William Henry Pierce, the eighteen-year-old son of a Scot employed at the HBC post of Fort Rupert on northern Vancouver Island and of a Tsimshian woman raised at Fort Simpson who died three weeks after his birth in 1856. According to young Pierce, when his maternal grandfather heard of his daughter's death, he "paddled all the way down the Coast in a large war canoe and going to my father in the Fort [Rupert], announced his intention of taking me away." Pierce recalled how his Scots father "told me afterwards that he went down to the shore and watched and cried as the canoe bore me away." [41] Only a quarter century later would contact resume between father and son. Raised at Fort Simpson and being a nephew of Arthur Wellington Clah, young Pierce got some schooling at Duncan's school until about the age of twelve, at which time he was taken on as a cabin boy on the *Otter*, whose captain taught him in the evenings. Spurred towards Methodism in Victoria through one of Thomas Crosby's fiery sermons during the late 1860s, Pierce was mentored, he later recalled, by Rev. Pollard's daughter Annie. William Henry Pierce accompanied Annie's father as interpreter when he went north in February 1874 to investigate the desire for a missionary at Fort Simpson, and he did the same for the Crosbys during their first six months there. [42]

Thus, in no way were the Crosbys on their own at Fort Simpson. The Dudowards, in particular Kate, taught at the day school and, like Pierce, interpreted for the Crosbys. So, from time to time, did Odille Morison, who also played the organ she and her husband lent for services that were initially held "in a large Indian house." [43] Interpreting was no easy task. Someone who heard Kate Dudoward engaged in this endeavour recalled: "Kate took on the task of interpreter, and what an interpreter she was! The writer has seen her sit on the platform, quietly listening to a full-length sermon, and then, when the minister finished, get up, and without a note, repeat the sermon verbatim. That there was no improvisation has been vouched for by those who could speak both languages." [44] All of these Aboriginal mixed-race people assisted Thomas until he learned Tsimshian. In the interim, he and Emma sometimes resorted to Chinook, the fur trade jargon whose limited vocabulary of several hundred words made it extremely easy to learn. During these years Chinook was almost universally understood along the Northwest Coast.

Intermediaries like Odille Morison, William Henry Pierce, and the Dudowards were key to the missionary advance on the north coast. Emma and Thomas quickly grasped, and took advantage of, their familiarity with both Tsimshian and English languages and with cultural practices. Whether or not the Crosbys chose publicly to acknowledge these people, this mixed-race generation, was fundamental to the missionary couple's well-being from their first hours and days at Fort Simpson. Unfortunately, almost all missionary narratives characterize these intermediaries as being the missionaries' accomplishment as opposed to being their partners or even their predecessors.

The support these intermediaries gave the Crosbys allowed Emma to quickly set about her work in the community, taking charge of Tsimshian health needs and ensuring that education and religious instruction got under way. She managed these duties alongside her commitment to establishing her own household, and in her letters she described not only the range of her participation but also the contributions of the Tsimshian men and women who ensured that the newcomers were made comfortable in their new surroundings. Within a month of her arrival, Emma already considered herself settled.

Fort Simpson, B.C.
July 27th 1874

My dear Mother,

We have just heard that our good ship the "Otter" is at a landing some distance away and will be here tomorrow about noon. It is half past ten now but I have several letters to write before she goes out tomorrow and might get at least one written tonight. The only trouble is there is so much I want to say to you, and my letter cannot be very long. Well, Mother dear, we are really settled in our own home. To be sure it has but three rooms in it, but they are not small, and make a real cosy, pleasant home though the walls are boarded and great beams run across the ceiling. The largest one, which serves as dining room, and for a great many other purposes, is after this wise – the floor is covered with cedar mats – I did not want to put carpets down in this house – the walls hung quite profusely with pictures & maps and other little things. It contains four tables, the melodeon, a rocking chair &c., an old-fashioned fire place, that comes away out into the room – though not very beautiful in itself, when there is a bright fire in it is the making of the whole. One of Auntie's large rugs lies before it. I was afraid of the cinders on my best rugs. The kitchen has the ordinary furniture in it, brought from Victoria. The bedroom is laid with mats & rugs, contains the bedstead, washstand, bureau, two tables meant for our parlor, a set of shelves for the glass &c. and numerous pictures &c on the walls. Your photo & my father's hang over the head of the bed.

I have that Indian boy to help me every day with the work. He can do pretty much everything, except some of the cooking and with that I have got on better than ever I thought I should at first. I had some trouble with yeast at first, but have had bread since that I am sure even Auntie herself would not be ashamed of. We have venison, salmon & halibut in abundance. Shall have other things I suppose after a while. For breakfast this morning we had fried venison & potatoes, toast & coffee. Mrs. Morrison of the Fort has very kindly supplied us with enough milk for the table every day – and many little things also from their garden. Our cow however is on the Otter now I believe, and some other things we sent for. Provisions are dear at the store, and some things we shall have to get from Victoria. The berries about here are not very good. Every day little girls come with gifts of berries for me, but very few we use. The morning school of about seventy children I am teaching. In the afternoon Mr. Crosby has about as many grown people. It will be impossible for him to keep this when the church & house are underway as they will be now immediately and likely for a while I shall take both. There really ought to be a teacher here immediately. There is so much to be done besides. Mr. Crosby has to visit & dispense medicines to the whole village. This is part of the work of every day. There is a great deal of sickness. I have made quantities of gruel & numbers of mustard plasters. Then hour after hour has to be spent in talking with them over their difficulties and troubles. They have to be cared for and dealt with like so many children.

It rains nearly every day & is almost always chilly & cold. We have a fire in our sitting room all the time pretty much. This was so disagreeable, but we are getting used to it now & never think of staying in on account of the rain, only I shall soon want new rubbers I am sure & waterproof & umbrellas. The people are anxious to learn and though they live in much wretchedness I hope they may show improvement before long. The young people are ambitious & promise well. I wish I could tell you more about them but it is really impossible. I did not get this letter finished last night after all – some letters were brought in, sent on from the Otter in a canoe and they must be read and then there was bread to be made up. There was no letter from you. I am in hopes of that today – surely there must be one by this time. There were letters from Eliza, Annie, Susie & the college. I am very anxious to hear from you. And now, Mother, let me assure you that isolated as we are we are yet very happy and comfortable. Our neighbours Mr. & Mrs. Morrison are as kind & friendly as can be. They often run in in the evening and sit a while with us & we always enjoy their visits. They were here for tea the other evening and also Mrs. M's mother a fine intelligent Indian woman who is quite a celebrated nurse about here. She is from the English Church Mission near by [at Metlakatla].

You would see by the [Christian] Guardian [published in Toronto by the Methodist Church] I suppose that there is some opposition from that quarter to our work – however, the people are almost all of them with us, and I don't think we shall be hindered much by it. I thought I should easily get letters written to Auntie & Sallie for this boat, but shall not do so now. Give them my very best love. Thomas would write to you but it is really impossible just now. You can scarcely think how our time is taken up – people are coming constantly. We are scarcely ever alone. I feel just as content & happy as can be. We take a world of comfort in our own home. I never feel lonely. I only wish you could see us here. Love to my father & yourself & Georgie. You have, be assured, the prayers & affection of both my husband and

> Your affectionate daughter,
> Emma

It may be a month or longer before we have another boat so do not be uneasy if you do not hear again very soon. Please send this at once to Susie.

According to Thomas, "our first class meeting was held in a little room inside the fort," but thereafter "Mrs. Crosby taught the school in the large house" belonging to the chief, which Thomas termed an "old heathen house with a mud floor." Some time later the school that Emma described in her letter moved to a large structure improvised out of "slabs of cedar." It was set on "the frame of an old Indian house, about twenty-four by thirty-six feet" that Rev. Tate had purchased while teaching there.[45]

> Fort Simpson, B.C.
> Aug. 15th 1874

My dear Mother,

Again I have an opportunity of sending you a letter. You have heard pretty frequently from us so far, have you not, more often I might almost venture to say than the daughters nearer by have written you in the same time. We were not expecting the "Otter" for another week but yesterday she was observed a long way out on her course northward – and will likely be back and call at the Fort by day after tomorrow (Monday). This hurries us as we had not begun writing. In the winter, of course, we shall not have communication so often – not oftener than once in two, or it may be, three months. It may seem dreary then. I don't know, but now the time passes so quickly, I never feel lonely. There is plenty to do and to think of. The school takes up most of the morning, in the afternoon I am alone, but that is my time for sewing & reading and writing &c. and sometimes Mrs. Morrison comes in to see me then. Two evenings in the week we have meetings and every Wednesday night a few come in to sing. I find the melodeon very useful on these occasions. Some of the people – the old ones especially – wish very much to have it in the church for fear they should die without hearing it. I feel so glad sometimes that I can play at all for

these people. It pleases them however poor as it may be. Then there is a great
deal of visiting the sick and so on. I wish very often that I knew more about
sickness than I do. The people look to us for advice of course. Thomas has had
a good deal of experience but there are cases where we really scarcely know what
to do. Our pictures are a wonder & delight especially the stereoscope. The
other day I sat by a chief from the American side, one who had been a terror to
all about him – had killed two American soldiers at one time. He was in our
sitting room and I was showing him the stereoscope with which he was very
much pleased, and he smiled most benignly upon me. His wife one day took
three young girls, cut their throats and left them to die on the beach. Of course
he is harmless & well-disposed now. A good many strangers like this come to
trade and most of them pay us a visit. We had a very pleasant picnic a few days
ago, a few miles away. We went by canoe, of course. Mrs. Morrison got it up.
We have had beautiful weather for three weeks, but I suppose it will not last
much longer. Two or three days it was quite warm, that is for Fort S. Only once
was I out without a sha[w]l round me and then I had a pretty warm dress on.
There is no extreme cold either, so we shall not suffer either way.

We get on very well as far as living is concerned. Venison is our stand by.
We got some beef from the Otter the last time she was here. Groceries are very
high and as we can get them in Victoria at wholesale prices it is cheaper even
to send there & pay the freight than to buy here – that is for some things – so
we sent for white sugar which is not to be had here, tea, biscuits & some other
things. A lounge came also by the last steamer so we have furniture enough.
Indeed a good many things have to be stored away – we have no room for them.
It seems probable now that our house will be put up this fall – the one we are
in is required. My good husband has as many things to think of & attend to
now as might do for three men. A quantity of lumber has to be got out & prepared here for the buildings & the Indians have to be directed & urged on at
every step. What had to come from the saw mill, a schooner has been char-
tered to bring from Victoria.

Thomas wants very much to write to you – he says there are a great many
things he wants to say to you – but really if you know how he has to attend all
these buildings, & visit the sick & bear on his mind & heart the affairs of the
whole village you would wonder how he ever did it. Whatever accident or
sickness or family or other trouble may occur he has to put right. But we are
happy as can be. Don't feel anxious about us, we are well, and quite content.
I have a young woman to help me in the house. She is clean & tidy & does her
best, only she has a great deal to learn. The boy is going to Victoria. I trust you
and my father are well and comfortable. I think of you so often, and often we
talk of you all. Love to Auntie & Sallie. I have a lot of shells & moss if I could

only send them. Thomas sends love to you both. My best love to my father, and believe me dear Mother

 Ever your affectionate daughter
  Emma

P.S. Just received your & my father's from Castleton.

Emma very soon became aware that letters home needed to be timed to the steamer's arrival. A fellow resident evoked the *Otter*'s meaning: "At times there appeared on the horizon the smoke of a steamer taking the outside passage, travelling either north or south bound. If the smoke remained in one place for a certain length of time we decided the ship was coming in and ... then the excitement ran high, till she came into port." [46] Fort Simpson might be, as one man who knew it well recalled, "about the largest settlement on the Coast, having at the time a population of two thousand souls," but it was still an extremely isolated place. [47] The *Otter* was Emma's lifeline to the world she had left behind.

       Fort Simpson, B.C.
       Aug. 31ˢᵗ 1874

My dear Mother,

It does not seem to me that the opportunities for sending letters come so very seldom after all. We are expecting the Otter again in about a week – but, of course, it is only at the summer season that she comes so frequently. After October I suppose we shall never know when to expect her. Three months we may be perhaps without a mail. Now it seems as though we no sooner get the papers of one boat out of the way before we have to begin writing for the next. It will likely be a week before we have one now but I do not want to be hurried with letters at the last.

 We are getting quite settled in our life here now. Besides everything else – now that the church & house are to be put up – Mr. Crosby has to superintend all the work. The ground is being prepared – it requires a good deal of draining, and leveling – and some clearing. Then there is hewing & sawing & getting out timber – about twenty men are at work. One Chinaman, two white men – the rest Indians. Six o'clock in the morning Thomas goes off to see them at work – except, of course, those off in the woods. Comes back about eight for breakfast and then is busy all day directing the men. It will be impossible to finish the church before the next summer, but the house must be ready for us to move into as soon as possible. The site selected is a very pretty one – facing north –

indeed the whole hill side on which the village is thought to be built faces
north. It is impossible to get any other frontage – but there will be a little
decline to the south behind the house that we hope may do well for a garden
when it is drained & dried. I have taken both schools for the present. It is quite
impossible for Thomas to attend while he has so much else to do. This takes
about two hours in the morning & as much in the afternoon. Then there are
the meetings to be attended & sick to be thought of – and I have to superintend every meal more or less – so altogether I have not much chance to be idle.
However I am well & the happier I dare say for having plenty to do. The Indians
are most of them away now gathering food – sea weed & berries & fishing, but
very many of them will return Saturday night for the Sunday & go away again
Monday morning. We had the melodeon at the S.S. Sunday before last to the
great delight of those present. It is altogether too small for such a place but they
were very anxious to have it so for once we let it go. Our Wednesday evening
practices are going on. Quite a number of new pieces have been learned. Anything that is lively pleases the Indians. "The Water of Life" is very popular and
"The Old Old Story."

The Indians mostly have an idea of respectful, polite behaviour with us, but
sometime[s] their curiosity betrays itself. I was amused one day, going into the
bed-room to find an old man gazing in at the window open on the Fort yard
upon that quilt you made – the log cabin – which was on the bed. He enquired
the price. I suppose he thought he would like to see himself arranged in such a
garb instead of his blanket. Another day a man stood a long time at the window
looking round at the pictures on the wall & expressing his admiration. Pictures
please them very much. The stereoscope almost takes their breath away sometimes. When they are all back – some time in the fall we shall likely have the
magic lantern. I wish I could send you some little Indian curiosities. Numbers
of things have been given us but mostly inconvenient to send away – heads of
bears, wolves &c. with the eyes made to roll about & the mouth to open & close.
They used to wear such things as these at their feasts & dances – some of them
frightfully hideous. We had sent by friends in Victoria by last boat a large box
of apples, some nuts, candies, and a little jar of honey & a few cucumbers. Very
kind, was it not! We have sent to Victoria for tea & biscuits & a good many
other things and are expecting butter from Chilliwhack. The freight will be
a good deal coming so far but cannot be more than the price we pay here for
butter – sixty cents a pound. It comes from near Victoria, I suppose. I was glad
to hear that Annie was safely over her troubles. You have been with her I suppose. I was very much astonished at the news.

I am going to do my best to write to Auntie this time – if I should not
find it possible give her & Sallie my best love. Love also to Mrs. Edwards, Mrs.

McD and any others. Thomas I hope will get a few minutes to write you. He will if possible & sends his kindest regards to you all. I was very glad to get my Father's letter. With much love to him & you & Georgie.

I am as ever yours affectionately
Emma

Sep 31st

A whole month this letter has been lying waiting for the Otter to come – we fully expected her three weeks ago but there is no regularity to her trips. Yesterday however she did make her appearance after an absence of seven weeks. She will likely make another trip next month and then not be here again until January. It seemed a long time to wait for letters – and delayed the work of building some – as the plans were to come by her – but the schooner arrived also yesterday with the lumber – so things will have to be pushed now, as much as can be. The heavy fall rains have set in though & we shall likely have very little more fine weather – so our house being ready before winter is very doubtful. It seems likely now that we shall remain where we are till spring.

The wet weather is rather trying but you know I do not take cold readily and on the whole have been very well. Mr. Crosby, strong as he is, is really more liable to cold than I am and being out often nearly the whole day in the rain I sometimes fear it may be injurious – still all that he does seems to be necessary and I trust his strength may be as his day.

We were between three & four weeks without a bit of butter owing to the delay of the Otter. However that is not likely to occur. We rec. a keg of sixty pounds from Chilliwhack yesterday & shall send for a little more from Vic so as to have a supply secure till the spring. Indeed we mean to depend on the Co.'s store for very little they are often so poorly supplied & the prices so high. The butter is now 75 cts. Quite a lot of things came upon the schooner – flour, hams, tea, eggs &c.

We had also sent to us by kind Victoria friends two boxes of apples, a dozen jars of preserved fruit & some other little things – and by the family we stayed with there a box of beautiful green gages and egg plums. It does me good to know we are remembered there. I am getting in a good supply of cran-berries also. They are very plentiful so we shall have fruit all winter I believe after all. I think none of your letters have miscarried. I see by this boat that from Cobourg & also one from Castleton. I was quite startled to hear that my scribblings had been read for the edification of the so august a body as the Miss. Con. & I see a letter of Thomas' in the Guardian that was written without any idea of publication. But I am glad these things should awaken much. Love to my father and yourself, from

> Your loving daughter
> Emma

Emma's letter evokes the power of visual images linked to the new technology of photography. The stereoscope paled before the "magic lantern" as a means to entertain and thereby to convert. The stereoscope gave biblical pictures or photographs a three-dimensional quality, but they had to be viewed individually, whereas the magic lantern used light to project hand painted or photographic glass slides onto a wall or a white sheet. If the slides were inserted fast enough, the images appeared to move and so tell a story. The use of a darkened room not only heightened the power of these "moving pictures" but also gave an almost supernatural quality to the event itself. Missionaries found this a very effective means of getting their message across.

> Fort Simpson, B.C.
> Sep. 3rd 1874

Dear Mother,

I have often promised myself to give you a short note but I have been so pressed with work I have not had time, and now it must be short. I have volumes I could tell you but I know Emma has kept you pretty well informed in a general way. I have only to say we are as happy as it is possible for us to be considering our work, isolation &c. And every day our happiness increases. Indeed it could not be otherwise for I believe we have been divinely directed in all our plans, journey &c. And surely if ever any two were in a good field for work for the Master we have it here. Yes and God blesses us in our work more and more. I often think of what Mr. Douse said to me on our way to Collingwood, "Take care of the Lord's work and he will take care of you" and so we prove every day.

Well but you will say how about the house keeping? Well, tell Auntie, we never once had poor bread and we have venison and fish done up in every way that is nice to the taste. And clam soup, &c. &c. We have had no bear or wild cat, as yet, but have been blessed with all that is necessary to make life happy. It is feared that some of the people here may be needing food before the winter is passed, as the summer run of salmon was very poor. We hope for the best. My dear wife has told you about her help and so on. We have had variety. We have a young girl now and I know if she stays long she will be able to keep a house clean and tidy.

Emma has had to take both schools of late for I have been so busy and shall be for another month till we get the house up, that I cannot take the work which I would. We must have help. The climate is very wet but thank God we are both well and happy and I have no doubt but while we do our duty and trust in God, all will work well.

    Love to Mr. Douse and all the rest.
    Your affectionate son-in-law
      T. Crosby

We have waited long for the Otter. Emma was unwell yesterday but is better. Mrs. Morrison and her mother are just in and she says I am to say that Emma has a mother at Ft. S. who will take care of her when she is sick.

    T.C.

The approach of winter gave relief from hot weather but made Emma realize more than ever the commitment she had made to another, still alien way of life. In her letters she carefully balanced the desire for an emotional outlet with the need to reconcile her mother to her decision, taken so precipitously a few short months earlier.

While Emma's letters did not mention her pregnancy, it is almost certain she made her mother aware of it. One way in which she might have done this would have been through inserting in her letter a small note intended only for her mother. During this time many women used this method to convey information whose intimacy was such that it could not be generally shared. Marked "Private," these "slips" would be removed from letters prior to their being circulated among family members.[48]

                             Fort Simpson, B.C.
                             Nov. 2nd 1874

My dear Mother,

The Otter came again day before yesterday (Saturday) and our letters are to be sent off by canoe tonight to catch her at a point below on her return. I have written to my father but would like to add a little to you. I am glad you have had so pleasant a summer. I hope you made a visit to Thomas' friends. They were expecting you I know. You speak of my health. It is I know of much importance I should keep well – but, I assure you there is no cause of uneasiness at present. I am very well now. Much better than I used often to be in Ont. The summer was a little trying, owing I suppose to the travel & change of climate but I have grown much stronger since. I had a cold, which Thomas spoke of when he wrote you but it only kept me in the house some two days. I dress warmly – have put on my lambswool vests besides all other flannels and shall likely never go without all the year round, as long as we are here. Thomas suffered very much some ten days ago from a boil on his hand. For two nights he scarcely slept the pain was so acute but it is almost quite well and within a week has him making almost super-human exertions to get the house up. We had five days of fine weather in which time the main part was put up & covered in, just in time to escape a heavy storm that came on Saturday. The lumber that was wanting the Otter has brought – so fires will be kept up to dry the lumber & the work pushed on, so that we may hope to be in it some time before Christmas.[49] It was only by getting some lumber out extra by the pit saw (if you know what that is – I only learned lately) that the building could be gone on with before the Otter came – and if that one spell of good weather had been lost likely nothing could be done till next spring. You know my husband is a "pushing man." We shall be very comfortable I believe when we get settled. I will send you a full description, all being well, when we are in it. The carpets I shall try to get made as soon as I can, ready to put down. There is so much work I want to do. We have it in our minds to get up a Xmas tree for the children. Quite a number of dolls & toys have been sent us from friends in Vict. and a lot of things to be made up. If I can only get the time – a great part of the work & all the direction I shall have to do myself. Mrs. Morrison will help me though, but then she has no idea at all of such work. My little girl does just as well as I could expect in the house, but of course she can take no responsibility – at all – & I have not the time I would like to teach her. Besides I want to make her neater & tidier than she is now and have to take time to show her how to sew all I give her. The washing & ironing I get done well & cheap. I scarcely trouble myself at all about that. There is no fear of my being hurt with hard work – if I propose anything of the kind my husband puts his foot down against it at once – and of course I have enough else to do. Pray, Mamma, do not trouble about snakes. Since I came to the country I have seen neither snake nor anything that looked like a snake. We are right on a rocky, sandy beach where a snake would die in a day, & even back from the shore the ground is covered not with grass much but a kind of moss – while the nearest woods are up on the hill sides, I suppose half a mile away – perhaps more. Indeed the timber for building was brought much of it about ten miles. All about here has been used for the firewood of many years.

We have supplies from Vict. for the house, flour, sugar, biscuits, hams, tea, coffee, raisins, currants, lard, butter &c. to see us I think well through the winter. Thomas is determined that no improvidence shall leave us without what we need. Mr. Russ of N. Westminster sent us a huge box of apples – hold a brl & half anyway. The friends we stayed with in Vict. sent also a large box of pears & another of apples which last however has as yet failed to appear. I hope it is not lost. Another Vict. lady sent a large cake & as this was the last boat this year a Xmas pudding, partly cooked. So you see we have friends who do not forget us. I sent to Vict. by the Capt. for a warm shawl. He brought me a very handsome one – more expensive much than I wanted but my husband says it is not too much – when it is for me. I send you a small gold nugget from the Cassiar mines up the Stickeen river. It was given me by a miner who had just come down and now this is the last chance I shall have to wish you a Merry Xmas & happy New Year. May God bless you all at home and be with us here. We expect the Otter again about the latter end of January. Love to Auntie, Sallie & all, and be assured, dear Mother, you have the true affection of your daughter & of her husband.

Emma Crosby

At the beginning of 1875 Thomas Crosby dispatched the first of what were to become regular public letters reporting on the Fort Simpson mission that were printed in the Methodist press.[50] Intended to elicit the maximum of emotional and financial support, the letters include passing references to "Mrs. Crosby" and may have benefited from her editorial assistance. Their content is not wholly inconsistent with Thomas's earlier published accounts but is much more sophisticated and nuanced.[51] The letters were very different from his private correspondence, which was rambling and grammatically incorrect, reflecting his sparse education. Whatever the logistics of their creation, the published letters reflect his state of mind and perspective. The information included about Emma, if refracted through a male lens, was factually consistent with the letters she signed as her own compositions.

Thomas explained in his first public letter how, the lumber having arrived, "our Mission-house was commenced by myself and Indians; and amidst rain and frost and snow, we worked on, until the week before Christmas we were so far on, that we were able to move in into it."[52] He referred to "the assistance of an old French-Canadian," whom he did not name and who must have been an HBC employee or former employee.[53]

The mission house was located "on the side of the mountain, about a quarter of a mile from the beach [with] four rooms on the ground floor and two up stairs, which are not finished, and a kitchen and woodshed behind the main building."[54] The house was not entirely for private use. Included was a "reception room for the Indians, where they find ready access and welcome at all times."[55] By the time the lumber for the mission house got to Simpson, Thomas also had, he reported, "got out nearly all the heavy timber for the main building of the church" so that its construction could begin as soon as weather permitted.[56]

There was also the matter of maintaining the schools and, just as important, of learning the language.

> We have tried to keep both schools going; Mrs. Crosby took them up to Christmas, and sometimes it was so cold in the old Indian house in which it was held, that it was really scarcely safe. Although the climate here is not so extremely cold, yet it is very damp and trying. Alfred [Dudoward] and his wife still assist ... They are a great help to us indeed; we could not proceed without them. I am trying to get the language ... I hope soon to be able to do without an interpreter.[57]

At about the same point in time Thomas described how "Mrs. C. has taken nearly all the time [at the day school, which enrolled about seventy-five adults and seventy-five children] with the assistance of Alfred Dudoward and Kate his wife, who have been invaluable helps as interpreters."[58] Visiting a few months later, Rev. Pollard reflected how "the efficient state of the school is no doubt owing, in a great measure, to the energy and wisdom of Mrs. Crosby, who, from the time of her arrival at the Fort, has taken a deep interest in training the native mind, and has had such a thorough training herself, she was especially qualified to give it the best possible shape."[59]

Emma Crosby quickly moved into her responsibilities as a missionary wife. She tended to the school and reached out to the Aboriginal community at Fort Simpson more generally. In doing so, she was assisted by Aboriginal mixed-race intermediaries who both literally and figuratively translated between cultures for her and for Thomas.

3
Motherhood

Emma's role as missionary wife became more complex with the completion of the new mission house and the birth of her first child. On December 23, 1874, just a few days after the Crosbys moved into their new home, she became the mother to a daughter they called Jessie, and who the Tsimshian named Ash-she-gemk, meaning the moon's leg, or moonbeam.[1] Thomas's first letter for publication signalled the birth in a coded fashion that would be explicit to any woman reading the text. "Mrs. Crosby was sick at the time [of the Christmas celebrations], and, though she had been preparing for it for weeks, could not be present to enjoy it."[2] Only several months later, with Rev. Pollard's report in the press following his visit to Fort Simpson as head of the Methodist Church in British Columbia, was the birth publicly recognized. "Mrs. Crosby and baby were well."[3]

Motherhood provided Emma with a new basis of authority within the mission. The move into the new home enabled her to exemplify the Victorian ideal upon which Aboriginal women were to model their homes, and the addition of a child to show them that properly practising their "maternal duty" was an important step towards becoming good Christian women who could be respected by white society. Emma illustrated what it meant to be a virtuous wife and mother. In the words of Dana Robert: "The missionary family was a living example of Christianity, and by its very existence was a sermon more powerful than that given by a preacher. In other words, the missionary man preached through word, but the missionary woman devoted to her family witnessed through deed."[4]

Emma's new role extended outward from her immediate family to the Tsimshian women and children for whom she increasingly took responsibility. The mission home and the birth of her daughter brought women to help with domestic duties and put young girls into Emma's charge. Historian Myra

Rutherdale has examined the images of motherhood in the mission enterprise, focusing largely on women who worked in the mission field on their own. She suggests that the institution of motherhood was particularly strategic in providing missionary women with the freedom to expand their work. "Motherhood became an essential part of the identity of missionary women and, to a significant degree, it justified their work. Moreover, notions of being a 'mother' to Aboriginal peoples gave women a feeling of both physical safety and superiority in the field."[5]

For missionary wives, such as Emma, maternal responsibility for the charges that lived in the mission home formed an important part of their obligations. A mother-daughter-like relationship could be nurtured without interference from the young girls' families, the members of which were thought, almost inherently, to neglect their children and to be incapable of providing adequate care or supervision. According to a contemporary description: "For several years these girls were clothed and fed at the Missionary's expense; and better still, Mrs. Crosby shared with these defenceless ones the mother love of her heart."[6] Only the guidance of the "mother of the mission" could save these young girls. "The metaphors of motherhood and family were relied on to organize a sustained structural intrusion into the lives of northern Aboriginal peoples."[7]

Emma accepted without question the need to protect those who came into her care. In Emma's mind, the girls needed to be saved not only from themselves but also from the influences of their surrounding community. As her husband explained, "they would come, one after another, and ask the Missionary's wife for her protection; and thus one and another and another were taken into the house."[8] Emma took her mentoring responsibilities very seriously, considering it her duty to have her charges adopt the ways she took for granted. Because, as everyone agreed during those years, the maintenance of the home was women's work, it was absolutely essential that the girls be prepared for marriage and motherhood. It was on these precepts that Emma's good intentions were directed towards the young Aboriginal girls whom she took into her care.

The role of mother was significant to Emma, and she shared with her own mother the joys, hardships, and challenges of motherhood. Thomas was not always so sympathetic. He described how, when the steamer *Otter* "arrived in the midst of a snowstorm" shortly after the birth of her first child and "we got hold of our mail bag we found, among the letters, a note with a cheque of fifty dollars from a friend in Quebec, saying that it was for some comfort and help to my wife as a momento of our last visit to them." Thomas then turned to Emma, who was caring for a premature infant, and said: "Look here, my dear, I am going to use this entirely for your comfort, for it is solely for your comfort that the School House is being fixed, and here is half enough to pay for the material."[9] And that is exactly what he did with the money.

Fort Simpson, B.C.
January 5th 1875

My dear Mother,

What do you think has happened! I have a startling piece of information to
give you – and even at the risk of stunning you all with astonishment, I must
give it right off. It is this – as I sit in the rocking chair writing there is lying on a
pillow on the lounge beside me a bundle of flannel and other garments inside
of which sleeps a wee little girl – just the sweetest, dearest little thing her
mother ever saw. I am her mother – you know. To say you will be surprised will
be putting it mildly, I suppose. We were rather surprised ourselves – not that
she should come but that she should come so soon. We were expecting her
about the end of February – but it is all right and we are both of us very thankful and happy.

    And now I want to tell you all about it soberly. We had been in our new
house a week, but were just beginning to get things a little settled – as it had
been free of workmen but one day. Then Christmas was right at hand and we
had ever so much to do to prepare for that – my chief burden was a Christmas
tree we were to have for the children for which I had been working for some
time. Wednesday the 23rd Dec. I proposed making a lot of cakes for the children – a young girl was coming to sew the sitting room carpet – and various
other things were to be accomplished – but "the best laid schemes" &c. I woke
in the morning feeling Oh! so, so – you know all about it. I was innocent –
thought I must have taken cold & feared inflammation and applied mustard &
hot flannels &c still clinging to the idea that I might by & by be able to get up
and make my cakes. About noon I thought it might do me good to get up, so
Thomas helped me to dress & took me out to the sitting room – but that did
not seem to do any good either. I could only lie on the lounge & wonder how
long it would last. It occurred to me once or twice that it might possibly be
what it proved to be – but I dismissed the thought as extremely improbable.
However in the afternoon Thomas had to go down to the village to a wedding
and I said I thought perhaps he had better go and ask Mrs. Morrison's mother
to come and see me. She is a woman experienced in nursing white ladies in the
Fort & elsewhere and always said she would take care of me when I was sick.
So she came, and after a little Mrs. Morrison came too. This must have been
near five o'clock. They seemed to understand it at once and when she said to
my husband, in Chinook, "You had better get everything ready," we understood it too. Well, this gave me something to think about. I had not finished
my sewing, and nothing I had made had been washed – and the house being
so unsettled, things were in every part of the house. However everything

necessary was at hand in a marvelously short space of time, and airing before the sitting room fire – powder & sweet oil & essentials such as those I had provided long ago – and it was chiefly the finery – day dresses, & the shawl, that I had left. I was waiting for the Otter to bring me trimmings. I had to tell where everything was to be found and Thomas was flying about pretty briskly for a while.

About half past five I walked into the bed-room & undressed, and by six, my little daughter was using her lungs most lustily and very shortly afterwards as I was lying comfortably in bed talking with my husband our little girl was brought in from the sitting room where she had been dressed in the clothes Susie sent, and a square of flannel pinned round her for a blanket. She was, of course, very small indeed, but is perfectly formed and thus far seems as strong and well in every way as ever a baby could be. She took to her natural food at once, and every day she seems to improve. She has never given us any trouble yet, night or day. She sleeps on my arm at night and except the first night when the nurse carried her round the bed to put her on the other side of me, no one has had to be up with her at all. She wakes once or twice to take some nourishment and goes off to sleep again. During the day she sleeps most of the time too – but of course I do not expect this to continue long.

Would you like to know what this far off little granddaughter looks like? Her limbs are long for her size but very thin – her face round and full. She will look very like her father, I think. She has a great lot of brown hair. It does not curl yet but it may by and by. Dark blue eyes and well defined nose and mouth – and rather a long chin. It is a very sweet little face to us, and would be to you too, I think, if you could see it. Her father makes a very good nurse whenever he has time to take her, and in case of necessity would be just as clever as any one could be in taking care of her, I know. Our baby will be a great comfort to us, I believe, if she is spared. We have a world of happiness in our home anyway. I often fear my heart is too much taken up with it. I cannot help now feeling a little anxious sometimes about baby, just because she came so soon and is so small, but I have really far more reason to be thankful & hopeful than anything else. She will be two weeks old tomorrow and thus far has appeared to be in most perfect health. We must do all we can to keep her well – and trust her to Divine keeping. The Indians seem delighted that we have – as they expressed it – "found" a baby at Fort Simpson. They come to see her – old men & boys, women and all – and take the tips of their fingers and turn aside the shawl to peep at her as she lies asleep, and exclaim "so small," and certainly compared with the great babies the Indian women have she is small indeed. She is known already by an Indian name they have given her – Asseh-e-gemk – which means Leg of the Moon – this is moonbeam. It is a name that could only be borne by a chief's daughter – and her father & I are spoken of, after their manner with themselves, as the father & mother of Asseh-e-gemk. Several curious little carved wooden dishes, one in the form of a duck, another a frog, have been given her – and a square of gray fur lined with white cotton. And now I think I won't write any more tonight. I will tell you all about myself and other things some other day – perhaps tomorrow.

Jan 6th – The baby is asleep and I have just finished a little sewing I had to do, so I will write now till my husband comes to dinner. I will write about myself now a while. I never told you about my expectations for I thought you might feel anxious if I did and there was time enough yet. I meant to send you word by the next boat. Susie I asked to send me some things I wanted but I said she had best not mention it to anyone else for a while. Whether she whispered anything to you or not, I don't know. It is all right if she did.

Last summer I suffered a good deal in the mornings with sickness, owing I think chiefly to the inconvenience of so much going about from place to place. After we were fairly settled here a while that ceased to trouble me and all the fall & winter I was as well as ever in my life. I got quite fat and was strong and well as could be. I had both schools all that time – was away from them only two days before I was sick and that was because I wanted to get on with the work in the house. Whether anything I did in the house brought on the event or not I scarcely know. We had plenty of people to help us and Thomas never would let me do any but very light work when he was by – but Christmas is such a time of play with them that as it drew near the day they did not care to work. The Monday before I was sick my washerwoman was sent for in the midst of her work to stand up at a wedding, so she left ever so much undone that I wanted finished that day. The kitchen was in a dreadful state of disorder and I felt as though I could not leave it so and therefore I proceeded to attack things myself. I took one brush and the little girl I have another & we scrubbed the walls &c. – not the floor – I did not attempt that – and by and by a satisfactory change came over the face of things, and a satisfaction to my mind also – and I did not feel so very tired though I had moved some pretty heavy things. The next day I was sewing on the carpets, and walked a good deal in the afternoon & evening and felt really very tired when I got home. Then the day after that was the eventful Wednesday. It may be that I exerted myself too much – but I was so well all the time and had so much exercise every day which I am sure was good for me that I did not feel afraid. Indeed I never felt any fear in the matter, either with regard to the nursing & care that would be necessary or anything else. I was very glad & happy in the prospect of motherhood, and always felt sure that all necessary provision would be made – that I should not be suffered to want for anything – and so it proved. Nature seems to do her work perfectly. There was no difficulty or trouble of any kind – everything seemed favorable – only, of course, the necessary pain had to be borne. I suppose I am scarcely qualified to judge, but my labor must have been an easy one for I did not feel at all exhausted when it was over as I had expected. I talked just as strongly as though I was not sick at all and felt as though it would be no trouble at all to get up and walk about. My nurse is I believe really clever and was very nice in her way of doing things. We felt both of us – I mean my husband and myself – very thankful that a kind providence brought us through this so safely and happily – so our way seems to have been prepared for us all through – we have never lacked anything that was necessary to our comfort and happiness. My recovery has been as steady and rapid as one could reasonably wish. I felt strong from the first, but, of course, I knew I must be cautious. The morning after baby came – I had ever so much to think about – her clothes had to be found and counted out before me for the wash – then the Christmas tree. I had to talk about that ever so much. The same afternoon I sat up in bed and combed out and braided my hair almost entirely by myself. Thomas was going to do it for me but he was called away so I went on with it myself. The next day was Christmas. Early in the morning the people came trooping up to the house in companies of twenty or thirty to wish us a happy Christmas, till I suppose as many as three hundred men, women & children had shaken hands with me as I lay in bed, had apples passed to them in the study and gone away. All day long they kept coming – sometimes the house would be thronged and I had to talk, talk, talk. Still it seemed to do me no harm. I grew stronger every day. Sunday they gave me a little beef steak for breakfast – my appetite was good from the first. I wanted to be careful, and meant to stay in bed patiently till the tenth day – but I began to feel that I should really be better up, so the eighth day I was dressed and Thomas helped me out into the sitting room and fixed me in a large rocking chair with a warm carriage rug thrown over it and my feet on a hassock before a fine open fire – and I enjoyed it I assure you. The view from the window was in itself a delight. It was a bright day & a quantity of fresh snow lay on the ground. Just below us is the village – then the sweep of water on one side of which stretches for miles a line of glistening mountains and here & there dotted with thickly wooded islands.

I did not sit up too long the first day – but the next morning got up again & did a little sewing. And so every day since I have seemed to gain strength. I feel very, very thankful that everything has gone on so well. No one could be kinder or readier in her attentions than the nurse I have. She is extremely careful about airing & warming everything for both me and the baby and is very nice & clean in her ways. Indeed the amount of washing she requires done is something appalling – but that is better than the other extreme. She washes & tends the baby very nicely and that I think more of than anything else. But she has very little idea of cooking and for a day or two I had rather a poor time. My gruel was either raw or thick with lumps and my tea tasted like nothing but lukewarm water with a great deal of sugar in it. But Thomas came to my rescue and by looking after things himself a little got the good woman to understand better so that now I have splendid gruel every night and very good tea. Then my good husband has been getting up in the mornings early and in a very short time has tea made & biscuits toasted for me. He brought them in to me ever so many mornings before my nurse was awake. It is late before the family breakfast and I seemed to need something earlier.

Jan 26th I am alone just now with my baby so I may as well go on with my writing. It may not be for long though that I can write – there are sundry noises proceeding from the rocking chair where we have made the little girl's bed which indicates she would like to be taken up. Thomas has gone to the meeting we have Tuesday evening and our little servant also. The nurse left us last Saturday – at the end of the month. She said she would come still & wash the baby but yesterday she went off to Metlakatla so I am left to myself. Excepting for the baby I did not care to have her stay longer. Her housekeeping was not after my heart. The bedroom she did keep nicely – but beyond that – alas! Of course I had made no arrangements so everything had to be left to her and the little girl. They did their very best, I believe, the house was swept about half a dozen times a day – that is the broom was flourished about in the middle of the room so as to send all the dust into the corners. With the one exception of the woman who comes to wash & do extra work for me I do not know an Indian who seems to have an idea of thorough cleanliness. The first sight I had of the kitchen made my heart go right into my moccasins. Then tea, sugar, biscuits &c. seemed to have wings, and the dogs ran away with the meat, and dishes were broken, and things in the wash were singed, and besides the constant use of one lamp and sometimes two, two lbs. of candles were used in four nights and candles are fifty cts. a lb. I did so long to be about again. Well, we struggled through, and now the house is quite settled and we have something like a regular order of work. My danger will be, I suppose, attempting too much – but I will try to be careful. This little girl we have is about fifteen – she is really a very faithful, devoted cheerful little thing and, I believe, will do very well. Indeed now she does very nicely as long as I can direct her a little. I have drawn on the inside of this sheet a plan of the house, which I hope will give you some idea of the place we live in. You must understand that it is entirely of wood. There is no plaster about it – except indeed about the fireplaces. It is lined with narrow boards which in time are to be either painted or stained & varnished. There is a good deal of work still to be done. The mantel pieces are not on yet – nor the sideboard nor the upstairs finished, but we have it now so that is very comfortable and it is not to be really finished till next summer when the lumber will be perfectly dry & can be made quite tight. You ask if we have a good bed. It is as good as I ever slept on I think. The bedstead is a new one & quite pretty one we got in Victoria. The mattress we got there too. It is made of something similar to wool. The bureau has a large oval glass, marble top & white knobs – the washstand of an approved pattern. So with the new carpet and some of Auntie's little mats & your nice one beside the bed, it is a cosy little room. The sitting room is very bright & cheerful with the bright carpet &c. There is a green lounge in it, an oval center table & a little stand, a rocking chair &c. The study & dining room are plainly furnished – the floors covered with cedar mats. The dining room has a couple of tables, cane-seated chairs & a little low seat made of a box for me when I tend baby. The study we use mostly for our sitting room. Thomas has to be there most of the time of course. It is hung with pictures & maps & contains the book cases, an oval table covered with green baize, a little dresser, the melodeon, my rocking chair, a couple other chairs & two stained & varnished benches &c. This is where the people all come. The space under the stairs we use as a wood-box, being just at hand for all the fires. A barrel sunk just outside the kitchen door – i.e. in the shed, gathers water from a little stream running underground. Altogether the house could not be more convenient – thanks to the builder's energy & good sense. I only wish you could see it.

Feb 11th Yesterday the "Otter" came to our delight after an absence of four months. We were O so glad to hear from you all & so thankful that there was none but good news. Many thanks for the handsome breakfast shawl, and also the little ruff. The shawl is just what I was wanting. Thomas wanted to get me one last summer but I would not let him. It is really a beauty so soft and warm.

And now we have only two days in which to do ever so much writing. I have told you nothing yet about the village affairs. Christmas was grandly celebrated. The whole village was decorated with flags & ever-greens, the bridge & walks arched over in many places. The [old] church, smoked & black as it is, was made quite beautiful, hung with white sails, trimmed & festooned with greens & decorated with mottoes. The Christmas tree was a great pleasure to the children. I should have been glad indeed of your help, but we managed to get enough little things for all. Then we had Christmas carols sung through the village. They came up to our house. Thomas was with them & sang for me & baby. About forty young men & boys had been practicing for some time & they really sang very nicely indeed. Christmas eve Mr. Morrison & Thomas together gave a feast to the whole village. A few of the young men managed the cooking &c., it consisted of rice sweetened with molasses, tea & biscuits. The largest house of the village was filled with tables – each person brought the dishes necessary for him or herself and speeches followed. Then portions were sent round to some forty sick who could not be there. For a week or more there was continual feasting & playing through the whole village, but without any of their old heathen practices whatever. New Year's night Thomas gave a Magic Lantern exhibition which was a great wonder & delight. Mr. Morrison & Mrs. M's brother helped to work it & it was managed very well. Of course, I could join in none of these things – but I was just as happy, in bed with our baby. I did feel sorry that I could do nothing to make a cheery Christmas for my husband at home, but he was so busy planning for the pleasure of the people that I do not think he missed it & he found his happiness in making others happy & in seeing the baby & me well..

We have had some trouble, or rather annoyance from the neighbouring English church mission. Mr. Duncan reigns a petty tyrant in his village. He is a J.P. which give[s] him a vast power – power to frighten the poor people of the whole region with his court & jail. Moreover he modifies & adapts the law wonderfully to suit himself & adjudicates in cases in which he has no legal right whatever to do so. It seems to afford him special delight now to bring up & fine the people of this village. He appears really almost demented on the subject of his power & authority, and resorts sometimes to the most brutal methods of punishment with his own people – over them he exerts the most absolute control. They cannot leave the village even to trade or procure food for a few days without his permission. That anyone should presume to come within fifteen miles and start a mission & gain any influence over the people drives him almost wild though for fourteen years he never came near the place except to frighten or punish offenders. Every Indian who goes there from Fort Simpson has to listen to a violent tirade against this mission and is told that it will soon fall, and so on. The fact is that before we came, he boasted that a missionary would never come here, that <u>he</u> had written to put a stop to it, and if one did come he would send him over to Queen Charlotte's Is. and all such nonsense as that. He always speaks of Thomas to the Indians by an Indian name which means a wild bad man. He insists upon being addressed himself by the Indian name of "chief." He seems to be constantly watching for an opportunity to give us trouble. Last summer it was found necessary to remove some graves from the site chosen for the church. Many of the people were away fishing at the time, but Thomas took the trouble to send word to those concerned and obtain their consent to the removal of the bodies of their friends & had them all nicely interred in the grave yard. However, it appeared afterwards there was one old man interested who had not been consulted and visiting Metlakatla some time after was, according to the old man's own story, put up by Mr. Duncan himself to lodge a complaint against Mr. Crosby for the violation of his friend's grave. This gave Mr. D. the opportunity – though he did not venture to issue a summons at once – to write some most insulting letters to Thomas threatening him with a summons unless he obtained a paper signed by all concerned to the effect that they were satisfied or would <u>forgive</u> the act, and this paper he – Mr. D. – would forward to the Government to obtain their sanction. The fulsomeness of the letter was really amusing. Of course, Thomas replied that he would relieve him of that trouble as he was himself in direct communication with the Gov. on the affairs of the village, and had already written the Indian Agent on the subject.

The old man who had complained was found and on the matter being fairly laid before him he was quite satisfied & at once became a warm friend to us. But in the meantime a woman was found in Metlakatla who laid another charge on the same ground. Her brother is a chief living here – and it so happened that she was with her brother at their fishing station last summer when Mr. Crosby sent him word about the matter and in the presence of a white man who wrote Thomas about it, she was consulted & gave her consent. So to put an end to it, Thomas one fine day went down to Metlakatla, taking the old man with him and with the woman & the man before Mr. D., two white men & one or two other Indians being present, he put the matter so plainly & cornered him so completely that I fancy he felt his own importance less than he had for many a year. It will be some other method of attack he will try next time. Thomas had to be away a night & stayed in the house of Mrs. Morrison's mother – of course the hospitalities of the Mission house were not offered him. Mr. [William Henry] Colinson a minister who assists Mr. D. was polite as far I suppose as he dared to be knowing the spirit of the "Chief."

The effect of this will not be, as we believe, to at all hinder our work here in the end, but for these poor, simple people to see that two missionaries cannot live peaceably together is not likely to do them good. Thomas gains constantly in influence over the people. They come to him with everything. I wish I had time to tell you about some of the cases that come up. But I must soon close. A teacher for the school here put in an appearance yesterday on the arrival of the "Otter." He is very tall, stoops very much, has curly hair, a slow dragging gait, and is a Scotchman, named [Angus] McKenzie, who appears to make one or two complete revolutions of his body every time he shuts a door behind him. I won't say anything more about him yet. We were not very well prepared to receive him – a part of the upstairs is curtained off for his accommodation at present where he has the necessaries of a bed-room.

Our baby grows finely, and is just as well as a baby could be, I think. Her hair is beginning to curl. She has a great quantity of it – and her eyes are big and so blue. She grows sweeter – to us – every day. It is a real pleasure to me to take care of her. I was a little afraid of washing her at first, but now I feel quite at home at it. I have been sewing for her a good deal, so now I think she has as many things as she will need till she is to be put in short clothes. She will be a great comfort to us, I am sure, if she is spared. Her father is never happier, I know, than when he has her in his arms – he makes a splendid nurse – nor prouder than when he carries her through the village and the old women and all come to look at her as children would at a peep-show. To take her into an Indian house makes as much commotion as would the advent of a royal child. It is wonderful how much these people seem to think of her. She has two cradles, both made by Indians in the village & given to her, and really very nicely made they are. One of them has posts that you would suppose had been turned & most elaborately, but they were cut all with a knife. I call them cradles, but we preferred them without rockers, so they are more like little cots. We have not quite decided what name we shall give her. We are thinking of Jessie. I do wish you could see her.

I am going to trouble you to get something for me. I find I have not enough of that crimson curtaining. Would you try to match it if you can, or as nearly as you can & send me two yards. Susie says she has some money to my credit. Please get it from her for it & send by simple post. When are you & my father going to have those photos taken? I have given your name to several in the village. They so often ask us to choose names for them. It is borne by a chief's wife & a little baby Eliza died the other day.

I had a very handsome little present from Miss Stinson by the Otter – a silver mustard pot lined with green. I feel as well as ever I did in my life. I am glad that Eliza has got over her trouble all right.

Now I really must close. Love to Auntie & Sallie & all friends in Barrie.

I must ask you to send this letter round to the girls. I cannot write them all as fully as I would wish. Thomas will write to you I think. I have astonished you, have I not? I do queer things, you know, sometimes. Love to my father and yourself – we so often talk about you. We shall have the boat now likely every month, so please write often.

> Again with love
> Your affectionate daughter
> Emma

Emma had good reason to fret over William Duncan at Metlakatla, as he was doing his best to thwart the Methodist mission. According to the British Columbia Indian commissioner, ever since the Crosbys' arrival, Duncan "openly expressed opposition to what he considers a rival establishment." [10] Duncan was a self-acknowledged utopian, whose model was the English village, where each

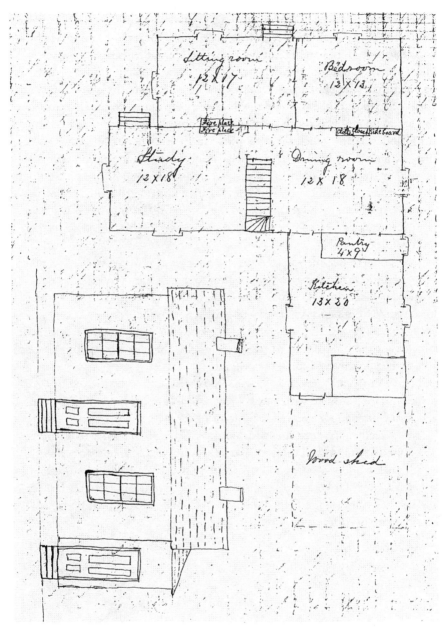

Emma's plan of the mission house, enclosed in her letter of January 5, 1875

nuclear family occupied its own small cottage. Duncan sought, as he put it, "a Christian village" set apart from "the deadening and enthralling influence of heathen customs."[11] Appointed a provincial justice of the peace in 1863, Duncan used the position to discourage Metlakatla residents from having any contact whatsoever with the outside world. Charles Morison, in charge of the HBC post at Fort Simpson and "closely acquainted" with Duncan, recalled: "He was the only magistrate on the coast, and had everything his own way. He ruled the Indians most despotically, flogging both men and women when he chose. He took [German ruler] Bismark for his model and … was a true autocrat."[12] Duncan's attempt to use his office to discredit Thomas for having opened up Aboriginal graves without getting the permission of all families and provincial authorities, as was required, was part of a more general campaign to discredit his rival in the eyes of potential converts.

Thomas Crosby irked Duncan in several ways. Duncan genuinely considered it "very prejudicial to the welfare of the Indians to allow them [Indians] to build a permanent settlement in the vicinity of Fort Simpson."[13] On his arrival on the north coast half a year before Thomas, Duncan's new assistant, a young Irishman named William Collison, had proposed to take up residence at Fort Simpson, to which Duncan "strongly objected, asserting that I would thus frustrate his [Duncan's] object, and prevent the Indians from joining the new station, where he was erecting a church capable of accommodating twelve hundred worshippers."[14] Duncan believed that, "but for his [Crosby's] interference and promises, a little over a year ago, many now remaining at Fort Simpson would have been at Metlakahtla … and in the matter of a few years not an Indian would have been left at Fort Simpson."[15]

Not only was Duncan's authority at stake, but also, there were important denominational differences between Methodists and Anglicans. From Duncan's perspective, Crosby confused immediate effect with a genuine shift in belief. Duncan characterized his Methodist rival as "very impulsive and emotional, a veritable shouter of shouters, who had managed to get some of the Indians into what almost amounted to a religious frenzy."[16] Another time Duncan lamented how everyone "prayed <u>aloud</u> at once … some in Tsimshian, some in Niskahh … each prayed whatever came into his mind at the time, and thus they turned the sacred office of prayer into a … Babel of tongues."[17]

On a personal level, Duncan was perturbed by Emma, fearing the extra advantage she might give Thomas. He took umbrage with the fact that, instead of a "master who was qualified for the work & could devote himself exclusively to it," the teachers at the Fort Simpson day school were "the Wesleyan Minister & <u>his wife</u> & the Native teacher & <u>his wife</u>." The emphasis on "his wife" was in the original letter, written in 1875 to the Department of Indian Affairs. The second couple was Alfred and Kate Dudoward. Duncan dismissed Alfred, his one-time

protégé, as "living two years ago as a heathen & a savage," with "neither the education nor training to fit him for a school teacher."[18] Duncan was not only sexist,
he was also racist.

                                        Fort Simpson, B.C.
                                        March 3rd 1875

My dear Mother,

I do not suppose you will be expecting to hear from me quite so soon again –
but now the boat is likely to come at least once a month regularly. So many are
coming up to the mines north of us [inland from Wrangell]. We got our mail
yesterday sent on by canoe from a point below and tomorrow we expect the
str. to call here on her way back to Victoria. A letter from Annie of Dec. 23rd
was the only one from home. I hope by next str. we shall have answers to our
last.
      Our baby is doing finely. She is really quite plump now and seems very
healthy. I do not know that she has ever had the least cold though we have had
her out in cold, rain, wind & fog – but of course we keep her well protected.
No baby could sleep better at night than she does – and during the day also
she sleeps a good deal – and every day she grows brighter and sweeter & dearer.
An Indian girl at Metlakatla made & sent her a very pretty little blue & white
hood – as nice a one as I could have got anywhere – but it will not fit her long.
I am feeling very well too – as well as ever I did. I find my time pretty well
occupied though. My husband insists upon my going out nearly every day – but
I have not been at church yet. The church is too cold to take baby there, and I
cannot leave her. We still call her Jessie. There is a possibility of Dr. [Enoch]
Wood's being here in the summer [from Toronto, where he was superintendent
of missions for the Methodist Church].[19] If we could depend on that we would
wait and have her baptized then, but it is so doubtful that as Mr. Pollard says
he will be up by next boat we may have the ceremony then. I should like to hear
from you all first if we could. The teacher jogs along. I don't want to be un-
charitable, but he is a negative sort of man and what positive there is about
him is not of the most agreeable kind. No great acquisition to Fort Simpson
society – but fortunately he is quiet.
      I do not know that I answered your last letter very fully. I had so little time
after I rec. it. You ask if we were warm & had dry wood. We had plenty of wood,
some dry, some not dry and kept up such fires sometimes as would terrify
Auntie. Then the house is quite comfortable and the weather never as cold as
you have it sometimes at home. There is no fear of our being cold or suffering
any domestic discomfort of that kind as long as my husband is able-bodied –

he would go to the woods & chop trees himself first. No, I never knew anyone that knew better how to make things cosy and comfortable than your son-in-law does, and he is always willing to help me. I often think I ought not to let him do so much as he does. He is the best nurse in the house.

Now, I must close. Love to Auntie – why does she not write to me? – and to Sallie – and all – and with best love to my father & yourself.

I am, dear Mother
    Your affectionate daughter,
      Emma

Emma's determination and strength of character is evident in the letter Thomas wrote at the same time. Most likely, he tucked it into hers.

                    Fort Simpson B.C.
                    [March 1875]

My Dear Mrs Douse

Emma says I must write this mail well it is not that I have not had a desire to write you but that I have been so crowded with other work. And now I sit to write a hundred things claim my attention and there is so much I would like to tell you but I know that my wife has sent you good long letters and I should perhaps be going over the ground again.

We have so much to thank God for in our life and experience of the last six or 8 months and although we were shut out from the rest of the world for 4 months yet I thank God we have been blessed and very happy in all work. Were I to recount the past 8 months work it would seem almost impossible that we could have [to] go through it and considering the climate and it being winter to [sic] but still by hard work and "never give up will" and above all the smiles and blessing of a rich providence we have got through.

Emma has been a noble help to me in it all. She took the schools till Xmas longer perhaps than she ought to but she would not give up. And if some of our Ont. friends had seen her with 70 & 80 pupils in a large Indian house with the wind whistling through it on all sides and sometimes so cold (she does not take cold easy) that it was impossible to keep warm and I need not say there never was a lot of peope [sic] made such rapid advance in such a short time. Well I had to attend to building and used to fear that it was too much for her at times but it was done for the Master and has its reward.

Well now she is kept more at home with our dear little daughter (she is very dear to us!) although we take a walk out near every day to visit our people.

And they all think a great deal of the Baby. She is always spoken of as the "Moon beam" and I need not say to you that we think a great deal of her to [sic]. But I trust we have given her to the Lord and if spared we pray that she may be useful. We are very happy in every way although our work is difficult and trying at times but we look for a glorious harvest. We often say it would be so nice if you and Mr. Douse could come in to see us but

We know you pray for us.

Truly yours T. & E. Crosby

Don't forget my love to Mr. Douse and Mr. & Mrs. Harrison Mr. & Mrs. King & Cusey [?]

The approach of the Crosbys' first springtime on the north coast encouraged Emma to begin another diary letter. She used it as a means of sharing her daughter Jessie's development, clearly aware that, except for her headstrong decision, her mother would have been directly involved in her upbringing.

Fort Simpson, B.C.
March 27th 1875

My dear Mother,

Baby is asleep just now so I take the opportunity of writing though it may be but a few minutes. It is not unlikely that the str. may be here some time next week, and I ought, if possible, to have all my writing done before she comes, as with her we are expecting Mr. Pollard – and to provide for his comfort and entertainment will take up my time pretty fully, I suppose, during the interval between our receiving our mail and the str. passing down again. Our mails seem to us quite frequent now they come every month. I am hoping for answers to Febr. letters but I know it is doubtful. There is a great deal I should like to tell you all but my time is not my own now – baby takes the largest share of it. We are all well, I am thankful to say, and happy & comfortable. My husband has had less driving work since Christmas and is the better for it. Baby does nobly. She seems to grow noticeably every day and is really fat – and is so bright. She still sleeps famously at night, and is always nearly all morning in the cradle. We have about decided to call her Jessie. I enclose a likeness taken by a local artist, Mrs. Morrison's brother who has been in Victoria and obtained a smattering of the art of photography. I do not suppose you will get a very clear idea of our daughter from it but it will at least represent her. She was asleep or nearly so. It would be impossible I think, to keep her quiet if awake. Her arms especially are always flying about.

29th – Monday A.M. I resume. Our village is almost empty just now. The people are off at a fishing station about forty miles away – where they spend five or six weeks every year at this season to get a very rich kind of small fish from which they extract great quantities of grease. My husband went last week to visit them and also some heathen tribes living beyond. He was away from Monday till early Saturday morning. Five Indians went with him. Having head winds it took them near two days to reach their destination – camping one night on the beach, though the weather was very cold. He took provisions with him and mats & blankets to sleep in but of course he was in the Indian houses. At a heathen village after a meeting of five hours & a half at which many speeches were made, he slept in the chief's bedstead with a new scarlet blanket that was lent him. This was after partaking of a supper of potatoes & dried salmon, the accompanying grease being untouched. Returning, the weather was very stormy. The route is dangerous but by the care of a steady crew and the blessing of Providence they came through safely, reaching here about five A.M. after being out all night, except two or three hours they slept at a little Indian hut a few miles away. It was something of a trial for me to have my husband go, but I saw the importance of it, though it was uncertain when he would get back – and I was the first to propose it. We were kept all well, and I was far less lonely that I expected to be – baby was such a comfort to me. An Indian woman, one who has been in Victoria a good deal & is very clean & nice stayed with me while Thomas was gone – for our little servant took a notion she must go off with her friends to the fishing. For about a week I was without any one to help me – except, indeed, Thomas – but we got on very well, and now the girl we had is back. She came with Mr. Crosby. I am stronger now, I believe, and able to bear more exertion than ever before.

April 10th The Otter came three days ago, bringing parcels but no letters – it must be that the latter have been delayed somewhere for I am sure you would write at once. I felt disappointed for I wanted very much to hear from you all and get your greeting to your little grand-daughter. I received a parcel from Barrie containing the curtaining, two dresses for baby & a pair of little boots – also a paper for Thomas. One dress, I see, is from "Ma" for which very many thanks – and indeed thanks for all, though I do not know exactly who the donors are. It does my heart good to know that our sweet little daughter so far away from those who would care for her & help her, is still thought of and loved. Then there was a parcel from Cobourg containing two jackets, two pinafores, two under flannels, a bib & a dress pattern – all just the very things I wanted – especially the little flannels. I mean baby to wear these always after she is shortened & I was at a loss for a good pattern. Many, many thanks. Besides these things she had sent her from Victoria – a little blue crocheted

jacket, a blue & white hood, a print dress ready made and five pairs of little
boots – one a very pretty pair of yellow kid to lace. She is at present in possession altogether of nine pairs of shoes of different kinds, including one pair of
tiny moccasins Mrs. Morrison gave her. I also received from Victoria a box
containing a large fruit cake, some pickles and a number of jars of preserves,
the last from that peculiar lady [Mrs. Trounce] we stayed with in Victoria last
summer. Besides these things the "Otter" also brought flower roots & rhubarb
ready to plant, some of the plants in bloom, and the Chairman [Rev. Pollard]
and a carpenter to build the church. The Chairman has to sleep in a bed on
the lounge in the sitting room as the carpenter & teacher are enough for our
one bedroom upstairs, as only one is yet partitioned off.

We had baby baptized yesterday. I wish my father could have done it but
that could not be. We were sorry that it should be when so many of the people
were away but thought on the whole it was best to have it done now. We had
decided to call her Jessie but the Indians were afraid of her Indian name being
quite superseded by the other & lost so we added it and she was baptized
"Jessie Asseh-e-gemk." We had a public service in the afternoon at which this
took place and Mr. Pollard addressed the people, that is, all there were home.
Baby cried a little during the baptismal service but was very good on the whole.
Her father kept her most of the time and she is generally good with him. In
the evening Mr. & Mrs. Morrison came up and we had refreshments – cake,
apples, little biscuits, raspberry vinegar & what I had of my wedding cake – I
did not know that there could be a more worthy occasion than baby's christen-
ing. She is growing brighter & sweeter every day and seems very well indeed.
She is very good too – and she laughs and coos so prettily. I only wish you
could see her Ma. I know you would say she is just as sweet a little baby as there
ever was. I wish some one, perhaps Susie could do it conveniently – would
send me some more flannel to make up for her. If there is any more of that
wide like I had, I would like three yards of it, also some fine cotton, and some
material for pinafores with trimmings. I would like too, some grey flannel for
night dresses as here flannel will be necessary all the year round. You would
laugh if you saw how our baby is fixed up for the night – something after Indian
fashion – that is, even her night dress. I wind her in a little shawl – that old
one of Ma's – brown & white – that was wrapped round something in packing
– pinned pretty closely round her throat and again the point wherever it
comes somewhere below her waist so that her arms, while not cramped are
kept quiet & she is warm. We believe she sleeps the better for it. When she
was very little the nurse used to roll her blanket round her in the day time so
that she could not get her hands out.

We have set up a boarding house – you see – as both these assistants – the teacher & the carpenter have no other place to look to.[20] This will, of course, give me more to do a great deal but Thomas says we must have some one to help us – whom we shall get I do not know. The carpenter is a dashing young fellow – the very reverse of the teacher. We get our provisions mostly from Victoria, and mind to look ahead. I shall have to ask you to send this letter to the girls as I have no time to write to them this time. I hope I shall have letters from you all next boat, I want to know how Eliza's baby is getting on.

Love from us all to Papa & Auntie & Sallie, my own dear sisters & brother & yourself, dear Mother,

Your affectionate daughter
Emma

We have no bills to send perhaps Susie will trust us.

The baptism of Jessie Crosby confirmed Emma's motherhood in the eyes of the Tsimshian people. The infant's gift of an Aboriginal name was no small honour, given that, during these same years, Thomas was encouraging the Tsimshian to adopt newcomer names. According to his memoir, the naming occurred on Christmas day just two days after her birth: "In one of the large houses three or four hundred people gathered, and they had a great ceremony in giving the baby a name. Amid clapping of hands and shouting, they said she was to have the name of King Legaic's daughter, 'Ashegemk,'– 'The Leg of the Sun or of the Moon,' that is, 'Sunbeam,' or 'Moonbeam.'"[21] The chairman of the British Columbia District, Rev. William Pollard, confirmed the honour by baptizing her as Jessie Aschekinka. He reported: "The second name was chosen by the Indians, and signifies a sunbeam, or ray of the sun. The Indians were very much pleased that the child was called by the name they had selected."[22]

Fort Simpson, B.C.
June 3rd 1875

My dear Mother,

I have another chance of writing you, but I may not be able to write very much. I suppose by the time you receive this you will be about settling down for another year. I trust you may be comfortable and happy wherever you are. Let me know, please, all the details of your arrangements. I was rather disappointed at not receiving more letters by this str. There was only one – that from Susie. I think mine of March must have been delayed somewhere as she evidently had not seen it. I had hoped too, to have had the things I sent for baby by this time. I trust they may come by next boat as I want to get her short clothes made. It is trimmed with bias pieces – piped with white – and looks very pretty indeed. Baby is very well and such a merry, bright, little pet. She wakes in the morning with a laugh and a crow – and all day is full of fun. We have taken another young girl into the house – she was without home or friends to care for her. It is a great care & anxiety to have these girls. We cannot trust to their truthfulness or honesty altogether but this seems the only way to help them. We had quite a ceremony about two weeks ago at the laying of the foundation of the church. A bottle containing various articles was deposited in a cedar block – Mrs. Morrison & the writer being honored in laying it.

Four days last week and two this, my husband was off with a lot of men about eight miles getting out the last of the timber required for the church. He went himself so as to hurry things on. I very much dislike having Thomas away, of course, but while it is necessary I try to take it cheerfully. He will have now to be at home, I think, steadily until the church is finished. The teachers in the college sent baby a very pretty little silver mug by the last str. My very best thanks to Auntie for that handsome dress.

I send by mail a small box, containing some moss and shells which you will please make over to Auntie, with my love – also two napkin rings – one for you & one for my father. They were made out of silver coin by a Hydah Indian who was visiting here. Putting the letters on was something new to him & he did not succeed so well with it but many of the Indians work very beautifully in silver & gold making bracelets, ear-rings &c. Please accept these with our sincerest affection. I will try to answer Auntie's letter very soon. Give my love to all enquiring friends and pray for us. Love to Georgie & my father and yourself from Thomas, Jessie and,

    Your affectionate daughter
    Emma

P.S. I am very glad indeed to hear that you are knitting some socks for baby. I wear no cotton myself so she will need none. But perhaps you will not have much time in which case please just b[u]y some & charge to me.

Just under a year at Simpson, Emma got her first taste of what it meant to be a public person. It was on June 7, 1875, that Emma, together with Odille Morison, wife of the head of Fort Simpson, was given the honour of placing "the bottle, etc." in the cornerstone being laid for the Methodist church. Thomas reported in his public letter how "the service at the site of the new church was necessarily very short, as heavy rain came on."[23]

Fort Simpson, B.C.

July 10th 1875

My dear Mother,

I was delighted yesterday when we received our mail & found two letters from you – the last dated Castleton June 16th. I had been wondering very much what you & my father were going to do about your place of residence, and indeed, yet, I have no decided idea. Annie says in a letter of June 21st that Georgie is going into an office in Barrie – in which case you will scarcely leave, will you! But I shall likely know all about it by next str.

Wherever you are I hope you will make yourselves thoroughly comfortable. Just make up your mind to have things easy. Have the house always warm and cosy with nice carpets & comfortable easy chairs &c. so as to really enjoy it. I don't see any reason why you should not – and do not undertake to do much work yourself. You ought to have a good girl that could do everything. Now do go on this plan – no one will be any the worse off for it – and your children & friends will all be the happier for knowing that you are comfortable. I hope Georgie will do well wherever you are.

I am sorry to hear that you were feeling uneasy about my letter not coming when you expected. If they usually come early in the month it must be by accident, for there is no certainty as to the time of their reaching Victoria, and from there the letters are usually sent to Portland, Oregon, and overland to San Francisco – instead of waiting for the fortnightly steamer. Indeed a delay of that kind should not be thought of anxiously, at all. There are so many possible ways of its occurring. I was very glad to get the photo you enclosed. Thank the girls very much for it. I want to write to Sally as soon as I can. The parcels you sent came all right – many thanks. The little socks I was especially glad to get. They will be just the thing for baby very soon. As yet she wears little woolen booties. I made her short clothes to cover her feet well, so they are warm enough at present. Indeed we are having quite warm weather just now – and very fine. We find it warmer where we are now – a little away from the water – both summer & winter than it is in the Fort which is built close to the beach. Still you would not call this warm weather at home. I still wear my flannels the same as in winter – only in outer clothing have I made much change. Baby – our little Jessie – does grow so fast and is such a fine healthy little girl. I would give so much if you could see her. She has such a lot of very curly brown hair and such a bright little face. She is full of fun and mischief as can be. She wakes in the morning with a laugh & a coo and is merry as the day is long. She is just the sunshine of the house, and such a comfort to us. Her father, of course, is very proud of her and they have fine frolics together. We feel very thankful indeed that she is so well and good. She is a blessing indeed to us. I began a few days ago to feed her a little once a day – more to get her accustomed to a spoon in case it might be necessary to feed her in that way than for any other reason – but it is only a trifle she takes. I tried corn-starch once – but sago seems to agree with her better. We are going to send to Victoria by this boat for some vaccine.

The church building is going on very well indeed. But it is a great undertaking. However most of the difficult work is over now, but it is only by the most persistent, plodding energy that it is carried on. Then there are worse difficulties than the building to contend with. I sometimes think surely this Pacific coast is the wickedest place on earth. White men living unmarried with Indian women is perhaps the chief evil. There are none in the village – but some not many miles away who come to the village & decoy away the young girls. It is dreadful. Of course my husband gives no uncertain sound on this subject and that is bringing him, and I suppose will continue to bring him in contact with these men under not the pleasantest circumstances. However duty is plain here – they are a craven lot of fellows too when there is an opportunity really to face them – but they can find ways to annoy and to hinder our work.

Our household arrangements have undergone no change since I wrote last but I find there is so little for three girls to do that I fear their getting into bad habits on that account. We think of sending one away – though I do not like to do it. If we had a house arranged properly we might have things more on the plan of a school and let them take turns in the kitchen – but as things are now that is impossible. Then the expense of keeping up such a family is not a little – perhaps more than we ought to undertake. One thing I must not forget to record – I have actually seen some white ladies! Two or three weeks ago on Sunday morning we saw a str. anchored in the bay and were surprised by a visit from Gen. [O.S.] Howard of the U.S. army & staff who had been on a tour of inspection up the Alaska coast. The Gen. and another officer came up very soon to the house. They had come in for the purpose of attending church and on reaching there we found quite an array of uniforms & children and two ladies. The Gen. and a Capt. had their families with them. Then after service there were all the Colonels & Captains & everybody to shake hands with and talk to. They had to re-embark immediately after the service so we accompanied them to their boat on the beach, and with some "gushing" and, I believe, not a little really kindly interest we bade a mutual farewell. The Gen. is a very philanthropic and religious man, and your son-in-law is "hale fellow well met" with every one. I believe he would ask the Prince of Wales to the house if he visited the village – and with equal cordiality would he offer the hospitalities of our home to the poorest miner. Another stray str. visited us a few weeks ago & a U.S. revenue cutter having on board a U.S. Indian agent looking up Indian curiosities for the approaching Centennial Exhibition. He took dinner with us & I should say was a fair specimen of the U.S. Indian agent as reputed to be – not inconveniently high-minded. But on this same str. there was a Lieutenant who visited us & whose visit was a real pleasure. He is a Methodist and after taking tea with us joined us in the class-meeting that meets in our house. He grew so fond of baby too! I liked him for that, of course – but indeed, everyone notices her. The Capt. of the Otter [Herbert George Lewis] brought his wife up with him this trip. She took tea with us. On their return they are to call here again & then I shall likely have another longer visit from her. She brought us some cherries which were a treat indeed. We had green peas for dinner today too – some a man brought who came on the str. We miss fresh vegetables & fruit a good deal. We have had some radishes from the fort – but nothing else from the garden.

Did you get the box I sent by last mail? I have got a lot of shells lately far prettier than any I had to send to Auntie before but I am half afraid to send them. I will enclose five dollars which will perhaps cover what I may be owing you and Susie. As I have written so long a letter I must ask you to send it to Susie. I fear I shall not have time to write her much. Best love from Thomas to you all. My love to my father & brother & Auntie & Sallie & all and especially yourself dear Mother.

Yours as ever
    Emma

The Crosbys' summertime visitors put their own expectations on Emma, if also giving her a respite from the everyday routines of motherhood. General O.S. Howard was the commander of the Pacific Division of the US Army and was en route from Sitka, Alaska, to Portland, Oregon. In describing the visit, based on what General Howard and his party related, the *Victoria Daily Standard* commended Thomas's "accomplished and estimable young wife, to whom too much praise cannot be given for the great change for the better that has been brought about by her in that place." It being Sunday the visitors attended religious services and the newspaper account noted how, "while at church they were greatly astonished by the interpreter, an Indian woman, who interpreted for Mr.

Crosby, word for word, all through the service, without any difficulty."[24] Once again, Kate Dudoward functioned as the critical intermediary.

The American in search of "curiosities" to display at the Centennial Exhibition of American Independence, slated for Philadelphia, was James G. Swan, a jack-of-all-trades living at Port Townsend, Washington Territory. An experienced collector of Aboriginal art for the Smithsonian Museum in Washington, DC, he had been designated a special agent by the federal Indian Bureau and given a budget between $3,000 and $4,000. Swan was travelling up the coast on a US revenue cutter and, according to historian Douglas Cole, Thomas did his best to impress him with his missionary exploits. He told Swan how he had persuaded many of the Tsimshian to remove the traditional poles standing outside of their houses. Some of these were already burned, but others were grouped "in a sort of museum," from which Swan selected for purchase a finely carved forty-foot pole. Thomas also acquired for Swan two more poles and a complete house front depicting a bear and whales, which he arranged to have repainted to enhance its commercial value.[25] Perhaps tweaked by Swan's interest, Thomas thereafter collected the very same items he was encouraging peoples to get rid of – everything from carved figures to dancing masks.[26]

Fort Simpson, B.C.
Aug. 5th 1875

My dear Mother,

The str. has come again, but brought no letters from any of you. However I hope there may therefore be the more next time. I will write to you as usual. I was hoping to hear by this boat where you were living – your plans & Georgie's were not decided when you wrote your last. I think about you all very much and wonder how things are with you. I think of all kinds of things, whether you are comfortably settled & well or feel the heat very much. With regard to heat I think Fort S. would suit you exactly. For a month or more we have had fine clear weather but not at all too warm – indeed excepting a very few mornings I have always had a little fire to wash baby by. I am glad of fine weather for Jessie's sake. I have her out as much as I can and she grows so fast. It seems to me I can feel the difference in her weight every day. I never attempt to carry her very far myself. If Thomas cannot go with me when I go for a walk I take one of the girls. But I often sit with her where she can see the men at work on the church and of course every one that passes us has a word for Jessie – while she laughs & coos at them all, quite irrespective of either character or appearance. She is so good and is such a splendid little sleeper – not one bit of trouble, only a comfort to me at night. I believe this is partly owing to her never having been accustomed to rocking. She generally goes to sleep – almost always – without any walking or special effort about it. Just settling herself down in the cradle or bed and closing her eyes as though she understood all about it. She is very lively and playful. What she always reaches out her little hands most eagerly for is the tassels attached to the window blinds as then she can shake the blinds which are new & stiff & make a great noise. If her father takes her the first thing is always to fasten a little hand in his beard & there she holds on while he frolics with her – rather a drawback to his pleasure. Her cheeks are pink as the dress you sent her and she is just the sunshine of the house. The Indians are going away now, many of them, for a month or so to their salmon fishing. Many strangers have been here lately, trading, Hydah's [sic] from Queen Charlotte's Is. & Sitkas from the north. They most of them come up to see us and attend church and of course Thomas takes these opportunities of casting in the seed. Chinook jargon affords a means, though a poor one, of communication with all these tribes. It is understood more or less on all parts of the coast, and all seem interested in what they see & hear. The work at the church has gone on well. The roof is shingled & the spire near finished & all is closed in but the tower & front end, but much inconvenience comes from having to send so far for what is needed, while the management in Victoria has not been the best. However I will say nothing about that.

We got a high chair for Jessie & some other things from Victoria this trip & some rhubarb & raspberries the Capt. brought and we are sending for fruit by next boat. I think it would be better for us all if we had more fresh things for the table – but we get on pretty well. We are sending by this boat for all the groceries &c. we think we shall need for the coming winter for there will likely be only two boats more this fall. It is astonishing what a difference it makes having two men boarding with us. However, the carpenter will likely be gone in about two months & the teacher I think means to put up some kind of a cabin where he can live by himself. Cheaper, I suppose, he thinks than boarding. He is a strange man. I believe he will be happier alone – though I don't think he will be very happy anywhere – till he gets to heaven. He seems to have no "faculty" for getting on & always to be dissatisfied, though I believe he is a good man & has some ability in his way. I have parted with the oldest of my girls – the married one – I saw one must go & thought she would be <u>safer</u> away than either of the others. I find now the work is done quite as well & with much more comfort than it was before.

Now I must close soon. Remember our last mail will likely be in October some time. My love to Auntie & Sallie. I suppose I had better send this to Barrie.

I don't know where else to send it. My husband & baby join in kindest love to you & my father. O if you could only see this little grand-daughter of yours! We are all well and trustful. I have not written to any of the girls this time. Love to Georgie.

　　Dear Mother,
　　　　Your affectionate daughter
　　　　　Emma

P.S.　I see by the Globe there was a great fire in Barrie in June but the particulars are not given fully. I hope Mr. Harrison is not one of the sufferers this time.
　　　E.

Emma's anxiety over not receiving letters from home each time a steamer docked was tempered a little, but not much, by the Ontario newspapers, which slowly made their way to Fort Simpson. She became increasingly anxious for news, aware that the distance to her family was lengthening psychologically.

　　　　　　　　　　　　　　　　Fort Simpson, B.C.
　　　　　　　　　　　　　　　　Sept. 13th 1875

My dear Mother,

We have just received our mail again. It came up before breakfast and made the repast quite secondary – and now having read all my letters – given Jessie her bath & seen her sweetly asleep in the cradle and set the dinner on the way I sit down to answer. The Str. <u>will</u> be back – likely tomorrow – she did not call in on her way up but our mail was sent from a point below. I had two letters from you to make up for none last time. They were the first I opened and the first I answer. We were glad to know you were well. I hope you may get a house to your liking in Toronto and be comfortable there. Write me full particulars, will you not? How I should love to see you and my father and all the rest. Those three babies that I have never seen I think about so often and it does me so much good to know that our little girl whom you have none of you seen yet is remembered so kindly by all. The parcel came all right – very many thanks. The stockings for Jessie will do exactly. I wanted some very much – those warmer ones you knitted I will keep for the very cold weather. They will all fit her very well I think. Her foot is very tiny – but when they are too large I fold them round her heel which seems to give her no inconvenience. She has been wearing moccasins lately but they soon get out of shape & soiled. I am going to send to Victoria for slippers or shoes for her – the smallest to be had. Our pet is still very well and so bright. I do wish you could see her as she sits in her high chair at the table by her father. I did not mean to let her come to the table for a long time but when once we began it was so nice to have her and she is always so very good, we cannot think now of doing without her. She plays with a napkin ring or a tea spoon and laughs & talks & shakes her head in a pretty little way she has till she is the life of the table. She has so many amusing little ways. Her love for singing is very marked – she will throw up her little hands and crow with delight when she hears it. She is very fond of being out. That comforter you sent will be just the thing for windy days – for we have many of them. It is so very pretty too and soft – and blue I think is Jessie's most becoming color. I enclose a photo of Jessie. Perhaps you will laugh at my sending such a poor dim thing but we cannot get a better just now & it may aid your imagination a little. She has on the pink dress you sent her & pinafore & bib just as you might see her any day at home. It was taken out of doors where the light was rather strong – and, as you will perceive, the picture was originally intended for a family group, but failed, only small portions of the other members being visible.

When are you & my father going to send us yours? In Toronto you will have a fine opportunity of getting really good ones. Those stockings you sent for me are just what I wanted – though I was not quite out yet. I have been wearing those half cotton ones during the summer weather.

I was glad you received the napkin rings all right. I had some misgivings myself about their going safely. I will send Auntie some more shells – I have much prettier ones now – when I have time, as those arrived all right. I am glad to know Sallie was in Chicago. It would do her good & be a pleasure to her I am sure. Dr. [Enoch] Wood is partly expected in B.C. this fall. I think a visit from him would be a great benefit to the district where all is not harmony & satisfaction – and I do hope he may be able to reach us. It would be such a pleasure to see him.

The church building has been going on vigorously & will soon be close[d] for the fall – though the seating, painting &c. will not be touched. The carpenter will not be here more than another month. The teacher I suppose will continue to board with us though we have heard indirectly that he thought of putting up a little house for himself, but I do not believe he has energy enough ever to accomplish it. He is so strange – very well informed – but so wanting, it seems, in frankness & sympathy. The school has decreased very much & his influence seems to be almost nothing – and yet I believe he is really a good man. There is a great deal to try us in our work & we feel more & more that we stand alone – yet not alone. It often is a great comfort to me to know that you all remember us prayerfully. Our love to Georgie & Auntie & Sallie & all. We shall likely have two more mails this fall so write an answer to this please. If Auntie can send anything for our Christmas tree it will be a great help to us &

I shall be very glad. My husband sends his best love to you both. God be with you & us – dear Mother.

> Your affectionate daughter
> Emma

P.S. Jessie has no sign of teeth yet. I feed her once a day on cornstarch. I tried arrow root but it seemed to disagree with her.

> E.

While Emma depended mightily on news and also material goods from Ontario, she increasingly found herself without the time to reciprocate through meticulously recounting her everyday life. She was aware of her shortcoming but simply did not have the time out of her busy days to remedy the situation.

> Fort Simpson, B.C.
> Oct. 9th 1875

My dear Mother,

I have only time to write a few lines but Thomas says never to let an opportunity pass without writing. It is near twelve Saturday night – & the mail goes early Monday. Jessie has been in bed a long, long time. She is still well and good and happy as a lark – God keep her so.

The work is near stopped on the church but Thomas wants to go to work on the house now. The carpenter goes away by this str. – so does the teacher so the school will be left for somebody. We have most of our winter supplies in. We received by this str. from friends a box of preserves, a box of pears & apples & a brl. of apples. The last time a lot of plums came, I have over thirty jars put away – besides some rhubarb & a little raspberry that was sent before. We have apples also and a great quantity of cranberries. I have chocolate on hand to take when I need it & also isinglass [a gelatin sometimes used to preserve eggs and other foods]. I do very well – we are getting vegetables now from the Fort. I suppose by this time you are quite settled in Toronto. I do hope you are comfortable. Now do take things & make them just as easy as you can. I hope you have a good girl. We expect another str. this fall when I will try to write more fully.

> Our love to you both.
> Yours affectionately
> Emma

Emma's life centred more and more on the mission and its needs, so much so that her letters home were as much pleas for assistance as they were intimate recountings from daughter to mother. Anticipating her second winter at Simpson, she was more aware than before of what it portended.

Fort Simpson, B.C.
Oct. 21st 1875

My dear Mother,

I must try to write a long letter this time because the last was so short and then this will be the last for this year, I suppose. The str. may be here now any day. I hope it will bring the usual letter from you – and then by the time our next mail comes likely in Jan. or perhaps Feb. I hope there will be sure to be another on the way. We shall think about you all very often you may be sure and talk about you, and pray for you. I wonder where you will spend your Christmas. I trust yours as ours may be pleasant & happy. Ours will be busy, I suppose. As I told you the school teacher has left. I don't think he was ever very happy here – but it was something to us to have the school provided for. Now Mr. Crosby has to attend all he can. He goes generally in the morning and I have been going in the afternoon. I do not like to leave Jessie but I put her to sleep before I go and she sleeps sometimes near all the time I am away. Her father is always either in or about the house and takes charge of her when she wakes. The girls are kind to her and often amuse her but we never leave her to their care. I am never away much more than two hours, and her father understands her well. It would be a great thing for us to have a really good teacher – and that must [b]e a missionary. The schools are promising and need more time than we have to give to them ourselves. A lady teacher of the right kind might be very useful. We have three girls in the house again. One who was in trouble and friendless almost had to be brought in – she is older than the others and not particularly bright but we do not choose. I find a great difference in the housekeeping now that our boarders have gone. It is really a relief to me and it seems so nice to have the house to ourselves.

Did I tell you in my last that we had a very good harmonium for the church. Some of the young men started the subscription for it quite of their own accord. It cost $150 and is much larger than I supposed could be got here for that price. It is really amusing to see how the people wonder to hear it and how pleased [they are]. It is placed in the new church which we do not use yet for service, only sometimes we have a sing there. Old & young are very fond of singing and I believe to the young especially it is a great blessing – unartistic as our singing is – in furnishing them with entertainment & keeping them from amusements that might lead to evil. We have part singing too, in quite a number of times. Mrs. Morrison's brother has a good ear for music. He can play a little – and he has trained a number of the young men to take the different parts. I often wish there was someone here really capable of teaching the people to sing properly. I believe the result would be more than ordinary. The work on the church is stopped now until a saw-mill that is being built [at Georgetown] about five miles away is running to supply lumber. This may be in a few weeks now – then all the buttress posts & some other outside work will have to be done. The ceiling & seats will likely not be put in before next summer. The former will be difficult work, it is quite lofty.

Thomas has been painting the house outside – with the help of some Indians. It is white with dark window casings &c. Whether he will get the inside finished this fall or not I do not know. I urge him to leave it – there is so much else to do.

Would Papa take the trouble to settle the bills which are enclosed. It is difficult to arrange these little things satisfactorily unless there is some one to look after them. Thomas holds also a policy of Life Insurance in the Etna Life Ins. Co. the premium of which falls due Feb. 4th. The amount of yearly premium is $113.60. If Papa would be kind enough to pay that also, Thomas will send an order on the Mission rooms by the first spring mail. I suppose it will not inconvenience Papa to find the money at the time. One of the bills I enclose Thomas thinks may have been paid though he has no receipt for it. Perhaps Papa could find that out at the Mission room. And about the Insurance. I forgot to say the policy is in the hands of Mr. Crosby's brother-in-law in Ingersoll. Thomas will write to him to send it to Papa.

Nov. 9th. We have received our mail since I began this. There was no letter from you but a good long one from Eliza which she said you wished to do instead of one from you. I hope you will be happy in Toronto. I was glad of the advice you sent me about Jessie's food. I only feed her once a day and I gave her corn-starch because she seemed to like it and I thought it good. We have always excellent bread and I am trying that now, but she does not take it well. She is used to nothing but fluid – however when she gets a little used to it, it will be all right I think. We have very nice little plain crackers in the house that I think perhaps I can roll and make smoother than the bread to begin with. I think she would be better for more variety of food than she has had. She has not a single tooth yet, but I suppose we must expect her to be backward. Of course she is small yet for her age, but she is well and so contented and happy. I believe she is just given us to be a comfort and joy in our home. She is very fond of going out and does not seem to mind the cold at all. Her father takes her with him near every day, and she is just the picture of babyish delight as he carries her off. She and her father are the best friends possible. Lately, before going to school I have made her food and left it for her father to give her and left him to put her to sleep. She is so good that as yet he has never had any trouble with her. And when she sees me come in she is always so delighted that it makes me happy too. We have been having some pretty cold weather lately so I have put on her those warm stockings you knit for her – they will be just the thing for her this winter – and some little black slippers I got from Victoria though still rather large are wearable now, so I think her feet are well provided for the cold weather. I have put on her a second flannel skirt also, and she is wearing the merino [wool] dress Susie sent her. That is the only warm dress she has, but I mean to make her another soon. Of course she has no idea of walking yet, indeed she cannot even sit without support but likely that is because I have never tried to teach her to sit alone. Sometimes I put her on the bed and place the pillows about her, but if she is left unsupported she is sure to tumble over.

Victoria friends remembered us well by this str. We received two boxes of apples & one of pears, a lot of things for our Christmas tree and for Jessie a doll and purple French merino for a dress. I think I shall scarcely need to sew at all for the Christmas tree – for which I am very glad for I really have no time for it. We have three girls now – one is soon to be married. I never told you did I, about a nice wrap I got! Thomas saw it in the store here one day and would get it for me. It is a large cape of the softest, finest wool very thick and warm – striped brown & white on one side & gray on the other. It is really a lovely thing.

Now, dear Mother, it will be likely a long time before you will hear from us again, but the Lord will watch between us. He is with us here I know – and though we have many trials among these people, some such as I could not explain in a letter – yet we are very graciously sustained and blessed.

About the Insurance Policy I spoke of, Thomas received it himself by this mail, so he will keep it instead of having it sent to Papa. God bless and cheer you both. Thomas joins me in warmest love to you and my father.

Your affectionate daughter
Emma

P.S.   Please send the enclosed $20 to Annie. I thought it safer to send it through because her letter had a little thing in it I was sending to Frank.

The Crosbys were never cash-rich. Thomas received an annual grant of about $1,200 from the Methodist Church's Mission Fund and additional grants ranging from between $600 and $1,400 "for Native Assistants, Schools, & c."[27] Just as Emma did not tell her mother what happened to the money sent at the beginning of 1875 for her "comfort," so she did not relate the incident's postscript, several months later. Thomas described in his memoir how "another cheque came from the same friend for a like amount, and thus we got the bills for our temporary School House paid." In his letters intended for publication Thomas repeatedly used Emma as a foil to get needed funds to build a new school to replace that "old patched-up Indian house" where classes were being held.[28] "Mrs. Crosby is taking the adult school at present, but I do not see how she can do so long, for we are provided with no better school-house this winter than last, and the old Indian school house we use is really too cold to be safe. I do hope the Missionary Committee will give us a school-house if possible." And that was not all Thomas wanted. "Could you not send us a teacher, a good young woman with a missionary soul, who would come here for the good she could do these poor people? Of course she would make up her mind to the isolation and want of society, etc."[29]

The classroom situation went from bad to worse when "the sickness of Kate Doudoward, left us entirely alone." Like Emma, Kate had, in the parlance of the day, to grow "sick" in order to give birth. The Dudowards already had William and Mary, who were now joined by Flora, who was soon to be followed by Ernest, Frederick, Rufus, and Charles. Alfred Dudoward ran a store at Fort Simpson, using his sloop *Georgiana* to get goods from Victoria, where his mother Diex lived. Emma continued to teach over the winter, as Thomas's next public letter explained:

> We could not think of giving up the schools ... my wife has taken the afternoon as she did last winter, but it has been very much more trying this year than last, on account of the very cold weather which has continued for an unusual length of time ... for a few days I thought it not safe to have a school in an old building which lets the snow-drifts through its huge cracks, till it lies in great heaps on the floor and seats ... I do hope we may get some kind of a school-house for next winter.[30]

While Emma remained committed to the school, the mission home increased her responsibilities. The arrival of Jessie gave new intimacy to Emma's relationship with her mother; a new dialogue entered into their correspondence – one centred on mothering and family. The role of mother also shaped her relations with the community around her. Necessity, combined with Christian duty, brought young Tsimshian girls into the mission home. The care required to maintain the mission home and its family came from these girls, for the most part, delivered by their families, who sought improved opportunities for them. Emma found the new help useful, yet chose to employ Christian rhetoric to explain why she took them. Her Christian obligation to protect these girls from the dangers she saw impinging on them provided her with the validation she needed to act upon her good intentions.

4

Emma Alone

The work of the mission was constant. There could be no lapse in school, sermons, or religious activity. Both Thomas and Emma had to remain vigilant in their duties despite any rest that might be needed following the arrival of Jessie and the completion of the mission house. The house was the heart of the mission. It was the place where visitors stayed, and it provided temporary quarters for those coming to participate in mission work.

More important, the mission house was the principal means by which civility could be modelled and conversion measured. Thomas emphasized its importance.

There is no better teaching than the object lesson of a good and well-ordered Christian home. If he is walking "in His steps," the teacher ... should be able and willing to show how to build a nice little home, from the foundation to the last shingle on the roof. Indeed, this is the only way to win the savage from his lazy habits, sin and misery. So soon as the Missionary gets the language of the people – and every Missionary should do so – he should make an effort to get them out of the wretched squalor and dirt of their old lodges and sweat houses into better homes. As soon as we were in our northern field, we had to build our Mission House.[1]

For Emma, the mission home was more than a place to ensure religious conversion: it was where the physical, social, and cultural transformation of young Aboriginal girls was sought. A boundary could be drawn between the girls' previous ways of living and the new lifestyle they were to adopt. The home provided the protection necessary to making their transformation complete. Inevitably, the public letter written under Thomas's name in early 1876 made the point in a manner calculated to secure sympathy and, thereby, financial support.

Perhaps there is no part of our work here that is more trying and yet more important than that connected with the young women of this place; they are exposed to
peculiar temptations, and up to this time there has been no restraint to their course
of action. But we feel they must be cared for, and in some cases, the only way to
save them is to take them to the mission house. We are doing all our room and
means will allow. I wish we could do more.[2]

This new aspect of the missionary enterprise was of interest to Emma for two
primary reasons. As "mother of the mission," she was bound by duty to oversee
the mission home and those who came to occupy it. In the home she could monitor the girls at close range and provide them with the moral supervision and
practical experiences important to their transformation. Emma incorporated
the girls into her daily round so they could understand what it meant to partake
in a civilized home. They carried out cleaning chores, prepared and gathered
food, made meals, and cared for the baby when needed. Emma saw letting the
girls be her helpers as her duty towards them. It was essential that they participate in all aspects of running a household. Many years later, one of the girls recalled for a reporter her experience of living in the Crosby home. "That's where
she learned to do things ... They taught her to do things in the house, you know,
sweeping, cooking, and things like that."[3] Emma also went out of her way to teach
the girls other skills, showing them how to sew, knit, and crochet, so that eventually their own dress and household decorum would attain the desired outward
transformation.

Convinced that Christian ways of life were the only right ways and that, until
indigenous peoples agreed, their actions were wrong-headed, Emma was always
anxious that the girls might revert to traditional Tsimshian practices such as arranged marriages and/or polygamy. And as the settler and trader presence continued to grow at Fort Simpson, Emma feared the girls might be led astray by
less principled colonizers. Increasingly, Emma came to believe that the end result of the protection she afforded the girls lay in Christian marriage. Women's
destiny lay in making a home for their husbands and families, and she believed,
as did others, that men were meant to have ultimate authority within the home.
Marriage of Aboriginal girls constituted an important mission strategy: it ensured Christian order in the family and community and contributed to goals of
assimilation. So long as Emma delivered each of her charges into the arms of a
man, she was fulfilling her good intentions.

The second reason the home was so central in Emma's life lay in her need to
fill the void left by Thomas's growing absences as he travelled to seasonal villages
maintained by Aboriginal groups or to settlements that did not have a resident
missionary. Increasing the number of "converts" was an indicator of the mis-

sion's success, and this kept Thomas on a regular route. The need to attend provincial conferences and fund-raising tours also resulted in lengthy absences. In his biography, Bolt writes: "Crosby was often away from home for weeks at a time, visiting missions or establishing new ones. His love of adventure and desire to spread the Word sent him on trips that covered hundreds of miles, entailed considerable risk, and involved numerous preaching encounters with Native people."[4] Tales evoking the nature and extent of his travels were useful fodder for his writings and letters to Ontario.

While Thomas was away, Emma took over his spiritual charges. Historian Margaret Whitehead describes how "the need for expansion, coupled with a shortage of male missionary help, not only enabled women to preach intermittently but also take complete charge of mission centers and to offer a full range of missionary services, including evangelical preaching."[5] As her husband's missionary zeal grew, Emma was left increasingly to her own devices.

Emma also had her duties as a wife and mother. Given that she calculated her second child was born a month to six weeks premature, she became pregnant again near the beginning of 1876. This time, she realized more clearly than before how alone she was at Fort Simpson. Her letters to her mother display the various nuances of her unhappiness, which resulted from Thomas's continual travel.

Fort Simpson, B.C.
February 8th 1876

My dear Mother,

It is time now to begin a letter which I want to make as fully as possible – our str. may be here now any time. I like to tell you even about very little things sometimes – and I know you will not think me foolish to do so – you know there are so many things I have no one to talk to about, except indeed my good husband and he has no time to listen to all the little things that go to make up a woman's life – and especially the life of a woman with a baby.

Then there are many very serious things which I must speak of too – for you know we have much to contend with, and much – to all human appearance – depending upon us. A very gracious Providence has been over us as a family – we have been kept in health with scarce a slight ailing to any of us – and our little pet – our Jessie – we have seen grow day by day sweeter and more interesting. She has been on the whole very well – though once she had a slight cold and once for a day or two she seemed not very well – I think from requiring a change of food. We gave her a little medicine and changed her food and she has seemed better since. Indeed we have much reason for thankfulness and I trust that, when we hear from you, we shall know that you all have been kept well and happy by the same kind care. Our thoughts and our words, too, so often fly to you – it comforts us to think that your prayers go up for us, and there is one home for us all beyond. I hope you and my father have been comfortable in Toronto. I often am afraid you perhaps feel lonely and are worried by little daily cares and duties – or perhaps are not well. And then I often think how pleasant it would be to have you with us – how much I should have to say to you – but it is all right, is it not? But I do wish you could see our home, and our little daughter – our little "moonbeam" as she stands now on a chair at the table when I write – one of the girls holding her – and pretending to read from an old envelope she has. She has so many funny little ways – she tries hard to talk – and to put on her own shoes and stockings. The pictures on the walls are a great delight to her. She is never tired of pointing at them and talking about them in her own words. She is so lively and full of fun. Singing is like a charm to her – you would laugh to hear her singing with us – at family prayers or anywhere she wants to join in. The girls are very fond of her and take charge of her a good [deal] – though seldom away from one of us – however lately I have been leaving her with one or the other of them Sunday afternoons while I went to S[unday].S[chool]. where teachers are so much needed that I could scarcely conscientiously stay away. That is the only public service I have been at for some time – I do not like to take Jessie while it is so cold – no fire & such a miserable house. She makes no attempt yet at walking alone but likes very much to have some one lead her about – I do not care to hurry her. She is growing tall but is thin rather, and has only three teeth yet. I nurse her now only at night – she has been taking as food chiefly sago and crackers with corn starch once in a while for a variety. I have given her also occasionally a little weak soup with bread in it. The bread as you sent me word – with boiling water and sugar – I could never get her to take well. We often wish we had good milk for her – but we are thankful she has been kept so well with what we have had to give her. Her father takes her out every day unless it is very stormy – sometimes, two or three times in a day, which is, I believe, a great benefit to her, and which she enjoys most heartily herself.

Feb 15th – My little girl is asleep and I have a chance to go on with my letter. I did not forget Georgie's birth-day, just passed, and hope and pray that he may have heaven's best blessings through a long life. O how anxious I am to hear from and about you all – and yet I almost dread as well as long for the coming of the "Otter." But I must cease my misgivings and go on to tell you some of the many things that it is on my mind to say. About our house – there have been many improvements made this winter. The lumber shrank so that the partitions and the lining of the walls had near all to be taken down and put together again. That was an awkward difficult thing to do but it was done. Then the mantel shelves were completed and the study and dining room stained and varnished. The stain is a light brown, the doors, window casings &c. being a darker shade. This was all done at very little expense and looks very well indeed. Then a neat little sideboard has been built into the recess intended for it in the dining room, which nicely stained and varnished is quite an ornament to the room. The up-stairs has been finished too – roughly to be sure – but nicely enough for any use to which it is likely to be put.

There are some rasp-berry and currant and rose bushes set out in the garden. I hope the cold has not injured them. I would like to tell you about a show we had last fall. The Indians were the exhibitors, and there were some curious things. They brought samples of Indian food – fish grease and dried salmon and seaweed and berries &c. – vegetables were also exhibited – and cedar mats – such as we use on our floors – many little carved wooden dishes – toy canoes – and a model of a steamboat that was very complete – the Capt. and officers all on board and the cook – and casks and bales of freight &c. Then there was a nice little rocking [chair] and patch work and book marks worked on card-board and bead work and stockings and gloves knit in most elaborate patterns of many colors – the more the better. Our Christmas time was celebrated much as the previous year. The singers went round and had coffee and biscuits served to them at the Mission house – then there was feasting – and the Christmas tree – and the companies coming Christmas morning to shake hands. We gave a tea to all the village. We made about seven hundred buns in the house & had besides rice and biscuits & tea. This of course was arranged in an Indian house – the largest in the village. But everything has not gone smoothly with us. I suppose it is best that there should be some things to try us. Our enemy at the Mission seems determined to leave no stone unturned to undermine our efforts here. The whole craft and cunning of his mind – and he evinces an uncommon degree of these qualities – seem turned to this one object and he loses no op-portunity of sowing discontent and making trouble among these people. He tells them they will never have any land unless they attach themselves to him and that ours is not the true church and so on – anything to weaken our hands. Just before Christmas a case came up in his court – though it was really a case in which he could have no jurisdiction – in which Thomas felt concerned so he went down and sat for three days in that little court and had to listen to a torrent of abuse all designed to bring him, if possible, into contempt with the Indians, who, of course, can be impressed often by what would merely amuse an intelligent man. The Metlahkatlah people are many of them friendly. Mrs.

Morrison's mother has a house there – though she is here most of the time – and there Thomas slept – while the widow of an old Indian chief and her daughter were extremely kind & made him very comfortable during the day. The missionary [William Collison] who is assistant to Mr. Duncan was also very friendly and almost cordial, when he had an opportunity – even going so far as to invite Thomas to call upon his wife, though in a way that said he was almost afraid to do it, but Mr. D. is all in all there. No one else seems to have much voice. All this sometimes makes me feel really badly – but I like to think that God's work can not be destroyed by man's devices – and if it is our own work and not <u>His</u> we are doing here, then let it perish.

March 6ᵗʰ – Our mail came three days – and O how welcome it was – I did long so to hear from you all, and we were very thankful indeed that from all there was good news. Thank you dear Mother for the pretty neck-tie and the gaiters but most of all for the little stockings for Jessie – she was needing them – one of the pairs you sent her before are too small now and are quite worn out. Thank Papa for settling the Book Room a/c – I enclose one sent by this mail, which however I suppose is the same as Papa has paid – if so, destroy it. I also enclose a Notice from the Ins[urance]. Company which is likely also worthless.

Our little pet has not been at all well for the last weeks. She seemed to have taken a severe cold – for two days she had a high fever – however that left her – and though she still has a cough it appears to be quite loose, and she seems very much better. But what makes me uneasy is this – she is troubled very much with constipation – she has always been more or less inclined to it. We have given her medicine several times but do not like to repeat that too often. She has the fourth tooth now, but no sign of the coming of the others as far as I can see. I am going to give her rice today for her food – to see if that change will help her – and I think we must try to wean her altogether very soon.

I think she must have taken cold in this way – I took her to church Sunday before last – it was a mild day and being used to the fresh air I thought it would not hurt her – but the next day her cold appeared. She is such a frail little body. I do hope we may soon see her as well as ever.

Will you please send this letter to the girls – I have not time to write much to them. I thought I should have heard from Auntie, but no letter came. My love to all at Barrie and especially love to my father. Dear Mother, believe me.

Your most affectionate daughter.
  Emma
Thomas sends love.

Dear Mamma – Would you some day when you are at the stores buy a <u>linen</u> picture book for Jessie – she is so fond of books & pictures but of course is very destructive of them. That will put me more in your debt but we will settle it. E

March 7th – Dear Mother – I enclose an order on the Mission Rooms which will cover I think all Papa has paid out. Any margin over will come in for probable future accounts. Jessie seems better this morning. I think she is getting quite over her sickness. We are just closing our mail.

    With love
      Emma

    Items of food available to Emma and her family at Fort Simpson were limited, and they varied by season and according to the generosity of others. Lack of demand meant that the HBC post did not, its long-time head Charles Morison recalled, stock many commodities. "One ton of flour and one chest of tea would last Fort Simpson for a year, no coffee nor bacon were kept in stock, but enormous quantities of rice, molasses and boxes of hardtack for their feasts." The Tsimshian "lived almost, if not entirely, on their native food."[6] A newcomer a dozen years later described "our foods" as "'pemican,' dried deer meet, cranberry and other wild berry desserts, the soap-berry (La brew), the dried and smoked Oolachans, baked brown beans and bacon and Iceland moss (jelly)," which "came by sealing schooners from the Arctic."[7] The fall fair Thomas organized at Fort Simpson was intended to showcase the variety of food items that could be produced and, it was hoped, to encourage local people to prefer some kinds of products over others.

    Food also played a role in the "good old English custom of carol-singing," as Thomas described in detail: "As a preparation for Christmas, from forty to sixty people would gather at the Mission House for practice in carol singing." That was only the beginning of a very long evening.

> They would meet in the church in the evening, about ten o'clock, and, after praying for God's blessing and direction, they would start out through the village, which was now all lighted up, the streets ready festooned with evergreens and the paths covered with white gravel. The singers would be accompanied by half a dozen watchmen, who would clear the way, so that everything might be quiet and peaceful in the village ... They would keep up the singing through the village until about four o'clock in the morning. They would then return to the Mission House, where coffee and cakes were provided.[8]

Fort Simpson, B.C.
March 29th 1876

My dear Mother,

The str. surprised us this evening – she is going no further north this trip and
leave[s] to return tomorrow morning. This leaves very little time. However
I have received no letters and mean to write only this. I have been very well
since my last – indeed I am, I think, the freest from ailments of us all. Thomas
has had a very severe cold – but is a good deal better now. Jessie has had another
little sickness – it appeared to be a cold – but not at all so severe as before but
[she] has got so very thin and pale. However for the last few days she has been
much better and seemed quite like her old self. She has only the four front
teeth yet and I can perceive no coming of any others. I have weaned her altogether now. Her father took that duty upon himself. For four nights I slept
away from her, it was done much more easily than I expected. She sleeps well –
indeed she has always done that which I believe has been an immense benefit
to her. We were somewhat disappointed that no teacher came up by this boat
– if one had come I think we should likely both of us with Jessie have gone
down to Victoria. The District meeting [of the Methodist Church in British
Columbia] is about to meet there. As it is it seems a necessity that Thomas
should go – there are matters in connection with the building here there must
be a better understanding about and with regard to the land reserve for these
people, Thomas must have information in order to properly advise and direct.
Our Missionary neighbor is, I believe, plotting all kinds of trouble for us in
this regard – it is very trying. So my good husband is going alone and Jessie
and I stay at home. It will be lonely perhaps, but I feel that it will be all right
with us. It would never do to leave these people all alone, besides the weather
is still so cold and unsettled I do not think it would be safe to take Jessie away.
Our interpreter Alfred [Dudoward] who used to be such a help and stand by
has been going down sadly lately and quite lost any influence for good he had
– he is in Victoria at present. His wife is faithful but she is in very poor health
and has a young child, so cannot do as much as she used to do.

Many of the people – perhaps the majority – are away now fishing and will
not return for a month or two. Thomas intends to be back by the next str. –
perhaps in five weeks. I hope I shall have letters from you all then too. We have
had another addition to our household – the last Otter brought from Queen
Charlotte's Island a half-breed girl, the daughter of a man in charge of the
H.B.Co.'s store there. He sent her over with her mother, a Tsimpshean woman,
seeming not to doubt that we would take her in – so what could we do. He
wishes her to have the advantages of better training than would be possible for

1

John and Emma
Douse, Emma
Crosby's parents

COURTESY OF HELEN
AND LOUISE HAGER

2

Emma Douse
(right) with an
unidentified
friend at Wesleyan
Female College,
early 1870s

COURTESY OF HELEN
AND LOUISE HAGER

3
Thomas Crosby
with his parents and
younger brother, likely
just before he left for
British Columbia in
1862
COURTESY OF HELEN
AND LOUISE HAGER

4
Emma Douse and
Thomas Crosby about
the time they met in
1874
COURTESY OF HELEN
AND LOUISE HAGER

5

Fort Simpson, 1879

PHOTOGRAPHED BY EDWARD DOSSETTER, GEORGE MERCER DAWSON/SANDFORD FLEMING FONDS,
LIBRARY AND ARCHIVES CANADA, C-023294

6

Thomas Crosby's congregation at Port Simpson, 1881

BC ARCHIVES, B-03538

7

The Dudoward family's "Eagle House" in Fort Simpson

8

Kate and Alfred Dudoward in early middle age

II

Fort Simpson's main street and firehall, 1890

12

Jessie and Grace Crosby, 1879

PHOTOGRAPH BY HANNAH MAYNARD,
COURTESY OF HELEN AND LOUISE HAGER

13

Matron Agnes Knight (on the right)
with Emma and Thomas Crosby and
charges at girls' home, 1888

BC ARCHIVES, B-06310

14

Emma and Thomas Crosby with teacher Susanna Lawrence (in top row with hat) and girls at girls' home, early 1890s

BC ARCHIVES, B-08046

15

Emma and Thomas Crosby just before his death in 1914

BC ARCHIVES, H-05316

her there. Of course he will clothe her – he is not poor – but we do the rest. She is a delicate girl. I hope she may do well.

I trust you and my father are well and comfortable. Kindest love from us both –

Yours as ever affectionately
Emma

The father of Emma's new charge was Martin H. Offutt, already in his mid-thirties when he headed west from Ohio to the California gold rush of 1849. Described as "a hard-living man, who had made and lost more than one fortune," he liked to tell how he once owned the land where Sacramento now stands and had kept a prosperous saloon there.[9] Losing his wealth, Offutt drifted up the coast, thinking of prospecting for gold in Alaska. Offutt stopped a while in Fort Simpson and there met a Tsimshian woman who became his wife. According to Kathleen Dalzell's history of the Queen Charlotte Islands: "The ways of her people offered Offutt the contentment that his battered spirit craved and he adopted their life whole-heartedly. Settling down among them he soon came to be viewed almost as part of the tribe."[10] It was his acceptance by the fiercely independent Haida that made it possible for the HBC to open a store under Offutt's charge at Masset at the northern end of the Queen Charlotte Islands. This store traded in fur seals, sea otters, and oil from dogfish livers. The Offutts had a grown son named John and several daughters, one of whom was Elizabeth. She was likely about fourteen when she was dispatched to Emma in early 1876.

Operating on their own understanding about what the Crosby home could offer their daughters, many parents made conscious choices about placing their children in Emma's care. They may have wanted to spare their children the hardships that resulted from the destructive consequences of encroaching settlement, such as loss of their subsistence economy, the loss of their land, and the erosion of their spiritual base. Others thought that the Crosby home could offer their children new opportunities. With new skills and knowledge, they could participate in the newcomers' world, gaining social and intellectual access to it through Christian means. According to Thomas: "Another case was that of a woman who had for some years lived a sinful life in the gold mines of Cassiar. She heard about our Home when she was staying at Fort Wrangle [Alaska], came the one hundred and sixty miles, and begged for admittance. We took her in and she stayed for several years with us. She was converted and became a most earnest Christian."[11] Some young women came of their own volition, knowing full well the advantages that being part of a Christian home offered. In some circumstances, the Crosbys may have been the only choice.

On Board the Str. "Otter"
April 1st 1876

My Dear Mrs. Douse,

I have often thought I would write you, but Emma has told you how busy I am. Now I have a moment as I am on my way to Victoria to attend D[istrict]. M[eeting]., and many other things that calls [sic] for my attention down there. I did hope so much that my dear wife and daughter could go along for I think that a change would do them both good but as no one came to take charge of the school and having those girls in the house it did seem that we could not both leave, and then the weather is very cold and stormy. We have been delayed 36 hours within 15 miles of home on ac/ of wind. Of course I wished that much more time could have been spent with them but that could not be. I hope to be back by the return of the str. perhaps 5 weeks and I hope you will not think I was unkind to leave Emma so long. Of course she and our dear Jessie are in the hands of a kind Providence and we trust they will be all well.

Emma is generally well in health not so apt to take cold as myself and would be very healthy I believe had we more fruit and fresh meat to live on. Jessie has done very well so far with exception of twice she has been a little sick. We wish much we had a cow on her ac/. But it is so hard to get the str. to bring one up. I shall do all I can to get one now. Jessie is a great comfort to us and of course we think there is nothing like her. May God bless her. We often say we wish you could all see her. She is such a happy little girl.

Our work is doing well considering we have so much to try us, but our trust is in God, the Living God. Of course I have a great deal of hard work on the church yet and do not know when we shall get through. Our neighbor likes to give us all the trouble he possibly can. But God is with us and we will not fear. Of course we often feel those things and often wish we could see you all. I believe we are as happy as we could be any where. And I do feel that God has given me a true helpmate in my dear Emma and I shall always thank God for directing us to each other. Love to yourself and Mr. Douse. I wish Mr. Douse could get me some Bibles and other books and send them out – perhaps by freight – would be best. but I shall have to write him further about it.

Yours affectionately,
Thomas Crosby

April 3 – I expect to get to Nanaimo 75 miles from Victoria tomorrow. Shall perhaps spend Sat. there and be in Victoria for the D.M. 14th. Will perhaps write from there. T.C.

Emma's letters continued to offset her husband's infrequent missals. His choosing to write while away doubled her need to assure her parents that she could manage in his absence. Her second pregnancy was layered onto the additional responsibilities she took on in Thomas's absence.

Fort Simpson, B.C.
April 27th 1876

My dear Mother,

My school is over and my baby is asleep in her cradle, and I am going to take a little time to talk with, or rather to write, you. I know you will be anxious to know how I get on while my good husband is away. It is pretty lonely to be sure but you know I can do without society – better than some people can – though I enjoy it when I have it to enjoy – and then our strength is as our day. The first week passed very slowly – but now the days go quite quickly and four weeks are gone today. In one week more I hope my grass-widowhood may be at an end, but of course in this I may be disappointed. Two days ago I had a letter from Mr. Crosby brought us from Victoria by some Indians in a little schooner they have but when that was written nothing was known as to when the "Otter" would leave.

Having the school everyday I think is good for me – it is small now, so many are away – so we have it in the house. I cannot feel easy to leave Jessie every day – the two older girls both attend the school so there is only a young girl to mind her during that time.

With the exception of a cold which did not take much hold of her, Jessie has been very well since her father went away for which I am very thankful. I should feel very anxious if she were sick while I am alone. And she is so bright and playful and has so many amusing little ways and is so affectionate there is a world of comfort in her for her mother. The four little front teeth are all she has yet though she is now sixteen months old. I think there must be something lacking in her food that she requires, but I do hope we may have a cow before long. Her father will make every effort to get one. The trouble is to get her brought here. When the steamer is crowded with passengers they cannot bring a cow very well. The Indians are very kind as far as they know how to be so. Some of them often come in to see how I am and to make my "heart strong." Then looking after the sick a little gives me something to think of. I attend the Sunday morning service and take care of it. The other services the people – those of them judged best fitted for it – conduct themselves. We have had quite mild and on the whole fine weather for some time, but rain has set in now and it looks as though we were about to have a spell of genuine Fort

Simpson rainy weather. Some currant & raspberry bushes that Mr. Crosby set out last fall are beginning to show signs of life, and a few plants in the flower garden are growing nicely but many I think have died.

May 10th – Yesterday morning the "Otter" passed up, dropping my husband opposite here only a little way out to come in by canoe. O so glad we were, I in particular, and the visit seems to have done Thomas so much good in every way that I cannot but feel glad that I had between five and six lonely weeks of it. Jessie did not know her father, of course, when he first came in, but very soon she understood it so well she could not bear to leave him. He was run down in health a good deal before he went away but is looking much better now. He brought a great many things up with him – fresh meat and vegetables – turnips, radishes, cabbage & cauliflower, a lovely bouquet of flowers, a lot of rhubarb besides a large supply of groceries & dry goods. He visited Nanaimo, N. Westminster & Chilliwhack as well as Victoria. Everywhere the people were very kind. Jessie, of course, had many presents sent her. Three merino dresses – a scarlet, a pink & a blue. The blue was from Mrs. Russ and is made up with a cape to match trimmed with white swan's down. She received also a little plaid shawl, some scarlet flannel, a water proof cloak, two pairs of shoes, a pair of stockings and a fine picture book – besides things that her father bought her. She had three pairs of moccasins given her lately too. O she is a wonderful little girl we think. She is so small – and so bright, and seems to find the way to everyone's heart.

Thomas wants me or at least advises me to go down this summer. The people, I believe, are expecting me, but I can hardly make up my mind to it. There was great excitement in the village yesterday – guns fired – flags flying – games & speeches on the green. I received your letter and the one Papa sent also came to hand. The book you say you were going to send Jessie has not come yet but such things are often longer than letters in reaching us. Thank you for it.

Would you send me, please, a little fine wool such as you sew for Jessie's stockings. She is well supplied at present but I can get no fine wool here and I would like some on hand in case of need. Get what colors you think best. I close with much love from us both to you and my father.

Your ever affectionate
Emma

P.S. I fear that teacher may not come after all. It seems Mr. Pollard saw fit for some wise reason of his own to write <u>disapproving</u> of her coming!

E.

May 11th P.S. As to the Ins. policy – it is here. If Papa thinks best Thomas will send it to him. Will Papa please give the enclosed bill to Mr. Rose. Today I have discovered that Jessie has another little tooth through. She has not been at all sick with it. I enclose five dollars for you to keep to fill any little requests.

Emma

The harried nature of Emma's everyday life is caught in the short note she dispatched home six weeks later. It makes clear her increasing reliance on the Aboriginal girls who lived in the Crosby home.

Fort Simpson, B.C.
June 8th 1876

My dear Mother,

I have only a few minutes in which to write. I had got all ready to go down to Victoria this trip and meant to write you from there but I find the str. is likely to be a long time on the way this trip, so I decided not to go. Indeed I can scarcely see my way clear to leave as things are now. Thomas has work and worry enough without taking any more – and to tell the truth I don't like the idea of going away alone. Jessie is very well and I should take a little girl to nurse her – but I am pretty sure I should be homesick. Our pet has improved lately very much. We have her out a great deal. She is very fond of walking about but does not go alone yet. She has eight teeth now, including two double teeth and has got them without any apparent trouble. The constipation has left her altogether. She is such a gay little blossom! I wish I could tell you all the good things Thomas brought home when he came – oranges and canned tomatoes & canned meat, and preserved fruit from a friend, and fresh meat and vegetables. You can get pretty much anything you want in Victoria for money – and Thomas says he will get these things. Would Papa be so kind as to see this account settled at the Book Room and get the receipts – and also to renew Thomas' subscription for the Weekly [Toronto] Globe which has run out.

Our united love to our father and mother,
Your affectionate daughter
Emma

The full extent of Emma's realization that she had to rely on herself and her Aboriginal charges, given Thomas's repeated absences, comes through in her next letter. So does the difference in priorities relating to dress that was beginning to separate her from her Ontario counterparts.

Fort Simpson, B.C.
June 30th 1876

My dear Mother,

Again we are preparing our mail to send away. I was glad to get your letter from Lefroy. You certainly lead no idle life going about and doing so much as you do. I am sorry Susie is poorly. I am sure her duties must require good health.

We are all well. Jessie has seemed to improve very much lately. She is out a great deal and, you will be glad to know, we have a cow now – so she has as much good, fresh milk as she will take. This cow came last week – by a steamer that goes up north and called here on purpose to leave her and some other freight for us. She came from Victoria and is a nice gentle cow and gives a good supply of milk. There is abundant pasture for her just about here. We find the milk so useful – every morning we have boiled wheat & milk for breakfast which we think delicious. I am going to try tomorrow butter making. I think I ought to be able to make enough for our use during the summer. Do not think we are ill supplied. We have always excellent bread and delicious butter from Chilliwhack – and keep a constant supply of groceries. We have never been without preserved fruit – and the fish we get sometimes is very fine. What we need most is fresh meat and vegetables & fruit. We have had no venison for a long time but it will likely be coming in again in about a month. We have tried getting vegetables from Victoria but the last that came up, a great sack-ful were mislaid on leaving the str. They were landed some distance below here as the str. would not call here on her way up – and got on board a little schooner that carried them about ever so long – till before they reached us they were, of course, quite useless. However when our garden is in order we shall be better off – and it has quite a start now. We had some radishes yesterday of our own raising. Our rasp-berry & currant and rose bushes too are in a very satisfactory condition. I believe we shall have a very pretty little place by and by. A root house has been added lately. Mr. Crosby is busy with the church. Last Sunday he was away about forty miles preaching. He started Saturday morning & returned Monday evening. I have decided not to go to Victoria. I don't see how Mr. Crosby could do with the house & all to look after & no teacher has come yet. Jessie is getting her teeth quite fast but very easily. She has been very well lately – loves to be out and is very fond of the milk. She runs about a great deal but always wants the chairs or somebody's finger to help her. I think she would soon walk alone if we taught her.

You say in one letter that my wardrobe must need replenishing – not at all except as be in plain dresses and of them I have a sufficient supply for the present. As to hats, I have worn that brown straw ever since we came. It is about worn out now though and I have a black silk handkerchief for my head such as the Indian women wear. I intend to have a fur cap for next winter.

We are always so glad to hear from you. Thank you, dear Mother, for writing so faithfully. With love to yourself and my father – from my husband and myself.

I am as ever yours lovingly,
Emma

After two years at Fort Simpson, Emma still used the arrival of the steamer *Otter* as an impetus for writing home. Her daily round increased as the summer ran its course.

Fort Simpson, B.C.
July 26th 1876

My dear Mother,

Again I have an opportunity of sending a letter. This last mail brought more from you but it is not very long since the "Otter" was here before. Annie said in hers that you had been in Cobourg and were to be there again to keep house for her while she was away. I suppose your own house is shut up – just as well for the warm weather, I should think. You would feel the heat very much I am sure, if you had everything to do yourself. We have had the warmest weather within the last week that I have felt at Fort Simpson. Still it was not what you would think immoderate at all.

Thomas is still hard at work. Besides the church building he has put up a new woodshed in which to store wood for winter – with accommodation for the cow at one end and also enlarged the old shed. Our cow proves a very good one. Her milk is very rich and I am making butter regularly twice a week. There would be a great waste of cream if I did not do this and it is very little trouble to me and the girls do all the churning. I merely over-see it, and I will say we have very good butter. We have no churn so we use an enamelled dish and a wooden ladle which serve I think as well as a churn. We have been making about five lbs. a week. If I skimmed all the milk closely we might have a good deal more but this is much more than we use so the balance I put away in brine for the future. And here where every lb. of butter costs about fifty cents, it is worth while to make it. There is plenty of wild grass about that can be cut for winter for the cow – but what other food she requires will be some expense. Jessie has grown quite fat on the milk. She is very fond of it. She grows more interesting every day – it seems to us. She chatters away at a great rate and can say a few words plainly – and will walk anywhere with some one's finger. She likes particularly to walk on the gravel path leading to the house – but she will not go alone.

We have been disappointed again about a teacher – and the half-breed woman [Kate Dudoward] who helped us is away now so we have the school on our hands. There is a young man who assists somewhat. Thomas goes to open the school in the morning and stays a while, then as soon as I can I take Jessie and go to relieve him and take the rest of the day. There are several places at some distance from us that Thomas wished very much to visit this summer but it is almost impossible for him to get away. The "Otter" brought us some fruit & vegetables. I was busy yesterday putting away cherries & currants – and we had also a few apples & tomatoes and a lot of green peas and beans. The trouble is to keep such things in good condition during the trip. The str. was five days on the way this time though she sometimes comes up in about three days. I hope I shall have a good letter from you by the next mail.

Our kindest love to my father and yourself. Remember us in your prayers, and

Believe me, dear Mother
    Your affectionate daughter
        Emma

Maintaining the mission while Thomas was away left Emma not only alone but also lonely for much of the time. She bore the added responsibilities that fell to her in his absence while carrying a second child. Born September 10, 1876, she was named Grace Eliza. Emma now had Jessie and a newborn in her care with only the assistance of her Aboriginal charges. Emma braved loneliness, assuring her mother that Thomas's absences were a necessary part of their work there.

The annotations in Emma's next letters reveal both the time it took mail to make its way to Ontario from Fort Simpson and the process by which her missals were passed around the family.

Rec'd in Cobourg, Nov 7th. Remailed to L. same day
First reading at Lefroy, Nov 8
Second dv. Nov 10
Sent to Barrie Nov 11

Fort Simpson, B.C.
Sept. 26th 1876

My dear Mother,

It seems a long time since I wrote to you and now I have a great deal to tell you. The steamer has been undergoing repairs in Victoria and we have had no mail since July but she will likely be here again in the course of a week or so. So I must begin in time to unfold my budget. Well, event No. 1 is the recent arrival of another little daughter. This occurred on the 10th of this month – another wee mortal, weighing, with her clothes, <u>five pounds</u>. She has quite a lot of hair, dark blue eyes, well developed features for her size, and although so small seems to be doing very well indeed. Jessie is very fond of her, always wanting to kiss her, but she thinks it very funny that baby cannot shake hands, that being one of Jessie's strong points. You must know that my baby is dressed somewhat after the fashion of the place – that is, her blanket is rolled round her and pinned as tight as is comfortable so she cannot get her hands out. I do not mean to continue this long in the day time but while she is so very small it is much easier and safer I think to handle her rolled up this way. She likes very much though to get a chance to stretch out her arms and quite often I let her have them free for a while. If she only gets on as well as Jessie has done we shall be very thankful. A healthier, merrier little girl you would scarcely find anywhere than Jessie is. She has been walking alone quite a long time now and her little feet never seem to tire of pattering about. She tries to talk too – she can say several Indian words plainly and about as many English.

Now that I have two little ones to care for I feel that my work must be almost wholly at home – this little baby will need great care all winter, if it is spared to us, and it is better for Jessie to be with me than with the girls. I was not expecting baby for a month or six weeks longer – perhaps that accounts for her being so small – or it may be I was wrong in my calculations. I do not know of anything I did that would be likely to hasten her coming. My sickness began about nine in the morning (this was Sunday) but was not severe till afternoon and baby's voice was heard about nine at night. It seemed pretty bad while it lasted but now it is over I think more lightly about it. I had the same attendance as upon Jessie's arrival and have got on very well indeed. At the end of a week, that is on the Sunday morning following, I was up and out in the sitting room. Last Sunday, that was when baby was two weeks old, I walked out a little and now I feel about as well as usual. My nurse only stayed two days with me as her son is lying very ill but she comes every morning to wash baby – and that is all I want. I would rather manage things myself in the house. I felt very much when I was lying in bed the need of some reliable person to take charge of the house. Mr. Crosby was so busy with the church that he could not be in the house much and though we have four girls – we took a new one lately – they had so little to do that two might have done far better than four. I have constantly to study to arrange work for them and keep them all employed when I am well. I have been teaching them lately some kinds of fancy knitting and crochet work and they do very well at it. Then Jessie had to be left almost entirely to their care and though, I believe, they did all they could for her still they cannot manage her properly. However I do not wish to complain – we have so very much to be thankful for I must not do that. Mr. Crosby has been also altering and enlarging the house somewhat, so as to give us another bedroom downstairs – but this is not yet finished. I think I must send you a plan of our premises & house. They have been so improved lately. The church has been a great burden to Thomas but I am glad to say that now the most difficult part of the work is very nearly completed, that is, the ceiling. It is so lofty and the scaffolding is so high I dreaded its being begun. However a few days now will likely see it finished including varnishing and only the seats and the walls to be stained sometime will remain which will be but light work. This church has really been such a labor and difficulty as but few men would have borne. Several times Thomas has almost broken down under it and now he is far from being well. Every little detail of the work has to be under his direction – of course, these Indians know almost nothing of such work. However the Chairman in the first place made great promises to the people while he far under-estimated the cost of such a church as this – and, though at the expense of his own strength and comfort, Thomas felt that to maintain our influence over the ignorant people these promises must be made good – and so he has labored on using every means to keep down the expense possible. But now that it is so near completion I do not want to grumble, only I wish the Chairman might have such an undertaking saddled to his back that he might know what it is. Thomas has been expending his own money on this too as well as time and strength. But enough of that. We have much to encourage us. Every summer numbers of the younger men go off to find work. This summer ten of our Tsimpsheans went to a place called Fort Wrangle in Alaska. It is on the route to the Cassiar mines and the most northerly point the "Otter" calls at. A small garrison of American soldiers is stationed here and it is the home of a large number of Indians and frequently white men stop there some time. Well, these Tsimpsheans began religious services which were very largely attended by the Indians and also by white men and the soldiers, and evidently much good has been done. Every one who comes down from there speaks so highly of this movement and the officer in charge of the garrison wrote to Mr. Crosby, saying he believed much good had been affected already and expressing his readiness to help in the continuance of these services. All but two of these men have returned now. They speak of the delight of the white man at their singing and how heartily they joined in it. Such a thing as a religious service was unknown in this place before these Indians started it. Mr. Crosby feels that something must be done to continue this. The Indians are wishing it as well as the whites and likely he will send two of our most intelligent and reliable men to carry on services and perhaps to begin a school for the Indian children during the winter – and we hope that some American church may be induced to undertake the work of a mission here where the door is so manifestly open for it. Thomas intends going up there when the steamer comes that he may know better what to do. This will take him from home three or four days.

There is a teacher [Caroline Knott] in Victoria, we hear, waiting to come up by the "Otter." We got word of it by a little sloop that reached here last week. I hope she will be an agreeable person and fitted to do good. We had school – I went to it – up to the Friday before baby came. There has been none since. We are expecting Mr. Russ from Victoria some time this fall, likely by the 2nd trip of the str. and we hope he may open the church.

An event which caused quite a little excitement amongst us was an unexpected visit from the Governor General and suite. It happened – unfortunately as we could but think – on a day when the village was almost empty. During the summer the people keep all the time going away after food & &c. so that a fine day will leave sometimes a mere handful of people at home. If we had had but a few days notice we might have sent for many of the Indians but there was no chance of that – and what seemed as unfortunate as the people's absence, Mr. Crosby and Mr. Morrison were both away too. They had been called away to a place about 40 miles distant and there was no white man to receive our distinguished visitors. There were two or three in the village but not such men as could do anything of that kind. So there was no one but Mrs. Morrison and myself to do the honors. Of course there was no time to arrange anything. The tide was out and a great raft of logs lay on the beach by the Fort gate which was the landing place of the vice-regal party and Lady Dufferin had to climb over these logs after walking across a rough pile of rocks. We met them on the beach & were duly presented to the Gov. & Countess. It was very easy to receive them after all and we accompanied them first into Mr. Morrison's house. Then, as they wished to walk through the village and see the church & school house, I set out with them. We went into two or three of the Indian houses also and the Gov. sat down on the church steps to take a sketch of the view which they admired very much. Then we went back to the beach. The Gov. addressed the Indians – those who were there – briefly, and we sat a while on some benches in the Fort yard and talked in a pleasant way. They were both very pleasant and genial and I really enjoyed their visit as I should meeting any agreeable people. I had Jessie with me – one of the girls carried her down –

and she sat on the Countess' lap and shook hands with the Gov. while one remarked what pretty hair she had and the other, what pretty eyes – very gratifying to her mother of course. After staying about two hours our visitors re-embarked. The flags were flying & guns fired but we could do very little. I was very sorry it happened thus – of course the Governor's object was to find out the condition of the Indians. Mr. Crosby felt very much disappointed when he reached home. He could have represented the Indians and given all information desired. However it could not be helped and I suppose was all right.

Oct 9th Our mail came day before yesterday (Saturday). There were two letters from you. One from Lefroy and one from Cobourg. I wish you could come & stay a while with me <u>as you do with the other girls</u>. Thomas left with the str. for Wrangle. He means to return by canoe so will likely be away ten days or more. The teacher arrived. I am pleased with her so far and trust she may be a great help and comfort to us. The children are both well and I am doing finely. Baby continues to improve. I have been washing her myself for about a week. I received the parcel of stockings and wool for which my sincerest thanks dear mother. I received also two letters from Annie, one from Eliza & one from Susie. I shall try to write the girls, but may not accomplish it. Please send this letter to them. A parcel from Eliza also came with a linen dress and a sash for Jessie, one from Susie with stockings & ribbon, and one from Annie containing patterns. The grey flannel came also. Thanks to Mrs. Brenton. Dear Mother I must close now – I am so busy. The mail is to leave tomorrow A.M. Write – again this fall. I think we shall have two more mails. Kindest love to my dear father, the girls and Georgie and much for yourself. Pray for us.

> Yours affectionately,
> Emma

Please mail this to Lefroy when read with two stamps on, then it must be sent to Barrie and taken care of.

The governor general and Lady Dufferin were on an official visit to British Columbia, which was intended to pacify separatist tendencies due to the delay in the construction of the transcontinental railroad promised on the province's entry into Confederation five years earlier. The principal goal of their trip up the coast by steamer was to visit Metlakatla, with which they were very sympathetic – not surprisingly, given their Anglicanism. William Duncan was well prepared for their arrival, firing a cannon as their tender approached and arranging for the singing of "God Save the Queen" accompanied by fifes. He took his visitors on an extensive tour of what Lady Dufferin considered to be "one of the most successful of Indian missions." Duncan was in her view "quite a model missionary."[12]

The Dufferins turned up unannounced at Fort Simpson by tender on Wednesday, August 30, 1876, at about 2:00 PM as an extension of their Metlakatla visit. The decision may have been spontaneous, given that neither the head of the HBC post nor Thomas Crosby as mission head was there to greet them. As Lord Dufferin penned in his journal, "We found, on arriving, all the men officials absent, but were received by Mrs. Morrison, of the H.B.Co., and Mrs. Crosby, the wife of the Methodist minister conducting the mission there, who conducted us over the place."[13] Lady Dufferin recorded how "Mrs. Crosbie [sic], the missionary's wife, took us through the village, where we saw for the first time some extraordinary monuments put up by Indian chiefs."[14]

Totem poles, if beyond the couple's comprehension, nonetheless piqued their curiosity. Lord Dufferin called them "curious poles with strange, goggle-eyed crests in them."[15] Lady Dufferin separated herself from the meanings others might attach to them: "The subjects are, I suppose, symbolical, but to us they appear grotesque." Emma showed her unannounced visitors through some Tsimshian houses, which, Lady Dufferin reported, "consist of one very large room, with the square fire at the centre, the rafters being made of the most enormous trees." Emma was accompanied, as she explained to her mother, by Odille Morison, who came to the rescue at a difficult moment: "His Ex. spoke to the Indians, and they made a reply, which Mrs. Morrison (who is a half-breed) translated."[16]

Lady Dufferin decided, not unexpectedly, that the "Indians [at Fort Simpson] are not nearly so civilised as at Metlakatlah."[17] Primed by Duncan, Lord Dufferin concluded that "Mr. Crosby has chosen a field for his labors rather too near Mr. Duncan, and would have been better at some other place where no missionary had been before, for Mr. Duncan began his labors at Fort Simpson."[18] It is revealing of Thomas's character, of his disinclination to admit he might have been in the wrong, that his next public letter made no mention of the visit.[19] As for Emma, she carefully kept all her life the *cartes de visite,* two-inch by four-inch photos that Lord and Lady Dufferin sent as a memento of their visit.[20]

For his part Thomas was more concerned with his own adventures. Wrangell had captured his attention. A number of Tsimshian from Fort Simpson, including a man named Clah (not Arthur Wellington Clah) who, on his baptism, had been renamed Philip McKay, had headed up the Stikine to the Cassiar mines in the spring of 1876. At Wrangell they "found the people here in utter darkness as regards the Saviour and his love." Taking a job there cutting wood for the American army garrison, McKay and a couple of others held Methodist services.[21] It was this sequence of events that drew Thomas's attention north.

The visiting cards that Lord and Lady Dufferin sent to Emma Crosby in 1876

NOTMAN STUDIO, OTTAWA, COURTESY OF HELEN AND LOUISE HAGER

Fort Simpson, B.C.
Oct. 30th 1876

My dear Mother,

We are preparing now for what we expect to be our last mail for this year, so you need not expect another letter until about February next. But I know we shall not be absent from your thoughts and prayers during that time and the same kind Providence that has cared for us hitherto will watch over us still.

I suppose you and my father are preparing for winter. Is your house a warm one? And don't you find it troublesome sometimes to look after all that house-keeping requires? I think you ought to have some one to help you.

When I wrote last Thomas was away. He returned sooner than I expected – the steamer having remained a day longer than usual at Wrangle, he was able to return by her. I was very glad of this for travelling so far as that (160 miles) by canoe at this season of the year is not pleasant nor always safe.

Our little ones continue well. Baby is thriving wonderfully – and is such a sleeper. She hardly has her eyes open half an hour in the day except when I give her her bath. She sleeps very soundly at night too. Jessie has had a slight cold for a few days but it is leaving her I think now. She is the life of the house, full of play and mimicking every thing she sees. Miss Knott seems quite content and thoroughly at home. I find it very pleasant having some one with me. She is good company, and I think we shall get along well.

After the Otter had gone last time I was pretty busy putting away fruit. We got a lot of [pears] up and a few plums – though the time for plums passed while the str. was so long in Victoria. I pickled a few [pears] and also a little cauliflower I got from the Fort garden. We are having plenty of good vegetables from the garden at the Fort now. Our church is, I may say, completed at last. All that remains to be done is the painting of the seats. The ceiling and walls are varnished, the lower part of the walls being also stained brown. The altar & pulpit platform are covered with a kind of Chinese matting that is very pretty & the step outside the rail covered with green baize. The aisles and space round the altar are covered with Indian mats made to fit – the work of the women of the village. The pulpit and altar are nicely stained & varnished. Lamp stands are set up and altogether we have a spacious and neatly finished church – and the expense of this summers [sic] work has been kept far below the estimate made by the architect in Victoria.

The Indians are delighted with it and are to have an opportunity of expressing their feelings tomorrow in another subscription. The opening services are to be in the course of about a week – perhaps next Sunday. We are hoping Mr. Russ will be up by the Otter – I mean to have the baby baptized at that time.

One of our girls is to be married in about a week, to a very promising young man. We are going to give the wedding feast which will likely include thirty or forty people. This is the girl who came to us first. I am rather sorry to lose her. She is a good nurse though not a very good worker, but of course it is best for girls to be married, Indian girls more especially.

Thomas has not yet been able to finish the house – but I expect it will be done as soon as the Otter has come and gone.

Nov 1st Our mail came in yesterday morning bringing a letter from you. I was glad to know you were well. Tell Jessie Peard I am sure those things she sent will please some of the children.

Mr. Russ failed to get here which was quite a disappointment, however Mr. Crosby will open the church himself next Sunday. Last evening he had a meeting to solicit subscriptions, and already near four hundred dollars have been given which will likely be increased some. Thomas thinks about going away next week to the Naas river, some sixty miles, where he has long promised to visit. Yesterday we had a visit from the Missionary who has been assisting at Metlahkatla [William Collison] and his wife. They had come here to take the str. for Queen Charlotte's Is. where they are about to establish a new mission. It was much against their own wishes that they kept aloof so long. They are earnest Christian people, I am sure. I cannot but regret that we were denied so long intercourse which might have been such a pleasure & benefit. They have two little ones – the elder two years old and they are going where they will have only an Indian house or such as they can put up themselves for the approaching winter. Our sympathies went with them strongly.

I know you will think of us during the long silence of the winter – and so shall we of you. Thomas joins me in kindest love to yourself and my father.

> Pray for us.
> Your loving daughter
> Emma

Caroline Sarah Knott, who was sent to teach at the Fort Simpson day school, was born in London, England, around 1843 and, hence, was half a dozen years Emma's senior.[22] She mentioned, a year later, that "Mrs. Crosby is the only white lady" at Fort Simpson other than herself.[23] The teacher boarded with the Crosbys, and this created a bond between the two women.

The HBC post overseen by Martin Offutt was located at Massett. William Henry Collison, who had been Duncan's assistant at Metlakatla, was on his way there to set up an Anglican mission. Collison, his wife, and two infant sons spent a day and two nights at Fort Simpson. On their arrival at Massett with only "a few boards and a tent, hoping to be able to induce one of the chiefs to permit us to have a corner in one of their large lodges," it was Offutt who rescued them. "I received a message from an old white man the only one on the islands, who was living with an Indian woman, and under her protection, stating that he could afford us shelter for the night." At first shocked by Offutt's unusual lifestyle, Collison grew quite fond of the man he dubbed "the Squire." Offutt reciprocated by inaugurating "a weekly prayer meeting at his house."[24]

> Fort Simpson, B.C.
> Nov. 28th 1876

My dear Mother,

As we are partly expecting a steamer in here to bring by special arrangement some passengers for Fort S., I want to have a letter ready to send in case the opportunity should come. If I should be able to get this off it will likely reach you about Christmas time – and let me assure you, dear Mother, that most heartily do we wish that you and my father, and all the dear ones may have a most happy time. I know you will think of us there though we are so far away. I cannot help wishing that you might spend it with us and our little children – but it is all right. We are much favored as it is. The children are both well.

Jessie was quite sick for a few days two or three weeks ago in getting her eye teeth but she has been well since. As for baby she thrives wonderfully. However, her temper is not always the most amiable. She sleeps always well at night and a great deal during the day – but when she is up she requires the best of attention or we hear loud complaints. But she is a sweet little baby for all that. We had her baptized – her father officiated at the church opening and named her Grace Eliza. The Indians are going to give her a name also, I believe. Jessie is the life and pet of the house and grows more precious every day. She and her father have great times. He takes care of her always at night. Thomas left us today to visit some village fifty or sixty miles away – which he had long promised the people to do. It is rather late in the season to take so long a trip, but he has a good crew with him and at present very good weather. When he will be back must depend greatly upon the weather, but I hope we may see him in the course of a week.

It is a great comfort to me to have Miss Knott here when Thomas is away. She is quite one of ourselves already. Our church was opened the Sunday after the "Otter" left last and a satisfaction and comfort it is to have so good a church. There is a broad road leading directly to it, and on a Sunday morning when the congregation have been dismissed it is a fine sight to see them thronging this road, as orderly and as neatly dressed people as you would find almost anywhere. We had an industrial show one day last week. I wish you could have seen the articles on exhibition. Vegetables, Indian food, silver work, wood carving, fancy work, knitting &c. bread, cakes, pies, pickles, preserves and raspberry vinegar. The entries for cooking, however were near all from the Fort and the mission house. Mr. Crosby gave out about sixty prizes most of them of course only trifles as he had no help except indeed from Miss Knott who contributed three prizes. There was one pretty piece of wood carving Thomas secured for me. It is a spool rack ornamented with birds and flowers, and is really a fine piece of work. The man who did this also carved a very pretty baptismal font for the church. As Christmas approaches the weddings and the feasts are beginning. There were two today. One thing that has occurred since I wrote you we cannot but regret – we have lost our cow. As the weather was cold Mr. Crosby put her one night into a shed that was not quite fixed as he intended to have it and either in an attempt to get away or in some other way she fell down and in the morning was found dead. We were so sorry about it. She was such a good cow and the milk seemed just the thing Jessie needed – and it is so difficult to get a cow brought up here that it is really a serious matter. However we must not complain. I use condensed milk for Jessie now a good deal, but it is not at all as good as the fresh. The bills I enclose Thomas would be much obliged by Papa's settling for him – and he would like also if Papa would pay the premium on his Insurance policy also which is due some time in February. I enclose an order for $200. Would Papa also renew the Globe subscription and send twenty dollars to Susie. I am owing her a good deal. So often I think of you all and how pleasant it is that you can meet to-gether so often but we have much to cheer us and as happy a home as, I think, you would find anywhere. It is a trial to me to have my husband go away, but I feel it is only right that, at times, he should do so. Our kindest love to my father and the girls and Georgie, and

> Believe me, dear Mother
> > Your most loving and faithful daughter
> > > Emma

Jan 6th A happy New Year to you all. O how much I have thought about you all, and I know you have remembered us. We are all well and have had a happy Christmas. Special meetings have been carried on for near a week with prom-ise of much good. I will try to tell you about our Xmas by the Otter. We had about given up this expected str. but one is in sight now. She may perhaps not remain longer than a few minutes so, though we expect our mail we shall likely have no chance to answer letters.

Baby is well and is such a sweet little pet. Jessie is very thin but seems well and we are greatly blessed. The winter has been remarkably mild.

> Love to my father and yourself & all friends from my husband and
> > Your affectionate daughter
> > > Emma

A month later Emma wrote again, in part to thank her family for Christmas gifts warmly received. Unlike some of her hurried earlier letters, this one de-scribed in detail her everyday doings and the two daughters who now vied for pride of place alongside her husband.

> Fort Simpson, B.C.
> Feb. 13th 1877

My dear Mother,

Again we are preparing for our opening mail. This is the first of my letters. We have been more favored than usual this winter with mails. Twice an American str. called here & once a schooner brought our letters &c. since the "Otter" was last here so the monotony has had very pleasant breaks. I sent you a letter by one of these opportunities early in January which I trust has reached you before this. I am anxious to get letters from you all – to know how you spent your Christmas and of your welfare in all respects and then it is such a comfort to me to read the kind words that come from home. I should feel far more lonely than I ever do if I thought I was not remembered kindly amongst you all. Only a few days after I had despatched my letter to you, another mail reached us bringing a letter containing two scarfs for which, thanks, and more for the letter. The book for Jessie reached us the same time. I wish you could have witnessed her delight. She has a great fondness for books and I told her you had sent her one. As I untied it she stood almost breathless and when she had it fairly in her hands her pleasure was unbounded. And having such a variety in it she never tires of it, and asks often to have her favorite pictures found for her by representing them herself. Indeed most of her conversation is carried on by signs and mimicry. She talks but little, but can make us understand almost anything in this way. She is a funny little thing – the life of the house. It would amuse you to see her with her doll. The poor thing has been without arms and legs a long time, but is no less precious on that account. She talks and sings and reads to her, scolds her, shows her pictures and her own new clothes, sometimes makes her look out of the window and in a looking glass, puts her to sleep, feeds her, gives her medicine &c. She seems well, but grows slowly and is very thin. Perhaps partly because she is so active for both bodily & mentally she is in constant activity. She is affectionate and unselfish in disposition, but has a strong will. I think she will be very like her father. Jessie and baby are like a pair of turtle doves, they are so fond of each other. Jessie's great delight is to get baby in her arms or to be left in bed with her in the morning and baby seems to like it about as well as Jessie. As for baby, our little Gracie, she is growing finely, is very fat and healthy and usually good. She is almost as large as Jessie. I put her in short clothes some weeks since. Our children are indeed a comfort to us. But I must tell you about something besides my babies.

Our Christmas passed very happily. The whole village were busy scrubbing, washing &c. the Saturday previous, for though the house may be disorder & dirt unmitigated all the rest of the year, it must be reduced to something that has a smack of neatness for Christmas. Midnight Sunday the bell sounded & guns were fired which were a signal for the putting up of evergreens and illuminating of windows the village over. An arch was put up over the church gate and the road leading to it decorated with evergreens & lit with lamps. Then the carols began – and very sweet the singing sounded. Our house was near the last visited, and the singers had coffee and biscuits served to them. Then when this was over we went to bed again a little while. During the morning the people kept coming to shake hands and a service was held in the church.

For dinner we had a fine roast of beef – an animal had been killed at the Fort – potatoes, cabbage, I think, tomatoes and an excellent plum pudding.

We sent parcels of tea, sugar, rice & buns to about fifteen or twenty sick people. In the afternoon we started out to visit from house to house – children and all. I gave out before we had been over the whole village, but Mr. Crosby and Miss Knott called at every house except one that stands some distance from any other. In the evening we were too tired to do much but rest. The Thursday following the Christmas tree was given. We had made a good many aprons and neckties and with some other things managed to find some little present for each of about 120 children – besides which each one received a parcel containing a couple of buns, an apple and a trifle of candy. A watch night service was held, and New Year's night the Magic Lantern was exhibited. A few days after this we gave a feast of biscuits & buns & tea and a few apples to some strangers who were spending their Xmas in the village, and to the Council, after which the sapunt [?] Council-men were pleased to bestow Tsimpshean names on Miss Knott and on Little Gracie. The former was called Kundoch – meaning an eagle seizing its prey. Baby was called Ihudathl – or a young woman. When the excitement of Christmas festivities was over special meetings were held in different parts of the village with apparently very good results. The difficulty with these people seems to be to show them that something more is needed than a mere outward change. This is especially the case with the older people. The younger men & women are many of them, I believe, really roused, and as they gain in knowledge, as they are constantly doing, we hope to see them become intelligent earnest Christians. The school is well attended, as are also all the services.

The winter has been a very mild one, but almost constantly we have had strong winds and very frequently most violent storms. The school being now provided for and that church building wound up, Mr. Crosby is free to go about visiting neighbouring places more than he has done in the past. This is attended however with considerable danger at this season of the year, on account of the prevailing storms and the rocky, dangerous character of the coast. Some weeks ago Mr. Crosby started for Naas, about 45 miles away, with a crew of ten men, but a contrary wind met them about half way to their destination and for two nights and a day they camped on the beach unable, through the violence of the storm, to move either way. We knew that it would be impossible for the travelers to accomplish their journey, and that they must be camped somewhere on the way – and also we suspected that their provisions would not hold out more than a few days. I was anxious to send a canoe to their relief but for a time that was quite impossible on account of the wind. However, Thursday morning – it was Monday Mr. Crosby left – one of the chiefs started off with a very large canoe, and eighteen men, and a large supply of provisions. That morning, though it was still very rough, Mr. Crosby & his men had ventured out and after passing some very perilous points, met the canoe that was in search of them. Their provisions were just about out – a very few dried salmon and a can or two of preserved meat were about all that was left. However both canoes sailed in finely in the afternoon, and were met with much rejoicing, flags flying &c. Since then Mr. Crosby has visited Naas but on his return was again delayed by the weather. He also made a visit lately to a village about 60 miles to the south of us. These Naas people sent a very urgent request that Mr. Crosby visit them, and they seem very desirous that a mission be established among them – and if it should be that the Society do not take it up as we hope they will, still Mr. Crosby will likely keep some one there on his own responsibility to begin a school and carry on services, while as often as he can he will visit there himself. I expect Mr. Crosby will make a trip to Wrangle before long, but that will likely be by the str. I cannot but feel sorry when we have to be left at home alone, still I believe it would not be right for Mr. Crosby to stay at home when there are calls from all sides, and while he is so kindly guarded, we are kept in comfort at home, and receive so much help and kindness from the people, what should I say? The children are a great help to me at these times, and Miss Knott is very good company, indeed, her being here is a daily comfort to me. She has taken our old bed-room down stairs now, while we have moved into a new room that was added to the house last summer. This latter room is about 14 x 14, has a fire place across one corner, has a large clothes closet and a small room we call the bath room opening from it. We sit here a good deal and I find it very cosy and convenient – the only drawback being that with the wind in one certain direction the chimney smokes, but this we hope may be remedied.

I am hoping that it may not be long before I shall be able to visit Victoria – unless some great obstacle comes in the way I mean to be there fore the summer is over. I may go with Mr. Crosby in the Spring if he goes to the Dis. meeting – if not, then later with Miss Knott. I am making things up for the children already with a view to this. I have a girl who is helping me with sewing. She is a Hydah girl who has lived a long time in Victoria but was lately married here. Her husband, Thomas [was] sent to Wrangle, so we took her into the house. She has a large machine & sews well.

Feb 17th. Last night the str. came in bringing your letter of Jan 30th. We were very glad to know you were all well, and comfortable. How I wish we could see you! Thanks for the bootees – they are very pretty. You need not have feared them being too small. My babies are tiny things, you know. You ask what would be most useful to me – well, dear Mother, any little things for the children come in useful – nothing more so than stockings. I do not know what the children would do without the stockings you have knit them. Baby wears Jessie's old ones now. I wear out very few clothes myself. If I go to Victoria I shall have to get a new bonnet – perhaps a wrapper and alter two or three old dresses a little – that is about all.

I shall have to ask you to send this letter the round of the family – and to Auntie. I have not been able to write fully to all. Our kindest love to both yourself and my father and kind regards to all friends who remember us in Toronto. Yours was the only letter from home by this mail.

With much love,
Your affectionate daughter
Emma

Emma got her long sought respite in Victoria in March 1877. After almost three uninterrupted years at Fort Simpson, she revelled in opportunities for small talk with women who were, like herself, the wives of Methodist ministers or missionaries.

Victoria March 29th 1877

My dear Mother,

You will see by the date of this that I am from home. We left home three weeks ago – had a comparatively pleasant trip down. There was but one other passenger – the weather was good – and though the "Otter" is not fitted up in first-class style – yet the Capt. gave us the use of his room all day and we were very comfortable. In less than three days we reached Nanaimo where we had decided to remain over for a few days. It was Sunday morning during service time that we arrived. Mr. Crosby went up at once to the church and soon was back with several friends to take us up to the Parsonage. Mr. [Cornelius] Bryant, the minister, and his wife were exceedingly kind but I cannot say I enjoyed my visit very much. The weather was wet and disagreeable. We all had colds and such a constant round of here for dinner, there for tea gave us no peace and made the children very restless. The following Friday we came down here – and have had a very pleasant time. The weather has been delightful – though not too warm for winter clothing or nearly that. The gardens are in bloom – that is, the early flowers are out in great abundance and the trees are in blossom. I have had a great many visitors and every day we are out. We have a pretty little carriage for Jessie. She can not walk very far yet nor very fast – and a little girl I brought down with me carries baby. This little nurse is of but little use to me but is better than no one. She is one we got on purpose to help me while away. The girls I had had in the house were all gone – three married and one we sent home. I believe this change will be a real benefit to me and to the children too. We are at the Parsonage with Mr. and Mrs. Russ who are kindness itself. There are two daughters in the family, the elder about fifteen, the other eight – and all seem to study the comfort of the children. Mrs. R. specially strives to secure regular hours for them and every comfort. She insists upon my going out to the evening services while she stays home with the children. I generally have them both asleep by about seven o'clock but I never leave them unless with some responsible person. Mr. R. and Jessie are the best of friends. Indeed our pets receive great favor wherever we are. Jessie is a funny, lively little thing, that attracts quite as much attention as is good for her, while baby is such a sweet-tempered little pet anyone could love her. We have had their photos taken. If I can get them in time tomorrow I will enclose one of each. We intend to have another of Jessie, which I will try to send you also.

Good Friday – 30th
A week ago today Mr. Crosby went up the Fraser river to see his old friends there. I should have liked to have gone with him but for the sake of rest and quiet for the children I thought it best to stay here. I expect him back tomorrow. Then next Thursday the District meeting is to be held here. The first trip of the "Otter" after that must take Thomas home, I suppose, and I think I shall be ready to go then too, though I am urged to remain longer. It will likely be three or four weeks however before we can get back as the "Otter" left for the north two days since and will not be going again probably within that time.

I am afraid Miss Knott will feel being alone a good deal, though we left her in good spirits. We left an Indian woman, one who had lived with me before, and her husband in the house so that she should not feel nervous at night. The people were most of them leaving for their first fishing and will likely be away until after we get back. I think I shall not be able to write to the girls by this mail, but shall try to do so soon.

I received a letter from my father a few days ago which I shall give to Thomas when he comes. Many thanks to Papa for his trouble. We are glad to get the papers. Tell me what you think of the children's photographs. With much love to both yourself and my father.

Believe me, dear Mother
    Your affectionate
        Emma

Rev. William Pollard and Rev. Amos Russ had once again changed places during Emma's first three years at Simpson. Rev. Pollard was now in New Westminster, and Rev. Russ was back at the Pandora Street church in Victoria.

Cornelius Bryant, who came out from England at the age of eighteen in 1857, taught school at Nanaimo until 1870. He then entered the Methodist ministry, serving in Nanaimo from 1874 to 1878 when he moved across to Burrard Inlet. The future Vancouver was still a small lumber town strung out along its south shore. Later he would have charge of Bella Bella.

Fort Simpson, B.C.
May 9th 1877

My dear Mother,

Another of your welcome letters came to hand yesterday, and I feel as though I have so much to say to you in reply. So many things occur that I should like to write about but when I am at a letter my time seems so short that I cannot write all I wish. I wrote you from Victoria acknowledging my father's letter. I am sorry to hear he has not been well. You must have work enough with your housekeeping indeed it seems to me you must do quite too much. I think you should do just so much work as you find necessary to keep you interested and no more. There are plenty of poor people in Toronto, I am sure, to whom it would be a charity to give employment and you ought to make your life just as comfortable as ever you can.

It gives me great comfort to learn from your letters that one and another of the good Christian people at home are praying for us. More and more do I feel the need of sustaining grace and long to be upheld by the prayers of those strong in faith. There are difficulties at every turn while the work continually grows. We are very sorry to find that a change is to be made in the management of the H.B. Co's store here. Mr. Morrison is to be removed to an out of the way place down the coast – while a stranger comes to take charge here. This latter is very unpromising. I fear he will be no help to us. His wife is a Spanish half-breed from the interior who cannot talk any English.[25] Mr. and Mrs. Morrison have been a real help to us and have had, I think, a very good influence on the Indians. Mrs. M. has improved wonderfully. Her house is kept as nicely as any-one's needs to be, and they live like people of refinement and good taste. They have decided, I believe, that Mrs. M. and the children – two little girls – are to remain here with her brothers & mother, while Mr. M. goes to his new post – only temporarily, I think, until he is prepared to return here to carry on business for himself. I must tell you about the latter part of our visit to Victoria. It was really a great pleasure to me, and the children improved very much while we were away. The people of Victoria were very kind indeed. I was kept busy visiting and the children met with universal favor. The Dist. meeting was held while we were there. Thomas, of course, was full of schemes of extension and had set his heart upon having a missionary for Naas, while word had been sent from the Mission rooms that no new work could be undertaken except by local effort, on account of that troublesome debt. When the appeal was made to the meeting this was how it was met – the sympathy of the ministers was roused and one promising young man was ready to go – but no money. Thomas came away, heavy in heart – even his own travelling expenses in visiting these people could not be allowed him – and feeling he could not say to these people that there was no one to take them the Gospel, and they begging for it – still hoping that some way would be opened. That (Saturday) evening he went to a small praise meeting held in a private house comprising perhaps twenty Christian people. Here he told his feelings about this matter, and a marvelous sympathy was felt. Then this young man, who was also there, declared his readiness to go and the tide rose higher and another young minister who has hitherto been very successful declared he was willing to go. By and by a colored man got up and said he thought they ought to do something practical. He thought fifty dollars might be raised that night. At once some one else said he would give half of that himself and subscriptions of fifty, twenty five, ten dollars & a few less were offered until in a few minutes between two and three hundred were promised without one being asked for anything. It was a wonderful time & those who were at the meeting seemed to think they had never felt anything like it. The next day other sums were promised, one poor & very old colored woman giving one dollar. At the Sunday night prayer meeting Mr. Crosby spoke again, but without asking for money. Again there was a strange and blessed tide of feeling over the meeting. It did one good to know that the hearts of the people were so much with us – as one and another got up and expressed their sympathy with this work and their purpose to stand by the workers. After the meeting several entire strangers – rough men – came to Mr. Crosby to add their subscriptions, and the amount was still further increased solely by spontaneous offerings till the result was the people of Victoria pledged themselves to support the Mission themselves for one or, if necessary, for two years. Monday morning Mr. Crosby went again, thus fortified, to the Dist. meeting and succeeded in getting the recommendation of a young man for Naas, which we think cannot but be sanctioned by the Committee.

This is really a very promising place for a Mission – albeit there is fierce opposition to be encountered from the English Church Mission some fifteen miles from the place selected for ours. This Mission is on the same plan as that near to us but the village numbers only about a hundred – all the Indians are invited to leave their own homes and come to this new village to live. This the Indians decline to do. The Missionary is also a trader and cannot command their confidence, and they urge that a Missionary be settled with them. Some of the things done, by the hands of these two missions, and by the Indians under their care with their sanction you would scarce be able to believe. Their bitterness towards us is most extreme. Mr. Crosby has visited Naas since we returned and is more than ever encouraged. Yesterday he left again for Wrangle, where he felt he must go as soon as possible, to oversee the work there. He went by the steamer and will likely be back in two or three days from now. Here he has kept up a school & services by having young men from here staying there for the purpose. This has been at his own expense chiefly though some money has also been subscribed on the spot. We are hoping that soon some permanent provision may be made for this place. Mr. Crosby has promised also to make a visit this summer to a place 150 miles south of us. I do not think I told you of this before. A young man of this village – which is called Kit-a-maht – having attended the Indian church in Victoria came home & began services among his own people. He is known as Charley [Amos]. Not long before we went to Victoria he, his wife, and two other young men came all that distance by canoe in a time of the year when it is difficult & dangerous to travel on this coast, to see Mr. Crosby and tell him that their services & school were creating much interest among the people and to beg that he would go to see them and "make their hearts strong." And of course he could not refuse. Thus the calls multiply and while it is a trial to me every time Thomas goes away, yet what can I say? And then I know you are all praying for us. But I must go back – I forgot to tell you about the end of our visit to Victoria. We went to New Westminster for a few days but had to hasten back to get ready for the "Otter" which we found was to sail much sooner than had been expected. Mrs. Russ urged that I remain behind with the children but I scarcely liked to take the responsibility of bringing them up alone. We had strong winds on the way up and all of us but baby were quite sick, but we got on very well, and were heartily glad to get home. We brought a lot of preserved fruit cakes &c., the gifts of friends, and best of all an excellent cow – so now we have lots of milk and make about six pounds of butter a week. Our garden is looking much better this spring than last & I believe in time we shall have quite a pretty place. The children are well. Jessie is learning fast to talk now and baby has two teeth. She is such a fine baby. I am quite proud of her. I have just begun to feed her twice a day. We have got a nice baby's carriage for her which is a great convenience. I wish you could see them both. Gracie will, I believe, soon be as large as Jessie. Jessie is so tiny and yet so bright. I sent you their photographs from Victoria. I will enclose another of Jessie now, but it is not good. I had one taken too, but by a poor artist. It is not worth sending, I think.

I received by this mail a parcel of stockings for which my most affectionate thanks are due you. Tell Papa Thomas' Policy of Insurance is here, if he thinks best we will send it to him. Mr. Crosby's brother-in-law had it but sent it to him some time ago. We are really under great obligation to you all for your kindness in many ways. The Lord keep you. Miss Knott appears to have borne her solitude very well, but was heartily glad to see us back. She took charge of everything most faithfully while we were away, and conducted the Sunday morning service always herself.

At present I have a hired woman to preside in the kitchen. She is clean & very trusty but very slow. We have also a young girl with us whom we found at Nanaimo. She belongs to this part of the country and it was for her good that Mr. Crosby brought her up. Now, I have written a long letter. I like to tell you all I can about our life here but I write much more fully to you than I can to anyone else.

Our sincerest love to both yourself and my father, and Believe me, dear Mother

> Your affectionate daughter
> Emma

Thomas Crosby recalled in his memoir how, when he thought his plans for expansion of his mission into the Nass had been turned down at the District Meeting in Victoria, "I felt almost brokenhearted; I sat down in one of the big seats in the church and had a good cry."[26] Thomas got his way, and the man who volunteered for the Nass, located about nine hours by steamer from Fort Simpson, was Alfred E. Green, a young English schoolteacher from Nanaimo. The consequence of expansion was another conflict with Anglican missionary William Duncan. Irishman Robert Tomlinson had, since 1867, served on behalf of the Anglicans at Kincolith, which was, like Metlakatla, a missionary-created village. The Methodist mission was established upriver, but not that far upriver, at the already existing village of Lack-al-zap, later renamed Greenville in honour of its first missionary.[27]

As for Wrangell, Thomas made an appeal for support to Methodist authorities in Toronto, which was turned down on the grounds that it was in American territory. After his request to the Methodist Episcopal Board in New York to dispatch an American missionary failed, Thomas sent Tsimshian Philip McKay, who was taken by Methodism and had already preached there. Thomas also continued to pursue his efforts to get an American Methodist mission at Wrangell. He wrote to General Howard, who had passed through Fort Simpson in the summer of 1875. The general handed the letter on to Dr. A.L. Lindsay of Portland, Oregon, who persuaded the American Presbyterian Church to send its first two missionaries to Alaska. One of those dispatched in August 1877 was a missionary's widow, Armanda McFarland; the other was Dr. Sheldon Jackson, who would become fundamental to the missionary effort in Alaska. With reference to Thomas, Jackson later stressed that "the Presbyterian Church owes much to him for his unselfish zeal and assistance."[28]

The impetus to expand into Kitimaat came from Charles Amos, who was born there with the name of Wahuksgumalayou in 1853 and was heavily influenced by Rev. William Pollard while visiting Victoria in 1876. Returning home to convert others, he travelled the next spring to Fort Simpson "with two canoes filled with men and women to seek a teacher." Thomas "promised to visit them."[29] Influenced by the Methodist tradition of itinerancy, Thomas felt justified travelling up and down the coast and inland to wherever potential converts could be found.

In order to accustom herself to her husband's constant travel plans, Emma had to make choices about the kinds of relationships she would forge with the girls she took into her home, the people of the community, and the world beyond Fort Simpson. Alone and lonely, her perseverance and unshakable faith in God and the importance of her work took her only so far. Though she may not have been fully conscious of the decisions she made, they led her to rely ever more on the Aboriginal women of the community and the girls in her care.

5

A Comfortable Routine

Back in Fort Simpson from her respite in Victoria, Emma began to appreciate the everyday pleasures of life in the mission field. Supporters of Crosby's mission visited the household, whether to view the new addition to the family, to bring needed supplies, or to see how the missionary's wife was getting along. Emma was valued. Her letters to her mother became more upbeat, as though she had come to take her husband's absences in stride. Any concerns she did express were about the mail she awaited from back home. She made sure her mother knew the value she placed on their correspondence, noting if a letter had not yet arrived and reminding her to keep up their connection. The parcels and packages that arrived for Emma and her children contained items that not only met their practical needs but that also signified to Emma her mother's recognition of her family and her work.

Emma's comfortable routine was made possible by the help of the girls in her home and of the Tsimshian community around her. The Tsimshian were as concerned for her as she was for them. Their attendance at services and school while Thomas was away kept Emma firmly rooted in the community. Kate and Alfred Dudoward, who were largely responsible for bringing the Crosbys to the area and who were instrumental in helping them to initiate their work, were becoming less available to Emma, who now had to rely on other sources of support in her endeavours.

The young Aboriginal girls in her home not only allowed Emma to assume a greater role in the missionary enterprise than would otherwise have been possible but also enabled her to engage socially with the increasing number of newcomers arriving at Fort Simpson. While Emma saw her role as providing the girls with salvation, her charges responded to her needs in ways she never anticipated. The missionary notion of these girls was that they were unhappy, weak, and couldn't possibly care for themselves. Yet, they provided companionship to Emma during Thomas's numerous, and sometimes lengthy, absences; maintained the home; and oversaw the Crosby children, engaging in a mutual exchange of protection that Emma never fully acknowledged either in public or in her private records. In essence, they made her life bearable: her loneliness was eased by their company, and her social life in the community was enhanced because they were there to care for her home and children.

Newlywed couples and young families were among the new arrivals to Tsimshian territory. Aboriginal women married to traders, teachers, and young missionaries provided company for Emma. Their stays were sometimes lengthy. Others passed through, moving on to surrounding areas. All enjoyed the hospitality of the missionary's wife, giving Emma a new sense of purpose. Social events such as dinners, feasts, weddings, and celebrations benefited from fresh faces, enabling Emma to showcase the efforts of the Crosbys in a much more public fashion than had hitherto been possible. Efforts to convert the young girls in her charge always remained Emma's focus, but new friendships contributed to her seeming contentedness in Thomas's absence.

> Fort Simpson, B.C.
> May 30th 1877

My dear Mother,

Our mail came in yesterday and with it a letter from you. We were glad to know that you were well and seemingly enjoying yourselves. When I hear of you all going about so much to visit each other it makes me – well – just think how I should enjoy the same thing if I might. I am very glad for you that Eliza and Susie are so near and I am sure it is a pleasure to them and their children.

Thomas has been busy again at the house, painting the ceilings – that had never been done – white and papering the sitting room and Miss Knott's room. We brought some very pretty light wall papers from Victoria which make the rooms look so bright and cheerful. Our sitting room looks really pretty – I wish you could see it – so does Miss Knott's room. Our cow proves a treasure and we make lots of butter – that is for us – non-professionals. I generally work it myself, to be sure it is fit to put away for I have already some ten or twelve pounds put in brine.

Our garden is looking well too, though we do not expect to get much from it this year. But our flower garden is nicely laid out and promises well for the future, though the climate is not warm enough to raise all kinds of flowers. At present we have quantities of pink daisies – English daisies – which are very pretty.

Jessie is well, and is growing quite fat – now she has so much fresh milk. She can say almost everything now, and is very amusing. Gracie has not been very well for a few days – likely her teeth are troubling her. She is indeed a fine baby and if you had seen such a tiny old-looking, wrinkled little creature she was at first, and then consider that she never had any but her natural food until very lately – now I feed her once a day – you would think I had brought her on pretty well. She is a sweet little pet, and grows every day more interesting. She likes her carriage much and is in it a great deal. I am glad you were pleased with the children's photographs. Jessie's did not quite satisfy us, though it is like her. It may perhaps be longer than usual before I have an opportunity of writing again. The str. is not doing much business this year and may not be up again very soon. Our kindest love to yourself and my father, and believe me, dear Mother,

Your affectionate daughter
Emma

Emma's trip to Victoria made her realize more than ever her obligation – as a missionary wife and mother – to be an exemplar. The wallpaper she brought back distinguished their house from those of the Tsimshian, just as the pinafores her mother sent distinguished her children from theirs.

Fort Simpson, B.C.
June 20th 1877

My dear Mother,

We have had another mail – it brought no letter from you but a parcel came containing three pinafores and a pretty pair of stockings for Gracie. How kind and thoughtful you are – and these things that you send so often are sure to be just the things that are useful to me. I like to see the children neat, so does their father. They are growing finely, both of them, and are a great comfort to us.

The str. came in night before last and left early yesterday morning for the north. Mr. Crosby has gone to Wrangle again to meet a young man [Dr. A.L. Lindsay] who has been sent from Portland, Oregon to explore with a view to beginning a mission there. He is highly spoken of by the Presbyterian minister of Portland – to whose church he belongs, and is introduced by Gen. Howard. He urged that Thomas go there to meet him and it seemed a necessity that they should confer together as all that has hitherto been done of mission work there has been under Mr. Crosby's superintendence. This young man is to return soon to Portland to report or Mr. Crosby would not have gone now –

he was loath to be away. Flags are at half mast in the village and if you walked through it you would hear most piteous wailing. Day before yesterday word came to the village of the loss of six men – probably all drowned. Near three weeks ago a canoe left the village for Queen Charlotte's island. It carried a Mr. Williams of the H.B.C. of Victoria who was up the coast inspecting the Co.'s posts and six Indians, and now one exhausted man is brought back by some Indians living to the north of us to tell a sad, sad tale.[1] They reached Queen Charlotte's Is. safely, remained at the Post there some days, then started to return. The course is a dangerous one, except in calm weather. They were about out of sight of land when a strong wind came up. They changed their course to escape its violence and sailed before it for some time, when a wave struck them and split their canoe from end to end. The bottom came quite out but all managed to get hold of the top of the canoe which was of course floating and they saved a sail & rope, a pole & knife. For some hours they drifted on in this perilous position, singing and praying and encouraging each other as best they could. The white man had just offered prayer when he was swept away and seen no more. After Mr. Williams sank, he prayed again.[2] This was about noon while it was some time during the previous night that the canoe had broken. The six Indians were still left – but before long one said he felt himself growing weaker and asked the others to sing and pray which they did and soon he lost his hold and was gone. Then another fell off – now four were left and they managed from the part of the canoe they had possession of to construct a kind of raft to which they somehow lashed themselves, and still on they went.[3] This was Saturday night or Sunday morning and on Sunday there on that little raft drifting on before wind and waves, these four poor men held a service while one of their number who often has led the service here preached to them. It was this Sunday night I think that one of these men, crazed I suppose with hunger & thirst and excitement madly cut the rope that held the raft together. On the foremost piece was the one man whom we know to have survived. The other three fell behind him and what became of them we do not know.[4] The one man – it was the one who had conducted the service – now sped on his solitary course. On and on he went – helplessly drifting – till about Monday night I think he was driven ashore. Exhausted & starving he could scarce move, however he found a little venison skin and bones. The bones he broke with stones and [ate] the marrow from them – and succeeding in getting some water he felt somewhat revived and when the tide went out dug a few clams from the beach. As soon as he was able he set out in search for some camp or village. After about three days he found a deserted camp or dwelling where a very small canoe had been left, but no food could be found. All he had was what roots & berries he could in his exhausted state gather in the woods, or clams from the beach. The canoe he took and started to find help. The next day, I think, he reached a village some distance north of us – this was Saturday and Monday some of these people brought him home.⁵ Such a shock we have scarce felt since we came to the village. These are about all the particulars we have been able to learn yet. Poor man is in such a weak state we do not like to ask him many questions now.

The gentleman who was with them leaves a wife and family in Victoria. But I am writing a long letter. I must close soon. We have four girls in the house – two came down from Stickeen, that is Wrangle, by the last str. for the purpose of living with us and we could not turn them away and we had two before.

The new people at the Fort prove more agreeable than we expected. The gentleman [Robert Hall] is a son of an English church clergyman in Ontario. His wife is part Indian, and speaks nothing but French. She can neither read nor write but is coming now every day to me to learn, and I think is capable of much improvement. Mr. Morrison and his family also remain in Fort Simpson. We have lately been receiving two copies of the Weekly Globe – perhaps through Papa's subscribing for us as he said he had done and the old one not being discontinued. Perhaps it would be well for Papa to speak of it. I suppose the conferences are not through their work yet.

We expect Mr. Crosby back tomorrow. With much love to yourself and my father, I am, dear Mother,

Your most affectionate
Emma

The caution with which Emma greeted the new family in charge of the HBC post was short-lived. Everyday social life of a kind she had not yet known at Simpson soon ensued. Englishman Robert Hall, newly in charge of Fort Simpson, and his wife were virtually the same ages as Emma. A year earlier, while based at the northern interior post at Fort St. James, Hall had assured his future with the HBC by marrying Rachel Ogden.⁶ Robert Hall's bride was not only the daughter of the chief trader in charge of the New Caledonia region but also the sister-in-law of the post's head. Rachel's father, Peter Ogden, was highly unusual in the fur trade, advancing to the upper ranks despite his mixed race. His mother was a Cree woman, his father the venerable Peter Skene Ogden, a major force in the fur trade across the Pacific Northwest. Rachel Ogden's mother was a Métis, Euphrosine Brabant, born at Fort Edmonton. The use of French as the Ogden household language is not surprising, given that Euphrosine's father was an HBC employee from Quebec and her mother a Métis whose father was also from Quebec.⁷

Fort Simpson, B.C.
July 30th 1877

My dear Mother,

We have been now some time without a mail. There is not much to bring the steamer up just now – but we hope she may be here within a week or two.

We have had on the whole a fine summer, with some, as it seems to us, very warm weather – though I suppose you would think nothing of such weather at home. Our garden is increasingly a source of pleasure to us – to be sure it is not yet very productive but it promises well. It is very prettily laid out with nice graveled walks, and as many trees set out as we thought well to have in this damp climate. We give a good deal of attention to flowers. Pink daisies, such as grow in England, have been the glory of the garden all summer. We have a great many of them and they are very fine. We have had also or have now – narcissus daffodils, wall flowers, violets, nemophila, mignonettes and roses – while quite a number of plants from seed are near flowering now. We set out this spring a number of rose bushes and some other shrubs and several pieces of ivy which grows well in this country. Thomas is all the time making some improvements on the place. The last is a trellis work fence to separate the garden from the wood yard behind. Before that he was busy constructing the necessary accommodations of a barn-yard. The yard is not stocked yet except by the cow which is the sole occupant but we expect chickens & perhaps one of those useful if not genteel domestic animals, a pig. Wild berries are very plentiful this summer. We use a great many with cream & sugar and there are some huckle-berries that I think would be nice potted. I intend to try some though the berries here are mostly of inferior quality. They grow in abundance all around us. We never walk down to the village without stopping to pick a few for Jessie. The children are well. Baby has four teeth and is a fine fat girl and very lively. Jessie seems every day to grow more interesting. She enters into everything with keen enjoyment and nothing escapes her. If wood is being carried in she must have some sticks tied to her back. When the girls carry in the hay she goes along with a little bundle across her shoulder. She sweeps and dusts and helps with the "puddinses" and the butter &c., while she reads & writes & sings and tends her baby as I do Gracie. She is very good-tempered too, and most affectionate. In fine weather the children are out a great deal – generally within our own enclosure – baby in her carriage while Jessie plays about. Baby has four teeth and has never had a restless night yet.

Aug 9th. The Otter came in day before yesterday, bringing two letters from you. We were glad to know that you and my father were well – but you must be lonely! Do not feel anxious, dear Mother, about me, in any way. Really with the one exception of a want of much society, I am very comfortably situated. A young man [Alfred E. Green] has come up to take the work at Naas, this new mission which Mr. Crosby has talked so much about. We are feeling most anxious about this place. There will be many difficulties to be overcome though perhaps not more than there have been here. I trust all the friends of these Missions will prayerfully remember this new undertaking.

Friends in Victoria sent up a great deal of fruit by this steamer – apples, pears, plums, cherries. I have put up a good deal.

Thank you, dear Mother, for being so faithful a correspondent. It is a comfort to be sure at least of a letter from you. I think Thomas has written to Papa. Kind regards to all inquiring friends. With warmest love from us both to my father & yourself,

> Believe me as ever
> Your affectionate daughter
> Emma

Thomas continued to spend much of his time away from Fort Simpson. In line with Methodist tradition and his own inclinations, he needed visible results. A later commentator described the behaviour that he fostered among his Aboriginal parishioners: "One rises while another is speaking, and that often seems a signal for a speaker to stop and give another a chance. Often 'the experience' is begun with a lively verse in singing, in which all join, and sometimes it is closed in the same way. They are sincere and simple-minded in their fellowship."[8] To the extent that men and women at Fort Simpson did not meet – indeed, could not meet – his expectations, he sought out new groups of Aboriginal peoples to convert. And he did this through that perennial Methodist favourite: the revival. "Our work at home is doing well, but I long to see a glorious revival here: it will come! I do not think the work here suffers in the least from our being away."[9] Crosby's absences put greater everyday demands on Emma, and they also left her in charge of Sunday, as he later acknowledged. "In the frequent absences of the Minister, his wife had to take charge of the services."[10]

If Emma carried her third child to a full term, she became pregnant again in late August 1877.

Fort Simpson, B.C.
Sept. 25th 1877

My dear Mother,

Our mail came this morning – the only letter from home was one from Annie – and the last mail brought none at all from home. I think surely you must have written and the letter missed. Annie's was of quite recent date and all seemed well when she wrote. Our mails will soon close now for the season – we may have but one more – perhaps two. We are all well, though Mr. Crosby is suffering slightly from a cold. We have had some very stormy weather lately and Mr. Crosby has been twice to Naas since I wrote you last. He was exposed also to a drenching rain during a whole night and parts of two days in getting some lumber up from the mill about five miles away. This was for the buildings necessary to be put up at Naas – a small house for the missionary and a school-house – and Thomas studies economy in every way – for he has no sources from which to draw for these expenses except the local subscriptions which are not likely to amount to much, and his own means. However he feels confident that all will come out right. Thomas and Mr. Green feel encouraged about this work. There are already signs of good work among the people.

It is likely Thomas will be away a good deal this fall. Our flower garden has done very well this year. The cold weather has found it all in bloom for our summer is short and we do not expect much more from it, but it has been great pleasure to us already.

The children are growing fast. Jessie is a great little prattler, while Gracie is just health & happiness. She begins now to climb up by the chairs, and tries to talk – indeed she can say a few words. I still nurse her at night but feed her during the day. We have now three girls. Our family is always large. It seems as though we could not help it but I pride myself upon being an economical house-keeper. However it takes a good deal to provide for so many. We have been laying in a large quantity of cranberries, of which Thomas is very fond and which grow in great abundance all around us. With what fruit has been sent me and what I have put up myself, we shall be well supplied, I think, this winter.

Our people are coming back now from their summer's fishing, and our house which is comparatively quiet during the summer begins to be thronged again – always some one coming on one errand or another. We are far from being quiet, I assure you.

I hope the next mail may bring letters from you all.

26th This str. brought a large box of clothing – chiefly children's things from the ladies of Moodyville, a village in the lower part of the province [later renamed North Vancouver]. There are many things which will be more useful to the children many of whom are very poorly clad. However this is more from carelessness and ignorance than poverty – and the children are very hard – that is those who are strong enough to survive the exposure of their infancy, but many of the little children die from inherited disease and want of care. Still there has been, lately, I think great improvement in the way they care for their children. They are anxious enough to have them and keep them. If an orphan is left there is always some one ready to adopt it.

I try to keep our children comfortable. They do not need much finery but I mind that they have neat warm well-fitting clothes. I have just made Jessie a dress out of that old purple merino wrapper I made before I left home from your dress, which has done me excellent service. I have stitched it with white and have a dress for Gracie also cut from the same. We have been rather poorly off for fresh meat this summer. There has been very little venison brought in but now we have in the house a whole sheep which was sent from Victoria, a present, two ducks & two fine geese. So we alternate between a feast and comparative famine. We have had word from Naas today. Mr. Green sends encouraging reports. He is a very good young man, I think, and I think, is likely to get on well. He is very fond of the children. He and Jessie are the best of friends. I shall perhaps not have an answer to this letter this fall but you will remember us as always.

Thomas joins me in most affectionate regards to my father and yourself, and

> Believe me, dear Mother,
>   Your loving daughter
>   Emma

Emma balanced her desire to share her life on the north coast with her family with the time constraints that sometimes bore down on her. This time she explicitly requested that her letter be circulated and made it clear that, for this reason, she would write less intimately than she otherwise would have done.

Fort Simpson, B.C.
Oct. 26th 1877

My dear Mother,

We are preparing now for what we expect will be out last mail for this year. I want to write a long letter but I do not know that I shall have time to write more than one long one, so I shall ask you to circulate it – that is if you think the girls will want to read it. There is a great deal to tell you, but I may not write very fully. However, Thomas is writing, and you may see something in the Notices. The weather has been quite cold. The mountains are covered with snow and this morning the ground all about was lightly covered with it, but is bare again now. Thomas has made his long-thought-of visit down the coast to Kit-a-mat. He was away about twelve days. It was a difficult trip – but little rest night or day. Still the weather, on the whole, was not unfavorable and Thomas pushes on, takes every advantage wind and tide afford, and generally makes his journeys with all the haste possible. Their visit was very successful as far as could be judged, though they found the people in the midst of their dancing and feasting. Just fancy – while they were gathered in one house – many of the people – just about to begin service Sunday evening – one of these crazed creatures, the conjurors, whose dire art it is to seize fire and fling it about in whatever house he enters – rushed from the house where he was confined – for they are allowed out only at certain times – towards the meeting house – his tongue protruding, eyes glaring, his body bent over till he walked more like a bear than a man, and uttering most unearthly yells. The children screamed and rushed about to find places to hide – and near every one in the house was in consternation. Mr. Crosby darted to the door prepared to exercise a little muscular Christianity if the man attempted to enter the house, but thinking it, I suppose, prudent not to do so, he passed on.

We hear some wild stories when Mr. Crosby comes home from these trips, you may be sure, but he is always treated with kindness and respect, even by the rudest. Do not imagine however, that any such wild scenes are to be witnessed here – indeed our village is more quiet and peaceable than, I believe, any place containing the same number of white people. There is no liquor to be found. Heathen customs have quite disappeared, and all feel themselves to be under the guardianship and authority in some sense of the Mission. Would you like to know how we prepare for these trips? Well, first a good supply of provisions is necessary, bread, butter, meat, cooked or uncooked, generally some canned meat or fish, plenty of tea, sugar, salt, pepper, a lot of pilot bread (especially for the men) salt fish, dried fish, potatoes, and anything else that can be preserved – pots, pans, knives, forks & dishes, to serve a comfortable meal for one person. These are all packed as neatly in boxes as may be. Often they get fish or wild meat on the way. Then a lot of blankets, a pillow and a comforter that you gave me (a real missionary comforter) are rolled up in a mat for bedding. All kinds of odd things are put into the canoe, and off they start. When they camp the first thing is to gather a lot of wood to make a fire – the larger the better – cook supper, then make the beds – with the canoe sails set up on poles as a protection on the windward side. If the weather is good this is quite comfortable, but when it is raining, you may imagine there are disadvantages.

While Mr. Crosby was away a wonderful revival began among the people. The whole village became in deepest earnest about salvation. Meetings were held every night in the church besides frequent ones in the houses. These still are going on and scarce one in the village remains un-moved. This is such a work as we have not seen before since we came. While every one was ready to come to church and prayer-meeting and a few were really in the enjoyment of religion – many had only the form without the power.

On the morning of day before yesterday our village was visited with the most violent wind storm we have seen here. About half past eight a part of one side of the church roof was blown off. It fell – a part of it – within a few feet of our house. Had the house been struck we cannot say what the consequences might have been. Before many minutes the remainder of this side and then the whole of the other side were rolled off like a sheet of paper. The excitement in the village was intense. The men rushed up, and though for some hours we were in fear that the whole building should fall yet the young men insisted upon mounting upon the rafters to brace them and fix ropes – nor did they hesitate to do anything though at the peril of their lives, I believe with a conscientious & loving purpose of thus serving God. We were in momentary fear that some lives would be lost but happily about noon the wind abated, having done no further injury than to remove the roof and some slight breaks in the ceiling &c. Heavy rain followed however, and, of course, streamed into the church to the ruin of stain and varnish and the endangering of the floor and walls. The building was, of course, much shaken, and is now in a very precarious position. The building must be repaired immediately or be a total or almost total loss. The people were unanimous about this and on the afternoon of the day of the injury a meeting was held in the school house – a most enthusiastic one – and a subscription started which the next day reached to over <u>five hundred dollars</u>. I do not believe the same number of people in the same circumstances could be found anywhere to act more promptly & liberally. Mr. Crosby thinks the required repairs will cost near a thousand dollars – though it is impossible now to estimate it very correctly, and feels confident that the money needed will be forthcoming from some quarter. He has secured a skillful carpenter living a few miles from here to take charge of the work, that it may be done properly. The burden will fall mostly upon Mr. Crosby, though – and the worry and anxiety to him is the part I feel most about. We shall have to be very economical to be sure this year, for besides this, the work at Naas will be quite an outlay – but I have no doubt we shall have all we need. We have a large family to provide for but the girls we have now are very careful in the use of things – and I need to spend almost nothing on clothes for myself, while the children's things cost but little. Mr. & Mrs. Hall of the Fort are very friendly. He gave a large subscription towards the church repairs. They have no children and make a great fuss over ours. Mrs. H. has just made a beautiful pair of little moccasins for each of them.

Jessie is growing very fast, and more amusing every day. She is very fond of getting a shawl round her and a black silk handkerchief tied round her face and then she is such a pale demure looking little lady with her big brown eyes. She will look very much like you, Mamma, I think. Gracie is fat and rosy, with mischievous blue eyes and such a curly head. She is a Crosby. She has been weaned and with very little trouble.

Nov 5th Our mail came in last week. I was glad to get your letter, and also my father's. We are much obliged to Papa for his trouble in attending to money matters for us. Where the missing receipt for the Insurance premium is Thomas cannot say exactly but that year he asked Mr. Brown – the stationer – to attend to it. He had it paid through the Mission rooms – so if the receipt is not lost it must be either with Mr. Brown or at the Missions rooms. I hope it may turn up all right. Thank you very much dear Mother for the parcel you sent. That flannel will be just the thing for my little girls. I use a good deal of flannel for them. The pinafore is very pretty – and the stockings will keep a cunning little pair of feet nice and warm.

Indeed I had so many things sent me by this mail. I really feel very deeply these kindnesses from my friends. Some mink skins I sent to Annie to be made up came back in first class style as a present from Harry Hough, with other things from Annie & Susie and a lot of fruit from Victoria and Nanaimo.

The work on the church has got on so well that about half the roof is shingled – but this is a great strain on Thomas – up between five and six every morning – and just driving the whole day. Every evening after the meeting a room-ful of people to be attended to, besides writing &c., then often called up in the night to go to see sick persons. And among an ignorant, inexperienced people like these there are, of course, numberless little trying worrying little matters arising that require almost endless patience & wisdom. A happy Christmas to you all. We shall be with you in heart and you with us, I know.

Dear Mother & father we send you our sincerest love,
    Your affectionate daughter
    Emma

In line with the obligation felt by women of the time, and certainly felt by missionary wives, to downplay their activism, Emma was modest about her own role in the revival that began at Fort Simpson during her husband's absence. The long-time secretary of the Toronto conference of the Methodist Church, which still had charge of British Columbia, did not share her reticence. In his memoir, which was published a decade and a half later, he lauded her role.

> On one occasion a remarkable revival broke out apparently without any human agency. Mr. Crosby had gone to visit outlying villages on a tour that would last several weeks. After his departure the Holy Spirit began to work mightily among the people. In the middle of the night several Indians went to the mission house, awoke the inmates, and asked Mrs. Crosby to give them the key to the church. Thinking it best to manifest no surprise, she gave them the key and they went away. Mrs. Crosby then lit a lantern and asked the lady who taught the school [Caroline Knott] to accompany her to the church that they might see what the Indians were doing. Softly opening the door, they saw by the light of the lantern some scores of Indians kneeling on the floor in the dark, and with sighs and tears pleading with God for salvation. For many days and nights in succession did these faithful women carry on the services, and by the time Mr. Crosby returned it seemed as though the whole village had been profoundly moved.[11]

Emma did not share in her letters aspects of her life at Fort Simpson that might not meet with ready understanding in faraway Ontario, and it may be for this reason that she did not explain her full role in the revival.

In her letters, Emma emphasized her support for practices that were in line with gender expectations. As the girls taken in by the Crosbys reached the age of marriage, Emma ensured that, so far as possible, the transition conformed to Christian practices. Five days after Emma tacked on the postscript to her letter to her mother, eighteen-year-old Agnes Hubbs wed twenty-one-year-old Amos Russ.[12]

Both Emma and Thomas were intimately involved with the wedding. According to an elderly Agnes, reported in the third person: "Mr. [William] Duncan and Mr. Crosby approved of the match ... They knew that they would be useful in a lot of ways to the church and things." Thomas performed the ceremony, but it was Emma who created an event that Agnes Hubbs, who was one of the girls living in her home, remembered all her life. Thomas likely gave the couple the Bible that Agnes treasured throughout her lifetime,[13] but "Mrs. Crosby provided the wedding breakfast and invited all the Indian chiefs of the district to attend," a touch deemed so significant that it even made it into the obituary of Agnes's husband.[14] By so doing, Emma ensured that the entire community witnessed this new, and in her view eminently superior, means of doing things. She may have been unaware that the presence of the chiefs to bear witness was consistent with Tsimshian tradition regarding the marking of important events. Emma and Thomas both took pride in how, as Thomas penned in his memoir, girls "have married Christian Indians, have helped to build up Christian homes, to civilize the people generally and to aid in developing their own neighbourhood."[15]

Such marriages had, just as did the Crosbys' marriage, a strategic aspect. Agnes Hubbs brought desirable genes, as well as status, to the union. Her daughter, who translated for her when she was being interviewed at age 103 in Haida, explained how Agnes's "father was an American" who "married the chief's daughter" while running a trading post at Masset prior to the HBC establishing its store there under Martin Offutt. Agnes's father wanted to follow the Cariboo gold rush of the early 1860s, but "her grandfather, who was the chief in Massett, and the grandmother wouldn't let the mother go unless they left the baby."[16] Charles Hubbs gave his daughter Agnes over to her grandparents to be raised as a person of high status, along with "a lot of slaves." She was then married off at a very young age to a chief who died before they had any children. Agnes's daughter described what happened next.

> They tried to marry her off to another chief, but she put her foot down then, and went with the family of the Hudson's Bay factor there. [Martin] Offutt was the name, and he had two daughters of mother's age. So when they moved to Fort Simpson she went with them to Fort Simpson. And then she entered Thomas Crosby's Girls' Home and that's where she learned to do things ... They taught her to do things in the house, you know, sweeping, cooking, and things like that.[17]

The man deemed suitable to become Agnes Hubbs's husband was even more special in the Methodist order of things, being the Haida namesake of Methodist minister Amos Russ. According to Thomas, the groom was "a prince of royal blood, the favourite grandson of the most powerful Chief of his race."[18] Born with the name of Gedanst at Skidegate in the centre of the Queen Charlotte Islands, he travelled to Victoria when young with fellow villagers, as was the Haida seasonal practice. In old age his wife Agnes recalled events: "Somebody got a hold of him. He got going to Sunday school, day school and things down there. Someone took an interest in him. And that's how he learned to read and write, and learned other things."[19] His obituary explained how "in baptism he was given the name of a pioneer Methodist preacher, Rev. Amos E. Russ."[20] The story passed down within the Methodist Church is that Russ returned home to face his grandfather's wrath at his having embraced Christianity. He took refuge among the Tsimshian at Fort Simpson, which is how he encountered Agnes Hubbs in Emma's household.

Such carefully crafted marriages were fast becoming a regular feature of Emma's life at Fort Simpson. Eight days later, on November 18, 1877, Elizabeth Offutt, whose father had, about eighteen months earlier, put her in Emma's care, was also married off. Her new husband had a similar background to her own. Paul Brentzen's father was a Norwegian who had long worked as a bricklayer for the HBC at Fort Simpson, and his mother was a Haida. A man who arrived at the post in 1868 was awed by "a splendid garden which that prince of gardeners, Hans Brentzen, kept in beautiful order and grew every kind of vegetable to perfection."[21] A newcomer of the early 1890s evoked an "old Indian woman" with "a lovely garden ... married to a Norwegian whom she always referred to as 'my Hans, my nice pink man.'"[22]

Such marriages strengthened an intermediate, or hybrid, way of life that swirled around the Crosbys at Fort Simpson. In the 1891 manuscript census "(Hf.Bd. [Half Breed])" was written after young Brentzen, replacing "(Ind),", which was crossed out.[23] Part of the reason for the change may have been his respectability: he worked at the HBC post as a clerk. Moreover, as to appearance, according to a contemporary, "Paul looked every inch a 'white man,' with fair skin and brown hair and moustache."[24] Skin tones mattered.

Emma's growing familiarity with the nuances of Tsimshian and hybrid life at Fort Simpson stood her in good stead upon the death of Philip McKay, the young Tsimshian man who had taught and preached at Wrangell. When he fell victim to consumption at the end of 1877, Emma felt compelled to write an appreciation, published under her name in the Methodist periodical *Missionary Notices* in February 1878. Its final lines testify to a deep missionary zeal: "While we feel our loss, still it is a precious thought that another of the poor Tsimsheans is safe at home with Jesus. E.C."[25]

Please forward to Lefroy then to Barrie.
All ok at Cobourg.

Fort Simpson
Feb. 14th 1878

My dear Mother,

It is time now that I began another letter to you, for the str. may be here any day. How many letters have passed between us. You are a good, faithful correspondent – indeed, I prize your letters highly, dear Mother.

We have all been well during the winter. Gracie was poorly for a week or two, from her teething, I suppose, but is very well now. She has most of her teeth, now, and has been walking since Christmas. She promises to talk also much earlier than Jessie did. She eats little else than bread and butter and milk. Jessie is growing fast. She goes out a good deal with her father which is a great pleasure to her. She takes a lively interest in all that goes on, and likes much to sweep & dust, wash and iron herself, with her own toy appliances. Christmas day she was made glad with a new doll in a little cradle, furnished with all necessaries, and a box of dolls clothes, besides a picture book and other little things. Gracie got a rattle and presents of money from her father and Miss Knott. Jessie gave some picture cards and pictures away to the members of the family. Miss Knott gave me a picture frame in which she placed that photo I have of you and my father together. It stands upon the sitting room mantel shelf.

We had Mr. Morrison, also Alfred & Kate [Dudoward] our interpreter for dinner with us. We got a quarter of beef a few days before Christmas, from a place about forty miles away – so we fared very well, with a plum pudding also. We have done very well this winter for meat. It is more scarce just now than it has been, but we have some canned in the house. The Indians celebrated Christmas about as usual – the carols were good. We had a tree for the children, and all seemed to pass pleasantly. The winter has been a remarkably mild one. Thomas has been gardening today. I hope no severe weather will come now, or I fear our flowers will suffer. The daisies have been in bloom all winter, and everything is starting now. I must not forget to tell you too that we have had celery in the garden all winter, which we have found a very good thing. Thomas has made one visit to Naas, where the work seems to be going on well, since I wrote you. The Missionary there [Alfred E. Green] seems to be an excellent young man, well adapted to his position. Last Sunday Thomas spent at a place some forty miles away where there are a number of Indians now staying. These people had sent an urgent request that he would visit and help them. Another village about fifteen miles away, in Alaska, he visited two weeks ago. The people there desire a school and Thomas means, if possible, to send them a native teacher.

Feb 22nd A young man [George Edgar] and his wife left two days ago for the Kit-a-mat village where Thomas visited last fall. Thus you see there is need for native or other agents at many places about us. This young man is to carry on a school and the services – and of course Mr. Crosby will visit there when he can. For the support of these agents Thomas is personally responsible, and although he never allows them to expect more than is just a comfortable living according to their own ways still it counts up. The Naas work has been a good deal of expense in this way. Do not think I regret this. The wants of the people are so urgent – it would, I am sure, be criminal delay to refuse to supply them until the expense might be provided for. Many opportunities would thus be lost and whatever we have, we believe, cannot be better spent than in this way. Still I hope these out-posts may receive some support from the Society. Our own expenses are, of course, likely to be more now than they have been. The stock of household articles we began with are beginning to show some wear and tear. Even my clothes are growing less plentiful though they hold out wonderfully. But we feel no anxiety on this score.

I think my last letter was written soon after the accident to our church. The people worked with a will and in about three weeks the church was ready for use again. The subscriptions given here were also sufficient to cover the outlay. We are still annoyed a good deal by our neighbours at the other Mission [of Metlakatla] – but I do not care to talk about this particularly. Our own people appear to be steadily improving and the work is extending to other tribes, for which we ought to be thankful.

March 4th – We were rejoiced to receive our mail two days ago. We had expected it much sooner. I am glad to hear you had so pleasant a Christmas – look out for us to join you some time. But really I often think I should be almost afraid to take Jessie home. She is such an impressible little thing I fear the excitement would be too much for her. Her book pleased her very much. I am sure she thinks Grandmamma a wonderful person. She wants very much to thank you for all you have done for her. The parcel containing the dress and three pairs stockings came safely. I see you have not given up knitting yet. Many thanks for these things which will all be most useful. We received a lot of fresh meat, fresh vegetables, and apples from Victoria sent by friends.

The Indians are about starting for their oolachan fishery and we shall likely soon have some of those most delicious little fish.

As to the Insurance policy, Thomas will be glad to have it attended to. If any further written application to the office is necessary or any writing to em-power Papa to do the business let me know and Thomas will send it. I fear I shall not be able to write to all the girls – not very fully at all events – so, if it is not too much trouble, please send this round. Our love to you all. O how I should like to see all those children – the cousins of whom Jessie is never tired of hearing. I received letters from Annie & Susie by this mail. I hope Eliza is well. I received a letter from her by a mail we received just before Christmas brought by an American str.

> With warmest love from us all to yourself and my father,
> Believe me, dear Mother,
> Yours as ever,
> Emma

In spite of the importance of intermediaries to the mission, Emma tended to overlook their role in the ministry. She failed to mention that, on Thomas's trip to the Nass, he was accompanied by newlyweds Amos and Agnes Russ, who translated for him on their "honeymoon trip."[26]

The couple Emma mentioned but did not name in her letter, and whom Thomas dispatched to Kitimaat in February 1878 in order to give assistance to determined local Charles Amos, was twenty-three-old George Edgar and his wife Marie, together with their two young children. William Henry Pierce had been responsible for introducing Methodism to his friend George Edgar seven years earlier. Edgar, like Pierce, was the son of a Scots fur trader and Tsimshian mother. Pierce apparently rushed to Edgar's house in Victoria's James Bay as soon as he realized the potential in the Methodist message, and the pair attended services together for "many months" before Pierce accepted the invitation to go north to interpret for Rev. Pollard on his exploratory visit to Fort Simpson in February 1874.[27] A missionary daughter who met the Edgars some years later at Kitimaat recalled him as "a self-taught man" who "spoke broken English and was remarkably eloquent in Chinook" and who "was a strong, sincere, humble and effective Christian." His wife, "Marie Edgar, a French half-breed, was a delightful person – intelligent, warm-hearted, generous and full of wisdom."[28] Her father was from Quebec, likely part Iroquois, her mother a Tsimshian woman. Unlike newcomer missionaries, the Edgars were not paid except for clothing, but expected somehow to earn a living for themselves at Kitimaat.

Fort Simpson
April 30th 1878

My dear Mother,

We were very glad indeed to receive your kind letters by this last mail. Really you are all so kind, I feel that I do not deserve one tithe of the sympathy I get. Compared to the lives of many engaged in similar work our path is easy and pleasant.

There is a great deal I should like to say to you, but I fear I can only write a short letter. The steamer is just in the harbor on her return trip and how long she may stay I do not know. Thomas has written to Papa, so I need not touch upon business. Many thanks for the five dollars. I value it the more coming from you. Please give our kindest love to Mrs. Cooney and thanks for her timely and generous contribution. It is always a comfort to us to know we have the sympathy of good people. I think I told you that the contributions towards church repairs raised here is sufficient to cover the outlay – so there is no debt and the Committee are asked for nothing for that purpose. However there is still painting to be done, and a new school house is much needed. I do not think we shall be likely to get into debt. Thomas has the faculty of making a little go a long way, and, of course, in many particulars our expenses are light.

I have been pretty busy lately. Mr. Russ from Victoria has been with us near four weeks. He and Mr. Crosby went to Naas together and brought Mr. Green back with them so we have had in all eleven in family.[29] We have enjoyed Mr. Russ' visit very much. He is about returning with his family to Ontario and expects to be at the Toronto conference so you will likely see him there.[30] He will be able to give you much information about our position and work. Should you meet his wife I am sure you would be pleased with her. She is a sweet and most excellent woman. The children are both suffering from colds and Gracie seems to feel hers a good deal. I think her teething tried her a good deal, though she was sick but little at the time. However when the weather becomes settled and they can be out more, I think it will be better for them. Jessie is a very active child, sewing, washing, sweeping, writing &c. She must always be busy. Gracie is serene and affectionate, and when well very good tempered. I should like so much to have their photographs again. Gracie especially has changed so much lately. She has such a wealth of little bright curls.

Dear Mother, I am sorry to know that you are not very well often – you must find it trying to be alone at such times. I do hope you and Papa will do all you can to make yourselves comfortable. With kindest love to you both.

> Believe me, dear Mother,
> Your most affectionate,
> Emma

The obligation Emma felt to write to her mother regularly was heightened by the fact that her husband's letters were few and far between. She continued to write, even as the final weeks of her third pregnancy weighed her down. With the passage of time her letters became less evocative, almost as though they had become an obligation as opposed to a means for vicarious intimacy.

> Fort Simpson
> May 16th 1878

My dear Mother,

I have only a few minutes in which to write but I do not want the mail that we are about closing to go without a letter to you. The str. returned sooner than usual this time – that is why there was no letter from you I suppose, but Thomas always thinks I must write you by every str. anyway.

We have been all pretty well – though the children have slight colds from changeable weather I think. Jessie has just been dosing her doll with sand in a toy spoon – she says her baby is sick. Gracie is out in the garden with one of the girls. They are full of play.

I suppose you will be preparing for the Conference by the time this reaches you. You will enjoy it I am sure but I hope you will arrange to have no extra work to do on account of it. Miss Knott intends to go to Victoria for a visit by the next trip of the str. Thomas will stay home, I think till her visit is over, then he contemplates some long journeys.

I have been pretty busy lately sewing – getting ready for summer. I have been well almost without exception, though I cannot stand much fatigue. Papa said in his letter to Thomas that he had attended to the renewal of the Globe subscription, but we have received none by the last two mails – that is, the last date would be some time in January. They came regularly before. I do not know what can be wrong. I will try to write more by next mail.

Our best love to both yourself and my father,
    Dear Mother, I am,
        Your loving daughter.

Emma's third daughter, named Ida Mary and known as Polly, was born on May 21, 1878. Two weeks later Emma shared the news with her mother.

Fort Simpson
June 3rd 1878

My dear Mother,

Your last kind letter I had the pleasure of reading early this morning, and I want to answer it tonight, though it is getting rather late. We have all been well since my last – and have added to our number a third little daughter. She was born the 21st of May, and is the largest, finest baby I have had to welcome. I say the largest, but perhaps you will think that is no great size when I tell you that her weight was six and a quarter pounds including her clothing, but she gives every indication of being a strong, healthy child. She sleeps nearly all day, and never wakes during the night. She has large dark eyes, and I think will look like Jessie, but, of course, it is hard to tell yet. The Indians were quite crest-fallen when they found it was another girl. They were hoping for a boy and I think almost feel a grudge towards baby, but I expect her to grow to be a girl to be proud of. Jessie and Gracie are delighted with her and never tire of kissing and talking about her. I have got on remarkably well. To be sure I was sick longer at the time than before and felt more exhausted but I have recovered more quickly than on the other occasions. I was up the seventh day and on the eleventh took a walk out. I feel now almost as well as ever. We have really great cause for thankfulness. The same woman attended me that I had before. She is here still, while Thomas and Miss Knott between them looked well after the children and the house.

The str. passed up last night and on her return – in a few days – Miss Knott means to sail for Victoria. She will likely be gone about two months. Mr. Crosby too is planning a trip. He did intend to remain at home while Miss Knott was away but he has several long trips to make and I fear that would bring him into the unsettled weather in the fall, and I think he will leave within about a week for Kit-a-mat and another place down the coast – Bella-bella. He will likely be away three weeks. I think Mr. Green will likely stay here while Thomas is away. The nurse would stay with me, I dare say, if I liked but I don't think I shall ask her. We have so many in the house – with four girls. The care of the children at night is the only difficulty I anticipate and I dare say I shall get on well enough. Auntie is quite mistaken in thinking that I meant by anything I wrote her that I was likely to be home soon. I do not remember what I said to her, but certainly I had no intention of giving her that idea. It is not probable that I shall be home without Mr. Crosby – the journey would be almost impossible, aside from other reasons – and I am sure he feels at present that he is more needed here than in Canada. Still, of course, we hope that some time Providence may open the way for a visit that would be so great a pleasure to us. It will be in good time we doubt not. I suppose by this time you are pre-paring for the Conference in Toronto. I hope Eliza may find a comfortable home. Is her health good now? We are glad to know that my father keeps so well. You should make things as easy and comfortable for yourself as you can, especially as you are not strong. Thomas joins me in kindest love to you both.

Dear Mother, I am,
    Your loving daughter
    Emma

Thomas's trip to Bella Bella was, like so many of the others, more complex than Emma revealed in her letter. In 1877 a Bella Bella man, Jim Starr, returned from Burrard Inlet, where he had been working in a sawmill, with the "good news" of his belief in Methodism. After building a church and teaching his fellow Bella Bella all he had learned, he travelled to Fort Simpson to seek Thomas's help. This was no mean distance for Thomas to go by canoe, even in one some thirty feet in length and manned by half a dozen of his converts. Bella Bella was over 200 miles away, the round trip to Bella Bella and Kitimaat that Thomas planned about 500 miles.[31]

Fort Simpson
July 10th 1878

My dear Mother,

There is a chance tomorrow to send off a letter to meet a str. that is to call in about thirty miles from here, and Thomas says I ought to take the opportunity of writing to you. He thinks you will be anxious to know how we are getting on with all our little ones.

I am thankful that it is a favorable report I have still to send. Jessie and Gracie are very well, and enjoying the privilege of running in the garden when the weather permits. Jessie says she wants to go to Canada. She is awaiting with much anxiety the arrival of the "Otter" when she expects to get a little dust pan that Miss Knott was to buy for her. Gracie is a funny little body, and very good natured. But this new baby I expect to surpass them both. She grows so fast – she is by far the finest child we have had physically. I wish you could see her large clear eyes and nicely formed features. She will resemble Jessie, I think. In general she is very good and has never failed yet of a steady night's sleep. I find my hands pretty full with three such little children and find it difficult to give the house as much attention as I should like but I am well, though, of course, I am not very strong.

Thomas returned a few days ago from his trip down the coast. He was away between two and three weeks, and encountered much unfavorable weather – nine days of heavy rains and head winds, six of which days were spent mostly or altogether in canoe, besides two nights of travelling. The furthest point he visited was about 230 miles away. This distance they accomplished on the return in a trifle over three days by travelling all one night and by coming in tow of a str. that was coming up the coast, for about sixty miles. This towing was at great risk – the wind was so high – but it was the only way to reach home Saturday night. It was an American str. not to call here, so that was all the help to be got from her. Thomas considered the visits he made successful, and does not seem to think much of these difficulties – but he is exposed to many dangers from which only a Kind Providence can preserve him. He had a good, though not very numerous crew with him, and his canoe is an excellent one and well rigged. Mr. Green was here for a week after Thomas had gone – then he left to catch a str. some thirty miles away by which he wished to reach Victoria.

I think Thomas will not be away again at least not for more than a few days, before Miss Knott is back. The str. that took Mr. Green away brought a mail with a letter from you. Many thanks for the pretty lace collar that was enclosed. The toys you sent by Jennie Morrow will likely come up with the Otter. We are anxious to hear about the Conference. Baby wants me so I must close. Our kindest love to my father and yourself, dear Mother,

> Yours as ever
> Emma

Emma's letters in the summer of 1878 were very child-oriented and were likely intended to assuage her mother for being so far from her granddaughters. Emma was caught up in motherhood in an almost idyllic fashion – something that, in good part, was made possible by the assistance of the Aboriginal girls and women in her home.

Fort Simpson
Aug. 2nd 1878

My dear Mother,

Your letter of July 12th came to hand last evening – we are always so glad to get your letters – and I cannot express my gratitude for your writing so frequently. I am sure it must often be done under serious difficulties. I sympathize with you in the oppressive heat you have had to endure. It would be most trying to me now I know, for it was always exhausting. Here we are spared that discomfort. The warmest day we have is only pleasant and this summer has so far been unusually cool – with a great deal of rain. When a bright day comes the children hail it with delight. They are so fond of playing in the garden which affords them a fine, large, clean play-ground. We have been off once or twice this summer for a picnic. Jessie and Gracie like this but Thomas has not much time to spare and I find it inconvenient to take baby off in this way. The children are all well – Jessie growing quite tall but very slender. Gracie is stouter, and of a more adventurous spirit by far than Jessie. She climbs on the tables and gets into strange dilemmas sometimes. However, she is cool and cautious and seldom gets hurt. The baby is growing to our entire satisfaction and invariably sleeps well at night but requires a good deal of attention during the day. I take her to church Sunday morning, and leave Gracie home. Miss Knott is not back yet from Victoria. Mr. Crosby was hoping she would be here as he wants to make another long trip up the Skeena River before going to the Dis. meeting in Sept. and there is no one to take the school or look after things. It may be he will not accomplish this.

You do not seem to have enjoyed the Conference time in Toronto as much as you ought to have done. It seems to me too bad that you should have so much to do. I wish you would make some arrangement to relieve yourself. I am glad you saw Mrs. Russ. Mr. Russ did not see things at their best when he was here – the weather was mostly disagreeable, and Gracie was poorly – and as it was not long before baby came, I was not feeling very well, and could not attend to things as I might otherwise have done. Still I don't think it would be at all a doleful picture he would give you.

Our garden is yielding quite a few raspberries this summer. We have all we need to use on the table. I don't know that I shall get any to put away. There is also a very nice blueberry that grows on our hill sides. We use a great many of them. The parcel you sent by Jennie Morrow came up by this str. I got it last night. I wish you could have seen Jessie's delight at the sight of those chairs &c. She has had nothing of that kind before. Gracie has been rolling the balls about. To Jessie Grandmamma is a wonderful woman. She often says she wants to go to Canada to see Grandmamma. Gracie too points to your photo on the mantel piece and talks about Grandmamma. She is a great talker already and knows many parts of the hymns we sing – especially of the Armour-bearer which is the children's favorite. Jessie can go through it entire. She appears to have an excellent memory. The Globe came again now. I suppose that Papa has spoken of it.

I should like very much to see Jennie Morrow – William Pollard, I believe, is doing pretty well in Victoria practicing Law. Thomas joins me in kindest love to yourself and my father.

Yours as ever most affectionately
Emma

Emma's joy at being a mother three times over was tempered by her husband's absences. She repeatedly put the best face on her lonely days and weeks.

Fort Simpson
Sept. 4th 1878

My dear Mother,

It is a good while since I wrote you so I had better avail myself of an opportunity we expect in a day or two by a str. that calls here occasionally. The H.B. Co.'s str. has been gone about five weeks now and may not be here again for some time yet. However this other str. I mention has brought the mail – a letter from Annie is all I received this time. She speaks of expecting you in Cobourg which is all very pleasant, I am sure – by the way why do you not go to one of these camp-meeting watering places in the summer? I should think you would enjoy that much, and there you would escape the intense heat, which, I am sure, you must find very trying in the city. We have had a very cool summer, with a great deal of rain and wind. Thomas returned a few days ago from a 16 days' trip into the interior. He walked 140 miles over a narrow trail or sometimes for miles over boulders or rocks. His feet were terribly blistered and swollen. He travelled about 300 miles by canoe also. His route was up the Naas river which lies to the north of us, then across the country to the Upper Skeena and down that river, whose mouth is about 40 miles south of F.S. I hoped he would be at home a while now, but he will likely be off by this str. for Victoria to attend the Dis. meeting. There are many urgent reasons why he should be present at this meeting still there are difficulties in the way of his going. Miss Knott has been away about three months and is not back yet – waiting for the Co.'s str. Mr. Green is also in Victoria, so there is no one to take the school or look after things here though the "Otter" may be here perhaps in a few days with Miss K. & Mr. Green. Thomas is yet undecided, but I think he will go. Mr. Green has been married, and brings his wife up with him. The children are all well. Baby is a fine girl, she grows so fast. Jessie is lively as ever. She is much interested just now in the Peep of Day which I gave her a few days ago. She knows more or less of the history of every picture, and never tires of hearing of them. Gracie is a great little talker, she can say almost anything now that she hears. I wish you could see her little curly head. I find time for very little besides taking care of the children until evening when I get them all to sleep. However I am not pressed with work. I had a woman staying with me when Thomas was away who is pretty handy, and I had her do a good deal of sewing for me. The Indians have been away from their homes a great deal this summer working and getting salmon, but are beginning now to come back.

A great many new houses have gone up lately. The whole appearance of the village will be changed before long. Some very neat houses are being built. I hope Annie will get on all right. Really your grandchildren are growing quite numerous. Eliza's boys must be almost young men now and indeed Jessie seems to grow so fast – it makes me feel old often to look at her. Our lives are passing.

I hope I shall hear from you by the next mail. Thomas joins me in kindest love to you and my father, and believe me, dear Mother,

As ever your most affectionate daughter,
Emma

The illustrated book *Peep of Day*, which Emma gave her eldest daughter at age three and three-quarters, was subtitled *A Series of the Earliest Religious Instruction the Infant Mind Is Capable of Receiving*. In simple and direct language *Peep of Day* narrated the lessons of the New Testament. From its initial

It was **GOD** Who made your Mother love you so much.

Illustration from *Peep of Day*

FROM DAVELL LEE MORTIMER, *THE PEEP OF DAY* (LONDON: HATCHARD, 1858)

publication in the 1830s, the book by English writer Favell Lee Mortimer enjoyed widespread popularity, its racialized, colonizing message being translated into Cree and Ojibwa, among other languages.[32] The copy may have been Emma's own. She may also have used it with the Aboriginal girls in her care and at the school.

Thomas's long trip in August 1878 was, like its predecessors, instigated by others. At the time the church was constructed at Fort Simpson, Thomas had been invited by a visitor from up the Skeena, whom he called "Blind Jack." Only now did he feel he could make the trip.

The changes that Emma reported in the village of Fort Simpson were no small thing. Missionaries encouraged single-family dwellings and, as Aboriginal groups were herded into a labour economy, more of them emerged. The Crosbys' home was intended to model the structures the Tsimshian should be building for themselves. Thomas later recalled:

> A great number of families now began, out of their small savings, to put up little "Christian" homes, of three to four rooms each, and thus got out of the old heathen lodges or community houses, where four or five families had often been herded together. This entailed much work in measuring plots or land, and in preparing plans for houses and streets ... We had no strict model, everyone building according to his own taste or ability.[33]

As well as new homes, the village's physical organization was being reordered. According to Clarence Bolt, "By 1877, there were thirty new houses; by 1881, there were ninety; and, by the end of the 1880s, all the old houses had been torn down along with their totem markers. The houses were laid out in orderly streets, lit by street lamps, and were decorated with picket fences, gardens, and shrubs."[34]

The destruction of totem poles by Aboriginals following Christian doctrines was interpreted by the missionaries as a victory. The Tsimshian were seen to be leaving behind "heathen" connections to the past and embracing Christianity. While this may have been true for some, Neylan cautions that the decision to destroy or remove totem poles must have been a difficult one. Either coercion played a strong role or the Tsimshian were negotiating their own outer transformation. "The burning of masks and shamanic objects may not have invalidated their purpose as physical manifestations of power; quite the contrary, it was a method of further empowering them or returning that power to the world whence it came."[35] Even Arthur Wellington Clah and the Russes expressed remorse about the acts of destruction.

Missionaries' desire for orderly progress led to the establishment of village councils that had the power to pass and to enforce laws. The watchmen were one of the means by which Thomas attempted to reorder Fort Simpson in his image. As well as outlawing gambling, "we also decided to allow no Sabbath-breaking, no dog-eating, no whisky-drinking, no quarreling, no fighting and no heathen marriages." Not only was the population under the surveillance of watchmen but punishments were meted out. "These laws were all put down in a big book, and fines or forfeits placed at the foot of each of them ... The fines or forfeits, as they accumulated, were spent in making roads and bridges through the village."[36] Despite Thomas's effort to refashion village life, physical or otherwise,

Tsimshian practices of communal living, property rights, and spirituality continued behind the scenes.

Fort Simpson
Sept. 30th 1878

My dear Mother,

Our opportunities of sending away letters will not likely be many more this fall, so I must not let this pass. I think I wrote you about four weeks ago before Thomas went to Victoria. He was away a week and ten days which gave him six days in Victoria. The rest of the staff came up with him. Miss Knott and Mr. & Mrs. [Alfred] Green, also a young man [Malcolm Matheson] who is at present to remain with Mr. Green, with a view to his commencing another mission on the Upper Skeena river where Mr. Crosby lately visited. This young man appears to have considerable ability and good address. He is very genial and good company. Mrs. Green is young and without much experience of the world but I hope she may do well and be happy. You may be sure I was glad to see them all after being alone so long. We had quite a houseful, and I thoroughly enjoyed seeing so many faces at the table – so different from the lonely days when I sat with Jessie one side and Gracie the other and no one else. They all stayed here a few days then Mr. Green and Mr. Matheson, the newcomer, started for Naas, leaving Mrs. Green behind until they shall have things somewhat arranged.

Another helper has also been raised up in the person of a man who was engaged at one of the salmon canneries this past summer. He had formerly been a Methodist but had gone astray, according to his own story, until the efforts he saw the Indians making to be Christians recalled him, and now he expresses himself as desiring only to be employed to help or teach them as he may be able. He seems to be a capable man, a good singer, a knack for doctoring, and knowing how to work at various trades. Of course we know very little of him, and cannot tell very well what to expect of him, but he seems willing to undertake humble work. He left a few days ago for Kit-a-mat, to help build the little church that is to be put up there. He is not regularly employed but works in a voluntary way. It sometimes seems wonderful to see how the work is extending on all sides of us – certainly we have reason to be thankful and encouraged.

Our children are well and a great comfort to us. We have not yet decided upon a name for baby but have talked of Gertrude. We shall likely have her baptized soon.

The weather is quite cold and I am feeling that the fall sewing must soon be done. We got a fine lot of pears from Victoria but I have not had time to put many away. I have only two young girls now, who both go to school, and our little people need a great deal of attention. I received a letter from you written at Eliza's a week ago when Thomas came up. You may expect to hear from me once after this, this fall. I trust you may have a pleasant winter. Thomas joins me in love to my dear father and yourself.

Yours affectionately, dear Mother,
Emma

The woman whom twenty-six-year-old Methodist missionary Alfred Green married was Elizabeth Gilbert, a twenty-one-year-old Englishwoman who stayed with Emma until her husband had a house built for her in the Nass.[37] His sister Mary Ann Green would join him to teach school there under his tutelage. Malcolm Matheson, who came north with the newlyweds, was from Dundas, Ontario. While in the Cassiar gold diggings he was apparently converted by Aboriginal companions from Fort Simpson who persuaded him to open a school at the forks of the Skeena River, site of the trading centre of Hazelton. Matheson would abandon the school the next spring in favour of becoming a bookkeeper for a Hazelton trader.

Emma enjoyed the company that came and went in their home and in the village. The girls in the home were also constant companions, and Emma sensed their closeness to her and her family. The mutual exchange of protection Emma and the girls afforded each other was escalating.

6

Adversity

The comfortable routine into which Emma had settled at Fort Simpson was disrupted at the end of the 1870s by a series of adversities. The first had to do with the escalation in the mutual exchange of protection between Emma and the Aboriginal girls in her home, the second with the departure of her long-time support Caroline Knott, the third with family loss.

It was not only Emma who took notice of the Aboriginal girls' influence on Jessie, Grace, and baby Polly. "Her own little children learned to talk Indian before they could speak English," ran a contemporary Methodist account Thomas included in his memoir.[1] Jessie and Grace had Aboriginal names bestowed upon them, and both little girls wore their scarves around their heads and had moccasins given to them, just like those worn by the Tsimshian women and girls they saw around them. Emma's observance of her daughters' behaviour revealed the nature and extent to which the Aboriginal girls' presence had come to bear upon her own children. She saw the way her children helped the girls with chores, took on similar dress, and even spoke their language. Uneasy with the girls' increasing influence on her young children, Emma's religiosity reached its limits. She took the girls into her home but she never came to accept that they belonged there. Her own children's best interests, as she perceived them, were paramount, so that when her good intentions (i.e., to care for the Aboriginal girls) clashed with her concern for her children, her good intentions were what gave way.

Emma's solution lay in building a home within a home. In this way, the girls could be separate from her daughters but still remain under her protection. Emma played up the more pragmatic aspects of her decision: over time the number of girls had grown, which increased her sense of responsibility towards them. Clearly, they were in need of more care than Emma could provide.

For Emma, the development of a separate home was a mission unto itself. It added to her responsibilities as she focused on promoting to family, friends, and Methodist connections back home in Ontario the need for a separate residence. She moved forward in her plan, playing on the notion that her decision to remove the girls from her home was consistent with the good intentions that she had always directed towards them. Whatever the extent she bought into this thinking, it was useful for convincing her counterparts in Ontario to provide funds. Fortunately for Emma, her requests coincided with the formation of the Woman's Missionary Society within the Methodist Church of Canada.

Historian Rosemary Gagan describes the evolution of women's associations within the Methodist Church of Canada. The idea for a separate women's missionary society was first mooted in 1878.[2] Great care was taken that the proposed society not be seen as competing with the existing broader missionary society. This was done by restricting its goal to "our degraded, down-trodden, uncared-for heathen women and children, lifting them out of the mire of heathen serfdom that they may recognize the truth that, 'even they,' are one in Christ Jesus."[3] Emma's requests for assistance came at an opportune time, as it was just then that women's role in Methodism was beginning to be recognized.

Victoria
April 8th 1879

My dear Mother,

You will think it a long time I have been silent, but our mail was very late in coming this spring. I wrote a line, I think, in a letter of Mr. Crosby's a month ago, thinking we had a chance to send a mail, but after sending our letters fifteen miles to catch the str., they were too late and were returned to us. We had not then received any mail, and received none until about two weeks ago. We were glad to hear from you all, you may be assured. How thankful we should be that we are all kept in so much comfort and peace. But I really think it would be a good thing if you could make your home where your health might be better suited.

April 14th This afternoon I received my father's letter with the fifteen dollars enclosed. We were much pleased with both. The parcels you have sent have, I think, all come to hand. The hoods you sent last fall served the children splendidly all winter. I acknowledged them before I am sure, also the grey flannel &c. in another parcel. This spring I received a parcel of stockings for the children, a most useful gift, which deserves my best thanks. You will see my letter is dated from Victoria. We have been here ten days. We did not intend coming down quite so early, but we had a good opportunity to come down with very few passengers on the str., and we did not know either but that this would be the last chance before the Dis. meeting. We had a very good trip down – fine weather, and made good time, and having the boat almost to ourselves was a great advantage.

Jessie and Gracie enjoyed it splendidly, and behaved beautifully. My little Polly is teething and has not been herself for a month or more – still she did not do badly. Since we have been here she was very poorly for a few days, but has cut two teeth and seems much better. As to the two eldest they are enjoying themselves just wonderfully, and are very well. They are to have their photographs taken tomorrow so I hope soon to send them to you. They are very good children. Their father is a great help in taking care of them or I should find it difficult sometimes to manage. As to little Polly – as we call baby – she wants no one but her mother. We intended to make our home with Mrs. Wm. Pollard junr., but coming by the first trip of the str. could make no arrangements beforehand, and found she was very poorly, so we have been at the parsonage thus far. We shall likely go to Mrs. Pollard's after two or three days. The Dis. meeting is not for ten days yet and, of course, we must stay in Victoria till that is over. Then we mean, if we have time, to go up the Fraser river to visit some old friends of Mr. Crosby's there. I think Thomas will not feel like staying down long after the D.M. is over.

Do you remember a little lump that showed itself on the back of my neck just before I left home? Well, it gave me no inconvenience and I paid no attention to it until last summer when I found it was increasing in size, and more recently I found some weakness and aching in the place. We thought best to have medical advice, and were advised to have it removed. Last Thursday it was operated upon by two doctors. They gave me chloroform so I was spared the pain of the operation which occupied about thirty-eight minutes. It was a tumour, but not of a malignant nature at all – merely a collection of fatty matter, in bulk perhaps equal to a small hen's egg. I think the operation was skillfully performed, at least the wound has healed very quickly. Today (Monday) the doctor removed the dressing and it is almost well. I felt very poorly for about a day after the operation, but am now about as well as ever. I feel very thankful indeed that I have got over this so well. Mrs. Smith and the girls were very kind in taking care of the children while I was laid up. If I can get up enough courage, I want to have all that remain of my upper set of teeth out and false set in before I go home.

We are having really a very pleasant visit. I have a carriage for baby so that we can take her out. I hope to send you photographs of all the three next time

I write. I trust you may see the originals some time. I am very glad to hear that this female home of ours is so favorably considered. We hope to have it in operation in some shape next summer.

Kindest love to my dear father and also to you dear Mother, from my husband and from

Your affectionate daughter.
Emma

think my letter was the only one that came this time.

May 2

Dear Annie,

I thought of sending you Emma's letter but did not know whether you had got one or not. I felt so relieved on receiving it, am thankful she got over it so well. Mr. [William] Sexsmith a missionary from BC called the other day. He had come direct from the district meeting where he has seen Mr. Crosby and Emma. He was to tell me they were all well. He says Emma has three beautiful children. They were going up the Fraser river to visit some friends. What an undertaking for Emma but hope it will do her good. I have been thinking about you this warm weather wondering if you were cleaning house. I have been packing up a little at a time, am almost through.

Love to all
Mother

The postscript Eliza Douse tacked on to Emma's letter before sharing it with Annie is a rare direct testimony to her ongoing concern over her faraway daughter. The Douses' visitor, William V. Sexsmith, was recruited from Ontario in 1874, served a year on rural Salt Spring Island, and had just completed three years' service in the gold rush town of Barkerville in the Cariboo.[4]

"This female home of ours" that Emma mentioned in her letter was intended to house Aboriginal girls like those she had cared for over the past five years. The addition to the mission house would physically separate the Crosby family from the young girls who had so long been an intimate aspect of their everyday lives. The addition also created additional space in the Crosbys' house for the company that was always arriving. Even though only half of the cost of $700 had yet been raised, the wing was constructed in the summer of 1879.

Fort Simpson

June 3rd 1879

My dear Mother,

It is high time I wrote to you, is it not! I have found it almost impossible to get
any writing done lately. I was glad to get your answer to my last a few days ago.
So you are about to move to Barrie – or, I suppose, you are there before now. I
hope you are comfortable and enjoying yourselves. I am glad you are free from
the burden of housekeeping, for however small a house and family you may
have there are a great many steps to take.

I have just got fairly into my household duties again. We reached home six
days ago, after being away about eight weeks. This was a longer visit than we
intended, but the steamers do not run regularly, and it is difficult to calculate.
Then we had a good deal to do in Victoria. We spent about ten days with Mrs.
Pollard. She has a fine large house. Then after the District meeting was over we
spent about two weeks in a visit up the Fraser River. This was in the country,
and the children enjoyed themselves very much. I was very sorry we had not
longer time to stay. Being inland, too, it was more of a change for them than
Victoria where the winds are almost as bleak and cold as they are at Fort
Simpson. When we returned to Victoria we remained at the Parsonage. I had
four teeth extracted and one filled. I meant to have more than this done but I
was feeling so tired out with so much traveling with the children that I could
not undertake more. We had a good trip home and I feel as though I should
never want to go away again. I think the next time I visit Victoria must be
when I am on that much-thought-of visit home, but we cannot tell.

Jessie and Gracie, I believe, are much improved by the change. They were
very happy wherever we went and made many friends. My little Polly is quite
poorly. I hardly know what is the matter with her. But it is likely the result of
her teething. I will send you their photographs. Poor little Polly strongly objected to the operation. She is so shy of strangers and had been crying – which
gives her that unhappy look. She looks merry enough sometimes and has many
funny little ways.

Mr. Crosby intends leaving for Naas tomorrow – to be gone, I suppose,
about a week. Then he has several long trips in view for the summer, besides
building &c. The "Home" is not completed yet, and the back part of our
house is to be rebuilt, and, if possible, a school house to be put up. We shall
be very glad to receive subscriptions towards the "Home."

The people gave us a very hearty welcome on our return. Miss Knott had a
lonely time while we were away, but she has good courage and is most devoted
to the work. I have two pretty good girls in the house. Baby takes most of my

time – she needs a great deal of care. Thomas joins me in kindest love to both you and my father.

Your affectionate daughter,
Emma

The decision to add a wing on to the existing mission house to make a home for the Aboriginal girls taken under Emma's care expanded her role in the mission beyond that of helpmate, teacher, and mother. She would manage this project until its completion. Young Aboriginal girls could find refuge there, at a comfortable distance from the Crosby children.

Fort Simpson
Aug. 4th 1879

My dear Mother,

I found a letter from you among the mail this morning. We were very glad to know that you and my father were both well and comfortably settled. I think you will be decidedly better than being alone. We were pleased also that you had something more to send towards the "Home." I will send an acknowledgment of the amount collected by Mrs. Jeffry to her. We have five girls under our charge, but two of them we keep mostly in our own house. Mrs. Green has been here for about two months. She has a baby about a week old – a boy – doing well. Mr. Green has been here about two weeks, besides several other visits previously, so with the woman that is waiting on Mrs. Green, we have in all a household of fifteen. Still we manage very well. I think Polly is a good deal better than she was. The others seem very well and we have had pleasant weather lately, so that they have been out constantly. Our garden is very dry and clean and pretty, as nice a place as they could have to play. Jessie talks a great deal about going to Canada. Grace looks like a rose – her face is so bright and rosy. Thomas returned a few days ago from a trip down the coast to Kit-a-mat. He went most of the way down with the str. the last time she was here, taking his canoe in tow, but had four and a half days' hard work coming back. He means to be off in another direction before long. Our garden is not doing much. The season was so late and cold, but we have a great many roses & other flowers, and the promise of abundance of raspberries, they are not ripe yet. Our kindest love to Auntie & all the family. Our most affectionate love to yourself and my father. Shall write again soon as I can.

Yours lovingly,
Emma

Lithograph of church and mission house at Fort Simpson

FROM SHELDON JACKSON, *ALASKA, AND MISSIONS ON THE NORTH PACIFIC COAST* (NEW YORK: DODD, MEAD AND CO., 1880), 309

If Emma carried her fourth child to a full term, she became pregnant again in mid-August 1879. With Thomas burning up the waterways and land routes to ensure Methodist gains, Emma carried out both her own and his tasks while pregnant. This necessitated her keeping several charges close at hand. So while the majority of Aboriginal girls stayed in the newly established home, Emma would often have a few of them live with her family, knowing full well she still needed their protection.

It was at about this time when Sheldon Jackson, who had taken charge of the missionary effort in nearby Alaska on behalf of the Presbyterian Church, made a visit to Fort Simpson. Jackson's account, published a year later, reproduced an engraving given him of the church and mission house alive with Tsimshian parishioners. It also evoked, in heroic detail, Thomas's far-flung exploits.[5]

Fort Simpson
Nov. 5th 1879

My dear Mother,

I was surprised to receive no letter from you by our last mail which came in yesterday, though it was with much pleasure that we both read my father's kind letter. You must try and not give up writing, for, you know, you are my most reliable correspondent. I hope, dear Mother, that the weakness in your arm may be only temporary. And if you cannot walk much, why not have the use of a horse and drive. It would do you good to get out. We are very glad to know that Papa is so well and comfortable. We are much obliged to him for looking after business matters, Mr. Crosby will leave his insurance in his hands to attend to. The "Mail" comes regularly, and the Guardian. As to the Globe it is not of much consequence when we receive the other. I received a parcel from Susie including a pair of stockings from you. They will be just the things for our little Gracie. By previous mail I received a parcel from Auntie, large piece blue flannel, and pair [of] stockings for myself. Were the latter your work also? Dear Mother you do a great deal for our comfort in these things. Please give Auntie my best thanks. I sent her a small box of shells and moss – the latter some Mr. Crosby brought from the Naas – by last mail. I hope she got it. I fear I shall not be able to write her now, indeed it is difficult for me to write at all. We have had a good deal of sickness among the children lately. Jessie has been poorly several times, though not seriously, and she seems very well now. Gracie had another attack of fever a few weeks ago. She was quite ill, but seems to be herself again now. Just as she was getting better little Polly was taken ill. She is very poorly yet – frequently vomiting, and very dull and heavy. I scarcely know what it can be that ails her. It was brought on I think by a cold. I have to nurse her almost constantly, and find it very difficult to attend to other things. There are now nine girls in the "Home." I find it quite impossible to give them the attention they need. I think we shall have to get some elderly Indian woman to superintend them until we can do better. Miss Knott was married here and went down by the last steamer. We are very sorry to lose her. A young man from Victoria [George Robinson] is taking the school at present. Of course he lives with us – until some other provision can be made. I hope there may be a good lady teacher here before long.

A lady in Victoria has sent me two large boxes of preserved & potted fruit this season, so with a little I put up myself we are well supplied. I have some pears also that I want to pickle & can if I can get time.

This is likely to be the last mail for this season, so do not look for letters from us again till spring. My best love to Auntie & Sallie & all the family. Dear Mother it is a comfort to know that you and my father and others are praying for us. Pray you have a happy winter. I trust I shall have a good letter from you by first spring boat.

     Your affectionate daughter,
      Emma

A second setback for Emma occurred in late November. She lost her great female support, Caroline Knott. The Fort Simpson teacher married thirty-seven-year-old Charles Tate from Northumberland. Nine years her junior, he likely met her during her visits down south. Tate, who prepared the way for Thomas at Fort Simpson and took over from him in the Fraser Valley in 1874, was ordained in the Methodist ministry in 1879. According to church practice, ordination gave the right to marry, which Tate did just six weeks later. The gendered character of the fur trade and then the gold rush meant that British Columbia contained three newcomer men for every woman. Choices for persons like Tate, whose wife had to have suitable Methodist credentials, were extremely limited. An older wife was preferable to no wife at all. Their wedding date, October 24, 1879, was three years, almost to the day, after Caroline Knott arrived at Fort Simpson, which was the precise amount of time she had agreed to remain there. Tate returned north for the first time in five years for the wedding, which Thomas performed in the Fort Simpson church. The witnesses were R.H. Hall, who was in charge of the HBC post, and Odille Morison, wife of the former head.[6] Tate returned with his bride to his ministry at Chilliwack.

The wedding put Emma back in the classroom to assist Caroline's replacement, who was not experienced enough to handle the school single-handedly. Thomas explained in his next public letter how "the children have been taught in the school-house by Mrs. Crosby and our teacher, with a staff of assistants." Emma also had the new girls' home to oversee for, as Thomas would write the next spring, "as soon as the building was fit for use, we began to take the girls in, and we have had twelve of them under our care most of the winter."[7]

Emma did all of this amidst deep personal loss. Ida Mary Crosby, known as Polly, died on November 20, 1879, at one and a half years of age. Thomas put the best face on his youngest daughter's death. "We had to part with the youngest member of our family, our little daughter of eighteen months, which tried us much. Yet I trust our hearts have been drawn nearer to the 'sympathising Jesus' and to His blessed work."[8] At the time of Polly's death, Jessie was five, Grace three, and Emma three months pregnant with her fourth child.

The letter Emma or Thomas wrote informing her family of their youngest daughter's death has not survived. Perhaps it was passed around the family and lost from view. Or perhaps it was so personal it was not kept.

Fort Simpson B.C.
March 10th 1880

My dear Mother,

After long waiting we find that the steamer passed up north yesterday but for some reason our mail is not to hand. The str. did not call in here, but usually in this case our mail is put off at some point below and comes on by canoe. The str. will be in on her way down, I suppose, likely tomorrow, but the time she may lie here will be too short to allow of much writing. And yet I feel as though I cannot write until I hear from you and know how it has been with you all during the long time that we have heard nothing. The str. is late in coming and I have felt very anxious for letters. I trust I shall find that all has been well. We have had much comfort during the winter. Our children grow dearer to us and more interesting every day. Of course we miss our little Polly – the memory of her grows more and more tender and precious, but we have so many, many blessings left we cannot but be thankful.

We have had an unusually cold winter such as has not been known for many years. During the early part of the season Jessie and Gracie were both very delicate, they could not bear the slightest exposure, and we felt very anxious about that, but lately they have improved wonderfully, and now that the weather has moderated and they get out every day they seem as well as ever I saw them. We have a very comfortable, cheerful home. The want of associates for the children we begin to feel some, for we cannot allow them to associate with the children of the village, but I supply the lack as well as I can by telling stories, and furnishing employment & amusement for them, and of course being so nearly of the same age they are company for each other – and company for me too. When their father is away, especially, I do not know what I should do without the children. Thomas has made several trips during the winter, and cold and stormy as the weather has been, a special Providence has seemed to give him prosperous winds and rapid transit. A little more than two weeks ago he left for a place about fifty miles away – with a large canoe and twenty people, a stiff breeze and a missionary spirit, and before we were looking for him at all was back to report a most blessed time among those whom he had gone to visit. It is wonderful how the people – the very best among them – rally round Mr. Crosby in these trips, which, especially in winter weather, mean hard work, and possibly great exposure and peril, but they seem to catch the spirit, and always return better Christians for their sacrifice.

We have had twelve girls under our care all winter so our "Home" may be said to be in fair operation. One was married a few weeks ago, but a little girl from another village, a heathen village, has since come to us to make up the number. Quite a family to look after is it not? We are seventeen souls in all, including the young man who has charge of the school.

March 11th – The Steamer came in this afternoon with the mail which had been detained on board by an oversight. I was glad to hear from you all but sorry to know that you were so poorly. You must find it trying, I am sure, but I trust patience and strength are given you day by day. I wish much that I could do something for your comfort, but, you know, dear Mother, we remember you and pray for you. Jessie has a little book mark that she wants to send you. She thinks a great deal of "Grandmamma" and talks so much about seeing you all. She is very fond of working little bits of cardboard. I mark the letters or figures for her and she can follow them very correctly. This was made when she was just five years old.

My father's letter is to hand and I was pleased indeed to read it, and to know that he was so well and happy. Many thanks for the Globe & Mail and other matters attended to. I received also a parcel containing two polka jackets & two comforters, also a small parcel with a pair of stockings, all of which I take to be from your kind thoughtfulness. Thanks again. I received letters from Eliza, Annie, Susie and Auntie, two pretty little valentines which pleased Jessie & Gracie much, and also the World and a splendid number of the "Graphic." I shall be quite unable to reply to these letters by this mail, so I will ask you, if you think it worth while, to send this to the girls, and I will try to write to them all by next mail.

We were much surprised and pleased to find that a lady teacher [Susanna Lawrence] had come up on this str. I am much pleased with her appearance and manner and I trust she may find a happy home with us, and be useful among the people. She expresses regret that she did not see you before she came away, but she was hurried having to prepare on short notice to come out with Rev. E. Robson. I am sorry to hear that Matt continues so poorly. Thomas and the children join me in kindest love to you all. Believe me, dear Mother,

Your very affectionate daughter
Emma

Send on to Annie. All well, Susie

Susanna Lawrence

COURTESY OF HELEN AND LOUISE HAGER

Thomas's trips continued over the winter of 1879-80. Early in the new year he visited the Nass, where he baptized fourteen adults and eight children, and married five couples influenced by the Greens. On the way he was caught in a blinding snowstorm and, for several hours, was in danger of being lost or driven by the floating ice onto sand bars. The next year, 1881, Green would be ordained, which meant that he could thereafter perform these tasks on his own.

The new Fort Simpson teacher, Susanna Lawrence, travelled west with Rev. Ebenezer Robson, who had been in British Columbia since 1859, when he was one of four Methodist ministers sent west from Ontario to what was then a "foreign mission." Rev. Robson moved back to Ontario in 1866 for his wife's health, returning to British Columbia in the spring of 1880 on her recovery. The new teacher who arrived from Ontario with him to replace the newly married Caroline Knott was the product of a very religious Toronto household.

Susanna Lawrence boarded with the Crosbys. In her Emma would find a cherished friend, recalling two decades later "how greatly Miss Lawrence endeared herself to us personally" during the several years that she was "a member of our

own household." Not only did Susanna Lawrence take a "kindly interest in every
family concern," but she also displayed "untiring devotion in times of illness and
affliction." She also took over tasks that had fallen to Emma. "The school was
her particular charge, but every day after school hours, and often in the early
morning would find her going about from house to house, visiting the sick, encouraging the mothers in their efforts at much-needed home improvements."⁹
Susanna Lawrence's presence supported Emma during the birth of her fourth
child, Gertrude Louise Crosby, on May 12, 1880.

> Fort Simpson B.C.
> May 14ᵗʰ 1880

My dear Mother,

I can just scribble a line as I lie in bed to tell you that another sweet little
daughter was born to us two days ago, on the 12ᵗʰ. Not a very large baby but
very strong & well. Thomas had just reached home the afternoon of the 11ᵗʰ
with Jessie, after a most prosperous four weeks visit away. Jessie had had a
delightful time and seems improved in every way. I have done remarkably
well – was sick only about two hours and am feeling quite strong.

  I am very sorry to hear of your being so feeble but I do hope you may get
some relief. We have received Papa's letter. With love to all dear Mother from,

> Your daughter,
> Emma

Emma's next letter, a month later, was written to her father. She underplayed
her growing concern over her mother's deteriorating health.

> Fort Simpson, B.C.
> June 9ᵗʰ 1880

My dear Father,

Your letter of May 12ᵗʰ came to hand this afternoon. We were pained that there
were not more cheering tidings of my mother's health. It is painful to me to
hear of her suffering but the "Lord doeth all things well."

  Thank you dear father for writing us so fully. Mr. Crosby read your letters
with no less interest than I. That you are so well and so happy in your own
mind gives me real gladness. The Lord is good. He blesses us much. About the
N.Y. Chr. Advocate – Mr. Crosby had subscribed for it before we heard of

your doing so, and paid for it – for this year. However, but one copy is sent so, I suppose, this could be put right. We received the book given as premium. We are much obliged to you for thinking of us in this way – the Advocate is well worth reading.

We are all well and our new baby a new joy to us. Jessie has taken great delight in working the little book mark enclosed, and asks you to accept it with her love. It is her own work. I merely marked the letters and gave her some directions. My husband joins me in kindest love to you. Love to Susie and family. I may not have time to write her by this mail.

    Your affectionate daughter
      Emma

Bookmark "For Grandpapa"

Emma became reticent in writing her mother, balancing her concern for her with the need to hold out hope. She used her young daughters to divert her mother from the seriousness of the situation.

                    Fort Simpson, B.C.
                    June 9th 1880

My dear Mother,

I was very sorry, and Thomas no less so, to hear that you were no better. I had hoped that we should hear that you had improved. You find it trying, I am sure, day and night to be in suffering, but, dear Mother, our God in whom you have trusted so many years will not forsake you now. O I do hope and pray that you may be sustained and comforted day by day with His abounding grace. I know you have the most loving care from our dear father and my sisters. Know I wish I could share with them in their service of love – but I must not speak of that. My little Jessie talks so much about you. She is very sorry to know of your not being well, and often tells me how she would take care of you if she were with you. Last Christmas I was struck with this – when I told her how you had not been able to go to Lefroy for Christmas she at once decided that when she is in Canada for Christmas, as she hopes to be some time, she would stay with you and let all the others go off for pleasure. She is a most affectionate little girl, and delights in making others happy. I missed her so much when she was in Victoria with her father. They were gone four weeks but she was so well and so happy all the time she was away that the recital of this rewarded me amply. Little Grace is growing fast and is full of fun. Our baby is strong and well –

the largest of the little flock at her age. She is very good usually. You would hardly believe, dear Mother, how rapidly I recovered after baby's coming. I have always done well, at these times, you know, but never so well before as this past time. I feel deeply grateful to God for His care over me. I am sure no woman is more happily situated in her home than I am.

Dear Mother, we commend you to our gracious Father above. I hope the next mail may bring tidings of your being better. Thomas joins me in tenderest love.

Yours affectionately,
Emma

Emma's realization that her mother was no longer able to comprehend a long letter caused her to write at greater length to her sister Susie in the hope that she would share its contents with their mother. Sadly, most of Emma's letters to her sisters have not survived.

Fort Simpson
July 6th 1880

My dear Mother,

I will write you just a few lines to tell you how we think of and pray for you without ceasing. We are sorry to hear that you are no better, but in this we rest, that the Lord will not forsake you, and while He is present all must be well. O how I should delight to be of some service to you now that you really need help. Dear Mother, be assured you have our tenderest sympathy. I hope we shall have another letter from my father soon.

I have written a long letter to Susie about what we have been doing – when you feel disposed, perhaps she will read it to you. My precious baby is such a comfort. She is so good, night and day, it is a real pleasure to take care of you [her]. Kisses from Jessie and Grace and be assured that my husband unites with me in sincerest love to both my father and yourself, dear Mother,

Yours as ever,
Emma

Emma's mother was her lifeline, a constant companion through their correspondence. Emma sent her continual encouragement and prayed that her health might improve. The frequency of Emma's letters home during the summer of 1880 gives evidence of her concern over her mother's deteriorating condition.

Emma must have agonized over how little she could do from such a distance, except to write and pray.

Fort Simpson, B.C.
July 29th 1880

My dear Mother,

I must write a few lines to you. I do not like to let any chance pass without some word to you. I have been hoping to hear of your being better – this mail brings me no news from home – but we shall likely soon have another. Thomas has just returned from a visit to Bella Bella, about two hundred and thirty miles away, where a native agent [William Henry Pierce] has been working a few months. The prospects of establishing a good Mission there are most encouraging but we hope that a minister may soon be stationed there, for the place is too far away to be connected with this mission.

My little baby is a real treasure – so bright and so good – and it is such a comfort to me to have her. She sleeps always so well all night and a great deal during the day. Jessie and Grace have been coughing lately – the weather has been very changeable – but I hope they will soon be better. I have been very well indeed since baby came. We have had a good many visitors this summer. Mr. & Mrs. [Alfred] Green & baby are here now – also Mr. & Mrs. [Charles] Tate and a man from one of the fisheries – but most of them leave by the steamer tomorrow.

I suppose my father has been away attending the Conferences. I hope we shall soon hear from him again.

Now, dear Mother, you may know that you have a tender place in my thoughts. May the Lord abundantly bless you with all grace. Our united love to yourself and my father.

Your affectionate daughter
Emma

The Methodist enterprise was becoming increasingly complex, with missionaries being moved from place to place rather like pieces in a chess game. Early in 1880 William Henry Pierce had been plucked from the Nass to begin a mission at Bella Bella. Since he was not ordained, Thomas travelled there to conduct baptisms and to marry several couples. Later in the year Charles and Caroline Knott Tate would open a mission at Bella Bella.

Seven Methodist missions with three ordained ministers and six Aboriginal or mixed-race assistants now dotted the north coast. Thomas Crosby was

William Henry Pierce

BC ARCHIVES, B-01288

stationed at Fort Simpson, Rev. Alfred E. Green at Nass, and Rev. Charles M. Tate at Bella Bella. The other missions were Port Essington, Kitimaat, Kit-wan-silk, and Kit-la-tamux, the last two under the charge of Nass. There were 675 church members and 1,020 pupils in seven schools. So much Methodist missionization had been effected that the coast was constituted as a separate district, with Thomas in charge.

Fort Simpson
Oct. 22nd 1880

My dear Mother,

This may be the last mail we shall be able to send away this fall, so I want to write you a few lines.

Dear Mother, I am grieved to hear that you are no better, and I feel how great a satisfaction it would be to me to be able to minister in any way to your comfort. But Providence has ordered it otherwise, and all I can do is to pray for you, and this I do without ceasing. Your letters to me were always so full of trust and faith, that I know well where your hope has been placed and I do trust that however your faith and patience may be tried now, that yet you can rejoice through it all. I hope our letters may be sent up during the winter, as they are sometimes, by a chance steamer, for I shall be very anxious to hear from you again. We are all well. Thomas has been away a great deal lately, but Mrs. Tate has been with us about three months, and has been good company for me. Jessie and Grace are growing well – and seem quite strong, though they are still small for their age. Their great delight is to go out with Papa. My baby is so strong and healthy – she does not seem like the others at all. She invariably sleeps well at night and is very good all day. Thomas joins me in love to yourself, dear Mother, and my father. Remember we are with you in our tenderest sympathy and most earnest prayers. God bless you my dear, dear Mother,

> Your affectionate daughter,
> Emma

The blow that Emma feared soon came. Eliza Douse died on March 4, 1881, aged sixty-nine, of "progressive paralysis."[10] Emma was more than ever on her own with three young children – Jessie aged six, Grace aged four, and baby Gertrude. The strain grew whenever one of them fell ill, as Thomas noted in passing two months after Eliza Douse's death. "Arrived home by Sat noon. Found all well excepting baby had been very ill for a week, and is still poorly." Perhaps for that reason he took his family with him on one of his next jaunts. "We have had a very pleasant trip to Naas. Spent a Sab[bath] at Bro[ther] Green. We were out three nights. Mrs. Crosby & the children enjoyed it much, and have felt much better for the trip."[11] If Emma carried her fifth child to term, she became pregnant again at about this time.

Increasingly, Emma's identity at Fort Simpson became caught up with the new girls' home. The need for more money to support distinctly female missionary causes was one of the factors leading to the formation of the Woman's Missionary Society within the Methodist Church of Canada. The WMS originated in June 1880 in Hamilton prior to the emergence of a national body. Made up largely of women married to businessmen and professionals, these "middle class 'club women' with the leisure and financial resources to sustain their extra-domestic pursuits" were keen on Emma's work.[12] At the first annual meeting of the Hamilton WMS in June 1881, all the monies raised were designated for the

Fort Simpson girls' home. As to the reason, a WMS history written a quarter of a century later explained the "special interest being felt in this work because of its relation to one who had formerly been a teacher at [the renamed] Hamilton Ladies' College, Mrs. Thomas Crosby."[13] The meeting minutes, taken by recording secretary Martha Cartmell, read: "The funds of the Society, which had been already prospectively devoted to the use of Mrs. Emma Crosby (wife of the Rev. T. Crosby), of Port Simpson, B.C., for the use of her (Indian Girls') Home, were drawn from the Treasury and entrusted to the Missionary Secretary, Rev. Dr. Sutherland, to be used by her. The amount sent was $200.25."[14]

One consequence of this donation was to give Emma a new responsibility – writing public letters of appreciation. Unfortunately, only a handful of these appear to have survived. Intended to garner and maintain support for the home, the letters incorporate elements of drama, which make them very different from her earlier letters to her mother.

Port Simpson, B.C., July 28th, 1881[15]

Mrs. H.M. Leland [Secretary of Hamilton WMS],

Dear Madam, – Your kind letter of June 27th, written on behalf of the Woman's Missionary Society of the Methodist Churches of Hamilton, reached me a few days ago. I need not tell you that it was with great pleasure and thankfulness that we read it, and with much rejoicing that we found we were remembered so kindly in the prayers and givings of the ladies of your Society, and that the Lord had put it into your hearts to help on a work that lies so near our hearts, and so heavy on our hands, as our "Girls' Home." The care of these young girls has been thrust upon us. Before we had any thought of undertaking such work in connection with the Mission, one case after another of urgent need was pressed upon us. Indeed the alternative was often coming under our roof or going to ruin, and, alas! to our grief, we found in the case of two or three girls whom we felt we were not prepared to take in at the time they applied to us, ruin speedily followed. A gay life in Victoria, or other places has led away many, very many, of the young women of these tribes. There are Indian villages where scarce a young woman can be found, the whole of that class having left their homes for a life of dissipation and shame, and only to come back, in nearly every case, after a few years, to die a wretched, untimely death among their friends. The temptation to this was strong, and we found it one of the most difficult things we had to contend with. Almost from the time we entered the Mission-house we had two or three, or four girls living with us; as one would be married – very few left us until married – another would soon come to take her place, and so the number be kept up. But we felt we could not well continue this, little as it was that we were doing, and as our own family increased we felt that our house was not the place for these girls. We could not abandon the work, so, after much prayerful consultation, we decided to build an addition to the Mission-house which should serve as a "Home" for the girls, and could be under our closer supervision, but entirely separate from our own family. We believed that, in doing this, we were following the direction of Providence, and that all necessary means would be provided. Two years ago next month the new building was brought into use. We began with four girls, but the number soon increased, and during the following winter we had twelve. The number has varied since that time, but during the last winter twelve were under our care, and twelve is our number now. We could easily gather in more, but have not felt ourselves in a position to do so hitherto.

Of course, as we undertook this "Home" entirely on our own responsibility, we had to move very slowly and incurred no expense that was not absolutely necessary. As yet the building is unfinished, and almost unfurnished, but we hope that the help Christian friends are now sending us will be sufficient to provide what is needed for the comfort of the girls and their training in some suitable industries. We have had difficulties and inconveniences all the way, thus far, but things look brighter now.

The care of the girls we have divided among us as best we could arrange it. Miss Lawrence, who is in charge of the day-school, gives what time she can to them, and Mr. Crosby keeps a constant supervision; but we feel that for the proper care and training of so many girls there must be a thoroughly practical and competent woman to give her whole attention to the work. Hitherto, of course, we have not been in a position to employ any one for this purpose; but now, we think, we should be justified in doing so, and it has occurred to me that the two hundred dollars your Society has voted to the "Home" would be well used if given towards the support of the Matron for the first year. I hope a suitable person may soon be found, with a heart for the work. Our plan would be to train the girls in general housework, in needlework of various kinds, in spinning, and weaving, if possible, and whatever else they might be able to turn to good account. We aim at making them capable Indian women, fitted for such a life as they are likely to be called to in after life. The most they can do is, as they leave us, to establish Christian homes for themselves where, as wives and mothers, they may show what industrious habits and a Christian spirit can do. What we desire most of all is that the heart of each girl who may enter the Home may be brought under the power of the Gospel; without this we fail, whatever else may be accomplished. It is most emphatically true among these people that "knowledge puffeth up," and is worse than useless unless true humility goes with it. How the glory of Christ and the good of man go hand in hand! Let me bespeak, dear Christian friends, your most earnest prayers, that every one of our girls may find the Saviour, and that the Lord may graciously abide with us.

We feel that we have been blessed in this work through all its course, and though we have met many difficulties and some sad disappointments, yet we feel thankful and encouraged. Most of the girls who have been with us have done well; very few have left us except to be married. One is in heaven. She was a Hydah girl, a native of one of the islands off the coast of Alaska and had been living in Wrangel, Alaska, a town composed of a few traders, a garrison, a tribe or two of Indians, and the stopping-place of great numbers of miners. While she was there religious services were begun by a few of our Christian Indians who were there seeking work. Matilda – that was her name – with many others, was soon much interested, and it was not long before she felt that she must get away from her old life, and decided to come to Port Simpson. This was before the Mission was established at Wrangel by the Presbyterian Church of the U.S., and while Phillip McKay, one of our own young men, was labouring zealously, and against great odds, to hold the place for Jesus till a Missionary should come. I cannot forbear to add that Phillip died, right here where the Lord had so honoured him in his work for his brother Indians, but not before he had seen the first Missionary in Alaska, Mrs. McFarland, on the spot, and with a good hold on the people. Since then, Mrs. McFarland has herself established a Home for girls at Wrangel, which is nobly supported, and doing a great work; but at that time there was no refuge there for such girls as Matilda, and when she came and told us her story – there was but one way for us – to take her into our family. She was very industrious, most amiable, and faithful in everything, and more than all, I am sure she loved the Lord Jesus, and rejoiced in what He had done for her.

After some time she was married to one of our Christian Indians, a young man in every way worthy of her. They were very happy together. Matilda's friends were still living in their heathen home, a hundred miles or more from here, and the winter following her marriage she set off to visit her mother. The weather became most intensely and unusually cold, and she was soon taken very ill. Thus her return was delayed. She grew rapidly worse, and it became doubtful whether she would ever see her husband and home again. Here she was in the midst of a heathen camp, with no friends to say a word of Christian comfort to her. How she longed for a hymn or a prayer. She made her friends promise that should she die there they would bring her body to be buried at Port Simpson. After some weeks of great anxiety a rumour reached her husband that she was lying very ill. (It is astonishing how news is passed, somehow, from one Indian village to another, when it would be hard to tell how it came.) At once eight or ten strong men volunteered to go with her husband to poor Matilda's relief. Against wind and storm they at last reached the dying girl. Imagine her joy. Though the weather was very severe it was her great desire to get back here before she should die, and after a few days they set out. For about eight days they travelled through cold and storm, but it was too much for Matilda's strength, and she died at a village about fifteen miles from here. How sad we felt! Yet we also rejoiced. To the last she urged her husband and friends to lay aside all grief for her, and said she was quite ready to die. She loved to have them sing with her, and talk of Christ and heaven, and she bade her husband tell us that our taking her when we did was the means of her being guided into a Christian life. Oh! how thankful we felt then that we had not turned her away!

Matilda is safe, but with others whom we have watched anxiously, the strife still goes on. You ask if Indian girls will stay Christianized and civilized. As to the Christianizing, while many mistake the form for the reality and so soon fall away, those who get the real "root of the matter" are mostly steadfast. There are those among our Indians here who for some years have adored the doctrine of Christ, and among our girls there are several who have long given every evidence of being true Christians.

Of course, the ignorance and inexperience of such a people as this, and the absence of the restraints thrown round a more refined state of society, leave them an easy prey to many temptations. Still we find St. Paul rebuking the churches of his time for just such sins as those poor Indians fall into. As to civilization these people are, many of them, very ambitious. Sometimes they try to take it on too fast, they want to play the organ before they know how to make bread, and a necktie is of much more importance often than an apron. Still, we can see considerable improvement throughout the village in the keeping of the houses, while the children are much better cared for than formerly. The people come to Church, almost invariably neatly dressed, and observe the strictest decorum. The girls are, as a rule, quick to learn, both in school and housework, though, of course, we find some who naturally lack all idea of order, and can never be thoroughly neat and clean. There is a girl in my kitchen now who makes bread that could scarcely be surpassed; very good butter, can do plain cooking well, and is clean and systematic about all her work. Less than two years ago she came to us from one of the most miserable houses in the village. Others have done equally well. There is a vast work, such as our Home is designed to accomplish, to be done among such a people, and we feel confident that so long as the Home is supplying this want, the means will be providentially provided, though, as yet, with the exception of two or three subscriptions, none exceeding five dollars, promised annually, the Institution has not pledged support.

You are greatly honoured in being the Pioneer women's Missionary Society of our Church. I hope you may not long stand alone. Pray for us, especially for the Home, and with many thanks, in which Mr. Crosby and Miss Lawrence most heartily join,

> Believe me, dear Madam,
> Yours most sincerely,
> E.J. Crosby

Having served a good half dozen years at Fort Simpson, Thomas Crosby requested a furlough to take the family back to Ontario. Part of the reason for doing so he attributed to Emma, whom he rarely described in his earlier personal letters but who now was repeatedly mentioned. In late August 1881: "Had a pleasant trip down [to Nanaimo]. Left wife & children at B[ella] B[ella] to visit with Mr & Mrs Tate. My wife had not been very well for some time. She needs a change much." A few weeks later: "Mrs C. needs a change very much. I hope it [the leave] will do her good." In Nanaimo: "I am hoping much in this trip home for my wife & the children."[16]

The family headed east in October 1881. They spent the winter in Lefroy and elsewhere in Ontario, where they repeatedly retailed their exploits to raise money for the new Methodist district. Thomas's special desire was a mission boat, which would markedly improve transportation between the various mission posts and also enable him to keep up with the Anglicans, who already had a vessel in operation. One of Thomas's biggest supporters was his long-time friend Rev. Amos Russ, who had moved back to Ontario four years earlier. According to Thomas, it was Rev. Russ's visit to Fort Simpson a few years earlier that led to talk of a steamer. The night that the two of them camped out on the trip to the Nass it snowed three or four inches, which caused Russ to declare that, unless Thomas had a steamer, "you will ruin your health and shorten your days in this kind of weather with this kind of conveyance."[17] During the Crosbys' Ontario visit, $4,000 of the $7,000 needed for a steamer was subscribed, over half of it coming from children in Sunday schools.

In Ontario Emma became a public person. Even as the family prepared to go east, her name was being used to promote the missionary effort. The letter of thanks that she wrote to the Hamilton WMS in June 1881 was read aloud a few months later at the annual meeting of the Methodist Church of Canada. She was validated to the delegates in two ways, first as the wife of "our dear Brother Crosby" and second as "a daughter of our venerable friend, Bro. Douse, who is here this morning. (Applause.)." It was virtually unheard of for a woman's voice to be so publicly acknowledged. The gender dimension was made doubly explicit in the introduction to the reading of Emma's letter:

I regret very much that we have not our dear Brother Crosby here this morning to give us tidings of his wonderful work in British Columbia. But in his absence the next best thing is to allow Mrs. Crosby to address the meeting [through the letter]. A few years ago, in writing to a friend, Mrs. Crosby remarked that the Missionary had to be everything – preacher, teacher, doctor, architect, carpenter, and a dozen other things besides; and you know, she said, when the Missionary is absent, all these duties devolve upon the second in command. That the Missionary's wife should designate herself the *second* [italics in original] is a wonderful circumstance, and one which does not hold good anywhere else (Laughter.).[18]

Emma was in Ontario at the time of the inaugural meeting of the newly formed national Woman's Missionary Society held in Hamilton at the Wesleyan Ladies' College in November 1881. The minutes recorded how "the presence of Mr and Mrs Crosby from Fort Simpson was a delight to all the friends, and a few words from the latter was a fresh stimulus to zeal and effort."[19] In the very same Centenary Church where her engagement had been announced, she once again held pride of place.

The small, pale, modest-looking lady – speaking evidently with diffidence, but with a sort of self-abnegation as though she had put herself out of the question and only lived for her chosen work – talked to us of the Indian Girls' Home, which with her husband it had been her lot to establish ... Mrs. Crosby states that fifty dollars a year will support one girl in the Home, giving her the plainest of fare and the plainest of homes.[20]

Emma was made a WMS life member, whereupon, "desiring to have all his family in this privileged class, Rev. John Douse immediately added to Mrs. Crosby's name those of his other [three] daughters."[21] The meeting resolved to support "the Girls' Home in Fort Simpson, B.C. by a sum not less than that sent last year by the Hamilton Branch $200.00."[22]

One of the reasons the Crosbys stayed on in Ontario may have been Emma's pregnancy. On March 29, 1882, her fifth child, named Annie Winifred, was born. In making preparations to leave Ontario after the birth, Thomas followed up on the opening that Emma had made with the fledgling WMS by recruiting Kate Hendry of Brampton as a matron for the Crosby Girls' Home. A single woman just entering her forties, she was to receive a salary of $400 a year, thereby becoming the first WMS-supported woman missionary. The WMS president went further. "From conversation with Rev. Mr. Crosby she thought he expected some money to be paid him for 'The Girls' Home' before leaving for Port Simpson," whereupon the WMS board voted that $500 be placed at his disposal.[23]

As for Emma, it proved no easier to leave family and friends in the spring of 1882 than it had in 1874. Thomas described how the day of their departure, June 29, "was a trying day for my dear wife," who had to part "with her father, her sisters, and all the dear friends at the Toronto station." The train "went on to Ingersoll, when my dear mother and two sisters came on and rode with us to St. Thomas; then we had another good-bye."[24] The sizable group that headed west together included Kate Hendry; Dennis Jennings, an English-born widower in his mid-forties who was to be the new teacher at the Port Simpson day school; and two missionaries bound for elsewhere in British Columbia. For the Crosbys the week-long train trip echoed its predecessor – Chicago; Council Bluffs, Iowa; Omaha, Nebraska, where the group stopped off for "the Sabbath"; Ogden, Utah; San Francisco. This time the Crosbys had four young daughters to mind – Jessie seven and a half, Grace almost six, Gertrude just turned two, and three-month-old Annie.

A pause over the weekend in San Francisco was followed by a three-day steamer trip to Victoria, whose difficulties are caught in Kate Hendry's letter to her sister in Brampton. "High winds & rough waves" caused everyone to become seasick, except for young Grace and the new matron. About "my first on briny Ocean," she wrote a bit triumphantly: "Most every passenger on board was confined to their berths near all the way. Brother & Sister Crosby with the rest oh what a funny picture I had to sympathise & help to take care of the children looking very motherly of course ... I had the upper berth not a yd wide & took Grace with me."[25] A weekend respite in Victoria was used to visit friends, buy provisions, and give Thomas opportunities to preach before heading north on the venerable *Otter*. During a brief stop at Nanaimo Thomas baptized a daughter of James Dunsmuir, "son of the proprietor of the Wellington Mines."[26]

Kate Hendry very soon learned that some people in British Columbia looked different than those with whom she had been familiar in Ontario, and she opted for disengagement rather than accommodation. During the trip up the coast the newly minted woman missionary discovered to her surprise that the "good comfortable meals" the group enjoyed were being cooked by a "big dirty looking black fellow," whereupon she decided "no more of his cooking for me however there was plenty biscuits & cheese so I made out all right."[27] Five days later and almost four weeks after heading off, on July 24, the Crosbys, along with Hendry and Jennings, reached their destination. As for how Emma fared during the trip, Thomas noted only that "all well, with the exception that Mrs. C. and children are very weary, and we long to get home."[28]

Emma was back to where she had come with so much optimism eight years earlier. The last two years had been filled with adversity, but she returned as committed as ever to the missionary cause, perhaps more so. Exacting funds highlighted Emma's growing role within the Methodist hierarchy. Among her contemporaries, according to Thomas, "she found a great many sympathizers, and indeed caused quite a stir in the minds of the women in the East."[29] Emma was no longer just a missionary wife: she was now also a public person, and through her published letters, a generation of like-minded women across Canada identified with her.

7
Changing Times

The trip home in 1881-82 proved to be a turning point for Emma. Their place in the missionary enterprise was attested by the reception she received from the Hamilton WMS and its enthusiastic commitment to her home and to the work she and Thomas were carrying out. Changes were also taking place in Port Simpson. The transformation in the community's outward appearance and of its Aboriginal and non-Aboriginal residents was becoming more apparent. But the most notable change related to the girls in Emma's charge. The protection that she gave them transformed into confinement as the character of the "home" became institutionalized.

Increasingly, Emma came to represent missionary wives as well as actually being one. She still had an onerous existence, but it now revolved around others' expectations of her. A long public letter from her that has not survived, "telling of their journey home and of the welcome given them by the natives," was read at the September 1882 general meeting of the WMS.[1] The opportunity that private letters to her mother provided for her, and for us as readers, to reflect on who she was and what she had actually accomplished disappeared. Now she was at the beck and call of a missionary enterprise that was much larger than herself – one that, in its own interest, found it useful to put her at its fore.

Emma did not return to a home of her own. Newly arrived Kate Hendry admired how the Crosbys' house was "all papered & carpeted & furnished as well as any one might desire large rooms bright & cheerful & a jolly company we are 4 ministers & 2 of their wives female & male teachers & my self."[2] The first Sunday back, morning church services were followed by "dinner at Mrs C's & back to church again at ½ past 2."[3]

As well as boarders and the girls' home, there were visitors. Emma was called upon to play the role of missionary wife at a moment's notice, as, for example, with Newton Chittendon, an American adventurer who came on the *Otter* in early September 1882. "Remaining here several hours discharging freight, I had the pleasure of meeting Rev. Mr. Crosby and his estimable wife, missionaries of the Wesleyan Methodist Church of Canada, of examining the mission church and school and attending an interesting service in the evening." Chittendon perceptively concluded that it was not only through Thomas's but, rather, "their noble self-sacrificing labors during the past eight years, [that] the marked improvement in the condition of these people is mainly due."[4]

The geographical isolation of the Crosbys' early years was abating. Several salmon canneries operated during the summer months on the Skeena River, with Port Essington and Inverness as their central points. As one report put it, "in the summer there are at least <u>350 white</u> people employed along the coast, the majority of whom winter in Victoria or elsewhere."[5] As well as the steamers running to Fort Simpson, steam schooners went up the Nass River. Fort Simpson was increasingly being called "Port Simpson" or simply "Simpson" by local residents who were disgusted that, all too often, their mail was ending up at Fort Simpson on the faraway Mackenzie River.[6] Thomas emphasized upon his return that "Simpson begins to have a settled town-like appearance."[7] Emma's letters were henceforth written from "Port Simpson."[8]

Simpson's physical face was changing. Newly arrived Dennis Jennings noted how once "the Hudson Bay Company's trading house was well fortified with cannon and small arms" but that now it "is no longer fortified, the fort-gate being open day and night."[9] Chittendon reported that many of the original, large houses "are still standing, strongly built of great hewn timbers and thick planks split from enormous cedar," but added: "The village contains at present about 800 Indians, most of whom live in comfortable houses and dress in civilized costumes."[10] Jennings described their appearance: "Most of the men here dress very neatly for Indians, much as men dress in the rural parts of Ontario. The women, or clootchmen, as they are called in Chinook, all come in very plain dress, with shawls, their heads covered with handkerchiefs, some one color, some of another."[11]

Most of the changes were directed towards Tsimshian men, not unexpectedly given the gendered society Thomas took for granted. Missionaries favoured the formation of brass bands as a means of countering traditional Aboriginal music and whipping up enthusiasm for the cause, and Thomas was no different. He used a number of expedients as well as the band to retain the interest of the young men whom it was his priority to convert. "We soon found there were a large number of young men who needed some amusement. Although they played football often on the beach, this was not thought enough, so we organized a Fire Company, and in their dress and parades and false alarms of fire, they took great delight ... Later on, a Rifle Company was organized."[12]

Aboriginal women were to be served primarily through the expanding girls' home. Emma's old associations in Hamilton and elsewhere in Ontario, as well as her family, were put to use to raise the funds that would see "a new Mission House built, and that the Indian girls should take full possession of the old house." Thomas later described how "the Missionary's wife had been writing to her friends, to her associates on the staff and to the student body of the old Wesleyan Female College, Hamilton, with which she had been connected for six years."[13] While it pleased Emma that monies came to support the project, the wait for its completion weighed on her.

Emma's growing distance from the girls who had once been so much a part of her everyday life was likely magnified in the letters that survive following her mother's death. They were intended for public consumption and were written for strategic purposes, being directed towards audiences that lacked any sense of the Tsimshian as living human beings. The public person that Emma had become realized that, if the home were to be supported, she had to play to her audience.

Port Simpson, B.C.[14]

Sept. 13th, 1882

My dear Mrs. [E.S.] Strachan [WMS Corresponding Secretary], –

As your annual meeting of the Woman's Missionary Society meets, if I remember rightly, early next month, it may be well for me to write you on matters connected with the "Home," in case you wish to consider them at that time. I hope this may reach you in time; you know our mails are very uncertain. I should regret it if you were inconvenienced, or at a loss for want of specific information. As you know, we began the care of these girls in our own family, and bore the expense as part of our own household expenses. The first subscription was made formally, when it was found necessary to put up an additional building to the Mission House, and bore the names of Miss F. Nott, Mrs. Tate, your correspondent, and a marriage fee of twenty dollars. The first contribution from any one not connected with the Mission is recorded April 14th, 1879 – "Friends in Toronto $15." Since that time we have kept a strict account of receipt and expenditure.

Contributions for 1879 .... $180.25

"   " 1880 .... 210.25

"   up to October, 1881 .... 562.15

The cost of the building put up, which is yet incomplete, amounted to $476.56. Some cast-off clothing was received from Victoria during this time, of which we were able to make good use. We kept the expenses as low as possible, supplied what was lacking when we could, and when leaving for Ontario last October, 1881, I had to the credit of the "Home" $11.17 ½. The boxes of clothing and material sent from Toronto had then just arrived, also a box of clothing and other articles from Belleville. The subscriptions which Mr. Crosby received towards the "Home" last winter being special, many of them not likely to be repeated, we have thought best to appropriate to the furnishing of increased accommodation. It has been suggested that, with the consent of the Missionary Committee, the Mission House we have hitherto occupied be made over to the "Home" for, say $700, which I think would be a fair valuation, this amount to go toward building a new Mission House. Some slight alterations in the building for convenience, painting, and other work still undone, and furniture required, would take $300 or more. Mr. Crosby received in Ontario in subscriptions, proceeds of special meetings, &c., $552.24. Besides this amount, other sums were sent to the Mission Rooms, which we have not yet received, and of which I can give you as yet, no exact account. We think, however, that the total would be sufficient to cover the outlay above spoken of, that is, $700 for building, and $300 for completely furnishing, &c; and, possibly, would also cover the travelling expenses of Kate Hendry, which amounted to about $200.

The $500 voted by your Missionary Society has not yet been received. I hope we may be able to appropriate it to current expenses. Since October last the expenses have been nearly $400. Our members have increased lately – we have now fifteen girls and expect more. It will be only by the utmost economy that fifty dollars a year per girl can be made sufficient, but I think we can do it. If we have, as we expect, as many as twenty girls with us, you will see what we shall require. Miss Hendry, I think, should not receive less than $400 per year. Out of that she could provide her own board. Our goods from Ontario have not yet reached us, which has given some slight inconvenience. When they are here, we shall have the means of carrying on more work in the Home than we have hitherto been able to do. I have given you these facts, my dear Mrs. Strachan, thinking they might be of use to you. If there is any other information you wish to have, let me know. I hope and pray that the annual meeting of the Society may be marked by perfect harmony of spirit, and that Divine wisdom may direct all your counsels. Matters of importance to the Society will have to be considered.

Mr. Crosby joins me in kind regards to yourself and cousins. In Christian love,

Emma Crosby

Indian Superintendent Israel W. Powell's visit to Fort Simpson, 1879
COURTESY OF HELEN AND LOUISE HAGER

Emma's public letter prompted the WMS to take at least part of the action she desired. It decided that, as well as paying Kate Hendry's salary as matron, it would support eight girls, at fifty dollars per year each, to be "given Mrs. Crosby."[15] Emma's release from the task of overseeing the girls came at a price. The Crosby Girls' Home became a WMS venture, but one for which Emma remained publicly accountable. Emma had an image to fulfill. Dennis Jennings, the teacher at the day school, observed how the "four white ladies at Simpson," in order to distinguish themselves from the hundreds of local women wearing "handkerchiefs" on their heads, "wear hats."[16]

Emma also had to deal with Thomas's growing preoccupation with the "Land Question," as it was becoming known. Across British Columbia Aboriginal peoples and newcomers were vying for the same land. Unlike the situation in the rest of Canada, in British Columbia a lack of treaties meant that there was no single means of reconciling competing demands. The Tsimshian were determined not to be deprived of land that they had long used. The Indian superintendent for British Columbia, Israel W. Powell, visited Fort Simpson in July 1879 and was impressed by the Tsimshian people's "intelligence and shrewd business capacity."[17] He responded favourably to their desire to protect their village sites at Fort Simpson and their fishing stations on the Nass and Skeena Rivers. According to Thomas, Powell "told them, in a meeting of four or five hundred people, that the land belonged to them."[18]

Indian Reserve Commissioner Peter O'Reilly was not nearly so sympathetic to Aboriginal interests as was Powell, either at Fort Simpson or through the province more generally. Arriving two years later to allocate reserve land, O'Reilly was handed a petition that had been written a year earlier and that requested "the whole country from the Naas River to the Skeena River, [which] has been in the possession of our nation from time immemorial," as well as the fishing stations.[19] The small amounts O'Reilly set aside in no way satisfied the Tsimshian, who increasingly realized that their adaptation to newcomers' ways, under missionary direction, had not brought them any measure of fair treatment, either generally or with regard to their most precious commodity – the land. Thomas's continuing efforts to defend Tsimshian interests not only took up time but also rebounded against him both with government officials and with the Tsimshian.

> Rev. T. Crosby
> On Board the Otter
> Nov 9th 1882

Dear Father Douse

You will see by this I am on my way to Vict[oria] expect to arrive there to night. I did not feel that I could get away handily at this time as all the [Tsimshian] people are getting home and it makes so much work for Emma as they look to her when I am away; and still I had to go down to see about the Land Question and money for the heathen and our winter supplies, and also I hope to see about a str boat. I hear there is one for sale, still I am short of money for that purpose and I do not wish [to] go in debt for it. Still I need the boat. I have traveled about 1000 miles in my district since our return.

Miss L[awrence]. who has been a great help to my wife for some weeks has left for Kit-a-maat 160 miles way [sic] with Indians alone she has about two weeks on the way. May God bless her she will not hear from us till next spring. Mr Jennings is doing very well but is new to every thing yet & so is Miss Hendry. This makes it hard for my dear wife and baby was not well when I left. So if Emma doesn't write the girls will know the reason. She had no time to write a line [to put in the] past mail and winter is now on us. The man Wood who comes out for Bella Coola left & went down to the Flat-heads so the poor

Bella Coolas are left. Mr. [George] Robinson has gone to Skit-a-gate on Q.C. Isl. I visited them last week.

Glad to see the Gen. Conf. is over so happy [sic]. Let me know why it is that Dr. S takes your place on the Sup[erannuation]. F[und of the] C[onference]. Glad that Dr. [Egerton Ryerson] Young is to Sup[erintend]. the N[orth]. W[west]. I hope the Marion will come and that we shall get some news. Our love to you all

Yours as ever

I told Emma I would write instead of her.   T Crosby

Victoria Nov 17th I have been here & at New Westminst [sic] on business for a few days and we go on board to night for home I wish I was with them for I feel that Emma needs me much I do wish I could get a woman to be with her as she needs help. I have tried to get some one here but failed. We have another young man [George Hopkins] out from Chicago who is going up with me to the work.

Yours truly

T. Crosby

I just got a letter from each of the girls. The boat is later than usual.

Four young children in the Crosby household in no way stemmed Thomas's roving. It was always the next new adventure that most engaged him. As he put it, "May God bless the seeds put down!!"[20] In November 1882 he wrote: "I have traveled 1000 miles in my district since our return in July," and he acknowledged that, although there was a school teacher and a matron to take charge at Port Simpson, "still they are strangers here among the people and it makes a great deal of work and care for Mrs. C. when I am away."[21]

Thomas was also taken up with staffing the mission field. The further he roved the more difficult it became to nourish the "seeds" he so enthusiastically sowed. In his memoir Thomas recalled proudly how he named Susanna Lawrence "the first white Missionary at Kitamaat," where the Edgars had previously served.[22] Skin colour trumped gender. George Hopkins, the twenty-year-old who travelled north with Thomas from Victoria in November 1882, had arrived from Chicago at his own expense on an emigrant train after hearing about the need for teachers on the Northwest Coast. As a missionary candidate, he would succeed Susanna Lawrence at Kitimaat after she fell ill. A year later he was transferred to Skidegate on the Queen Charlotte Islands and in 1886 ordained. About the same time, Dennis Jennings, who had come west from Ontario with the Crosbys, was sent to Port Essington as a probationer for the ministry. Missionary activity in Port Essington harked back to the community's founder, Robert Cunningham, whose wife Elizabeth had long run a Sunday school there, as well as to versatile mixed-race missionary William Henry Pierce, who had built a church there in the late 1870s before, at Thomas's behest, moving on to other missionary assignments. In the fall of 1883 Thomas dispatched Pierce to Bella Coola for a year.

The Methodists' entry into the Queen Charlottes renewed competition with the Anglicans centred in Metlakatla. William Duncan's former assistant, William Collison, had opened a mission on the north end of the Charlottes at Masset, and it was expected that the denominations would not overlap. There were complexities, however. Some time after Haida Amos Russ wed Agnes Hubbs, his grandfather permitted him to return home to Skidegate to preach Methodism. In late 1881 Russ asked Thomas to send a missionary. Thomas at first resisted, being overstretched financially. Then the man who was teaching at the Port Simpson mission school, George Robinson, volunteered to go. Thomas could not resist, and the Russes interpreted for and gave Robinson accommodation at Skidegate.

The Russes were likely Methodism's most effective agents at Skidegate. They modelled the new ways that missionaries like Thomas Crosby propagated, "building a modern house" as soon as they arrived – a house that "had rooms in it." In the words of their daughter Gladys: "I remember my father cutting down beautiful totem poles and cutting them down for kindling wood and firewood. He wanted to do away with all those old things if they were going to become Christians." The Russes' eleven children were not permitted to "go to any of the village does and dances" or to "the old time dances they put on now and again" but only "to church and Sunday school and these kinds of things." Gladys did not "remember any pleasures." [23] At the same time, even families as devout as the Russes walked a middle course in continuing to observe traditional hierarchies. Their eldest son Willie, who was educated by the Crosbys, became a hereditary chief through his Raven Crest mother.[24] When hereditary chiefs were dispensed with, Amos Russ acted as an elected chief, "and then when my father got too old, my brother was the chief councillor for years." [25]

Amidst all of the toings-and-froings, Emma continued to act as the public face for the girls' home. A letter that has not survived was read to the WMS board at the end of February 1883. In it Emma recommended, once again, "the building of a new Mission House for the Minister the present Mission Home to be purchased by this Society for the Girls Home at Fort Simpson." According to the board's minutes, the request was deferred: "In reference to proposition or suggestion made by Mrs Crosby, the Cor. Sec. was requested to write that at present the Board felt that it was wiser for them to make a certain appropriation each year but not burden themselves with the care of real estate until they were

older and richer."[26] Emma was not deterred, regularly reminding the WMS of
what was being accomplished at Port Simpson and what more was possible given
adequate support.

Port Simpson, B.C.[27]
March 20th, 1883

[To Mrs. E.S. Strachan, WMS Corresponding Secretary]

Your letter of February 5th came to hand about a month ago. Excepting a few
letters forwarded by friends in Victoria by casual vessels, this was the first mail
we had had since November. Two large mail bags were turned out on the sitting-
room floor, and every one took a hand in sorting. It is always with some anxiety
that we open our mails, and very thankful do we feel when we find that all is
well. I was very glad to know, from all I could gather from the [MISSIONARY]
OUTLOOK, which is almost my only source of information – and one number
of it is missing – that the various branches of the Woman's Missionary Society
are active and vigorous, and that, as Providence may open up the way to new
undertakings, from time to time, and responsibilities thus increase, your resources will be equal to the growing need, and you will feel, more and more,
that yours is a work which is bound to triumph.[28]

I felt much in sympathy with our dear Miss [Martha] Cartmell, as I read of
her departure for Japan [as a missionary under WMS aegis]. I am sure many a
prayer has gone with her, and certainly she is honored in being permitted to
thus show her love to the Saviour and her trust in Him; and after the tedious,
perhaps tearful, sowing, if only it is faithful, is sure to come the joy of harvest.
One of your own number being right in the field, must give an impetus to your
sympathies and efforts, and I trust, to the efforts of every auxiliary.

In our own work in the "Home," we have had cause for encouragement, while,
at the same time, trials have fallen upon us such as we never experienced before.
Our numbers increased to seventeen – and though much inconvenienced for
want of room, we could not well refuse those who desired to come in. A revival
that was felt through the entire community in the early winter deeply impressed
many of the girls, and in some, I believe, the blessed effect still remains. Others,
we are pained to see, soon grow careless again. O I hope in your monthly meetings you will pray earnestly for the conversion of these girls!

Shortly before Christmas measles broke out; scarcely a home escaped.
There were thirteen cases in the "Home." Most of these recovered rapidly, but
two of our dear girls, after about six weeks' illness, apparently the effect of the
measles, were taken away. This was the first time that death, or serious illness,
had visited us, and we could not but feel it much. But, thank God, there was

hope in each case. One who died was a young girl about sixteen years of age, named Jane Jeffery.

She was put in our care nearly four years ago by her mother, who was dying in consumption. This poor mother, a Tsimshean woman, had come all the way from Washington Territory, whither she had wandered, and where she had lived for years, though in a dying condition, for the sake of leaving her four children among those she could trust to care for them. She lived but three weeks after her arrival here. Jane was a delicate child, but always amiable and obedient, and possessed of very tender feelings. She mourned the loss of her mother very deeply, and I am sure her heart was drawn heavenward by this early trial. Quick and intelligent, she made good progress at school, and we looked for the time when she should be very useful as a teacher and a leader among her own people. But that hope was to be cut off.

During her illness, which appeared to be rapid consumption, brought on by a heavy cold in connection with the measles, though she suffered much from her cough, she was always patient, and so thankful for any kindnesses shown her. Miss Hendry was with her almost constantly, and tended her like a mother. She was quite resigned, and repeatedly assured us that Jesus was most precious to her, and loved to join, as her strength would permit, in hymns. Shortly before she died, after expressing her gratitude and love to those who had cared for her, she added, "But I love Jesus most." Dear Jane! we feel sure she is safely housed.

The second to be taken from us was a little girl we called Martha, about eleven years old. She had been with us but a short time, and was not so well instructed as Jane, but she knew of the Saviour's love, and it was a great comfort to her. Her mother was with her during the latter part of her illness, and seemed much comforted by the child's expression of faith in Christ. Martha, too, we believe, is with the blood-washed throng.

We felt it a great trial to lose these girls, yet we could not but feel that we had cause also for thankfulness. A much sorer trial has come upon us since. A spirit of restlessness and discontent took hold of some of the girls, encouraged, we fear, by some of their friends outside, and two went so far as to leave the house without permission. [An]other two seemed so discontented, that we feared their influence would be injurious to the others, and thought best to let them go to their own friends. But we shall by the help of God, follow these girls, and we hope yet to see them in a better mind. Since these departures the utmost harmony and cheerfulness have prevailed, and though our numbers are reduced to eleven, that is really as many as we can conveniently provide for at present. It is very hard for some of these girls to stand restraint for any length of time, so accustomed are they to a life of freedom and change. And we must expect trials – we have found them in the past, such trials, often, as one not knowing the character and circumstances of the people could form no idea of.

But the past encourages us to feel that the Lord can bring us through, whatever may assail, and He will take care of His work. I know many are praying for us. Your suggestions that I should send monthly or bi-monthly letters is a good one, and I will see what I can do to carry it out. I have been asked to write to different places; perhaps it would be well to address each in turn, with the option of forwarding to other Auxiliaries, if it was thought worth while. I should deem it a favor if you would send this on to some member of the Toronto Branch. It should have been finished and might have been sent off before this, but a little sick child of mine has needed my attention, and it has been written by snatches. I wish I could do a great deal more to show the need of earnest Christian work among these people. Thank you for your letter. It is very cheering to hear of your continued sympathy and effort.

[Mrs. Crosby]

The letters of matron Kate Hendry to her sister elaborated the deaths at the home: "My 2 sufferers are at rest Jane Jeffrey a half breed & Princess in her 18th year good & obedient but always delicate."[29] The events that resulted in two other girls' running away from the home were more complex than one would gather from Emma's summary, which is fraught with cross-cultural misunderstanding. According to the matron, Thomas wanted lumber cut for the construction of the new girls' home. No boys were available so "he had 2 of the girls cut some Lucy the eldest of the 2 being a Princess felt it beneath her dignity." So she and another girl ran away. The two were found next morning but would not return. "They said they had to work too hard." The constable brought them back the next night "& they were locked in our work room nearly a week where I fed, talked to & prayed with my 2 prisoners every day."[30]

Aboriginal girls continued to express their individuality in multiple ways. Kate Hendry wrote home how "I have only 11 girls now as 4 have gone with their Friends for small fishing season."[31] Writing in June 1883 she explained how, for various reasons, one girl was sent home to her mother, another to her father (in one case after a fight over whether or not she had stolen some clothes). Hendry put the blame on the girls and their families: "I had a mother love for these poor girls & it has been the saddest trial of my life ... They are a very suspicious thankless people no matter what you do they think you should do more."[32]

Emma's public letters were critical to ongoing WMS support for the Crosby Girls' Home, which explains, in part, their upbeat tone. They testified to dollars well spent, even when reporting on children's deaths, as WMS minutes summarizing their contents affirm: "Two of the 17 girls in the home had died recently and had left behind testimony to the power of Christ to forgive sins. Both died peacefully in the sure and certain hope of a blessed resurrection."[33] The fall 1883 general meeting voted to continue to support eight girls at fifty dollars each per year as well as to pay Kate Hendry's salary.

If Emma carried her sixth child to full term, she became pregnant again in mid-May 1883. To the extent that she had household help, it came through older girls from the home. Kate Hendry explained how "Mrs C took 2 of the girls into her kitchen as her domestic had left."[34]

Port Simpson B.C.
Nov. 15th 1883

My dear Father,

I was much pleased to receive by our last mail another letter from you, and thankful to find that your health continued so good, and, better still, that you are kept in quiet and peace of mind. This is indeed a matter of thankfulness to us all, and a pleasure to us to witness. May it continue, and by the goodness of our Heavenly Father, I feel confident it will, until a fuller joy shall take its place! Being in Toronto, as you expect, for the coming winter will give you privileges that you will enjoy – and be an advantage to Susie and the children as well. I hope the change may do you all a great deal of good. You will often see the family at Cooksville. I[t] must be quite a trial to Mr. Brown and to Eliza that he should be laid aside, but I trust they may find all things work together for their good.

Thomas has been away a good deal lately. He made a visit to Queen Charlotte's Is. lately, where a mission has been begun [at Skidegate], and so far been carried on with apparently great success. It is inconveniently far removed, however, from any other of our stations, and may yet be handed over to the [Anglican] Church Miss[ionary]. Society, who have a Mission established on another part of the Island [at Masset]. Just across the Alaska border also a small church is to be built – the subscription was begun by the people themselves who have many of them spent considerable time here, and wish a place at their own village where they can gather to worship.

Mr. Jennings has gone to his appointment at Essington, about forty miles from here and our school is under the care of Mr. Hopkins, a young man who came out from Chicago to this country, paying his own way, for the purpose of engaging in the Indian work – of which he had heard something from a friend who formerly lived in Victoria. He has spent some time at the Evanston College – seems ready to adapt himself to any kind of work, is a good singer, and we hope may be very useful.

We have not a large number in the Home just now, and until we get out of the house do not know that it is best to have very many. We may have the new Mission House finished, or a part of it some time during the winter so that we may move in. Mr. Crosby is working hard at it. The children are well – the elder ones have their lessons with me daily. Gertie seems to be growing much stronger than she need to be, while our little Annie has had less sickness so far than any other one of them at her age. I am much better than I was. Thomas is troubled at times with asthma, especially in wet weather. Thank you very much for the Globe & Mail which comes regularly – the Advocate we are always glad to see.

I hope you may all have a very happy Christmas. We shall think of you all, and pray for you and I know you will not fail to remember us. Mr. Crosby and the children join with me in warmest love to you, and to all.

Your affectionate daughter,
Emma

The new mission house was finally finished in time for Christmas 1883, matron Kate Hendry reported: "Friends Crosby moved into their new house the 12 of Dec so I have charge of a large house now & like it very much better." The old mission home became the new Crosby Girls' Home. There was "upstairs the girls bed rooms 2 large store rooms & some dark corners to put the naughty children in."[35]

Kate Hendry's letter home at Christmas 1883 reveals, largely unwittingly, the full extent to which the holiday embodied elements of tradition alongside outward adherence to the new ways being thrust upon the Tsimshian. She described a feast given "on the 28 by Kate Dudoward (a princess) just for women quite a large gathering some were dressed up & called themselves princesses." As for the entertainment: "They made speeches & had plays which were very noisy & foolish. I forget to say we had tea biscuits, candies & tea 10 or 12 biscuits given to each one to eat or take home with us."[36]

The very next day, at another event to which the matron was also invited, "in the same house the women were painted & dressed in their skins blankets & other old fixtures & went through some of their old performances which were both noisy & ridiculous." As to the rationale, "they said they done it to let me see what they used to do before they heard the gospel." Not only was Kate Hendry made to witness but she was also asked to make a speech, "so I spoke to them of the happy change which had taken place reminding them of the time when they would not want to see me at their feasts & I would have been afraid to go."

Just as Kate Hendry did not understand the layered meaning of the events, so did she not grasp the echoes of the potlatch in the gift-giving; rather she took pleasure that "we could eat & drink together & feel that we are brothers & sisters in Christ Jesus an idea that pleased them very much." Then, "as I was about to leave they presented me with a basket of goodies & dressed me with it on my back as they carry them there formed a procession & cheering as I was leaving them they gave 3 as hearty cheers as you ever heard." She did not realize the significance in reporting how "from the feasts I had 53 tea biscuits."[37]

Yet another feast followed on New Year's Day, when, flattered by being virtually commanded to attend, Kate Hendry found herself in a place of honour: "As soon as I entered the large building, which was crowded such a cheering & clapping of hands why I almost forgot myself for a while & as the chief (a fine looking gentleman with a curled mustache high beaver hat & black coat with silver buttons) came forward & armed me to the table of royalty the house was brought down with cheers." This time Kate Hendry was, as the evening progressed, troubled with the turn of events and left as soon as she could after the meal.[38]

Port Simpson, B.C.[39]
January 24th, 1884

[To Woman's Missionary Society]

We are rejoiced to hear of the growing activity of the Woman's Missionary Society of our Church. I am sure it will be a great blessing to the Church at home as well as to those for whom it may labour abroad. I have watched the reports from Japan with much interest. Miss Cartmell would naturally feel appalled at standing face to face with such deep darkness and heathenism, but the sweet trusting spark which her letter so beautifully displays will arm her with power Divine. The name of Jesus is the all-conquering name and however we may have to lament our own mistakes and failures, we need never be ashamed to proclaim Jesus. The discouragements and difficulties among a people so ignorant and unstable, and so low socially as these, are not few, and sometimes they seem very many; yet we are filled with thankfulness to see some who give good evidence of having really laid hold of Christ, and of having His love to their hearts. We had a most blessed time at the sacrament recently, a time refreshing to us all, and we feel there is a living Church in our midst, but there has been no general revival such as we should have been glad to see and such as we hear of at some of the other missions. Miss Lawrence returned to Kit-a-mat last fall. Shortly before her arrival there, while a native agent and his wife [George and Maria Edgar] were laboring among the Kit-a-mats, a powerful revival broke out, which seemed to reach almost every one in the village, some of the most bitter opposers were led to yield, so Miss L. can rejoice over the spiritual prosperity of her charge.[40] We heard from her a week or so before

Christmas; she was far from well, and was still quite poorly when she wrote, the result apparently of exposure while on a visit by canoe to a neighboring tribe. We are anxious to hear again from her, but communication is uncertain.

By the same mail which brought your letter Mr. Crosby received from the Mission Rooms the amount in full which you had transmitted for the Home vi., $300 on last year's account, and $450 on the present year. I am sure the ladies have dealt kindly and liberally with us, and I trust the money so voted may be the means to much good. Mr. Crosby succeeded in getting the new house so far on that we have been occupying it since Christmas, and he is now busy making the necessary alterations in the other building for the use of the Home. The necessity for such an institution is as urgent as ever – one young girl after another goes down morally – yet for some reason we have not had so many applications as formerly for admission. We feel this work a great responsibility and anxiety; do not cease to pray for us. My own health has been poor lately, and with such indifferent help as I can get here the duties of my own household are sometimes more than I can manage well. Then my four little girls need all the attention I can give them, not that I have anything to complain of, no, we feel that we are most graciously cared for by a loving Father. But under the circumstances I cannot give the personal attention to the Home that I should like to do were I more free. Mr. Crosby gives such oversight as he can from day to day. May God richly bless the Woman's Missionary Society.

[Mrs. Crosby]

George Edgar, who acted occasionally as Thomas's interpreter, as, for example, at a revival meeting held at Fort Simpson in 1878, was incredibly committed to the Methodist cause. On being dispatched to Kitimaat he was expected to earn a living for his family of five while evangelizing on behalf of the Methodists. Later in 1884 Edgar considered settling down in New Westminster, where he could get steady work at the local sawmill, build a house for his family, and be able to send his children to the local school. It was only when Thomas realized that Edgar would be out of reach that he took him seriously. Thomas offered Edgar a job as interpreter at a salary of fifteen dollars per month, with the prospect of becoming a regular missionary. Instead of going to public school in New Westminster, the Edgar children were subsumed into the missionary day school at Port Simpson. The next February Thomas escorted the Edgars to Gold Harbour on the west coast of the Queen Charlottes, which had been promised a missionary. There he tried to pass Edgar off as "a white man," which was what had been requested, but the local Haida would have none of it, considering him a Tsimshian.[41] Edgar persevered, did eventually get ordained, and ministered at numerous outlying northern missions.

Emma's sixth child, named Mabel Caroline and known as Winnie, was born on February 17, 1884. She joined sisters Jessie aged ten, Grace seven and a half, Gertrude almost four, and Annie about to turn two. As Emma explained in a rare surviving letter to her sister Susie, she had her hands full.

Port Simpson
April 1st 1884

My dear Susie,

The Steamer is in and leaves they say in an hour, but I must scratch a line to you. You have heard likely that our numbers have increased. The little new-comer is quite equal to any of her predecessors – we think – and is just as precious – indeed it seems to me she is the sweetest we have ever had, and is growing finely. She takes a good deal of nursing however, and is not by any means a model baby. I had an easy time as such things go and though, of course, I had not all the attentions that were so kindly lavished upon me on the preceding occasion, I had really good nursing. Jessie & Grace were most devoted, and were like little mothers to Gertie & Winnie – while Thomas gave himself to the general superintendence of things. Jessie cooked and brought me with great pride the first fresh egg of the season. Baby came on the 17th of Feb. Our children are all such a comfort to us. I only hope she will be as sweet as the rest of them. Winnie is the brightest, happiest little chick you could imagine – with lots of energy. Jessie & Grace are very early risers and bid fair to be far better workers than ever their mother was.

I read E. Prentis's while I was getting better, with great interest, but after all don't you think she failed. Is not Miss Havergal much more logical & scriptural? Thomas hands me the envelope & says he wants to go. We have had no mail since early Jan. Love to Winnie, Frank, Dollie & Fred and also to our father, to George & yourself.

As ever affectionately,
Emma

The outside world more and more intruded on Port Simpson. The *Otter*, on its early August 1884 run, carried a photographer. As Kate Hendry enthusiastically reported: "The steamer has returned from Naas & stays till midnight ... there is a photographer along & we have had my Home photographed with the Crosby family, myself & the girls all on & around the verandah. I hope to send you some when we get them if they are good."[42] The photo, particularly that half

The Crosby family, 1884. This is a cropped version of a larger photograph (see Plate 10 and cover of this book) that also includes the Crosby's Tsimshian charges

of it featuring the Crosbys, would become a widely known image of a missionary family standing tall whatever the adversities.

Emma had become a celebrity of sorts. At the fall 1884 WMS annual meeting, various branches, including the one at Montreal, told of receiving the "most cheering letters" from her.[43] The president reported how "Mrs Crosby was still ticking at Fort Simpson."[44] Kate Hendry increasingly apprised the WMS on ongoing events, but Emma was doyenne. Her letters to the WMS were copied and distributed to various branches to inspire them to take on the support of one or more girls in the home. One woman later mused how "we auxiliary members at home gave one dollar a year in aid of her work, and we thought we were doing nobly!"[45]

Port Simpson
Jan. 28th 1885

My dear Father,

We were very glad indeed to receive your last letter, as we always are to hear from you. We rejoice with you in the peace of mind which you enjoy, and it is a great help to our faith and hope to know that the way has grown so increasingly bright and happy with you. We give thanks on your behalf. I had written you shortly before your letter came.

Mr. Crosby was away still in Victoria where he had been detained much longer than he had expected awaiting the completion of the "Glad Tidings." He found it very trying being kept away from home and from his work here so long but the people were kept in quietness, and everything seemed to go on well, while Mr. Crosby found it a great advantage to be on the spot to superintend the fitting out of the Str.

It is a fine little vessel, said to be one of the best in the country, and we believe it to be a child of Providence. An excellent ship carpenter [William Oliver] who was converted in New Westminster, undertook to build it as Missionary work, at a low figure. He did his work admirably, and has attached himself to the str. so that he seems bent on keeping with her. Though not a qualified engineer, yet he has made himself sufficiently acquainted with the machinery to run it very well – and when not busy on board is ready to do any work that offers on shore. He is a devoted Christian & worker – a most valuable man in every way. The weather was so stormy when we were expecting the str. up and it was so delayed that we felt a good deal of anxiety. The Indians, who are easily excited, would come to me & say they thought surely something must have happened, and if Mr. Crosby did not come before much longer they would start off in their canoes to look for him – but for my part I could feel confident mostly that a kind Providence would watch over him & over the vessel built for his service & bring them here in safety. And so it was, after a pleasant & prosperous journey – Mr. Crosby himself being pilot – they reached here on the 11ᵗʰ Dec. on a lovely day. There was great rejoicing – cannon fired – colors flying on shore & on board, and our native brass band out to escort Mr. Crosby to the Mission house.

We had a very pleasant Christmas, great harmony among the people. The unsettled state of their land has disturbed them somewhat, but most of them look at the matter reasonably. No treaty has ever been made with the Indians of this country – and this they desire should be done before they accept any portion as a reserve. They intend to appeal to Ottawa in the matter & if necessary to England.

The newspapers you have ordered reached us. We thank you very much. You speak of my sending for anything I need and you will pay for it – it is very kind of you to think of it. I do not feel that I ought to burden you in this way – but there are sometimes little things I cannot get to advantage here – and if you would be so kind as to give Susie two or three dollars to spend in stockings for the children I should be much obliged. There are so many little feet to cover.

We have been mostly well. Thomas had a severe attack of asthma soon after he came home which kept him in the house nearly a week. He will be away a good deal I expect, if all is well, visiting the Missions. The children are doing well – but Jessie suffers a great deal with head-ache.

I hope you have not suffered with the cold as much as you did last winter. It would, as you say, be delightful if you could visit us here. I believe you would see a great deal that you would give thanks for, and we should feel it an honor to have you here. I trust we may all meet above. We have indeed great cause for gratitude. Our love to Susie & all the family and to Georgie, and my husband & children join me in most affectionate greetings to you, my dear father.

Your loving daughter,
Emma

Thomas finally got his long-sought steamer. After failing to find one to purchase, he was put in touch with William Oliver, a recently converted Scots boat builder from the Clyde who offered to build a boat for him.[46] On the completion of the vessel, christened *Glad Tidings*, Oliver took charge of it as engineer, while Thomas acted as skipper and "a native lad as deck-hand and cook."[47]

The land question dogged Thomas. Indian Reserve Commissioner O'Reilly had left out of the Tsimshian reserve, which he had laid out in October 1881, land coveted by two of his friends, who managed to acquire it some eighteen months later through a manoeuvre that was shady at best.[48] This "land grab," as

Thomas Crosby's steamer *Glad Tidings*
BC ARCHIVES, A-00391

it was termed, more than ever convinced the Tsimshian that they had been duped. They had kept their side of the "civilization" bargain, inviting in a missionary and then acquiescing to the demands put upon them, only to be deprived of their most valuable resource. Taking for granted that Aboriginal people were "like children," incapable of thinking and acting for themselves, government officials put the blame for growing Tsimshian unrest on Thomas and urged that missionaries be prohibited from meddling in secular matters.[49]

For a time at least, public dissension paled before private tragedy. Mabel Caroline Crosby died on June 8, 1885, at sixteen months. She was followed a week later by Annie Winifred Crosby at just over three years. It was Thomas who broke the news to Emma's father.

Aberdeen
July 6th 1885

My dear Mr Douse

We are here for a few days hoping it will do my dear wife good after the sor [sic] trial we have had.

I left home some 6 weeks ago with the Glad Tidings for a trip to Victoria and calling at all the missions along the way. Taking Jessie & Grace with me we had a most delight full trip and the children enjoyed the visit to the city so

much. We were there one week and I spent a Sat with Rev. Robson at Nanaimo
on our way back. And all went so well and happy till we got within 150 miles
of home on our return when we saw a canoe come off from shore with a black
flag and told us that more than a week ago they left home and that one of our
children was dead and another was not expected to live, you may be sure we
put on all speed and ran all night got to Inverness 30 miles from home by 9
a.m. next day when they told us that our dear little Mabel and Winnie were
both gone and that another was not expected to live. I cannot forget the three
hours it took us to run that 30 miles. We got home and now we found it was
too true for my dear little Winnie the strong spirited little girl that she was &
so full of life when we left had been lain in the grave the day before. I found
my dear Emma wonderfully sustained by grace divine in this sor [sic] trial. B^ros
Green and Jennings had come to their help & every one had been so kind that
it had some what lightened the burden for my dear wife. But – oh I thought –
if I could only see those dear little girls again. But – no they are all right. And
although the home seemed so lonely without them for when we left they were
so happy and well. And we had often said that no one was blessed with brighter
happier little girls than us. Mabel was so sweet with her large blue eyes and
would since Aug get up to her high chair and sit on one side of me at the table
and then Winnie on the other so full of life would sit on the other, and at
prayers she would sing so sweetly & so happy & Mabel would hold the book
and try to sing to [sic]. And they were both so well and in short 4 weeks from
that time both of them taken home and now there lies three sweet little girls
side by side in the Indian grave yard on the [Rose] Isl[and]. It seems the week
after we left Emma in her kindness had gone to visit an Indian family and took
the disease from the children and brought it home had it herself and gave it
to Mabel & the rest. Of course she did not know it was diphtheria. I believe
everything was done for the dear pets that could be. We thought it best not to
allow Jessie & Grace to go to the house so after the Sub. [?] I brought them
down here about 50 miles from home. Mr. & Mrs. Dempster have been so
kind to them. After all Mrs. Grant and Hannah the girl that was so sick had
got well enough to be out, I thought it would be well to get Emma away from
the place. So last Sat although she was so poorly on finding that I found it
would not do to take her out. Yet we came had a fine day got her in the evening.
And she has been some better the last two days. I took Mr Jennings' work
yesterday and we should stay here at least a week and it may be more. I wish
Emma to try the hot springs. She is nearly prostrated with the great strain of
watching &c. oh you know of nearly three weeks. Nothing but the divine
hand kept my dear Emma up and then she had the disease herself and did not

do any thing for it and her throat is still sore but I do trust she will be better soon. Our three dear girls left to us are very well and very happy. And we do pray that they may be good & wise and useful. And I also trust that our hearts will be serene and now given up to work for the Master. Oh heaven is made richer by our dear pets home there. Half of our dear children are now in that better land, and we shall all meet them. Oh that we may be faithful unto death! The Glad Tidings our missionary ship is a great help to us in getting about the D[istric]t. and is doing better than we had expected in every way. She can carry lumber to help the poor people to build their homes and she is strong and safe and the man B^ro Oliver who runs her is a real good Christian and does good wherever he goes. If it were not that Emma gets so sea sick I would take her with me now for it would do her good. We have traveled some thousands of miles with her now and find she rides well the storm as well as a calm.

I am writing a letter now to pay the last debt and I hope she will pay her own way by & by. Could you get some of your friends to send us papers &c that would be good to distribute amongst settlers where we go, or some suitable books for a little library for the boat. Oh how much we should like it if you were closer to come and spend the summer with us. Our love to all the dear friends and our dear Grandpapa. I know you pray for us. Emma & all the children share [?] in love.

Your son
Thomas

I would like to get the Missionary in all lands by the M.E. Church New York.

The Crosbys' visit was to the Aberdeen salmon cannery, which was located about two miles up the Skeena River from Port Essington. The cannery's proprietors, the Dempsters, were New Brunswickers of Scots ancestry and were close to the Crosbys in age. Dennis Jennings was now a missionary at Port Essington.

A week after writing the letter to his father-in-law, Thomas described Emma's plight to his long-time Methodist minister colleague Ebenezer Robson.

I came here to the mouth of the Skeena a week ago to get Mrs C. away from home. She has been much better the last few days but it was a great trial to her. Still our Heavenly Father is so good & kind that we have only to cling sure to Him to find how blessed he does comfort those who trust him. Oh that we may be faithful unto death. All the rest of the children are now well. And Hannah the girl is better thank God.

At the end of the letter Thomas commented: "Mrs C. & the children join in love to you all. I know you pray for us.[50]

It was not just private grief that had to be borne. The Methodist press turned the Crosby daughters' deaths into a morality tale, much as Emma had done with the deaths at the girls' home. "A private letter" told readers of the monthly *Missionary Outlook*: "We are sure that Rev. Thomas Crosby and his estimable wife will have the sympathy of thousands all over this country in the sore affliction which has befallen them in their far-off field of labor, on the border of Alaska." The article concluded: "But the consolations of Divine grace are as rich and abundant at Fort Simpson as elsewhere, and it is delightful to hear that in the midst of this sore affliction our beloved sister and her husband have been wonderfully sustained."[51] To the extent Emma was consoled, it was by Susanna Lawrence, who had lived with the Crosbys prior to becoming a missionary at Kitimaat. A decade and a half after her daughters' deaths, Emma recalled that "her untiring devotion ... when bereavement came to our home, we can never forget."[52]

Even as the Crosbys were reeling from the loss of their two youngest daughters, the mission was coming under scrutiny. The Methodist Church in British Columbia was still part of the Toronto Conference, which, in the summer of 1885, dispatched its general secretary, Alexander Sutherland, on a two-month tour of inspection. He arrived at Port Simpson shortly after the family's return there, on July 29, where he found "a civilized and well-ordered community, and a Church numbering 238 full members, and as many more on trial" to determine whether they were worthy of membership. For Sutherland external change provided the measure of what had been achieved: "Twelve years ago this spot was the site of a heathen village, with all the darkness, poverty, filth, cruelty and vice characteristic of such a condition. Now there is a Christian village of 800 inhabitants. All the old heathen houses have disappeared, and have been replaced by street after street of neat cottages of various designs."[53] Sutherland could not resist adding a denominational comparison: "At Metlakhatlah the houses, almost without exception, are of one pattern; but at Port Simpson variety of style has been encouraged, giving a pleasing appearance ... That would do no discredit to any Ontario village." Sutherland pointed out that the new mission house was "plain and modest, as becomes a missionary's home, but neat and comfortable."[54] One of the few signs of caution was "the 'Girls' Home' with about a dozen inmates, and room for more."[55]

Thomas's mission had an underside. Secretary Sutherland pondered whether the mission had been extended along the coast and inland faster than it could be serviced. As various young Tsimshian men informed him at a council meeting, Thomas had neglected his base at Port Simpson. David Swanson explained: "Mr. Crosby has too much to do. He is often away, and we fear sometimes we will lose him." In Swanson's view, a bargain had been struck but not kept.

It is eleven years since we gave up our old way, and no one has visited us to help us in anything connected with the improvement of our village. When it was first proposed to build a house for God, we all gave our property to help; and when we wanted a bell, and an organ, and lamps, we gave our money again. We also built our school-house. When the storm took the roof off God's house, we again gave our property, and put on a new roof without help from any one. When the missionary was away, we made the road up to the church without help. Then with one heart we made the bridge over to the point. We persevered in our poverty, and got up our houses as far as you see them. We have done all we could to help ourselves ... This is all I have to say.

There needed to be another missionary and also someone "to administer medicine, – some one who understands it." [56]

Another Tsimshian, Thomas Wright, went further, claiming Tsimshian ownership of the feats for which Thomas took credit.

When the Word first came to us it was wonderful how it was run. Alfred Dudoward went to Victoria, and he and his wife came back bringing the Word of God in their hands; so we see the necessity of having some [one] taught to preach. The Tsimpseans opened the way to Kitimaat, to the Bella-Bellas, and to the Naas people; also to the Wakeenos, and they are opening the Word to the Bella Coolas. They also opened it to the Stickeens ... I tell you this because the white men say they were the first; but it was the Tsimseans.

The Tsimshian had at each stage taken the initiative. Like Swanson, Wright believed the Tsimshian had done all they could by themselves. "You see by our village we have been trying to help ourselves. You see the roads about the village; we made them with our own hands – no one helped us. We wish some of the great chiefs would send us some lamps for the streets, so the old people could see at night to get to the house of God." Wright had a request: "We ask for another missionary and teacher to help Mr. Crosby to teach the people. We ask for a man to teach, not because the women who have taught have not done their duty, but we think a man would do still better. We are not taught trades, nor is there a large school to teach native missionaries." [57]

Other Tsimshian had additional complaints. Matthew Shepherd explained the economic situation, in particular the lack of "labor or other means to keep our people at home." Men had to go off to find work, and when they returned they were being swindled. "Our young men are able to earn some money for their work, but they go to the [Hudson's Bay] Company for food, and the money is all gone ... All the time we have been a mission, no Christian trader has come. This is why all your children speak as they do." [58]

Charles Price turned the secretary's attention to land claims: "Words are always coming about our land, saying it is not ours. This is our great trouble." [59] James Wright explained how "God gave this land to our people from the beginning." How could it belong to someone else, given that no one had "bought our land" or "fought ... and [taken] it"? Wright ended with a warning: "God will not blame us if there is trouble about our land. He will blame the men who take it from us in this way. We have said now what is in our hearts."[60]

As always, Thomas had a ready response. He would have another adventure, perhaps at Hazelton on the forks of the Skeena River. The secretary observed how "Mr. and Mrs. Crosby have volunteered to go ... and establish the mission, if the authorities so desire."[61] In the fall of 1885 William Henry Pierce went with Thomas to see about beginning work there. Nothing came of it, likely because Thomas was infatuated with his new steamer, *Glad Tidings*, but perhaps because Emma had reached the limit of her endurance. Sutherland noted in his report that, after Sunday services, "I go with Mr. and Mrs. Crosby to visit one or two sick people, and then across the bridge to the little cemetery [on the island] to visit the graves of their children." [62] The next day "Mrs. Crosby and children" went along on the *Glad Tidings* to visit nearby villages and canneries, including Aberdeen, and then down the coast to Victoria. This unusual inclusion of a missionary wife on an official visit related directly to Emma's condition, the secretary explained in his report: "The anxiety, the watching and the grief had told somewhat severely upon Sister Crosby, and we united in urging that she should come with the remaining children on a brief visit to Victoria and New Westminster. She yielded to our entreaties, and I was afterwards glad to find that she had profited much by the rest and the change."[63] No further mention was made in Secretary Sutherland's report of how Emma and the children fared during the numerous stops that were made on the way south so that the men could preach.

Another woman integral to the Methodist mission on the north coast was also on the trip, as Sutherland revealed in passing when discussing the sermon he gave during a stop at Port Essington.

> I preach to the people as best I can, and find an excellent interpreter in Kate Dudoward, a Tsimpsean half-caste woman, one of the first converts in connection with the Port Simpson work. The discourse in English occupies altogether some 35 or 40 minutes. When about a third of the discourse is over, I pause, and Kate Dudoward, commencing with the text, repeats what I have said, almost verbatim. The remainder of the discourse is given in the same way, with only one other pause, and the brethren tell me that not a thought, not an illustration, and scarce a word seemed to be omitted in the process of translation.[64]

While at Port Essington Sutherland ordained Dennis Jennings. Six weeks later, Jennings, a widower, married Carlotte Godby, an Ontario woman living in Nanaimo.[65]

At Port Essington Sutherland held another council, at which he was once again told in no uncertain terms about whose initiative had led to the success of the north coast mission and about the obligation that this placed upon the Methodist Church. Chief Neeshot, or Albert Nelson, from Port Simpson reminded him:

> The Tsimseans were the first to start in the new way, and we asked the Methodist missionaries to come, and although all things do not go as we would like them, we have not repented of sending for the Methodist missionaries. We would like to have a missionary who could teach our children all things [trades, etc.]. Mr. Crosby does not stay at home; he goes to visit other places.

Chief Neeshot reiterated how the Tsimshian had used their own time and money to build up the village and that now "our strength is gone." Like the others, he ended on a note of respect: "We thank you very much for listening to us."[66] Chief Paul turned the secretary's attention to education, asking "why the Tsimsean children are not taught to speak English as Kate [Dudoward] was."[67] The bargain the Tsimshian made by inviting in the Methodists, at the Dudowards' initiative, was not being kept. Thomas Crosby had let his ambition override his commitment to them.

Amidst the growing turmoil over the mission, Thomas, at least occasionally, took notice of Emma's difficult circumstances following the deaths of her two youngest daughters. Writing from Bella Bella in October 1885 he noted in passing how "Mrs C. is some better though not well." A month later, from Port Simpson: "Mrs C. joins in kindest regards. She is not well yet – her teeth still trouble her."[68] Emma's grief is also indicated by the WMS president's comment, made later in 1885: "Owing to the great affliction which has fallen upon our beloved brother and sister Mr. and Mrs. Crosby, and the change of matron at the orphanage, we have few particulars from Port Simpson."[69]

Emma was in the midst of another transition with the Crosby Girls' Home. Two months after the children's deaths, matron Kate Hendry married the Methodist minister in the Nass, Edward Nicholas, an Englishman six years her junior.[70] In her early forties at the time she became matron, Kate Hendry had briefly contemplated the possibility of joining forces with mixed-race missionary William Henry Pierce. She described their first encounter in the spring of 1883: "W.H. Pierce one of our Indian preachers is with us & is to remain 7 weeks as bro. C will be away we think just as much of him as of any white br in the place.

Agnes Knight
COURTESY OF HELEN AND LOUISE HAGER

You will see some of his letters in the Guardian." A few lines later, Hendry added a bit coyly: "Some of the Indian friends propose that I will marry a Tsimshean so I will belong to them."[71] In the event, Kate Hendry soon found another prospect, whom she wed as soon as her commitment to the WMS came to an end. Just as had her predecessor, Caroline Knott, she served out the requisite three years and then made her own life. As Kate Hendry explained, "Bro Nicholas another of our missionary workers is here he is a fine young English man has travelled nearly round the world & is well informed."[72] The marriage took place at Port Simpson on September 15, 1885, with Thomas officiating. The couple replaced William Henry Pierce at Bella Coola.

The WMS, to its credit, had already found a new matron for the Crosby Girls' Home. It felt that it had found "a worthy successor in Miss [Agnes] Knight, from Halifax, N.S."[73] Born in Ontario, Knight was in her late twenties.[74]

Port Simpson
Jan 28th 1886

Dear Mr Douse

Your very kind letter came to hand by the last mail telling us that you had renewed the the [sic] sub[scription] for the papers it is really very kind of you and it is a great comfort to have them. The Advertiser & Missionary in all lands, are very good, and it is good to be posted on all those subjects and we are very much shut out here. Our work has been in a good state this winter but we are having opposition from the white men more than we used to have and the fact that the H.B.C. have a license to sell liquor here is very bad and is bound to do harm among those people in the long run. But the Lord blesses His own land and I think we never felt more that blessing of God upon our labours than this winter. The class meeting and prayer meeting and public sinners have been well attended. And our S[unday]. School has been a real comfort to us and the people, and has been well attended. Our children attend and like it much. The dear girls we shall soon have to do something for them in school some where else. We have been pleased to hear that you were so well and hope you may continue to be as happy and as well as ever.

We have longed for a genuine revival all this winter it has not come, and our people are scattering home again.

I am glad to hear that Mr Green had called on you. He is a good fellow and has done great good.

You will be glad to hear that our mission ship Glad Tidings is about paid for, and she ran 9000 miles last year and paid her own expenses and was the means of taking the gospel to many who would never have had it.

Emma says she will write you she has never been so well since our little pets left us. It may be necessary for her to have a real change before she will get back her strength.

Pray for us.

Yours respectfully
T. Crosby

If Emma came to full term with her seventh child, she became pregnant again in early February 1886. She was thirty-six years old.

The improvement in Emma's health is suggested by her letter to her father, which was written in April. At the time she wrote, Thomas was about to head to Victoria to attend the founding meeting of the Methodist Church in British Columbia, which had been given permission to separate from the Toronto Conference. William Henry Pierce and George Hopkins, both of whom would be ordained at the meeting, went with him on the *Glad Tidings*. At the meeting the province was divided into four districts, one of which was Port Simpson. Out of a total of 1,975 Methodists enrolled across the province, fully 1,269, or almost two-thirds, were Aboriginal persons.[75]

Port Simpson
April 16th 1886

My dear Father,

It is a good while since I wrote you, but Mr. Crosby sent you a letter lately and as we always hear from Susie how you are getting on we do not feel that we are at all cut off. We are very thankful to know that you have come through the winter so comfortably, and been spared any serious illness. You have been a large family at Susie's, but it will be a pleasure to you, I am sure, to see your children and grand-children about you. Annie and her family being in Toronto too must have made it very pleasant for you all. I did think at one time that I saw a prospect of reaching Ont. before long, perhaps the coming summer, that was if the proposed removal of Mr. Crosby to the interior [to Hazelton] should take place, but now it seems more than doubtful that such a change will be made at present, the District meeting now being held hesitate to recommend it, and if we remain here there will not be the same occasion nor opportunity of my going East.

The children get on pretty well with their studies, but I feel it would be a great advantage to them to be associated with other children in a good school. They are good company for me especially when their father is away, which is very often. A week ago he returned from a trip of about 900 miles with the Glad Tidings, bringing with him the members of the District meeting from their various stations.[76] Mrs. [Charlotte] Jennings is here also, but the other ladies whom we expected failed to come. This gives us quite a houseful, but within a week I expect they will all be gone. Within that time Mr. Crosby intends, all being well, to leave for Victoria, which will keep him from home probably four weeks. There is to be a convention of representatives from the three Districts in this country at that time in Victoria. Miss Knight who has charge of the Home is a most excellent person. I find her very good company, and it is nice to have such a neighbour. We were very glad to get those packages of cards you sent about Christmas – we find such things very useful to encourage the children to learn verses, and as Christmas presents &c. Thank you also for the "Life of Miss Havergal." It is a book I have read with great profit.

The Advocate & Gospel in All Lands come regularly, also the other periodicals which you have ordered for us. You remember us with great kindness. Our people are nearly all away just now on the Naas where they go to fish at this season. On the whole they have done well lately. I am sure there are some very earnest happy Christians among them especially among the old people. Some of the younger people are careless. But the leaven is working, and some of the younger missions are very promising.

We write in love to you my dear Father, hoping that your way may grow brighter and happier with every day.

As ever your affectionate daughter,
Emma

Emma suffered another loss with the death of her father, Rev. John Douse, in Toronto on May 8, 1886.[77] Thomas found a temporary solution to his desire for freedom in the face of Emma's new grief by parking her and the children in Victoria for the summer of 1886. As he explained in mid-September: "I am just back from a hurried trip to Victoria for winter stores, and to bring my family back. Mrs. C. and the children have been much refreshed by nearly a three months' visit."[78]

Thomas was still enamored of the *Glad Tidings*, which fed his desire to travel faster and to go longer distances. Just as he had done when he was a young man, he got up at 4:00 AM; however, now it was "to make an early start" in his boat.[79] Thomas visited logging, mining, and fishing enclaves and took one trip around Vancouver Island. Wherever he stopped, he preached, as powerfully and dramatically as ever, with forceful gestures and thundering voice. "Not only was every tribe on the Coast visited, but also many a logging, mining or fishing camp. Usually the men seemed glad to meet us, and listened to the Word."[80] The difficulty was that, without a missionary to follow up, the enthusiasm he stirred up inevitably withered away.

As the Tsimshian were so very aware, Thomas was caught in the inevitable bind of missions. He had to do more and more, at an accelerating pace, in order to stay in the same place. The novelty of claiming converts was in itself insufficient to raise the funds upon which the missionary enterprise depended. The accomplishment of yesterday became the norm of today: something additional had to be added even as the status quo was maintained. Thomas increasingly relied on busywork to keep those in his midst out of mischief, as a description of a New Year's Day parade at Port Simpson indicates.

The first procession, headed by the Riflemen's brass band, included the Temperance Society and the Band of Hope. The second procession, headed by the Fireman's band, was composed of the village councillors ... It made a grand sight for here; the Fireman's Band in their blue uniform, Riflemen in navy blue, the Temperance Society with their bright regalias, and the children with their badges and sashes, the councillors, all in black skirt coasts, roles of MS in their hands, spectacles on their noses.[81]

The *Glad Tidings* was the most dramatic in a series of ever larger concentric circles by which such practices extended out from Port Simpson.

Emma was not long home in the fall of 1886 when another family tragedy struck. The Crosbys' seventh child, Emma Jane, was born on November 8, 1886. Just a month later, on December 8, she died. Agnes Knight, matron at the Crosby Girls' Home the past sixteen months and almost as close to events as was Emma herself, wrote in her journal:

Dec 10th Sat. night.
This has been such a sad, sad week for God has allowed another heavy sorry to come to dear M[r]. & M[rs]. Crosby, the darling baby was such a joy & happiness to the whole household, we were all so glad when the wee pet came, but she only stayed a month with us & then God claimed again His precious loan. Wednesday before five Mr. C. came down for me & I went up at once, found baby had been very sick all night, it seemed to be inflammation of the lungs, we did all in our power for the little darling, but by ten that night she was taken – taken to be with Jesus I know, but after we had prepared her for her last resting place & I stood looking at the sweet little face I could not help asking could you not have spared this little one to them Father – God knows best, the quiet submission of the dear mother is so touching, my heart never ached so for any one as it does for her – may our loving, sympathizing Jesus comfort her thro' all the lonely hours of heartache that will come to her. They buried her baby today it seemed so hard to cover up the lovely little face in the cold earth – oh, how unbearable this life of sorry would be if it were not for the life & joy awaiting us by & bye.[82]

Emma had buried four daughters at Port Simpson. She was left with a husband enchanted with a boat and three growing children. Jessie aged twelve, Grace ten, and Gertrude six-and-a-half vied for her attention with the Aboriginal girls, who now resided on the margins of the Crosby mission, yet were still formally in her care.

8

Good Intentions Gone Awry

Through all of the changes of the mid-1880s, Emma remained committed to the Crosby Girls' Home. She oversaw its operation with the help of the matrons who, under the guise of protecting them, were hired to guide and guard the girls. In practice, the girls' confinement increasingly resembled incarceration, with strict rules, restricted activities, and direct instruction being hallmarks of the care provided for them. For all Emma's good intentions, the direction of the home had taken a considerable turn, impinging on any freedoms the girls may have known previously. Her good intentions went awry for another reason as well. The Methodist mission that Thomas headed, and Emma competently managed, lost its utility for the Tsimshian people.

The various matrons who had charge of the Aboriginal girls formerly under Emma's care had their own good intentions. Unmarried and without children of their own, they sometimes transferred their maternal desires onto their charges. For example, Kate Hendry took pleasure in how "they often call me mama," another time she commented that "my family have all been so well." When two girls were permitted to return home to their mother, she could not quite understand why they were so eager to do so: "I believe I had a mother's love for those poor girls & it has been the saddest trial of my life but thank God I have been enabled to lean hard on the strong arm of Jesus."[1] These women's convictions were undoubtedly sincere, perhaps too much so, as they set them up for a fall.

The matrons were paid employees who had been hired to do a job. Forced to watch over ill children during her first Christmas on the Northwest Coast, Kate Hendry told how "the enemy tried hard to tempt me by telling me I could be very much better employed than waiting on poor ignorant rude Indian girls."[2] However good their intentions, and there were many indications that they empathized with their charges, the string of women who managed the girls' home from the early 1880s onward found it incredibly difficult to get beyond their racist assumptions.

The solution to the matrons' almost innate distrust of their charges was to enforce a strict routine. Organization was paramount, as Agnes Knight explained in 1886: "We do everything by rule. We have bedroom, dining-room, kitchen and wash-room rules, also general rules, or a time-table giving the hour for everything, from the rising-bell to bed-time."[3] As to whether or not the girls could, through this regimen, become Christian and civilized, great doubt existed. She wrote in her memoir: "I had some girls who used to 'get converted' regularly every few weeks, would cry and mourn over their bad behaviour and make a great profession of repentance in class meeting and in a day or two be as bad as ever – I never respected such conversions – tho' I might have had quite a list in the course of a year – it wasn't the kind of conversion I waited for."[4]

Surveillance was key to the enterprise. One summer the girls were taken on a camping trip to compensate for their being "so used to migrating from place to place" with their families. The home's annual report to the WMS emphasized how "it was not much of a rest for the teachers, as ears and eyes must always be on the alert as well as hands to keep things as they should be."[5] As to surveillance's benefits, Agnes Knight explained these at the beginning of 1886:

> On the dining-room wall I have two large sheets of paper containing the names of all, for good and bad marks; I find they have a very good effect upon them. Knowing that if a rule is broken there will be a bad mark for the disobedient one, makes them very careful and often saves them from more severe punishment ... Sometimes there is stubbornness hard to conquer, but when such is the case I let Mr. Crosby undertake for me, and the naughty one is soon penitent.[6]

The girls, for their part, continued to believe, perhaps had to believe, that their surrogate mothers in their new "home" were teachable. Agnes Knight described how the children "have a wonderful facility for finding something to eat every time they go out; sometimes it is mussels off the rocks, sometimes roots or young shoots, or various plants which they tell me 'the people eat,' so they know they are safe."[7] Come the spring, "they are very anxious to borrow a boat and go for fish eggs."[8] The girls were enormously resourceful at retaining skills, Agnes Knight recalled: "The children used to delight in gathering large quantities [of berries] which we preserved for winter use – In the late winter they always begged to take our walks on the beach so they could gather clams and mussles [sic]." The girls also maintained the familiar in other ways:

> They weren't as fond of romping as white children ... they seemed to enjoy a quiet walk & talk best – While passing through the village I always had them walk in

order but once out in the bush or on the sea-shore the older girls would join me & they would tell me of their earlier life or legends of their people, or I would tell them tales of the white folks of my own childhood – & I used to enjoy it as much as they did, & any treasures in the way of sea-shells, wild flowers or fine berries were always saved for me.[9]

Perhaps it was for this reason, but more likely simply because it was more economical and less stressful, that eventually "native food is purchased for the children of the Home – salmon, sea-weed, small fish and game."[10]

One of the most difficult things for the girls was trying to maintain communication with their families. Some of them tacitly or deliberately effected a trade-off, as matron Sarah Hart, hired in 1888, unwittingly revealed: "It has been cheering to have some of the girls who have always refused to pray in public, of late pray with the sick ones, as we visit from house to house together. We usually take two with us when visiting in the village; the children deem it a special privilege to accompany us."[11]

As to how it was that the various women in charge could be so certain of their perspective and remain so largely unaware of the girls' strategies for handling their confinement, Kate Hendry explained: "My Savior comes & talks with me & sweet communion there have we. He gently leads me with his hand for this is Heaven's border land." It was not that the job was so wonderful. Tempted by the devil to leave, Hendry "soon drove his majesty back by telling him I was quite willing to do my Father's work whatever that work might be & had no desire but to do the whole will of God. Oh it is grand when we have the right weapon of defense & ... I may run with patience the race that is set before me looking onto Jesus."[12]

Sarah Hart was equally convinced of the rightness of her ways with the Aboriginal girls in her charge: "Their dispositions and habits are so very different from those of white people that we need not expect the same results from our efforts to improve them."[13] Any lack of response to her efforts reflected on the girls rather than on her: "They do not appreciate it very much, it is true, but that is nothing to us; our work is for the Master; and I hope it will meet with His approval."[14]

Emma long struggled with the meaning of the Crosby Girls' Home, over which she still exercised general oversight. Whereas she once incorporated the girls into her daily life, and vice versa, her successors sought to bend them to their will. If Emma ever realized the full extent to which her good intentions had gone awry, it went unrecorded. At least publicly she never had any moment of reckoning. She could not have done so in any case, for she herself was in good part responsible for the changes that had come about. The closest Emma ever came to being visibly ambivalent was when, in 1885, in a public letter that has not survived, she

Sarah Hart (left) at girls' home, 1890

broached the notion of giving the home "more the character of an orphanage" as opposed to that of the institution it was fast becoming. She wanted to do this because "there are many children in different parts of the country – chiefly half-caste, who are left without proper care, and might be gathered in such a refuge."[15] Among them was Minnie Offutt, granddaughter of Masset trader Martin Offutt. On her father John's death in 1887, this "little fatherless girl ... between seven and eight years of age" was, as had been her aunt Elizabeth a decade earlier, almost as a matter of course put into the home.[16]

Emma did not have only the home with which to cope. If she carried her eighth child to term, she became pregnant again in early June 1887. Her last child and first and only son, Thomas Harold Crosby, was born on March 7, 1888.

By now times had changed. Emma had, as she wrote in her last letter to her father, hoped to visit her family in Ontario in the summer of 1886. The newly completed Canadian Pacific Railway gave Emma the confidence, six months after the birth of Harold, to head east on her own with the children. The purpose of the journey was to put the two oldest, Jessie almost fourteen and Grace twelve, in school in Ontario. They would attend the Ontario Ladies College, a solidly Methodist girls' school founded in 1874 in the market town of Whitby, about thirty miles east of Toronto. Much like its Hamilton counterpart, the college offered a range of courses leading, if desired, to the Mistress of English Literature and Mistress of Liberal Arts degrees.[17] It was customary for missionary children to leave the mission site to attend school abroad or in places where family and friends were anchored. What is surprising is that Emma waited so long to move her children back home.

In Ontario in the summer of 1888 Emma drew on her public image to make the missionary case for Port Simpson. Competition was growing for financial support. The new fashion was Asia, both as a mission site and in terms of persons of Chinese and Japanese descent living in British Columbia. At the same time that the WMS sponsored Kate Hendry as first matron of the Crosby Girls' Home it sent Martha Cartmell to Japan, and her work quickly took priority among a number of branches. By the mid-1880s the WMS, if continuing to put $800 a year towards the girls' home, gave over $4,300 a year to the Japanese mission.[18] WMS priorities were made explicit in the declaration that the Crosby Girls' Home was "not our special work" as it had been formed prior to the WMS, whereas "Japan was our own daughter."[19]

Not only were Asians viewed as more exotic than Aboriginal people, but they were also perceived as more biddable and trustworthy. Indicative of this shift in focus are the first sentences of matron Agnes Knight's memoir: "There is no romance, friends, in the Indian mission work. We have not even the distance that lends enchantment to the vices ... not the same as Japan."[20] Aboriginal men and women were too persistent in retaining their ways of life and, from the Church's perspective, insisted on dying at too rapid a rate. In 1890 the General Board of Missions of the Methodist Church of Canada explained that, "in the Indian work the Church ministers to a dying race, whose poverty and helplessness, no less than its spiritual destitution," means that "there are no returns in kind for the money expended on these missions."[21]

The tide was turning, and Emma, like her husband, had to do more and more in order to maintain existing levels of support. The flourishes that found their way into her public letters were part of the rhetoric that was necessary to keep funds coming in. As early as 1884 the Nova Scotia WMS was at pains to explain that "we have not lost interest in the Crosby Girls Home," and it detailed what was expected of Emma if its support was to continue: "The vivid pictures we have had of the degradation and oppression of poor Indian girls have enlisted the heartfelt sympathy of our members."[22] In Ontario Emma worked hard to make the case for her Aboriginal girls. At the WMS's annual meeting in the fall of 1888, she "spoke for a short time on the work being done for the Indians, and the opportunities for increased helpfulness to them." When she finished answering questions, "the ladies showed their appreciation by rising."[23]

Thomas joined his family in Ontario over the winter of 1888-89. The timing was strategic. He had gotten more and more publicly involved in the growing dispute over land, so much so that a joint government commission charged Methodist missions on the Northwest Coast with fomenting Aboriginal unrest.[24] The Church's general secretary visited British Columbia in 1888 and agreed that "politically, the [government's land] policy was a blunder; on ethical grounds, it admits of no defence."[25] All the same, it was politic to lessen Thomas's identification with the Tsimshian and, perhaps for that reason, before heading east he was given charge of a new "Glad Tidings Mission."[26] The official announcement described how "Bro. Crosby will become missionary at large, and with the steam yacht, *Glad Tidings*, will visit all accessible villages around Vancouver Island and up the coast."[27] The family's home base remained Port Simpson.

The chimerical quality of the past fifteen years was laid bare. Shortly after the Crosbys' return, Rev. Alfred E. Green, having filled in at Port Simpson for several months, described in the mainstay Methodist monthly, *Missionary Outlook*, how "for several years there has been a backward movement at work in this mission." The Tsimshian were "always talking of their own great power, instead of seeking power from on high." There was disregard of the Sabbath, drinking, and, worst of all, "a taking up of the old feast again, with some of the potlatch features." Rev. Green explained how "the leading chiefs want absolute liberty to do as men please" in the interests of "the well-being of the community at large" rather than to "obey the dictates of a conscience illuminated by the Word of God."[28]

Returning to Port Simpson, the Crosbys found themselves increasingly irrelevant. Various vessels besides the *Glad Tidings* plied the coast. Mostly they served the numerous canneries that now dotted the coast, while some carried curious "excursionists." According to a resident of these years, "a great many tourists" wanted to gawk at Port Simpson.[29] For an American woman travelling up the coast by steamer in 1890, Port Simpson "was the treat the Captain had in store for us, and a real treat it was." At the HBC store Septima Collis peered at "indigenous curiosities" and then, "note-book in hand," trekked to the village.

> The population is almost entirely native, consisting of fifteen white people and nine hundred and fifty Indians; [who] seemed to be superior to any we had yet seen, their houses having neat outsides, though the interiors afford much room for improvement. It boasts of a Methodist church, an exceedingly plain structure of four walls with a cheap lot of benches, and a simple decoration of "God is love" behind the pulpit ... The totem-poles are by far the most remarkable feature of the place; they are of large size and grotesque sculpturing.

Port Simpson was, as summed up by Septima Collis, "the home of the totem-pole and of every type of Indian life and custom, civilized and savage."[30]

Port Simpson's old isolation was giving way to a relatively comfortable everyday life. Emma's personal circumstances were less confining with only Gertrude, who was about to turn ten, and Harold, who was a toddler, to mind. She played the primary role in their care and also acted as an intermediary with their father, who was often away and, when at home, could be overpowering. Emma's nephew considered Thomas to be "very domineering, austere, & often harsh in his judgments." He recalled how "as a boy I was a little bit afraid of him" and reminded Emma that "your girls own up to a little of this feeling."[31]

Newcomer women were now in sufficient supply for Emma to have diverse opportunities for sociability, alongside her continuing oversight of the Crosby Girls' Home. Robert Hall, who ran the HBC trading post, and his wife Rachel had two children, Carrie and Robert, as well as Hall's mother and one or two sisters living with them. Also sometimes present in the Hall household was the

Hudson's Bay Company head Robert Hall with his extended family

COURTESY OF HELEN AND LOUISE HAGER

family of James Lindsay Alexander, a Scots HBC officer whose first wife, Sara Ogden, was Rachel Hall's younger sister. In partnership with Hall, Alexander attempted cattle ranching on the nearby Queen Charlotte Islands before settling with his family at Port Simpson in the early 1890s. Another newcomer was Janet Lockerby, a Scots woman Emma's age. She cared for the infant child of her brother Gordon, the post's accountant, by a mixed-race wife who was said to have "left her husband and went back to her Indian relations on the reserve."[32]

The missionary contingent was also growing in numbers. Agnes Knight, eight years Emma's junior, and her much younger assistant Sarah Hart, a Nova Scotia minister's daughter who arrived in March 1888, ran the Crosby Girls' Home. Two years later, Agnes Knight married Robert Walker, who had come from Ontario the previous September to teach in the day school.[33] As with her matron predecessors, Knight was older than the man she married, in her case by eight years. Sarah Hart was promoted to matron, assisted by Kate Ross, an Englishwoman in her mid-thirties.

Also newly arrived was Maggie Hargraves, a missionary teacher from Toronto who also took on the task of improving the English of William Henry Pierce, ordained a Methodist minister in 1886. When the couple announced their engagement, Thomas was, a contemporary recalled, absolutely opposed to the unexpected turn of events: "I was a child at the time and remember hearing that Mr. Thomas Crosby, then missionary in charge, did his utmost to stop the marriage. Perhaps because William had an Indian wife."[34] In 1876 Thomas had married Pierce to a Haida woman named Emma Leusate, with Kate Dudoward as one of the witnesses.[35] Whatever happened to Emma Leusate, "the white teacher was determined and the wedding came off" in August 1890, adding to the pool of missionary wives.[36]

Another new addition was Nellie Bolton, who arrived from Ontario with her doctor husband in November 1889. After being told that the Methodist Church was not undertaking medical mission work, they came on their own initiative.[37] Nellie Bolton kept a diary in 1890 and 1891, whose entries give glimpses into the social life of what she termed "the white residents" of Port Simpson.[38] Newcomer women visited back and forth to share meals, to sew, to go for walks, or just to chat.

Emma Crosby, along with her husband, remained the principal authority figure in the Crosby Girls' Home. The matrons had charge of quarterly reports that told the women of the WMS what they wanted to hear. These reports took care to emphasize Emma's status: "When Christmas work is talked of, the first question always is, 'What shall we make for Mrs. Crosby?'"[39] Emma was there to take charge in moments of crisis, such as when a parent wanted to take away a daughter before "her time was up."[40] Parents were expected to commit in advance that they would not attempt to retrieve their children until ten years had passed.[41]

The Boltons with their daughter Isabel, Susanna Lawrence (left), and the
hospital nurse

Agnes Knight fretted about how a newly arrived "little girl, not quite six," who
was admitted to the home by her mother "in accordance with the father's dying
wish," was "only in for five years, too short a period by half." From her perspective
"in five years the hardest part of training the child will be done, and yet she will
not be old enough to have fixed principles, nor fitted for anything useful in future."[42] Another matron considered such departures "the most trying part of my
work, for sometimes, just when we see that the child is being influenced for good,
why something occurs that she must go home."[43]

The Crosby Girls' Home now competed for the Crosbys' attention with a
boys' home on which construction was begun in the summer of 1889. A handful
of boys who, as a temporary measure, had earlier been admitted into the girls'
home were transferred to the new building in October 1890, with the Boltons in
charge. The discussion now turned to a new building for the girls, who were still
housed in the Crosbys' old home. In May 1890 the WMS decided to purchase
two acres of land for that purpose, only to encounter "the opinion of some in

Thomas Crosby with boarders and day students, 1889

BC Archives, A-04182

British Columbia that a more suitable place than Port Simpson might be chosen for the new Home."[44]

Emma was determined to retain the girls' home at Port Simpson and used every means to do so. Martha Cartmell, the first WMS woman missionary to Japan until ill health forced her to transfer to Victoria to work with Chinese families there, was dispatched to Port Simpson to appraise the situation. Her selection gave the advantage to Emma as they were acquainted from their Hamilton days. As Cartmell later enthused, "I first heard of you, as the promised bride of the missionary Rev. T. Crosby whose burning words had so moved me in the Centenary [church] so long ago."[45] Martha Cartmell no sooner arrived in September 1890 than "Mrs. Crosby came in to say I would be welcome to a room in her house; and out of consideration for the ladies [at the girls' home] whose hands are so full, and who have everything stirring by 5.30 every morning, as well as for myself, I thankfully accepted."[46] Emma used her social set to put the mission's best face forward. Nellie Bolton recorded in her diary that she "Dressed & went over to the Crosby's to take tea with Miss Cartmell." The next day, "Miss Cartmell here for tea."[47] As to the school's location, the cosseted visitor could see "no argument in favor of its being taken from Port Simpson."[48] Indeed, the day before her departure, Nellie Bolton wrote: "The afternoon I went over to Mrs Crosby's & we selected things that were needed for the Home."[49]

Emma also marshalled her sister Susie in Ontario to use her influence in the WMS to push the society to choose Port Simpson. Emma's letter emphasizes how much she still considered the home to be in her charge or, as she diplomatically put it, that of her husband.

Port Simpson
Sept. 16th 1890

My dear Susie,

I was glad to get your letter – cannot reply fully just now. Some few things I want to reach you without fail before the [WMS] Board meets. Miss Cartmell is here – came last Friday morning – this is Wednesday – intends to leave by a boat that is expected today or tomorrow. She has made her home with us as there is no spare bedroom in the Home. She comes introduced by a "resolution" which she gave us to read, but just by what it was passed I have not learned – but she has such a sweet spirit that it is easy to get on with her. I had a feeling, I confess, that she was coming to criticize, but I must say she has manifested nothing of that, but has met everything in a most reasonable, conciliatory spirit. The site for the new building is one of the points she wants all possible information on & has also looked into the working of the Home – with a view to reporting, I suppose, officially. She has I believe, been very frank and so have we. I think her visit may do much good. It has been a point with her to assure us most emphatically of the confidence & sympathy of the entire Society – and expresses the great pleasure the "ladies" feel in being able now to take more responsibility in the Indian work than they have hitherto been in a position to assume. Query, what change has put them in this position? Is there anything of a reaction elsewhere? It is evident that the strong feeling that the energies of the Society have run too much in one direction is forcing recognition, and some change of policy has to be made. I hear too that a change in the presidency is more than possible. Probably you know of that. We thought it only right to acknowledge that we had felt there was a want of interest in the Indian work, and I gave a little of my experience to show how coolly the President could ignore the whole work, and had done so, but at the same time I assured Miss C. that as far as [WMS Recording Secretary] Mrs. Strachan was concerned, while I thought I had missed of late the sympathy that there used to be in her letters, yet that she had always been frank & straight-forward, and business-like & we had no fault to find there. Then we talked over our relation to the Home, and Miss C. says she sees how Thomas must remain connected with it, for we had told her that we had felt that the Ladies would rather have it quite out of our hands – and Miss [Kate] Ross, without saying so, acted as though we had nothing to do with it. Miss R. has not a happy manner – perhaps that partly accounts for it. Miss [Sarah] Hart thinks Thomas should in no wise give it up, and at present I do not see how it can be. But considering everything, we feel that there must be an expression on the part of the ladies & a clear understanding as to our, or rather, Thomas' relation to the Home, and that it ought to come before the Board. Now I want you to be prepared for it. Miss Hart has been appointed Treasurer – that is all right – let her hold the funds & keep the accounts & whatever may be sent directly to us from private subscribers we can hand over to her. And as to internal arrangements the Ladies in charge can be guided by the wishes of the Society, but in dealing with the parents & friends of the children, and as general advisor & referee at present Thomas ought to keep the position he has held. Miss Ross has not got on very smoothly – perhaps mostly from want of experience – and Miss C. seems to comprehend the situation and has given good advice, so that I hope things will improve. No one seems to know much about Miss Ross – she is active and pushing I think, and when she understands things may do very well – but she was inclined to find fault &c. till it was very trying for Miss Hart. Of course these personal matters are for yourself only. Miss C. is certainly very nice, and has a good deal of tact, and a great deal of patience. The weather has been mostly very stormy since she came, so we have not been out much, but her visit has been really very pleasant to us. I invited Dr. & Mrs. Bolton and the ladies from the Home for tea one evening so that we might all be together. I have been taking the day school in the mornings for some time. Miss Hart takes it in the afternoon. The building such as Miss C. has in her mind will cost much more than we estimated, but if the Society are inclined to work vigorously why all the better.

One evening last week we had the ladies from the Fort to spend an evening, including Mrs. Hall senior, the two daughters & Carrie – Mrs. Hall junior stayed home with the children. Everyone was very pleasant, and we had a nice evening. I did my best at the tea. The Missionaries were all invited too, so we had quite a gathering. I suppose the children are settled now at Whitby. I am so glad they keep well. Write freely about them. As to there being any preference between Whitby & St. Thomas I fancy there is not much – then if they were at the latter place it would seem to me they were among strangers.

Gertie & Harold had each a little sick turn week before last – but are quite well now. I have been very well lately. I am so sorry Eliza keeps poorly. How are you yourself?

Love from all to all, yours as ever,
Emma

Thomas is intending to go to Victoria right away. I do wish there was a teacher here – my own work is getting quite behind. If Eliza is a [WMS] delegate let her know the situation. Do so any way when you have a chance. Be moderate, I know you will.

On Thomas's September 1890 trip to Victoria, which Emma mentioned in her letter to her sister, she and the children went along on the *Glad Tidings* as far as Bella Bella. There they stayed with the local missionary until picked up by Thomas on the return trip north. The family made a stop at Port Essington to give the missionary there a furlough.

Emma returned home to another round of letter writing. As well as her public letters to the WMS, she wrote more informally to supporters. Her letter of thanks to the "mission band" in Barrie, Ontario, for clothing was printed for general circulation. The newsy letter, which points up Emma's good intentions towards the Aboriginal families that gave legitimacy to the mission, is likely indicative of the many letters she wrote that have not survived.

Port Simpson[50]
November 26, 1890

[To Mission Band,
Barrie Ontario]
Dear ––– ,

Your letter and parcel makes me hasten, for they must be acknowledged at once. The things will come in very useful – the aprons and neckties and handkerchiefs – and please give our best thanks to all who helped to make and send them. There are so many of them, and some of our little girls are quite too small for the aprons, so I feel almost like taking some of them to give to the village children, which I suppose would not be against the wishes of the ladies if they know just all the circumstances. There are so many children in the village, and we have very little for them. We have to prepare for nearly two hundred. However, I am not sure that we shall have a tree for them this year, and we will consult together and try to make the very best use possible of the Barrie gifts. I will ask Miss Hart to mention this in her quarterly letter, which should reach every Auxiliary, and the OUTLOOK may possibly hear from Port Simpson soon also, as we have just formed an Auxiliary among ourselves, with Miss Hart as Secretary, and Mrs. Bolton and Miss Ross and I each with an office.[51] As yet we have only three other names, but we intend to ask the ladies at the Fort (three of them) to join us, and a few of the Indian women will probably do so also.

The Home children are all well. The boys have been placed in the new building, under the care of Dr. and Mrs. Bolton, which leaves Miss Hart's family somewhat reduced. She has, I think, fifteen girls, and there are six little boys in the other house. One of the girls, who was a long time in the Home, and afterwards lived with us about a year, is helping Mrs. Bolton, who has a babe a few weeks old. This girl is very useful. Miss Ross, who came out last summer, has taken hold of the work vigorously. We are all kept pretty busy. The Doctor finds a great deal of work in professional duties, besides the charge of the Home. Then we have been without a day-school teacher since last summer, and with so many children the school cannot be given up, so we have had to manage as best we could between us. Miss Hart taught for a time; at present I take the morning session and the Doctor the afternoon.

We had quite a live time one evening last week. The whole mission community, numbering thirty-one, including Baby Bolton and our own family, took tea with us in the Mission House. We had three tables for tea; but it was not much trouble, and the children were delighted and had a very good time, playing games, looking at pictures, etc.; and certainly every one looked as well and neat as could be, and behaved very nicely. I was very glad you saw Jessie and Grace last summer – they told me about it. Gertie and Harold are growing so fast. I was so thankful that they have all good health.

Mr. Crosby reached home two weeks ago, after a trip to Victoria, taking in the missions by the way. He finds plenty to do at home. There is a large number of people here, and will not likely be away much during the winter. The want of a teacher makes it more difficult for him to get away. The services lately have been full of interest, and many of the people seem much in earnest. They are improving very much in their homes and living. In sight of our windows is a very pretty two-story house a young Indian has built lately, and into which he has removed his family. It would be a nice little house in the street of any town of white people. You pray for us, I know; do not cease to do so. I find a book, also, from some one in Barrie – thanks to the giver. Mr. Crosby joins me in kindest love and prayer that you may be comforted and borne up day by day.

Emma Crosby

At its annual meeting in 1890 the WMS voted to erect a new girls' home at Port Simpson "under the entire control of our Society."[52] The design of the two-story structure by a Victoria architect and its economy of construction – "curtains [to] be used instead of doors" in the dormitories "to reduce expense" – makes clear the full extent to which the care of Aboriginal girls had become a professional undertaking.[53] It was no longer the personal initiative of a missionary wife seeking, directly or indirectly, to protect girls by taking them into her home.

Now, the WMS decreed, "children be not allowed to return to their homes during the summer school vacation."[54] Two years later, in 1893, the federal government undertook to support the "Crosby Home for Aboriginal Girls" as an Indian residential school at its standard annual rate of sixty dollars per year per child.[55] The shift from care to confinement to incarceration was complete. The penitentiary nature of the Home reflected the conditions of industrial and residential schools for Aboriginal children.[56]

Emma still had an important role to play. It was taken for granted that she would fill in at the home and also in the mission whenever need arose. The teacher of the "village school," which enrolled a good hundred Tsimshian children, left in the spring of 1890 when Emma's youngest child was just over two years old. In September, Emma took "the school for an hour and a half" every morning, the matron doing the same in the afternoon.[57] A contemporary recalled how Emma would also take the Sunday school for "all the white children" for two months each summer to relieve the regular teacher: "She was such a dear little thing, I remember her well."[58] Emma filled in during emergencies in the girls' home, such as a bout of whooping cough in 1891: "Mrs. Crosby stayed with the sick ones while I took those who were able out for a short walk." The next day, "Mrs. Crosby came in and stayed quite a time" to give the matron a rest. After one of the girls died, it was Emma who was left to deal with a "room ... full of Indians." Sarah Hart explained how Emma "came in shortly after the mother did," whereupon "we talked to the mother, but of course she feels terribly, and said some very hard things."[59] At the same time, Emma's responsibilities were somewhat eased by the return to Port Simpson of her two eldest daughters, Jessie and Grace, from Ontario.

Port Simpson
Aug 19 – 91

My dear Susie

I did think that this mail would have brought a letter from you, but I suppose you find enough to do. I hear from some letters to the children that you have quite a number of visitors. I do hope you will make your stay at the Point a real rest, you need it, I am sure. Jessie and Grace take hold of the work very well, and relieve me a great deal. I think it was the right thing to bring them home. They have changed a good deal certainly, especially Grace and I think I shall understand them better now, and I hope be able to direct them more intelligently. Their journey was accomplished so safely and pleasantly. I felt not a little anxious about their coming so far, and would imagine possible mishaps, but they got on as well as anyone could. We have been trying to sew, and Grace has some underclothes made already, but I cannot do very much and it does not go very well. Then we have had a good many visitors. At present our household numbers fourteen including the girl & a washerwoman. One or two of these may be gone before night. The boat came in last evening. Miss Hart is back from Victoria and looks well. Miss Ross intends to leave the Home as soon as the ladies release her. I feel rather sorry for this – she has lots of work in her, and has done remarkably well while she has been alone the last six weeks, but she is peculiar in some ways, and she and Miss Hart cannot get on together. This is for your own information and not for talk's sake. Finding she had sent in her resignation, Thomas asked her to take the school at B. Bella, to which she agreed and intended to be there early next month, but now [WMS Corresponding Secretary] Mrs. Strachan objects to her leaving till some one else is found for her place. Work is going on at the site for the new Home. I hope they may have fine weather enough to get it up.

There are nine boys in their Home – nice boys too. We are still in suspense as to our movements. We hear of no one coming as yet, and if it drifts on till another Conference I shall not be surprised. If we knew it would be a convenience in many ways. An engineer has come up for the Glad Tidings, so she will have soon to go to Victoria for her new boiler, I suppose. Thomas has been home a good deal this summer. The people are coming & going.

We had a visit of about ten days from a Presbyterian young minister [John A. MacDonald], a friend of Dr. Bolton's who is to take up work among the Indians of the West Coast of Vancouver Is. Thomas was away part of the time & he preached & led the meeting like a Methodist. He was visiting the Missions to see their working and left us to go by canoe to Port Chester, Alaska, Mr. Duncan's new place, a distance of about sixty miles. I am glad to hear Eliza is or has been at the Point. Tell me how her health is now. You must have a delightful time. I have written to Auntie. Give my love to Sallie & Georgie and tell me about the children. How does Eliza like their new [preaching] circuit? Love to all,

Emma

Not just Emma's but also Thomas's good intentions had gone awry. Fur trader James Lindsay Alexander's stepdaughter Martha O'Neill, born in 1880, described how, during her youth, the Tsimshian accommodated themselves to the newcomers in their midst rather than being transformed by them: "They were a most intelligent and ambitious lot of natives. Already many had built new homes though they still clung to their totems and tombs on the premises ... The Tsimpseans are an itinerant tribe, always on the move and seldom at home." Her detailed description of their seasonal round was virtually identical to Emma's much earlier passing comments in her letters home and to accounts going back to the HBC's arrival in the 1830s.

> Their first outing in the year was a journey to the Naas River in March to engage in the Oolachan fishing. The small candlefish were salted, smoked and dried and the oil extracted while the fresh fish was shipped to the markets ... The grease is a deep cream color with a strong fishy smell. This product is used in place of butter or dripping by the Indians and trading with neighboring tribes for other articles of food and clothing. This industry usually lasts a month or six weeks when Mr. Indian returns home ... until it is time for the salmon cannery season, which opens about the 5th of June. Then the canoes are put in good shape and these people are on the move once more. The men engage in fishing while the women clean and prepare the salmon for the tins.[60]

Next came a new aspect of the yearly round, one that took many of the Tsimshian even further afield in response to economic opportunity.

> At the close of the salmon run, the Indians boarded the Coast steamers for the hop-picking season at Chilliwack or across the boundary into Washington. By the time the natives return home, the hunting season was on, so they went away to the mountains or islands for bear and deer for their winter supply of meats and fats. Those that didn't hunt gathered cranberries and wild crabapples or dug their potatoes.[61]

Thomas used the Tsimshian seasonal round and preference for established ways as a means of excusing himself, alleging that their sojourns away from his ministrations brought them into contact with "demoralizing influences." In reality he had spread himself so thin over the years, with his constant travels to convert new groups and his predilection for the "big bang," which he associated with vivid preaching and revivals, that he lost his staying power. Young Martha O'Neill recalled the man during the early 1890s:

> Mr. Crosby was one of those sensational and revival preachers. During a sermon he dashed back and forth with such speed on the platform, his coat-tail flew, he pounded the desk, waved his arms, squatted and stared at his flock. Then all of a sudden shouted, "Am-sky-ka-mas-ka-shum" and everyone stood up for his blessing. He was a tall square built man, fine large blue eyes, brown curly hair and long beard. I remember the white men of the place saying the Rev. Crosby should have been a 'Bull Puncher.'[62]

Fort Simpson women at a "tea party" of their own making, c. 1890

On a Sunday about this time Thomas wrote proudly: "I preached seven times, and closed two other services. I started at 6.30 in the morning, and was through at 6.30 in the evening ... This was one of the happiest days I ever spent."[63]

Thomas's conversion policy relied as much on threats as it did on substance. Elsewhere in British Columbia, about one in ten adherents to Methodism was on trial in any given year, as opposed to being full church members; however, even into the 1890s Thomas kept a third or more of the 350 to 500 members in Port Simpson on trial, supposedly to monitor the sincerity of their conversion.[64] Such men and women became openly critical of how they "had been deprived of the sacraments of religion," saying that their children were "growing up in ignorance."[65] Part of the explanation for this state of affairs lay in Thomas's lack of follow-up, part in Tsimshian disinterest. Thomas's inability to secure Tsimshian land stripped him of much of his power and authority. He lost his utility. Numerous Tsimshian flirted with the Salvation Army, which they brought north from Victoria in a fashion reminiscent of how Methodism arrived two decades earlier. In 1895 a letter signed by a dozen Tsimshian was sent to the Methodist Church, requesting Thomas's replacement. Although some of the individuals later claimed that their signatures had been forged, the point was made.[66]

Thomas's rocky relationship with the Dudowards was emblematic of his changing stature in the community. Not long after Thomas arrived at Fort

Kate Dudoward in middle age

Simpson, he put Alfred "on trial" as a church member, along with a goodly number of other Tsimshian, and in 1880 he put him "back on trial." Unlike in earlier years, in 1881 Kate was not listed as a class leader; that is, as a person considered capable of leading one of the small groups that met regularly for prayer and, more generally, for exhorting others to conform to the Church's expectations of them. By 1889 Alfred was back as a full member and Kate as a leader, although the next year Alfred was again on trial and, a year later, in 1891, Kate was no longer a class leader. In 1892 both the Dudowards were on trial, and the next year they, the most influential family in the community, threatened to leave the

Methodists altogether. By 1894 the Dudowards had, Thomas reported, "gone to the other church," by which he meant the newly arrived Salvation Army, although local tradition suggests they simply dropped out altogether.[67] Thomas acted at his own peril, given that, as a missionary contemporary recalled, "they were a striking couple when they walked about their village, attended services in their church, or entertained in their home."[68]

The Dudowards had good reason to stand tall, for they operated the most diversified commercial venture at Port Simpson. As well as running a sealing operation, the family's sloop *Ringleader* transported furs to Victoria and picked up merchandise for trade and sale at Port Simpson. The Dudowards' ties with Victoria were strengthened by the fact that Alfred's mother continued to live there with her Scots husband Robert Lawson, a customs officer.[69] A Canadian visitor to Victoria in the late 1880s was awed by how "Mrs. Deix, who is still a woman in the prime of life, and of great energy of character ... related in fervent words her Christian experience – first in English, then, as her heart warmed, in her native tongue."[70] Martha O'Neill described Alfred in the 1890s as "a tall handsome half-breed, French and Indian," who "commanded great respect from his tribe." By this time he was "the Chief of the tribe, [and] Chief Dudoward lived at 'Eagle House' with his wife and seven children." Martha O'Neill recalled how "Eagle house was erected and donated by the tribe. It was a modern home of three stories and tower facing the sea."[71] Its impressive Victorian detail put the mission house in the shadow. Both in their person and in their possessions, the Dudowards dwarfed the Crosbys.

The Eagle House was much more than a residence. Susan Neylan reminds us that, while Tsimshian homes took on aspects of newcomers' pioneer homesteads, many of them remained spatially consistent with Tsimshian culture, including with regard to class-based and rank-based social living arrangements. This duality could be observed in the Dudowards' home, which was modelled on large multi-story Victorian homes built back east. "Taking responsibility for members of ones' community, reflecting a village's wealth, and demonstrating diligent industry were indications of a good chief, whether accomplished by Indigenous or Euro-Canadian means." Neylan points out that "the establishment of Christian missions in Tsimshian villages meant the further introduction of colonial spaces among the people, a process underway since first contact with Europeans. For First Nations, the distinction between Christian and non-Christian was sometimes made at the architectural level, but certainly never in ways as clear-cut as the missionaries viewed them."[72]

Even the mixed-race families so central to Thomas and Emma's good intentions continued to exist between worlds. Alfred and Kate Dudoward's eldest son William married Emma Brentzen of the long-standing HBC family at the end of January 1891. Nellie Bolton recorded in her diary: "In the afternoon I went over to the church to see William Dudoward & Emma Brentzen married. After went to the feast."[73] By her presence, Nellie Bolton legitimized an event that drew from Tsimshian as well as from Methodist cultures. Three months later, Emma Dudoward's brother Henry, employed at the local HBC post, married Agnes McIntosh, whose father had, like the senior Brentzen, come to British Columbia with the fur trade, in his case from Scotland, and whose mother was a Kitwanga.[74] Again, Nellie Bolton and likely Emma were in attendance: "I went to the church to see Henry Brentzen & Agnes married then Dr & I went over to House & had tea with them a very good spread."[75] The Brentzen children's lifestyles indicate the range of behaviour that was coming to characterize Port Simpson. According to a contemporary: "Henry built a fine ten roomed house on the hill overlooking the harbour. His family attended the public school and had musical training. The girls dressed well, but could not get their mother away from her handkerchief and shawl which she was accustomed to wear. She said she could not wear a 'hat' as it made her feel foolish." Henry Brentzen's sister Emma went to live with her husband William Dudoward in Eagle House, along with her parents-in-law and the other Dudoward sons and their families, which "made her an Indian of the 'Eagles.'"[76] In due course her husband, William Dudoward, became chief.[77]

The intermediate lifestyles of Port Simpson families come through in Martha O'Neill's description of a typical wedding:

> The first Indian bride I saw was dressed in a lemon colored silk dress, trimmed with royal blue ribbons. The bridal couple and party wended its way to the rifle hall, headed by the band. The hall was decorated with flags and the wedding party took their places on the dais at one end of the room. At the bride's table, was also seated the missionary and wife, the Hudsons Bay Manager and his wife and some Government officials including myself.

This was no austere Methodist happening but, rather, a community celebration: "We enjoyed a full course dinner while some 200 Indians sat at a long table on the floor of the house and were served a good venison stew, apples and hardtack. The band played during the feast and then followed the speeches, women and all spoke in their own dialect of course." Echoes, perhaps an imaginative reinterpretation, of the potlatch were present, just as they were at the Christmas feasts that Kate Hendry had described a decade or so earlier. "One old man attempted his discourse in English ... remarking about all the flea (free) clackers (crackers), flea lice (rice) ... Indians leaving a feast, always loaded up their handkerchiefs with the leftovers from the table. This was doing honor to their host as to their custom."[78]

It was not just the Tsimshian and mixed-race people who were, so far as possible, finding their own middle ways. By their actions Methodists and other

Fort Simpson, 1890
BC ARCHIVES, A-04180

newcomers also gave the lie to the promise that conversion would lead to some
kind of rough equity between themselves and Aboriginal people. The social life
that comforted Emma served to set her and other newcomer women apart within
their own enclave. More and more, and not just at the Crosby Girls' Home, separation became institutionalized. From the summer of 1891, if not earlier, Thomas Crosby held a separate Sunday afternoon "service for white people at 4
o'clock."[79]

Increasingly, Port Simpson resembled other small communities around British Columbia. Its "dirt roads and wooden sidewalks & lanterns" were commonplace across the province. The year 1892 saw the opening of a public school, among
whose twenty-some newcomer and mixed-race pupils was twelve-year-old
Gertrude Crosby, who was recalled as being at the top of the class but "delicate"
and unable to "join in our games." A fellow student described the building as
"one room with a dais at one end ... a few good sized maps, a globe and some
good blackboards." There were seven classes, which, in practice, meant that "the
primers almost knew as much as the Readers."[80] The teacher was Caroline Hall,
sister of the long-time HBC head. She had been cajoled west from Toronto,
where she had taught, by the promise of free board and room at the post.[81] Her

personal contribution was to decorate the walls with large red-print mottoes that emphasized such newcomer assumptions as "Manners Maketh Man" and "Laziness Shall Clothe the Man with Rags."[82] Serving also as a community hall, the school became yet another area of sociability that lay beyond Thomas's grasp.

Even as the school was preparing to open, the continuity provided by the Hall clan was broken with Robert's transfer to Victoria, although his sister stayed as teacher until 1897. Hall's successor, Charles Clifford, was a self-described "Irish gentleman" a couple of years younger than Thomas.[83] Lured to British Columbia by the gold rush, he eventually went to work for the HBC. While running its trading post at Hazelton at the forks of the Skeena in the 1880s, he courted and married Lucy McNeill, a dozen years Emma's junior.[84] She was descended not just from William Henry McNeill, a long-time Boston sea captain who had charge of Fort Simpson during the early 1850s, and of his chiefly Haida wife, but also of another long-time Port Simpson employee, Scots fur trader Donald Macaulay and his Tsimshian wife Margaret Snaach.[85] Her aunts and cousins made up much of the fur trade elite. Young Martha O'Neill recalled how Lucy Clifford "was nearly six feet tall, and carried herself like a queen." Her self-confidence – "one almost had to be related to Royalty to be invited to the fort while she reigned" – obviated any need to rely on the Crosbys for sociability or acceptability.[86]

All of these shifts gave growing credibility to, as one Methodist put it in 1892, "the idea that creeps about, to the effect that Domestic Missions have had their day."[87] To the extent that Aboriginal people still mattered, their circumstances were dramatized, as in a leaflet published the same year for WMS members.

> Among many tribes, particularly in British Columbia, slavery still exists, man-eating and dog-eating are still carried on, as well as witchcraft, conjuring, and heathen feasts, and Pot-Latch. Witchcraft has a strong hold on many of these people ... Who knows how many a little fevered child has been tortured to death by the hideous rattle and frenzied antics of the medicine man, who plies his vile arts as long as a blanket can be extorted from the parents ... Sometimes children have been taken by heathen parents from the mission schools and forced to go through these heathen rites.

Such sensationalism gave legitimacy to the Crosby Girls' Home's transformation from a place of protection to a place of confinement to a place of incarceration. From this perspective, the only solution lay in "boarding-schools of an industrial character," as at Port Simpson, which, the WMS noted confidently, is "now entirely under our own control."[88] Emma's good intentions were a world away.

So was Thomas's dream for the Northwest Coast. He was aging alongside the *Glad Tidings*. The vessel experienced such frequent breakdowns that it became a financial liability. Thomas turned fifty in 1890, and the years of frenetic activity began to tell on him. The glory days were over. He was no longer immune from open criticism. After a particularly laudatory article appeared in the popular Methodist publication, *Christian Guardian,* in 1893, one of the younger missionaries on the Northwest Coast dared to respond that it expressed "altogether too exalted an opinion of the work of Rev. Mr. Crosby."[89] Emma's nephew, who knew the couple well, emphasized that "Uncle Thomas was not a very <u>popular</u> man on the Coast."[90]

Most contemporaries were more circumspect about the turning of the tide than was the matron at the Crosby Girls' Home in 1895: "The work here has been hindered by the unrest and disaffection among the people ... It has affected both our Home and Church work."[91] It was not the fault of the Tsimshian but, rather, the nature of confinement that resulted in some of the most traumatic setbacks. The girls incarcerated at the home continued to die from illnesses they lacked the resources to resist. The policy of returning girls to their families when death was imminent, as with sixteen-year-old Minnie Offutt, who was ill with tuberculosis in 1894, did not keep the home from being blamed. Her reported wish, "before dying, 'to go to Heaven to be with Jesus'" may have comforted devout Methodists but it did little for the home's reputation among parents.[92] The new building could house fifty girls, although the actual number did not rise above thirty or forty, depending on how many could be cajoled to go there.[93] The problem became acute in 1895, "information having been received that on account of the inefficiency of the School in the P[ort]. S[impson]. Home parents have removed their children and sent them to the public school."[94] Particularly for families of mixed race, who were not under the control of the federal Indian Act, which prohibited children from attending public school, the decision whether to send offspring to the home or to the local school was theirs to make. And they made it.

While Emma continued to play a public role at Port Simpson, she was increasingly replaced as a missionary presence by her two oldest daughters and so could venture further afield. In May 1894 Emma travelled to Vancouver to address the annual convention of the provincial WMS. Her talk was summarized thus: "For twenty long years the struggle had been carried on in loneliness and isolation. In the early days she had been the only white woman in that part of the country, and a brief visit from Mrs. [Caroline Knott] Tate was an event never to be forgotten."[95] Emma was elected second vice-president of the provincial group. She could accept the position because Jessie and Grace Crosby relieved her at Port Simpson. A visitor "saw Bro. Crosby and his daughter visiting from house to house, among the poor and sick Indians, often where it could not be very congenial to the tests of a refined young lady to go."[96] It may be that only now was Thomas becoming aware of the toll that missionary life took on many

Young Thomas (Harold) Crosby with Isabel and Grace Bolton,
Port Simpson, c. 1896

women, reflecting to a missionary friend on "good missionary's wives who had
to leave the field because of broken down health, by been [sic] so much alone in
a lonely place where often in the absence of their husband they had to do all the
work of the mission alone."[97]

Thomas was manoeuvred out of Port Simpson in 1897. At the annual meeting of the British Columbia Methodist Conference in May, he was elected president. The honour was double-edged, recognizing his contribution to the Church
but also compelling him to leave the remote mission field that he had claimed
for himself for almost a quarter of a century. The family departed at the end of
June. A woman very familiar with Thomas's exploits considered it "a hard trial"

for them to say good-bye: "The service in the church when nearly the whole congregation pledged afresh their allegiance to Jesus Christ; the school children, most of whom Mr. Crosby had christened, gathered to say good-bye; old people who had been brought out of paganism parted with the missionaries until they would meet again in their Father's house of many mansions."[98] Thomas's successor as chairman of the Simpson district wrote in his diary three days later: "Wed. 30 [June]: Mr Crosby, wife & Harold sailed in the Glad Tidings at 8 a.m. ... Mr C. was suffering from a cold & asthma & fatigue. I am sure his heart is sad at leaving the scene of 23 years of faithful toil. The few Indians here have bidden him an affectionate 'good bye.' May God be his guide."[99]

Perhaps most difficult of all for Emma was the realization that she was leaving four of her children behind. Thomas described how, "as we came away, many of them promised to take good care of the four little graves we left in the Indian graveyard on the Island."[100] Not only that, but also, their eldest daughter Jessie stayed on to teach in the Methodist mission at Bella Bella. On the way south, the steamer stopped at every mission Thomas had established along the coast to enable them to engage in farewell "fellowship" and visits to "happy Christian homes."[101] Response was muted. There was no great outpouring of sadness. The Methodist press did not even acknowledge the trip, much less use the opportunity to praise the Crosbys. The WMS, be it the meeting minutes or publications, was silent.

The Crosbys' departure signalled the end of an era. Thomas had cobbled together a vast fiefdom at the expense of Emma and his family, never mind the Tsimshian. He claimed as accomplishments on the Northwest Coast the girls' and boys' homes, three hospitals, the mission steamer *Glad Tidings*, thirty churches or places for preaching, and about 1,500 church members, including 400 at Port Simpson itself. No one else was capable of taking over from Thomas, nor did the Methodist Church want anyone to do so. On his departure the territory he had colonized for the Methodists was divided for mission purposes into four parts – Port Simpson, including the Queen Charlotte Islands; the Upper and Lower Skeena; the Nass missions; and Bella Bella, extending south around Vancouver Island. In a bow to Thomas's role he was made chairman of the Bella Bella district and was to be stationed at Nanaimo, where the family lived their first two years after leaving the Northwest Coast.

Emma's voice was not wholly lost in this transition. Thomas, as president of the conference, presided over the meeting of the British Columbia Branch of the Woman's Missionary Society in May 1897. Emma gave the report on the Crosby Girls' Home, illustrating it with "specimens of needlework (which were much admired) and letters from the Indian children at Fort Simpson." Her report was so interesting that she was "requested to embody the facts in leaflet

form and place them at the disposal of the Literary Committees."[102] The national WMS had for some time been publishing pamphlets of eight or so pages
on aspects of missionary activity, which were intended for wide distribution
among women belonging to local WMS groups across Canada. It was to this
series that Emma was invited to contribute. Even as the leaflet was being printed,
Emma was honoured at the annual national WMS meeting in Kingston, Ontario, with a motion that she be "given all the privileges extended to returned
missionaries," whereupon she "thanked the Board for including her with its missionaries."[103] *How the Gospel Came to Fort Simpson* was first advertised in the
WMS's *Monthly Letter* of December 1898.[104]

OUR WORK, No. XI
How the Gospel Came to Fort Simpson
By Mrs. Thomas Crosby, Victoria, B.C.

HEATHENISM, with its superstition and witchcraft, had a strong hold of the people.
Food and drink were thrown on the fire as an offering to the unknown divinity, while the
ascending smoke bore the prayers of the poor blind worshippers. Certain mountains, and
rocky, dangerous points, where the waves raged, and tossed the frail canoes, were looked
upon as the abode of spirits which had to be propitiated by offerings of food. Superstition
held the people as slaves, while witchcraft kept them in continual terror. A few hairs, or
scrap of a garment that had been worn next the person, falling into the hands of a witch,
might become the charm that would bring illness and death to the victim. The hideous
medicine rattle hurried many a one to death; conjuring flourished; the dog-eaters tore the
flesh from living dogs, while others made a pretence (only a pretence) of eating the flesh of
dead human bodies. When trade with the whites began to be carried on, strong drink became a new factor in the heathen orgies. At times the whole tribe would be in a drunken
debauch. To obtain liquor was sometimes difficult in face of the stringent liquor law. No
effort was too great to get it. So it came that in the latter part of the summer of 1873 a large
canoe set out from Fort Simpson for Victoria, a distance of some six hundred miles, to
procure a supply of liquor for the winter feasting. A young chief and his wife were among
the party. The mother of this chief was living in Victoria. The daughter of the most powerful chief of the nation, when she was quite a young girl, was required, according to custom,
to become the head wife of a chief (whose head wife had recently died), an old decrepit
man, with several other wives of lower rank. This was so repulsive to her that she ran away
and became the wife of a white man. After various vicissitudes she was settled in Victoria,
and being of strong personality and kindly spirit, was a woman of influence.

A few earnest Christians of Victoria, among them Mrs. A.E. Russ and the now sainted
"Father" [William] McKay, touched by the destitution of the Indians who found their way
from various places to the city, many of them for immoral purposes, hired a room that had

been used as a barroom, and began an Indian Sunday School and gathered the poor people in to hear the story of the cross. Soon a revival followed. Mr. Crosby and Mr. Tate visited Victoria occasionally and helped on this work as they had opportunity. One after another was converted, and soon the Tsimshean chieftess, "Mrs. Deaks," as she was called (Deeks being her Indian name), came to the meeting, was amazed and touched, and was soon rejoicing in the Saviour. Now her heart went out to her friends in the north, and she prayed earnestly that in some way they might be brought to the light. Just at this time her son and his wife arrived by canoe in quest of liquor. She induced them to attend the services, and soon they were both converted. Her brother, also a chief, at Fort Simpson, for whom she had prayed most earnestly, came down by steamer, impressed that he must go to see his sister; and he, too, was converted, and now there was quite a little band of Christian Indians. They wanted no liquor now. They had something so different to take to their people. Reaching home, they at once began to preach Jesus; and soon the entire people, numbering some eight hundred, agreed to send an appeal to Mr. Pollard for a missionary. Mr. Crosby, who was then in Eastern Canada, after twelve years' work among the Indians of Vancouver and the Frazer River, was appointed to Fort Simpson.

In February of 1874, Mr. Pollard visited Fort Simpson, found the young chief, Alfred Doudoward and his wife holding services, and nearly the whole village eager for the "new way." He baptized a few and encouraged them to go on, promising a missionary as soon as possible. Mr. Tate was sent as a supply for three months, until Mr. Crosby should return to the country.

In the latter part of June, Mr. Crosby arrived. The journey from Victoria was made in the Hudson's Bay Company's steamer *Otter*, a small vessel which went north as far as Wrangel in Alaska. The steamer was not to call at Fort Simpson till her return from the farther north, so the missionaries were put off in a canoe in the channel, with two or three Indians, to make their way to the village some eight or ten miles distant. It was a lovely June morning, calm and radiant on the sea and shore.

Soon we met a canoe from the village, whose occupants learning in answer to their enquiries, that the new missionaries had arrived, begged that we would delay an hour while they should return to the village with the news and make ready to receive us. So we pulled in to a lovely bit of beach on an island, and sat down to wait awhile, at our feet the blue waters, and opposite us, behind the mainland shore, the rugged line of mountains that was to grow so familiar through the years to come. Reaching the village, we found old and young on the beach to welcome us, all in their best attire and with a hearty, joyous greeting. We had at once the entrance to every house and access to every individual. A day school taught by the missionary, assisted by Chief Doudoward and his wife, who both understood English somewhat, was attended by both children and adults. Mr. Tate, who had been supplying, now went away. Our work began in earnest. I took the school while Mr. Crosby was kept busy preparing for building, giving out medicine, counselling with the people, etc.

An old Indian house of 50 x 60 feet, fitted with rude benches made of slabs and a little reading desk, served for both school and services. So many came to school that we were

= OUR WORK =

No. XI.

HOW THE GOSPEL CAME TO FORT SIMPSON.

By Mrs. Thomas Crosby, Victoria, B.C.

HEATHENISM, with its superstition and witch-craft, had a strong hold of the people. Food and drink were thrown on the fire as an offering to the unknown divinity, while the ascending smoke bore the prayers of the poor blind worshippers. Certain mountains, and rocky, dangerous points, where the waves raged, and tossed the frail canoes, were looked upon as the abode of spirits which had to be propitiated by offerings of food.

Front page of Emma's eight-page mission publication, selling for one cent
COURTESY OF HELEN AND LOUISE HAGER

obliged to take the children one half of the day and the grown-up people the other half, while three times on a Sunday and two evenings of the week the place was crowded with eager, delighted, half amazed listeners and worshippers. With a natural gift for singing they quickly learned many of our hymns, and made this place ring again. Indians of distant tribes visiting the place heard of Gospel story with astonishment; and carrying the news home, opened the way for missionary work in many places. This was only the beginning of a long conflict between Gospel truth and error and sin, yet a great change was evident. The law of God, as laid down in His Word, was acknowledged as the rule of faith and practice –

to love one another and live in peace was the first duty, and forgiveness of injuries began to take the place of ancient rivalries and jealousies.

In the old time, before the reign of English law, when one of a chief's family died one or more slaves were put to death to attend him in the spirit land, now all were recognized as brothers, and the old superstitious dread of death gave place to glad anticipation of the rest and glory of heaven.

Published by the

WOMAN'S MISSIONARY SOCIETY OF THE METHODIST CHURCH, CANADA,

Room 29, Wesley Buildings, Toronto, Ont.

Prize 1 cent each; 10 cents a dozen.

The pamphlet that Emma wrote in the WMS's "Our Work" series was intended, along with its predecessors, to spread the missionary message to women across Canada. Its appearance at the end of 1898 signalled, perhaps more than any other single event, the end of an era in Emma's life. By writing as she did, Emma, in effect, bequeathed her public self to the missionary cause. The WMS history written early in the new century evoked a heroic Emma, larger than life: "From the atmosphere of a minister's home, a graduate and teacher of Hamilton Ladies' College, Mrs. Crosby had been transferred to a heathen Indian village, and for many years was the only white woman of the place. What this life meant to Mrs. Crosby, and what her beautiful, Spirit-filled life meant to this benighted people, only the future will reveal."[105]

Having willed her public image to the church, the private Emma turned her attention to herself and to the family that had for so long existed in the shadow of the missionary enterprise. She had left four of her children at Port Simpson – Mary Emma Jane at one month, Ida and Mabel Caroline each not yet two years old, and Annie Winifred just after her third birthday. To the extent that she was comforted, it was by the news from time to time that "a new fence around the grave plot" was in the offing or that "the graves were well kept."[106] Emma still had four other children in need of her care. In early 1898 her eldest daughter Jessie married a Vancouver lawyer, but as so often happened, pleasure was soon followed by anxiety.

A year later, just as the Crosbys' youngest daughter Gertrude was getting ready to take her high school examinations, hoping to become a teacher, she took ill. Shortly thereafter, the family moved from Nanaimo to Sardis in Thomas's old Fraser Valley stomping grounds, and Gertrude was diagnosed with tuberculosis. Thomas described in a letter to a friend how Emma was again put to the test: "Mrs. C. has been kept up and sustained wonderful for the last two months. She was by the dear child night and day for our dear one suffered so much and only at times could she talk and sink & pray so her mother wanted to be with her when

Emma Crosby in middle age
COURTESY OF HELEN AND LOUISE HAGER

ever those bright moments would come to her."[107] Gertrude died on August 23, 1901, aged twenty-one.[108] A few years later the Crosbys' son Harold headed off to the University of Toronto to study electrical engineering.

As for Emma's husband, Thomas did not know how to stop. He may have been reacting against what historian David Marshall has described as a general sense of disenchantment towards the missionary enterprise amidst growing secularization.[109] Thomas berated the Methodist Church in British Columbia, insisting that it "let us stand by the old doctrines and stand by the old ship."[110] At the turn of the twentieth century the Methodist press described how "his spontaneous shouts of 'Amen' and 'Hallelujah' remind his younger brethren of that earlier type of Methodism."[111] In 1906 Thomas was honoured with a doctor of divinity degree from Victoria College, Toronto, and, while there on missionary work, his health collapsed.[112] He rallied to return to British Columbia and in the

Thomas Crosby posed with Sudalth (also known as Victoria Young) in Tsimshian regalia, c. 1876. His regalia ended up, minus the headdress, in the collection of the Canadian Museum of Civilization.

BC ARCHIVES, G-07293

fall of 1907 was given a church pension. The Crosbys retired to the Kitsilano area of Vancouver at 2535 West Second Avenue.[113] His conversion efforts took the form of writing. Almost certainly with Emma's assistance, Thomas published his first volume of missionary reminiscences, *Among the An-ko-me-nums of the Pacific Coast,* about the pre-Fort Simpson years. Perhaps to raise money he sold what historian Douglas Cole has described as "a large collection" of Aboriginal art to a collector who was about to create the Museum of the American Indian in New York City.[114] Six years later a new Methodist mission steamer was named the *Thomas Crosby* in his honour.

2535 Second Ave West[115]
Vancouver Oct. 11th/13

Rev. W.L. Hall
   Revelstoke

Dear M[r] Hall

Thank you very much for your kind message of sympathy. When I read it to M[r] Crosby he responded so brightly and expressed his gratitude. Indeed all through his long illness the kindness and sympathy of his friends and especially of his brethren in the ministry have been a very great comfort to him.

He still continues very feeble, though he has recovered to some slight extent from the bad attack of nearly four weeks ago.

It is good to know that many are praying for him, and to feel sure that in three days and nights of weariness, and sometimes distress, the loving care of our Father is always about him.

Thanking you again and with kindest regards to yourself and M[rx] Hall,

Believe me
Yours very sincerely
Emma Crosby

Emma's ministrations were critical during her husband's long illness, but even she could not keep him alive indefinitely. His second volume of memoirs, *Up and Down the North Pacific Coast by Canoe and Mission Ship*, was still in the editorial stage when he died on January 13, 1914.[116] A Vancouver newspaper described him as "typifying the great missionary zeal of the Church in the nineteenth century."[117] Thomas Crosby had become a historical anomaly in his own lifetime.

Widowed in her mid-sixties, Emma continued to make her life in Kitsilano with her unmarried daughter Grace. Harold and his family lived just a block away, and across the street was the Kitsilano Methodist Church.[118] Emma was regularly in attendance and explained how "I do not hear very well much but what I do hear is very sweet."[119] According to Harold's daughter Helen, born in 1917, her grandmother was "a great believer." Helen recalled how "we had certain things we did on Sunday, I had a doll I played with only on Sunday." Her grandmother "would come over for a Sunday night dinner and at Christmas." As a young child, Helen was allowed to visit Emma on her own.

I would usually go by myself. As a little girl I was allowed to walk to grandma's on my own. On a certain day she'd make gingersnaps. Oh, I just loved her to pieces, she was so good to me as a little girl. I could have any number of gingersnaps she made. I would help her make the gingersnaps. We would eat them in the kitchen. I could hardly wait to get them out of the oven.[120]

Perhaps it was only now that Emma Crosby had the leisure to do as she would with her family. At some point she, together with her older sister Eliza Browne and their daughters, travelled to Port Simpson and the girls' home, where they visited the four lonely graves.[121]

Emma's social life came to centre on simple pleasures, as she explained in letters to her daughters that focused mostly on routine private matters: "We ran down town yesterday morning. I had promised Jessie to have my hair fixed and I also indulged in a pair of new shoes, also in Spencer's [Department Store] Roof Garden we had each an ice cream soda, so you can see we are having quite a gay time."[122] Five years later, when Emma was seventy-five years old, she wrote:

> Grace and I made a trip downtown a few days ago, the first time I had been down for months. We took our lunch at the H[udson's].B[ay]. and then went to shop. What I wanted particularly was a nice pair of light shoes, which we found, and looked for some other things which we did not find. However, it was quite a little adventure for me, and I was very glad to find that though we walked about quite a bit I was no worse for it, only rather tired for a day or two.[123]

On the union between the Methodist, Presbyterian, and Congregational denominations in 1925, the church Emma attended across the street from where she lived was renamed Crosby United Church in honour of her and her husband.

Emma came to live more and more within the circle of her family. As she confided to her eldest daughter Jessie, her thoughts drifted back to her children's younger years and to her life at Port Simpson.

> The older I get the more vivid seems to be my recollection of the old times, and the more precious. The years up north with the little ones about me. There were five of you at one time. Then change came ... Nothing can deprive me of that while memory lasts ... "Surely goodness and mercy" have followed us all our days. I am an old woman now, and I am often in doubt and perplexity, but surely I may trust my Guide to lead me safely home. I usually wake very early in the morning, and it is then particularly that I lie thinking and praying for those I love.[124]

Emma wanted to keep busy. As Grace recalled, "often I did not want her to do things that she wanted to do."[125] In the summer of 1926, as in previous years, the seventy-seven-year-old Emma looked forward to the two of them getting away from Vancouver for a holiday: "If we can get suitable accommodation we may go to Sidney Van. Is. – not to the sanitarium but to a boarding house near by."[126] While there Emma went swimming, got a cramp in her leg, climbed the stairs back to their room, and fainted away into death, possibly from a blood clot. Emma Douse Crosby died on August 11, 1926, at Sidney on Vancouver Island.

9

Repatriation

Emma Crosby's granddaughter, Helen Hager, and her great-granddaughter, Louise Hager, engaged in a true act of repatriation in placing her private letters in the public domain and encouraging their publication. Emma's letters reclaim an important legacy for the Crosby family, for other missionary wives, and for the Tsimshian people. The letters allow for the building of a bridge across time.

Emma's letters give us a glimpse into the personal records of this wife, teacher, mother, friend, and missionary. Helen and Louise Hager were aware that these letters are unique. As Louise said, "these letters are not only part of my family's heritage, they are part of our provincial history; they are part of a history here in Canada." She explained how "the collection of letters has always been kept in back rooms and always in the back of my mind." Louise and her mother Helen made the decision that the letters should be shared so that others might see the gendered and domestic perspectives of missionary life. Helen knew the time was right to have a balanced view of the missionary endeavour: "The analysis twenty years ago would have been so black and white. Now we can look at them in the context of the time."[1]

The letters give Emma Crosby a voice that has for too long been subsumed within that of her husband. Helen and Louise Hager shared with us what they learned growing up as descendants of the Crosbys. As Louise explained: "I always thought that she did more than he did. She was 'the strength behind the throne.' He couldn't have done what he did if not for her. He had the name, but she was on the home front. So he had something to come back to. There wasn't anything she couldn't do." When Helen Hager talked about her grandmother's early history and her years at Fort Simpson, this was not based on what Emma had told her but, rather, on the stories that had come down through the family. "She didn't talk much about those early days," Helen said of her grandmother, "she was a quiet kind of person." But Emma's contribution was well known within the Crosby family. As Helen observed: "I often wondered how she ever survived up north. She was such a gentle, kind type of person. He'd go off for days on end and she'd be left all alone among the Indians."[2]

Thomas Crosby's adoration of his own exploits inevitably put Emma in the shadows, even though she was integral to the mission. And, indeed, many in the Crosby family besides Helen and Louise saw Emma as pivotal to the work of the mission. At the time of Thomas's death, Emma's nephew reminded her:

> Aunt, you truly helped, so did your daughters, he, my Uncle Thomas, accepted this as a tribute to a cause, not as a help to him ... [He] had one purpose & never ceased in all his long life to pursue it & keep it always in front of him. This was hard on you sometimes ... The last time I saw Uncle Thomas, he said to me, "I could never have got on without Emma."[3]

We each bring our own inheritances and insights to Emma Crosby's letters. In taking up the invitation to publish her correspondence we draw on our respective backgrounds as an Anishinaabe woman concerned with Aboriginal responses to contact and a historian of British Columbia seeking to broaden approaches to the past. We are joined by our interest in better understanding the missionary phenomenon.

Historical writing has tended to construct two sides to missionary work. The first side is that of the male missionary, which, to a considerable extent, still structures our thinking about missionary activity. The mirror image is Aboriginal peoples as objects of conversion, brought to "salvation" by the work of these missionary men. The reasons are fairly straightforward. First-hand accounts were almost all written by missionary men. Their reports to their home churches and other organizations that supported them financially perforce emphasized all they had achieved in the missionary spirit and the vast amount of work that remained with regard to searching for new converts. In creating a space for Emma within the missionary discourse, we situate her within a framework that attempts to understand gender roles and race relations at a time of increasingly complex encounters between Aboriginal peoples and newcomers.

Just as Helen and Louise Hager have read and re-read these letters to better understand their family legacy, so we have read Emma's letters through our different lenses, bringing our own insights and inheritances to understanding the missionary enterprise. As scholars we view Emma's narrative within the larger story of women's participation in mission work. "Women's experiences in and with the missions," Mary Taylor Huber and Nancy Lutkehaus explain in *Gendered Missions*, "was so often officially unrecognized and unrecorded."[4] The endeavours of missionary wives tended to be subsumed within their husbands' chronicles.

In his memoir, *Up and Down the North Pacific Coast,* Thomas Crosby did acknowledge Emma as an important, albeit subsidiary, part of mission work. Other accounts, such as Clarence Bolt's *Thomas Crosby and the Tsimshian: Small Shoes for Feet Too Large,* have been less inclusive. Valorizing Thomas's exploits, Bolt depicts Emma as, if anything, a hindrance: "It is particularly significant that [in Thomas's letters] Emma Crosby was either 'sick,' 'worn out,' or doing 'badly' for most of her years at Port Simpson ... She was always 'in bed,' and this fact, combined with the lack of reference to a specific disease, seems to point to chronic depression."[5] Emma's eight pregnancies, termed in the language of the day "sicknesses," do not count because they are not identified as men's work. Bolt's characterization negates the obligation of missionary wives to bear and raise children and also to maintain their households alongside their other responsibilities. As Hilary Carey reminds us, "however important or whole-hearted their involvement, missionary wives were never given official recognition, funding or thanks for their contribution."[6]

Motherhood had many tragic implications for missionary wives. They railed against death during difficult births, suffered at the loss of their children from sickness and disease, faced separation from their young whom they sent away to be shielded from their surroundings, and cared for their children in poor living conditions. As Dana Robert reminds us, "although a desire for usefulness drove women into mission work, the actual conditions of missionary life quickly turned motivations for usefulness into the realities of self-sacrifice."[7] For Emma, all this was too true, as the gravestones at Port Simpson attest. Yet, Emma persevered despite the fatigue and sometimes disappointment she experienced; she remained committed to teaching at the school, organizing activities, and preparing young women who came to live in their home for domestic and Christian life.

If the presence of missionary wives was long suppressed in the mission discourse, the voices of Aboriginal peoples, so "noble, wretched, and redeemable," have, until recently, been equally silent.[8] A close reading of Emma's letters reveals the ways in which they understood their own reality, dealt with cultural intrusions, and constructed their own world. We have been particularly struck by Emma's use of language, the messages she conveys, and the images she evokes in her writing. Her words make visible the inherent contradictions and voids between her world and that of the Aboriginal peoples of Port Simpson. A "reading against the grain" attests that the Tsimshian were effective agents in shaping their world, in taking advantage of the conventions that the missionary enterprise offered and using these to claim and maintain status, land, and access to the newcomers' world. As Neylan reminds us with regard to the Tsimshian, "the identities they assumed as part of this process illuminate the extent to which conversion entailed negotiation."[9] The Tsimshian could judge at close range the value of this encroaching group of missionaries and choose from what they had to offer.

Retrieving the Aboriginal perspective also involves "reading the unwritten." Emma knew precisely what she could reveal about the nature of her involvement in the missionary enterprise. Particularly in her public correspondence, she situated herself in her husband Thomas's shadow, assuming a role that centred on "women's work," in particular the care of Aboriginal girls. The times in which she lived determined that this would be so. Many of the images she evoked of the Tsimshian are linked to stereotypes prevalent in writings concerning Aboriginal peoples. Like most newcomers of the time, Emma associated Aboriginal women with "savagery" and "sexuality." While her attitudes and assumptions towards the Tsimshian are revealed in what she put on paper, what is absent has just as much to offer us in our attempt to understand Tsimshian society. Emma's correspondence, though conforming to colonial rhetoric, permits new insights into the roles of Aboriginal people and the construction of the mission. Through her letters we are also introduced to her husband's conduits into the mission field. As we discovered in following up on the leads that Emma's letters provide, Aboriginal and Aboriginal mixed-race men and women were important participants in the missionary enterprise.

Among Tsimshian voices in the present day is that of Caroline Dudoward, who remains very conscious of the link that bound her family to the Crosbys. It was Caroline who so forcefully reminded us that the Crosbys have not entirely left Port Simpson. The church built at the beginning of Thomas's tenure burned down in 1932, the residential schools originating in Emma's good intentions closed in 1948, but tangible links remain. In what is another act of repatriation, Caroline tracked down the graves of the Crosby children. Amidst the overgrown tumble she located their headstones, as impressive as they must have been on being erected by their bereaved parents. We glimpse Ida Polly aged one and a half, Annie Winifred aged three, Mabel Caroline aged two, and Emma Jane Crosby aged one month, all of whom died at Port Simpson between 1879 and 1886. The Crosby family still resides at Port Simpson.

Caroline's family history, passed down through the generations, confirms that her great-great-grandparents Kate and Alfred Dudoward were in good part responsible for the rich harvest of souls at the Methodist mission. Not only did they invite the Crosbys onto their territory but they also succored them upon their arrival. As Alfred ascended to leadership among the Tsimshian, his relationship with Methodism deteriorated. Kate remained closer to it, even though she, like Alfred, had doubts. Both remained their own persons all their lives, secure in an identity that went beyond denominational affiliation. The family's power and prestige is acknowledged by Caroline: "They lived between two worlds as man and wife, interpreters, translators, entrepreneurs, teachers, and hereditary leaders who promoted Tsimshian interests through literacy and the written word of 'God' to guide and sustain our daily lives." Overall, as Caroline

Headstones of Ida, Mabel,
and Annie Crosby in the
Port Simpson cemetery

PHOTOGRAPHED BY CAROLINE
DUDOWARD IN 2002

reminds us: "Too many voices have been silenced. The voices of Aboriginal people need to be heard."[10]

Caroline Dudoward not only repatriated the images of the Crosby children's graves, she scoured the family's photo collection for appropriate images to accompany Emma's letters. It is through her generosity that Emma's letters are accompanied by images of Kate and Alfred Dudoward, of members of the Dudoward family, and of the Eagle House. The mutual exchange that Emma initiated with the Tsimshian women and girls of Port Simpson is alive and well in the present day.

It was the Tsimshian people, notably Caroline's great-great-great grandmother Diex, who invited the Crosbys to Fort Simpson. The reason for this may be found in their desire for newcomers' knowledge, which would enable them to compete in changing times. In many important ways Thomas responded to their desires rather than the other way round.[11] In taking up the invitation, Thomas had no second thoughts about the possible consequences for a wife or children. He was already in full flight at the time he and Emma married. Thomas did what he liked and liked what he did, even though he may have done it for the Lord. As historian Terrance Craig explains, missionary men were "in the habit of self-description and self-justification ... They knew they were interesting people, engaged in often fascinating and challenging work."[12] One story tells of Thomas being asked to tell "the most thrilling incident of his career," whereupon he recalled "over a dozen incidents of a character such as never fall to the lot of the average man."[13]

The Tsimshian people also invited the Crosbys to leave Port Simpson once the missionary couple had lost their utility. The breadth of Thomas's adventures came at the sacrifice of depth. The centrepiece of the mission unravelled as he cruised the coast, looking for yet another place at which to make a splash. Emma provided a stability that, at least for a time, masked her husband's inability to accommodate to the mundane. The Tsimshian realized much sooner than did the Crosbys that their good intentions had gone awry. For all of Thomas's genuinely decent desire to do so, he could not save Tsimshian land. For all of Emma's good intentions, she put the interests of her own children above those of the girls she took into her home. The eventual result of her good intentions was residential schooling, which was as disastrous to the Tsimshian as it was to Aboriginal peoples across Canada.

Emma played her role in the missionary enterprise willingly and knowingly. Just as much as was her husband, she was driven by two imperatives that today we find unacceptable but that at that time were simply assumed. Virtually everyone accepted as a given the superiority of their religion and the superiority of their skin colour. This potent combination was at the heart of the missionary phenomenon. The notion of a hierarchy of skin colour, drawn from the ideas of

Charles Darwin and others, reflected biblical images of light and dark, which added to the seeming potency of Christianity. The colonization of indigenous peoples around the world only seemed to confirm the superiority that persons of the dominant societies already took for granted. In keeping with this theme, we have been careful to think of Aboriginal people who engaged in Christianity as something other than converts. Despite the term's historical currency in writing on missionary work in Canada, we believe it overstates the case.

Women and men like Emma and Thomas Crosby felt compelled to do God's work whatever the personal cost. Theirs was a delicate balance. Not to bring indigenous peoples to Christianity was to condemn them to everlasting hell. The conviction held by many, including one matron at the Crosby Girls' Home, was that Aboriginal peoples were doomed to disappear. This belief gave an urgency to their mission: "These people are dying. In a few years, comparatively speaking, there will be few Indians, and are we Canadians going to let these people die in heathen darkness ... Our time to help is fast passing from us."[14] Missionaries' pale skin tones coloured their obligation to convert those whom they believed could not help themselves. Dennis Jennings, a teacher at the Port Simpson day school, expressed this sentiment in reference to what he termed Aboriginal peoples' "great depths of sin and iniquity": "What other could be expected of savages!"[15]

Yet differences in pigment – "race" as it is usually termed – could not be interpreted by missionaries as so great that the objects of their concern were without agency. Methodists in particular believed that each person had to have their own private conversion experience, which heightened the tension the Crosbys felt towards the men and women whom they considered to be in need of their ministrations. One means of reconciling the irreconcilable was to refer, in describing Aboriginal people, to their "simplicity" and to the child-like quality of their faith, hence Emma's references to "these poor, simple people" and "these simple ignorant people."[16] To use such language very conveniently strengthened the missionaries' appeal for continued financial support in their endeavour to ensure that Aboriginal peoples did not risk returning to their former, or true, selves. As Jennings, a Northwest Coast missionary and Methodist minister, intoned: "peculiar tact is required to manage them, their prejudices and superstitions being welded into their very nature."[17] The inevitable consequence of all this was that Thomas ended up having far too many of those who took up Methodism on trial. After a decade and more of tutelage, the growing self-confidence of the Tsimshian should have been commended but, instead, it was routinely condemned. The "children" that Aboriginal people were perceived to be could never be permitted to grow up for that would have been to accept them as racial equals.

The potency of race helps to explain Emma's attitude towards the Aboriginal girls she took into her home. Her commitment, grounded in Christian belief, to protect them from the dangers she saw impinging upon them provided her with the validation she needed as a missionary wife. It was when their presence began to have some bearing on the lives of her own, paler-skinned daughters that Emma modified her position. In July 1881 she explained how "as our own family increased we felt that our house was not the place for these girls." Seeking to lessen the influence these girls would have on her offspring, Emma gave priority to the latter, separating them physically from the Aboriginal girls in the house. She led the move to secure separate quarters for the Aboriginal girls in the Crosby home and then to secure for them their own home, which continued to be identified with the Crosby name well into the twentieth century, long after protection had become confinement and then incarceration. Her good intentions went dreadfully awry.

The messages the Crosbys gave were particularly potent in reference to Aboriginal mixed-race persons. In her letters Emma routinely named newcomer missionaries but glossed over those who were of Aboriginal descent. William Henry Pierce, George and Marie Edgar, and the Dudowards flitted through her life and letters. Alfred and Kate Dudoward in particular shadowed Emma's life at Fort Simpson. It was at their instigation that she and Thomas went there in the first place, yet, at least to her mother – perhaps as part of her strategy to shield her from the realities of her life at Fort Simpson – Emma was unable to acknowledge their influence. By rarely naming them she diminished their power both on paper and perhaps also in her own mind.

For the most part these intermediaries were used as needed and then cast aside. Men like George Edgar and William Henry Pierce were incredibly committed to Methodism, especially given the treatment they received. From Thomas's perspective, they were his creatures, to be used and named however best suited his own purposes. When he needed Aboriginal converts, Aboriginal they became; when he needed a white man, they became white. George Edgar, whom Thomas once tried to pass off as white to appease the Haida, was reduced by a fellow missionary to "a native teacher, George Edgar, a Tsimshean."[18] William Henry Pierce became, in Thomas's memoir, "our native Missionary."[19] The shifts were enormously convenient for they permitted Thomas to take full credit for having raised them up from the "savagery" into which they had supposedly been born.

Alfred and Kate Dudoward were less easily reduced to Aboriginals, for whose conversion missionaries like the Crosbys could take full credit. The alternative was to belittle their mixed race. In April 1885 Alfred was a signatory to a letter to the editor regarding a dispute with the Nass people.[20] A judicial report dismissed his intervention out of hand: "The man A. Dudoward, whose name appears on the letter of complaint, is an idle, untrustful and mischievous halfbreed, who lives with the Indians at the place."[21] The full extent to which this assessment was race-based is indicated by that fact that the Dudowards were one of the hardest working, most successful families at Port Simpson.

Race and racialization were always close at hand. The mother and child in *Peep of Day*, which Emma read to her young daughter and also likely to the Aboriginal girls in her care, could not have been whiter. Within that context, the questions posed by the young Aboriginal girls in the Crosby home were not nearly as "curious" as matron Agnes Knight made them out to be: "'Why did God make black men?' 'How did white men get their skin white?' 'I thought God didn't make Indians. He only made white people.'"[22] Emma modelled racial difference most visibly in giving priority to her own children and, as they grew, in wanting to separate them physically from the Aboriginal girls who had previously mingled with them in her home. Her strong religious commitment to the Aboriginal girls in her care did not lessen; however, by creating a separate home for them she was able to continue to be comfortable in her racial assumptions.

The Crosbys also modelled a gender hierarchy. One indication of this is Thomas's comment in 1882 with regard to the first woman he sent to a mission on her own: "Miss Lawrence left for Kit-a-maat – 150 miles away from here in canoe all alone with Indians she was two weeks on the way May God bless her, I could not get a white man to go."[23] Susanna Lawrence was better than a mixed-race person but inferior to "a white man." Thomas accepted without question the gender assumptions of the day – indeed, he took them as absolutes. His perspective on women missionaries echoed his attitude towards his own missionary wife, as is revealed in her letters. Emma was useful to the Lord's work in ways consistent with the nature of woman as Thomas saw it and as it was understood at the time. The Aboriginal girls who did housework and looked after children formed the impetus for a girls' home – an initiative absolutely at one with woman's role as domesticator par excellence. Not without reason, a little girl at the Crosby Girls' Home was absolutely convinced, so a matron reported, that Thomas was "on earth when Jesus came."[24]

The last quarter of the nineteenth century, when Emma wrote her letters, coincided with the emergence of women missionaries. The process was gradual and partial. By 1874, when Emma set her fate, change was in the air, as indicated by her letter to her mother in which she described her future self as "not exactly ... a missionary on my own responsibility."[25] Half a dozen years later the Woman's Missionary Society was formed within the Methodist Church of Canada precisely so that women could participate in the missionary phenomenon without threatening male dominance. Thereafter missionary wives and women missionaries existed side by side in the mission field. Women missionaries to Port Simpson boarded with the Crosby family until the construction of new quarters for the school. Their common religiosity and their status as the very few newcomer women at Fort Simpson also joined them to the Crosbys.

At the same time, fundamental differences divided women missionaries and missionary wives: the former were single, the latter were married. The former gave up one life for another, the latter layered one life on top of another. The former made a commitment of three or five years, the latter of a lifetime. The former received a salary, the latter had to stretch the few dollars that came her husband's way (in Emma's case through repeatedly leaning on family members). The former was assigned a specific task, which, however daunting, had its limits, the latter had, at one and the same time, no task and every task. The former had a certain status that was lauded in accounts from the mission field, the latter was almost wholly subsumed within the husband (who, given the nature of the task, had to praise himself at every opportunity).

In the event, most of the women missionaries sent to Port Simpson became missionary wives. They served out their agreed term and immediately married. The paucity of newcomer women in British Columbia provided them with opportunities that would have been denied them at home.[26] Mostly well into middle age, which helps explain their decision to become missionaries in the first place, they were often considerably older than were their husbands, who were most often neophyte missionaries or ministers who were being urged to get themselves a wife. Some of the women missionaries who served with the Crosbys simply wore themselves out and died alone.

Women missionaries' decision to wed was likely more complex than can be accounted for through social expectation, desire for companionship, or sexual satisfaction. Their status as single women residing at the bottom of the missionary hierarchy did not encourage them to remain where they were. Aware of gender expectations, they realized they could better do God's work in tandem with a male missionary than on their own. At the end of the initial time period for which they had committed themselves to stay single, three of the first female additions at Port Simpson – Caroline Knott, Kate Hendry, and Agnes Knight – each wed a man a good half dozen years her junior. They then went off to tend their own flocks. Mary Ann Green, Sarah Hart, and Margaret Hargrave also married missionaries.

The sense of obligation these women felt to marry the male missionaries in their midst did not always come to fruition, though not for lack of trying. Susanna Lawrence remained single, despite her successor Kate Hendry's manoeuvring on her behalf. In 1883 Susanna Lawrence returned to Port Simpson from her missionary post at Kitimaat in order to assist Kate Hendry in the girls' home as well as to replace as teacher one of the missionaries who had come west with her – Dennis Jennings, then in his mid-forties.[27] The two women took the Aboriginal girls camping, during which they exchanged confidences as they "knelt on a stone beside a log & had a gracious season of sweet intercourse with Heaven, oh the delights of such an hour." Among the topics of conversation were, so Kate Hendry reported, the possibility of Jennings proposing to her compatriot: "I expect Sister L will be with me all winter unless Bro Jennings make her his wife."[28] As it happened, he settled on someone else, and Susanna Lawrence went on to a long career as a missionary in British Columbia.

Intimacy grounded in religious fervor had its limits. For all of his accomplishments on behalf of Methodism, William Henry Pierce transgressed racial boundaries by daring to become intimate with Maggie Hargrave. Two female contemporaries considered it a kind of natural justice that Pierce's marriage did not work out as he had hoped. According to one of them, in conversation with anthropologist Marius Barbeau:

> She was one of these freaks from England, who thought that an ordained Indian (he was by this time ordained) was a thing much to be desired ... It was much to the surprise of many people who thought that a white person should not have married a half breed. But soon after her marriage she became an invalid and went to bed and stayed in bed for thirty years, refused to go out of bed ... Some said that she went to bed in sheer disgust after she thought the thing over.[29]

The other female contemporary was somewhat kinder in recollecting a steamer trip: "We stopped a few minutes at Kispiox Indian village and spoke to Rev. Wm. Pierce, the missionary. Mrs. Pierce, as we expected, was in bed. She had been in bed several years then ... So many remarked later how poor William got the worst of the bargain."[30]

The assumptions of the day concerning religion and race, which Emma and Thomas Crosby put in place at Port Simpson, continued long after their departure. It was during their last years there that more and more missionaries looked for a solution to the dilemma that Aboriginal people posed through persisting in being their own persons – despite their inferior skin tones – in the residential school. By 1890 Susanna Lawrence was convinced that "there seems to be only one way of saving the children, and that is to take them entirely away from the influence of their parents and the temptations around them."[31] A decade later, the school's matron wrote confidently: "Our home life is a very happy one, though the discipline is strict, and exact obedience is required of every people, irrespective of personal inclination."[32]

The Crosbys and other missionaries missed the point. Thomas accepted it as his due that "in some cases they would ask for a School, so that their children might be taught to read and write," and he did not question how "they would call each other 'School people' in preference to 'Mission people.'"[33] The Tsimshian and other Aboriginal peoples understood well the dramatic changes being thrust upon them. The power that literacy gave was not lost on them, and, if they had to obtain it through the medium of missionaries, then they believed, at least at this early point in time, that they could do so and still retain their self-respect. Thomas had a wholly different agenda, one that seemed to work for a time at Fort Simpson and then diminished in appeal, both because of the nature of the changes he demanded and because he lost interest. Not all missionaries were as determined as was Thomas to have access to greener pastures, although the character of the missionary phenomenon encouraged them in this direction.

Emma's letters emphasize the great extent to which she was privy to, and understood the implications of, each aspect of the missionary endeavour. The tradition out of which she emerged made her as zealous as was her husband. Her father got his impetus in Canada as a missionary among Aboriginal people, and she did not flinch when the opportunity came for her to follow in his footsteps with a man who, in so many ways, resembled him. After meeting Thomas, Emma never looked back. Perhaps because her decision did not meet with her family's complete approval, she did not, in her letters home, express any discontent with her circumstances; rather, she used her private correspondence to assure her parents she was doing important work.

Emma made her decision, and she accepted the consequences. It may, from her perspective, have been God's will, but it was *her* will that got her through the days and weeks and years on the Northwest Coast. In responding to the desire among so many women of her time to enter the mission field, albeit by a side door, Emma Crosby became part of a movement much bigger than any single individual or couple. As the woman behind the missionary, she was caught in a web of assumptions and obligations that would have daunted, and overcome, a lesser person. Emma Crosby comes across as a woman to be admired, regardless of the perspectives we hold today on the larger issues of Aboriginal participation in the missionary enterprise and on the missionary impulse in general.

Afterword

CAROLINE DUDOWARD

It is an honour and privilege to share a personal perspective on the Dudoward family. The Dudoward family is a chiefly and noble, high-ranking family who essentially established Methodism in Fort (Port) Simpson. My family originates from Lax Kw Alaams, which translates into "Area of Wild Roses," which is Tsimshian territory. There are two significant missionaries who travelled into Chief Legaic's traditional territory. William Duncan was the first, and Thomas Crosby the second. Each one was important in a different way to both sides of my family. Essentially, Christianity introduced a new form of power and authority in relation to status and prestige.

I am very blessed to be born in the land of plenty. The Tsimshian spiritual leadership and expertise is related to family structure and house relationships. Personally and professionally, I know where I come from and where it is that I need to go. I am very fortunate to have had the teachings of my great-grandparents Charles and Louise Dudoward. As the eldest great-granddaughter of the duo, I was privileged beyond my expectations. I am also thankful for the many elder women on both sides of my family. Each woman is/was powerful in her own right. I stem from a very rich heritage.

Life represents a complex web of relations. On the Northwest Coast, First Nations women were especially important as they were the principal caretakers of our families. During pre-contact times matrilineal societies were predominant. Chieftainship was a serious matter and was never taken lightly. Training and education was essential to any leader. Long ago, my great-great-great-great-grandparents Shas and Ballah represented the ultimate reflections of their families. Each nation was distinct on the coast, its lineage design specific. Even the character of the canoes in which they travelled was different, the range exceptional and diverse. The pride and esteem of one's family is built upon generations of oral tradition based on specific stories, songs, and dances.

The most notable woman in my family heritage since contact is my great-great-great-grandmother Deiks, who is avidly recorded in a number of different texts. Deiks was an important woman from the Gitando-Gispaklots tribe. Reverend Thomas Crosby describes her in his book *Up and Down the North Pacific Coast by Canoe and Mission Ship* as "this remarkable woman [who] was thus a princess of royal blood." As I know it, she is the daughter of great head chief Shas, from Haida Gwaii, and Ballah, who was Tsimshian. One illustration comes from her girlhood, when she lived at her uncle's house and was trained to observe the customs and manners befitting her position. As a young girl she had a slave who was never to leave her side. One day she spotted canoes in the distance bearing gifts. Deiks knew nothing about this, and she questioned her slave, who explained that she was to be wed that very day to an old decrepit chief. She was not impressed, so she fled immediately to Chief Legaic's territory to seek refuge.

This is how Deiks ended up at Fort Simpson and met Felix Dudoire. Felix was a Frenchman from St. Denis, Quebec, who was employed as labourer, tailor, and middleman by the Hudson's Bay Company. His travels took him to Fort Vancouver, on the Columbia River, as well as on journeys on the steamer named *Beaver*. He created the first sails for canoes and is last recorded in 1859. Before then Deiks and Felix had two children named Charlotte and Alfred, but Alfred was the only one to survive.

Deiks was a matrilineal leader and pioneer who adapted well to the changing times. Due to her relationship with Felix, she was the first of her kind to be dislocated and dispossessed from her motherland. The alliances created by my grandmothers continue to be undermined through colonization.

Deiks moved to Victoria with her son Alfred, who, due to his mixed ancestry, was afforded a formal education. Meanwhile, Deiks worked for a Judge Pemberton. Later Alfred moved to Metlakatla where he became William Duncan's personal servant. William Duncan, who arrived in Fort Simpson in 1857, relocated to Metlakatla in 1862 along with the Gitlan tribe. My matrilineal relations were the first of his followers who vowed to abide by the fifteen laws he created. Named David and Rebecca Auriole, they brought their three children, named Lucy, Joseph, and Caroline, with them to Metlakatla.

In 1871 Chief Legaic sent his best paddlers to Fort Victoria so that Alfred Dudoire (hereafter known as Dudoward) could be married to Mary Catharine Holmes. Mary was the daughter of Captain Holmes and Dool, whose brother was Chief Shakes, another hereditary leader among his people. Mary's mother Dool died on route to a feast, and records show that Mary arrived at St. Ann's Convent in Victoria in 1865. There Mary (hereafter known as Kate) was taught to speak, read, and write English. Kate, who, at the age of fourteen years, is known as the youngest chief of her time, returned to Fort Simpson in the late 1860s to establish a school to teach the Tsimshian European skills. The day and evening sessions, at first held in the longhouse, began with seventy-five adults and 100 children.

Described as "a woman of commanding appearance and of great force of character who exerted a powerful influence over her people," Deiks was continuously concerned about her son and the well-being of the Tsimshian. When Alfred ascended to leadership of the Gitando due to his lineage relations, Deiks ordered a *hyets* for him. The abundance of Tsimshian knowledge and wisdom is symbolized by the *hyets*, which was a copper shield depicting a thunderbird with its wings folded. There was a killer whale at the centre and, at the base, a bear holding a shield, which symbolized their wealth.

While in Victoria Deiks attended Methodist services and was baptized Elizabeth in October 1872. When her son Alfred and daughter-in-law Kate visited Victoria both found favour in Methodism. These described conversions began a rich harvest for the Methodist mission. Deiks was one of the first forty or so taking to Methodism in Fort Victoria and was the first to request missionary assistance. In February of 1874 Reverend William Pollard visited Fort Simpson and hundreds attended the services he held. Later that same year Thomas Crosby was sent to assist the Tsimshian. By then he had married Emma J. Douse, who was the daughter of Reverend John Douse and a teacher in the Wesleyan Female College in Ontario. Deiks is recorded at James Bay in Victoria in 1881 with a new husband, who was a Methodist customs officer. Elizabeth outlived three husbands and preached to her people until 1903, when she died.

Alfred and Kate Dudoward lived at Fort Simpson. Proud parents of five sons and two daughters, they lived between two worlds. Alfred became the spokesman for Tsimshian land claims. Rich oral traditions link existing nations with specific territories defined as both secular and spiritual places. For the Tsimshian the land is a source of power, prestige, wealth, and honour. The Queen disregarded our power and authority by giving us away, like children. The discourse is very real for us as Aboriginal peoples of this land. All First Nations across Canada have been marginalized. It was only in 1888 that the Sutherland Commission was appointed to inquire into the condition of First Nations on the Northwest Coast. Still, it did not recognize the broken promises and stolen dreams. First Nations continue to be treated like fourth-class citizens in our homelands. We never ceded, relinquished, or sold our land. It was stolen by the powers that be. Thanks be to the Queen?! And the injustices continue in various shapes and forms.

Power struggles between the religious denominations were evident as Crosby and Duncan competed endlessly. This rivalry resulted in divisions among the

Tsimshian. In 1887 William Duncan and 823 of 948 people at Metlakatla departed for Annette Island and created a New Metlakatla in Alaska. Those who followed included Joseph Auriole and Caroline (nee Auriole) Haldane, but my great-great-grandmother Lucy (nee Auriole) Ryan stayed at Old Metlakatla.

Without people like Alfred and Kate Dudoward and others like them, the missionaries would not have made it anywhere on the Northwest Coast. Without First Nations assistance, non-Native people would be non-existent. My great-great-grandparents were the interpreters/translators for the missionaries who first came to this bountiful coastline. They also witnessed death and destruction through foreign diseases, like smallpox, tuberculosis, and the like. A few of the Crosbys' children also died. People during this time felt these great losses beyond our wildest dreams. This transformation is recognized by the physical structure of the households themselves. Chief Sgaguade's traditional longhouse was transformed to the Victorian-designed, Dudoward Eagle House. Today, stained glass windows can be seen in the United Church at Port Simpson attesting to Alfred Dudoward bringing the Word of God to the Tsimshian.

Over time Alfred and Kate Dudoward's relationship with the Crosbys deteriorated. Kate was not paid for quite some time for teaching school. By 1880 Alfred was placed on trial and dropped from the Methodist list. A suave and handsome leader, Alfred joined the Salvation Army in 1895, which ultimately added to the religious rivalry and dynamics of competition. One of the last great hereditary leaders of his time, Alfred died at age sixty-four on December 15, 1914.

The chieftainship passed to my great grandfather Charles Henry Dudoward, the youngest of Alfred and Kate's seven children, born March 1, 1888. Charles was a multi-talented individual who could accomplish anything he set his mind to and who travelled worldwide. He was a very industrious person. He owned and operated his own businesses at Port Simpson, one of which was the Thunderbird Shoppe, as he was artistically talented as well. He married my great-grandmother Louise (nee White) when she was twenty years old and he was in his twenty-ninth year. They were a handsome couple and had three children: Audrey, James, and Beatrice. When their first grandchild, my father, was born, he was raised as their own.

Colonization and the pursuit of assimilation have been neither kind nor just to Native Canadians. They wreaked havoc throughout matrilineal societies. Paternalism is neither kind nor just, nor is the elected system of governance, in which Tsimshian are no longer validated as extended family structures but as individual families.

The repercussions can be felt today. The health of Aboriginal peoples involves a complex web of physiological, spiritual, historical, sociological, cultural, economic, and environmental factors. We must heal our nations in order to move towards a healthier co-existence. Culture among the Tsimshian involves continuous acculturation through acquiring skills, abilities, and knowledge. To exist in to-day's world we must be educated, which involves leaving our homeland and family. All this is necessary in order to survive within a complex, dynamic world.

As I assert my voice and agency, I hope to give credit to my ancestral relations. My great-great-grandparents are deserving of their rightful place in the course of history. Alfred and Kate Dudoward lived in between worlds as man and wife, interpreters, translators, entrepreneurs, teachers, and hereditary leaders who promoted our interests through literacy and the written word of God in an effort to guide and sustain our lives. We need to rejuvenate the importance of family and continue to heal our nations, one by one. No longer can we be denied our power and authority over this amazing and beautiful land we call home. Our voices need to be heard, individually and collectively. We as leaders must rise to the occasion just as our relations have done in the past. Knowledge is empowering, depending on what we do with it. May God bless all our relations and help us to become the best we can be!

Notes

INTRODUCTION

1   Letters that were wholly of a report nature were not included, as with Woman's Missionary Society (hereafter WMS), *Annual Report*, 1887, 64; and *Missionary Outlook* 10, 1 (January 1890): 13-14. Some of Emma's later letters to her children have been excerpted for relevant information. None of the reproduced letters is edited or altered in any way. Words and phrases underlined in the text were so underlined in the originals.

2   Thomas Crosby, *Up and Down the North Pacific Coast by Canoe and Mission Ship* (Toronto: Missionary Society of the Methodist Church, 1914), 29.

3   Emma Douse to her mother, Hamilton, February 18, 1874, University of British Columbia Library, Special Collections, Crosby Collection (hereafter UBCCC), as reproduced in chronological order in this volume.

4   Dana L. Robert, *American Women in Mission: A Social History of Their Thought and Practice* (Macon, GA: Mercer University Press, 1996), 3.

5   Hilary M. Carey, "Companions in the Wilderness? Missionary Wives in Colonial Australia, 1788-1900," *Journal of Religious History* 19, 2 (1995): 227-48. Carey examines the role of missionary wives who lived among the Australian Aborigines.

6   David B. Marshall, *Secularizing the Faith: Canadian Protestant Clergy and the Crisis of Belief, 1850-1940* (Toronto: University of Toronto Press, 1992), 99.

7   S. Phillips, Recording Secretary, WMS, to Emma Crosby, Toronto, February 4, 1914, UBCCC.

8   "Founders of B.C.," *Victoria Times*, April 22, 1967.

9   Clarence Bolt, *Thomas Crosby and the Tsimshian: Small Shoes for Feet Too Large* (Vancouver: UBC Press, 1992), 36. In "Creating Textual Communities: Anglican and Methodist Missionaries and Print Culture in British Columbia, 1858, 1914" (PhD diss., University of British Columbia, 2001), Gail Edwards offers a more nuanced interpretation of Crosby's missionary activity within the broader contexts of Methodist and Anglican initiatives during the same time period.

10 See Emma Crosby's letters of November 5, 1879, and July 30, 1877.

11 Robert, *American Women in Mission*, 68.

12 Letter of March 29, 1876.

13 Crosby, *Up and Down*, 85.

14 Susan Neylan, *The Heavens Are Changing: Nineteenth-Century Protestant Missions and Tsimshian Christianity* (Montreal and Kingston: McGill-Queen's University Press, 2003), 106.

15 Letter of July 28, 1881.

16 Crosby, *Up and Down*, 92-3.

17 Patricia Grimshaw, *Paths of Duty: American Missionary Wives in Nineteenth-Century Hawaii* (Honolulu: University of Hawaii Press, 1989); Robert, *American Women in Mission*; Amanda Porterfield, *Mary Lyon and the Mount Holyoke Missionaries* (New York: Oxford

University Press, 1997). An exception pointing up the difficulty of locating first-hand sources is Carey, "Companions in the Wilderness?"

18 Robert, *American Women in Mission*, xvii; also Barbara Welter, "She Hath Done What She Could: Protestant Women's Missionary Careers in Nineteenth-Century America," in Janet Wilson James, ed., *Women in American Religion* (Philadelphia: University of Pennsylvania Press, 1980) 111-25.

19 Among other sources, Mary Taylor Huber and Nancy C. Lutkehaus, eds., *Gendered Missions: Women and Men in Missionary Discourse and Practice* (Ann Arbor: University of Michigan Press, 1999); Lesley A. Orr Macdonald, *A Unique and Glorious Mission: Women and Presbyterianism in Scotland, 1830-1930* (Edinburgh: John Donald, 2000); Patricia R. Hill, *The World Their Household: The American Woman's Foreign Mission Movement and Cultural Transformation, 1870-1920* (Ann Arbor: University of Michigan Press, 1985); Leslie A. Flemming, *Women's Work for Women: Missionaries and Social Change in Asia* (Boulder: Westview, 1989); Susan M. Yohn, *A Contest of Faiths: Missionary Women and Pluralism in the American Southwest* (Ithaca: Cornell University Press, 1995). For Canada, Ruth Compton Brouwer, *New Women for God: Canadian Presbyterian Women and India Missions, 1876-1914* (Toronto: University of Toronto Press, 1990); Rosemary R. Gagan, *A Sensitive Independence: Canadian Methodist Women Missionaries in Canada and the Orient, 1881-1925* (Montreal and Kingston: McGill-Queen's University Press, 1992); Margaret Prang: *A Heart at Leisure from Itself: Caroline Macdonald of Japan* (Vancouver: UBC Press, 1995); Kathleen L. Lodwick, *Educating the Women of Hainan: The Career of Margaret Moninger in China, 1915-1942* (Lexington: University Press of Kentucky, 1995); Margaret Whitehead, "Women Were Made for Such Things: Women Missionaries in British Columbia 1850s-1940s," *Atlantis* 14, 1 (Autumn 1988): 141-50; Margaret Whitehead, "'Let the Women Keep Silence': Women Missionary Preaching in British Columbia, 1860s-1940s," in Elizabeth Gillan Muir and Marilyn Färdig Whiteley, eds., *Changing Roles of Women within the Christian Church in Canada*, 117-35 (Toronto: University of Toronto Press, 1995). Myra Rutherdale examined women missionaries and missionary wives as a single, coherent entity in *Women and the White Man's God: Gender and Race in the Canadian Mission Field* (Vancouver: UBC Press, 2002); "Revisiting Colonization through Gender: Anglican Missionary Women in the Pacific Northwest and the Arctic, 1860-1945," *BC Studies* 104 (Winter 1994-95): 3-23; and "'I Wish the Men Were Half as Good': Gender Constructions in the Canadian North-Western Mission Field, 1860-1940," in Catherine A. Cavanaugh and Randi R. Warne, eds., *Telling Tales: Essays in Western Women's History* (Vancouver: UBC Press, 2000), 32-59, as does Vi Keenleyside, *They Also Came* (Duncan, BC: Vibook Committee, 1987), which contains some thirty laudatory biographies of Methodist missionary wives and women missionaries, including Emma Crosby.

CHAPTER 1: COURTSHIP AND MARRIAGE

1 E.A. Davis, "The Philosophy of Methodism," in E.A. Davis, ed., *Commemorative Review of the Methodist, Presbyterian and Congregational Churches in British Columbia* (Vancouver: Wrigley, 1925), 38-9.

2 "Late Mrs. Emma J. Crosby," clipping, and "Rev. John Douse," Minutes, Toronto Methodist Conference, 1886, both in "Rev. John Douse," Minutes, Toronto Methodist Conference, 1886, in United Church Archives (hereafter UCA), Emmanuel College, Victoria University, University of Toronto, John Douse fonds. For the history of Methodism in Canada, see Neil Semple, *The Lord's Dominion: The History of Canadian Methodism* (Montreal and Kingston: McGill-Queen's University Press, 1996); also William Westfall, *Two Worlds: The Protestant Culture of Nineteenth-Century Ontario* (Kingston: McGill-Queen's University Press, 1989).

3 John Douse to Richard Reese (Spitalfield, London), Salt Springs Mission House, Grand River, near Brantford, August 26, 1834, Library and Archives Canada (hereafter LAC), MG19-F18.

4 Douse to Reese, August 26, 1834. According to an obituary, John Douse was born October 8, 1801. "Rev. John Douse."

5 "Rev. John Douse."

6 Eliza Milner was born just outside of Hull. Death registration, Innissfel District, Simcoe County, p. 156, 01837, Ontario Provincial Archives (hereafter OPA). The Douses' first child, a son, was born in 1839 and died three years later. Information in UCA, John Douse fonds.

7 John Douse was listed in George H. Cornish, *Cyclopaedia of Methodism in Canada* (Toronto: Methodist Book and Publishing House, 1881), 85-6, as being at Grand River 1834-35, St. Catharines 1836, Coburg 1837 and 1848, St. Clair 1838-40, Belleville 1841-44 and 1861-63, Hamilton 1845-47, Kingston 1849, Toronto West 1850-52, Barrie 1853-55, London 1856-57, Guelph 1858-60, Ottawa 1864-66, St. John 1867-69, and Paris 1870-72, at which time he was superannuated, or retired.

8 John Douse to his wife, Eliza Douse, Leeds, July 22, 1862, UBCCC.

9 See Andrew Frederick Hunter, *A History of Simcoe County*, vol. 1 (Barrie ON: County Council, 1909).

10 Annie Douse Hough to her sister, Emma Crosby, January 14, 1914, UBCC.

11 September 17, 1854, entry in Robert Orchard, diary, reproduced at http://members.home.net/billwarnica.

12 Annie Douse Hough to Emma Crosby, January 14 and 18, 1914, UBCSC.

13 John Douse, *A Register or Alphabetical Arrangement of the Wesleyan Methodist Ministers and Preachers, in connection with the Canada Conference* (Toronto: Guardian, 1853), preface.

14 See, for instance, Methodist General Conference, *Centennial of Canadian Methodism* (Toronto: William Briggs, 1891), 91.

15 "Death of Father Douse," *Christian Guardian*, May 12, 1886.

16 Information on Wesleyan Female College and its staff and students is taken from its *Annual Catalogue* (Hamilton: Spectator), available from Canadian Institute for Historical Microreproductions; and *Dictionary of Hamilton Biography*, vol. 1 (Hamilton: Dictionary of Hamilton Biography, n.d.); also Johanna M. Selles, *Methodists and Women's Education in Ontario, 1836-1925* (Montreal and Kingston: McGill-Queen's University Press, 1996).

17 Hamilton's development has been examined in Michael B. Katz, *The People of Hamilton, Canada West: Family and Class in a Mid-Nineteenth-Century City* (Cambridge: Harvard University Press, 1975); and Michael B. Katz, Michael J. Doucet, and Mark J. Stern, *The Social Organization of Early Industrial Capitalism* (Cambridge: Harvard University Press, 1982).

18 John C. Weaver, *Crimes, Constables, and Courts: Order and Transgression in a Canadian City, 1816-1970* (Montreal and Kingston: McGill-Queen's University Press, 1995).

19 Henry Browne to his aunt Emma Crosby, Alberni, BC, January 23, 1914, UBCCC.

20 "Deborah Kirkwood, "Protestant Missionary Women: Wives and Spinsters," in Fiona Bowie, Deborah Kirkwood, and Shirley Ardener, eds., *Women and Missionaries: Past and Present*, 23-42, esp. 28 (Providence, RI: Berg, 1993).

21 Carey so titles her article on missionary wives in Australia.

22 "One of Our Pioneer Missionaries," *Missionary Outlook* 19, 2 (February 1899): 33; also Davis, *Commemorative Review*, viii; Charles M. Tate, "Autosketch of My Life," 6, typescript in UCA, Vancouver School of Theology, "Pioneer Missionary to Pacific Dead," *Mail and Empire*, January 15, 1914; "Dates in the Life of Rev. Thomas Crosby," typescript in UBCCC.

23 Thomas Crosby, *Among the An-ko-me-nums or Flathead Tribes of Indians of the Pacific Coast* (Toronto: William Briggs, 1907), 26.

24 Crosby, *Among the An-ko-me-nums,* 23-4, 28.

25 Thomas Crosby, letter written on fortieth anniversary of Methodist missionaries to British Columbia, Toronto, January 18, 1899, British Columbia Archives (hereafter BCA), H/D/R57/C88r.

26 E.O.S. Scholefield and F.W. Howay, *British Columbia from the Earliest Times to the Present,* vol. 3 (Vancouver: S.J. Clarke, 1914), 1099.

27 Scholefield and Howay, *British Columbia,* 1099; also Thomas Crosby, "Indian Tribes," Methodist Church, *Annual Report,* 1870-71, xxi-xxii; 1871-72, xix-xx.

28 Edmund Hope Verney to his father, Sir Henry Verney, HMS *Grappler,* Nass River, October 6, 1864, in Edmund Verney, *Vancouver Island Letters,* ed. Allan Pritchard (Vancouver: UBC Press, 1996), 226. See also Adele Perry, "The Autocracy of Love and the Legitimacy of Empire: Intimacy, Power and Scandal in Nineteenth-Century Metlakahtlah," *Gender and History* 16, 2 (2004): 261-88.

29 Terrence L. Craig, *The Missionary Lives: A Study of Canadian Missionary Biography and Autobiography* (Leiden: Brill, 1997), 30.

30 Conversation between Helen Hager, Louise Hagar, Jan Hare, and Jean Barman, Vancouver, October 30, 2000.

31 "Open Letter to the Members of the W.M.S. of the Methodist Church," *Missionary Outlook* 17, 5 (May 1997): 76.

32 James Allen to Emma Crosby, Toronto, January 17, 1914, UBCCC.

33 "Funeral Services for Rev. Dr. Crosby," undated clipping (January 1914), UBCCC; and "Great Missionary of Methodists Is Dead," *Province,* January 15, 1914.

34 William Pollard, "Victoria," Methodist Church, *Annual Report,* 1873-74, xviii.

35 Thomas Crosby, "Indian Tribes," Methodist Church, *Annual Report,* 1873-74, xxiii.

36 Crosby, *Up and Down,* 29-30.

37 Ibid., 30.

38 Annie D. (Mrs. Frederick C.) Stephenson, *One Hundred Years of Canadian Methodist Missions, 1824-1924,* vol. 1 (Toronto: Missionary Society of the Methodist Church and Young People's Forward Movement, 1925), 167.

39 Made of wool.

40 Maria Orme Allen to Emma Crosby, Rochester, NY, April 4, 1914, UBCCC.

41 Henry Browne to Emma Crosby, January 23, 1914.

42 Crosby, *Up and Down,* 11.

43 F.E. Runnalls, *It's God's Country: A Review of the United Church and Its Founding Partners, the Congregational, Methodist, and Presbyterian Churches in British Columbia* (Ocean Park, BC: n.p., 1974), 26, 46-9, 55; William Pollard in *Missionary Notes,* June 1875, 55. Runnalls, *It's God's Country,* is a very useful general history of the Methodist Church and its missions in British Columbia.

44 Located in UCA, John Douse fonds, box 1, file 7, 86-088C.

CHAPTER 2: ARRIVAL AT FORT SIMPSON

 1 Martha Washington (O'Neill) Boss, "A Tale of Northern B.C. from Cariboo to Cassiar," 23, typescript in BCA, Ms. 771.

 2 Charles F. Morison, "A Recollection of the Early Days in Northern British Columbia" (1919), typescript in UBCC, Imbert Orchard papers, box 2, file 9.

 3 Boss, "A Tale of Northern B.C.," 89.

 4 J.C. (Jessie Crosby), "Missionary Work in British Columbia" (c. 1893), UBCCC.

5   Margaret Seguin (Anderson), ed., *The Tsimshian: Images of the Past, Views of the Present* (Vancouver: UBC Press, 1993), ix-x.

6   See Jay Miller, *Tsimshian Culture: A Light through the Ages* (Lincoln: University of Nebraska Press, 1997), 21-4. Miller describes the significance of the house as a building, a membership, a territory, or a repository for hereditary treasures that formed the basic social unit. Within the house system kinship ties were expressed through the four clans of Orca, Wolf, Raven, and Eagle; they were passed matrilineally and were accompanied by a sacred narrative, or *adawx*. The paternal side of the house took responsibility for the wonders and privileges of the house.

7   Crosby, *Up and Down*, 15.

8   Morison, "Recollection."

9   J.C., "Missionary Work."

10   Neylan, *The Heavens Are Changing*, 44.

11   Robert Galois, "Colonial Encounters: The Worlds of Arthur Wellington Clah, 1855-1881," *BC Studies* 115/16 (1997/98): 134. Clah's diaries offer an Aboriginal perspective on various points of contact between the Tsimshian and newcomers on the coast. The diaries span fifty years and represent a sustained and detailed account of economic expansion and mission activity on the north coast.

12   Galois, "Colonial Encounters," 135.

13   Furtwangler, Albert. *Bringing Indians to the Book* (Seattle: University of Washington Press, 2005), 116. Furtwangler examines the extension of literate institutions, such as missions, into non-literate societies, focusing on missionaries in Oregon in the United States. Also moving mission studies beyond just their Christian proselytizing efforts to focus on teaching Christianity and literacy is a compilation of essays by editors Jamie S. Scott and Gareth Griffiths in *Mixed Messages: Materiality, Textuality, Missions* (New York: Palgrave Macmillan, 2005). Works in this book demonstrate how missions engaged Indigenous peoples around the globe, including Canada, through written texts.

14   Peggy Brock, "Building Bridges: Politics and Religion in a First Nations Community," *Canadian Historical Review* 81 (2000): 72.

15   C.M. Tate, "Fifty Years with the Methodist Church in British Columbia," in E.A. Davis, ed., *Commemorative Review of the Methodist, Presbyterian and Congregational Churches in British Columbia* (Vancouver: Wrigley, 1925), 65.

16   Church records, St. Andrew's Catholic Church, Victoria, 1849-1934, BCA, Add. Ms. 1.

17   R. Geddes Large, *The Skeena: River of Destiny* (Vancouver: Mitchell Press, 1957), 91; and Bruce Watson, fur trade biographical dictionary in process.

18   The Dudowards' story is told most fully in Archibald McDonald Greenaway, "The Challenge of Port Simpson" (B. Div. thesis, Vancouver School of Theology, 1955); see also church records, St. Andrew's Catholic Church, Victoria, 1849-1934.

19   School Register, Fort Simpson, 1857, 1860, in UBC Library, Duncan Papers.

20   William Duncan to Church Missionary Society, February 24, 1874, Correspondence Inward, Church Mission Society, North Pacific Mission, UBCDP; and William Beynon, "The Tsimshian of Metlakatla, Alaska," *American Anthropologist* 43 (1941): 86.

21   Criminal charge, November 25, 1871, William Duncan, Civil Office, UBCDP.

22   "St. Ann's Academy, Victoria, B.C. 1858-1923, Pupils' Registration," St. Ann's Archives, Victoria.

23   William Pollard, Victoria, March 19, 1874, *Missionary Notes*, August 1874, 384.

24   Crosby, *Up and Down*, 21-2.

25 See E.W. Wright, ed., *Lewis and Dryden's Marine History of the Pacific Northwest* (New York: Antiquarian Press, 1961), 46.

26 See Charles Leroy Andrews, *Wrangell and the Gold of the Cassiar* (Seattle: L. Tinker, 1937).

27 As well, everyone sang "'Shall we gather at the river,' a hymn that they had lately learned at the revival in Victoria." Crosby, *Up and Down*, 38-41.

28 William Pollard, July 24, 1874, in *Missionary Notices*, November 1874, 401.

29 William Pollard in *Missionary Notes*, June 1875, 55; Crosby, *Up and Down*, 39.

30 William Pollard, July 24, 1874.

31 Ibid.

32 Crosby, *Up and Down*, 161.

33 William Duncan to Meredith, Ottawa, June 5, 1875, Department of Indian Affairs (DIA), Black Series, RG 10, vol. 2614, file 4083.

34 Post Office Inspector to Postmaster General, Victoria, April 6, 1979, LAC, Post Office Inspectors Reports, RG3, series D-3, vol. 2, file 1879-449, reel C-7225.

35 R.C. Mayne, *Four Years in British Columbia and Vancouver Island* (London: John Murray, 1862, repr. 1969), 308.

36 School Register, Fort Simpson, 1857.

37 Brian C. Hosmer, *American Indians in the Marketplace: Persistence and Innovation among the Menominees and Metlakatlans, 1870-1920* (Lawrence: University Press of Kansas, 1999), 140, and wedding certificate in family possession; Catherine Holmes to William Duncan, Victoria, July 31 [no year] in UBC Library, Duncan Papers.

38 Crosby, *Up and Down*, 37.

39 Morison, "Recollection."

40 School Register, Fort Simpson, 1857.

41 William Henry Pierce, *From Potlatch to Pulpit* (Vancouver: Vancouver Bindery, 1933), 8. For another perspective see Gail Edwards, "'The Picturesqueness of His Accent and Speech': Methodist Missionary Narratives and William Henry Pierce's Autobiography," in Alvyn Austin and Jamie S. Scott, eds., *Canadian Missions, Indigenous Peoples. Representing Religion at Home and Abroad* (Toronto: University of Toronto Press, 2005), 67-87.

42 Pierce then returned to Victoria to attend school both day and night, and, when his money ran out, he got a job in a sawmill at Port Laidlow in Washington Territory, where he helped to launch a temperance society. *Missionary Outlook* 20, 2 (February 1900): 35-6. Pierce detailed his life story in *From Potlatch to Pulpit*.

43 Morison, "Recollection."

44 Large, *Skeena*, 92.

45 Crosby, *Up and Down*, 40, 43.

46 Boss, "A Tale of Northern B.C.," 89.

47 Morison, "Recollection."

48 Jessie and Annie McQueen used what were referred to as "slips" to share intimate knowledge with their Nova Scotian mother after migrating to British Columbia in 1887-88. See Jean Barman, *Sojourning Sisters: The Lives and Letters of Jessie and Annie McQueen* (Toronto: University of Toronto Press, 2003), 63.

49 Crosby later described how the lumber "was all thrown overboard – as there was no wharf – rafted alongside the ship and towed ashore." There were no horses or oxen at Fort Simpson so that "we had to get all the lumber and timber up the hill and, soaked as it was with salt water, every piece had to be packed on men's backs." Crosby, *Up and Down*, 40-1.

50 Thomas Crosby, Fort Simpson, January 20, 1875, in *Missionary Notices*, April 1875, 36.

51 See, for instance, Thomas Crosby, "Indian Tribes," Methodist Church, *Annual Report*, 1870-71, xxi-xxii; 1871-72, xix-xx.
52 Thomas Crosby, Fort Simpson, January 20, 1875, in *Missionary Notices*, April 1875, 36.
53 Crosby, *Up and Down*, 41.
54 William Pollard, report on visit, in *Missionary Notices*, June 1875, 55.
55 Alexander Sutherland, "Special Report," Missionary Society of the Methodist Church, *Annual Report of the Auxiliary Missionary Society of the Toronto Conference*, 1885, xii.
56 Thomas Crosby, Fort Simpson, January 20, 1875, in *Missionary Notices*, April 1875, 36.
57 Crosby, January 20, 1875.
58 Thomas Crosby, "Fort Simpson," Methodist Church, *Annual Report*, 1874-75, xix.
59 William Pollard, report on visit, in *Missionary Notices*, June 1875, 55.

CHAPTER 3: MOTHERHOOD
1 Information on Crosby family births and deaths comes from Crosby family Bible, UBCCC.
2 Thomas Crosby, Fort Simpson, January 20, 1875, in *Missionary Notices*, April 1875, 36.
3 William Pollard, report on visit, in *Missionary Notices*, June 1875, 55.
4 Robert, *American Women in Mission*, 72.
5 Rutherdale, *Women and the White Man's God:* Chapter 5 looks at motherhood as an essential part of the identity of missionary women. Though Rutherdale's work refers to women who joined the missionary effort to become missionaries in their own right, the image of women as "Mothers of the Church" and as mothers of Aboriginal children applies very much to missionary wives and is therefore helpful. See also Myra Rutherdale, "Mothers of the Empire: Maternal Metaphors in the Northern Canadian Mission Field," in Alvyn Austin and Jamie S. Scott, eds., *Canadian Missions, Indigenous Peoples. Representing Religion at Home and Abroad* (Toronto: University of Toronto Press, 2005), 46-66.
6 Mrs. Platt, cited in Crosby, *Up and Down*, 87.
7 Rutherdale, *Women and the White Man's God*, 100.
8 Crosby, *Up and Down*, 85.
9 Ibid., 43-4.
10 J.W. Vowell to Minister of the Interior, Victoria, September 5, 1875, DIA, Black Series, RG 10, vol. 2614, file 4083.
11 William Duncan to David Laird, Minister of the Interior, Ottawa, May 21, 1875, LAC, Dufferin correspondence, FA127, reel A-420.
12 Morison, "A Recollection."
13 Albert Furtwangler, *Bringing Indians to the Book*, 116. Furtwangler examines the extension of literate institutions, such as missions, into non-literate societies, focusing on missionaries in Oregon in the United States. Also moving mission studies beyond just their Christian proselytizing efforts to focus on teaching Christianity and literacy is a compilation of essays by editors Jamie S. Scott and Gareth Griffiths in *Mixed Messages: Materiality, Textuality, Missions* (New York: Palgrave Macmillan, 2005). Works in this book demonstrate how missions engaged Indigenous peoples around the globe, including Canada, through written texts.
14 William Henry Collison, *In the Wake of the War Canoe*, ed. Charles Lillard (Victoria: Sono Nis, 1981), 56.
15 Duncan to Meredith, June 5, 1875.
16 Cited in J.W. Arctander, *The Apostle of Alaska* (New York: Revell, 1909), 245.
17 William Duncan to Church Mission Society, February 12, 1875, cited in Bolt, *Thomas Crosby*, 43.

18 Duncan to Meredith, June 5, 1875.

19 Dr. Enoch Wood held an honorary Doctor of Divinity degree. See George H. Cornish, *Cyclopaedia of Methodism in Canada* (Toronto: Methodist Book and Publishing House, 1881), 153.

20 "Great credit is due to Mr. Bennett, of Hamilton, builder, for the quiet manner in which he worked with the Indians." Thomas Crosby, Fort Simpson, November 3, 1875, in *Missionary Notices*, March 1876, 95.

21 Crosby, *Up and Down*, 78.

22 William Pollard in *Missionary Notes*, June 1875, 56.

23 Thomas Crosby, June 7, 1875, in *Missionary Notices*, October 1875, 67.

24 Crosby, *Up and Down*, 161.

25 Douglas Cole, *Captured Heritage: The Scramble for Northwest Coast Artifacts* (Vancouver: UBC Press, 1995), 22-3, 29-30.

26 "Indian Curios, Collected on the North-West Coast of British Columbia and Alaska Between the Years 1874 and 1894," UBCCC.

27 Cornish, *Cyclopaedia of Methodism*, 620.

28 Crosby, *Up and Down*, 44, 46.

29 Crosby, November 3, 1875, 96.

30 Thomas Crosby, Fort Simpson, February 16, 1876, in *Missionary Notices*, April 1876, 129.

CHAPTER 4: EMMA ALONE

1 Crosby, *Up and Down*, 74.

2 Crosby, February 16, 1876, 129.

3 "Local Lady's Great-Aunt Is 'Grand Old Lady of Q.C.I.,'" *Omineca Herald*, July 25, 1952.

4 Bolt, *Thomas Crosby*, 48-9.

5 Whitehead, "'Let the Women Keep Silence.'" Whitehead reported on missionary women of the Methodist, Presbyterian, and Anglican churches in British Columbia who expanded their roles beyond domestic and educational responsibilities to assume preaching duties in the absence of their husbands and/or male missionaries.

6 Morison, "A Recollection."

7 Boss, "A Tale of Northern B.C."

8 Crosby, *Up and Down*, 77-8.

9 Kathleen E. Dalzell, *The Queen Charlotte Islands, 1774-1966* (Terrace: C.M. Adam, 1968), 76; Collison, *In the Wake of the War Canoe.*

10 Dalzell, *Queen Charlotte Islands*, 76.

11 Crosby, *Up and Down*, 90.

12 Marchioness of Dufferin and Ava, *My Canadian Journal 1872-8* (London: John Murray, 1891), 261.

13 Marquis of Dufferin and Ava, *Journal of the Journey of His Excellency the Governor-General of Canada from Government House, Ottawa, to British Columbia and Back* (London: Webster and Larkin, 1877), 38.

14 Marchioness of Dufferin and Ava, *My Canadian Journal*, 264.

15 Marquis of Dufferin and Ava, *Journal of the Journey*, 39.

16 Marchioness of Dufferin and Ava, *My Canadian Journal*, 264-5.

17 Ibid., 264.

18 Marquis of Dufferin and Ava, *Journal of the Journey*, 38-9.

19 Thomas Crosby, Fort Simpson, November 1, 1876, in *Missionary Notices*, January 1877, 179.

20 Morison, "Recollection." The copies intended for Odille Morison were lost en route.

21 George Weeget and four others to Thomas Crosby, Fort Wrangel, August 27, 1876, reproduced in Crosby, *Up and Down,* 169, also 167-8.
22 Marriage certificate, 1879-09-003-2820, BCA, Division of Vital Statistics (DVS), GR 2962.
23 Caroline Knott, Fort Simpson, September 20, 1877, in *Missionary Notices,* December 1877,
  266.
24 Collison, *In the Wake of the War Canoe,* 78-9, 146-7.
25 The incoming head of Fort Simpson was married to a daughter of Peter Ogden, which makes
  the reference confusing, unless a different name was being mooted.
26 Crosby, *Up and Down,* 201.
27 See E. Palmer Patterson II, *Mission on the Nass* (Waterloo: Eulachon Press, 1982).
28 Sheldon Jackson, *Alaska, and Missions on the North Pacific Coast* (New York: Dodd, Mead &
  Co., 1880), 131-2.
29 Crosby, *Up and Down,* 252.

CHAPTER 5: A COMFORTABLE ROUTINE

1 According to Crosby, "the Hyda people begged the party not to go, as there was going to be
  bad weather," but they left nonetheless and were carried by a southwest wind "out near to
  what is called 'Rose Spit,'" when the wind changed direction. By this time, they realized they
  had to get to shore but were unable to do so. Crosby, *Up and Down,* 130.
2 The sole survivor was Matthew Hat-lead-ex, who was one of Crosby's earliest converts. He
  later gave his own account of events. "We all got on the broken wreck, as the thwarts and
  withes held the pieces together at the bow, and the great bottom slab was still attached to the
  two side slabs which looked like wings. Mr. Williams had caught hold of one of the wings,
  and Chief Sick-sake was clinging to the other. For some time Mr. Williams held on with his
  head down on his arms. It was very cold and after a time Mr. Williams said, 'Boys, pray'; he
  bowed his head and we all prayed. Mr. Williams then threw up his arms and dropped off and
  we saw him no more. We could not see any land at this time." Matthew Hat-lead-ex, cited in
  Crosby, *Up and Down,* 130-1, 134.
3 Back to Matthew Hat-lead-ex. "Soon our Chief and guide got cold and weak, let go his hold,
  and disappeared. After this, we succeeded in cutting in two a pole or mast that was still attached; and, with the ropes hanging to it, we got the slabs of the canoe together. We lashed
  one piece of the pole at each end and the planks were still attached by the withes of the bow.
  Now we felt better, as we had a raft; but one paddle and a broken oar were all we had with
  which to pull. Darkness soon closed around us, and we prayed again to God to take care of us
  for the night. Before daylight Saturday morning, another of our number got weak and fell off
  the raft." Matthew Hat-lead-ex, cited in Crosby, *Up and Down,* 131.
4 "Far on in the night, one of our brothers got out of his mind. He jumped up and shouted, 'I
  see a fire, let me get ashore.' Either he cut the rope with a knife or the ends of the raft parted,
  and there in the darkness I was left alone on one slab of the broken canoe. I saw my friends no
  more." Matthew Hat-lead-ex, cited in Crosby, *Up and Down,* 131-2.
5 "I got a flat piece of stick or board to serve as a paddle, launched the canoe and paddled along
  till I came to Old Tongass village, where I broke into one or two houses in hope of finding
  food, but there was none there. I then started to paddle across to Cape Fox. While crossing the
  channel, a steamboat came from the north; and my heart jumped with joy ... but the steamer
  went on, and my spirits sank very low. By hard paddling I reached the village of Cape Fox
  [about seventy-five miles from Masset in Alaska]." Matthew Hat-lead-ex collapsed, but a day
  later, "on Sunday I spoke to the people from God's Word in Chinook," and the next day he
  returned home to Fort Simpson. Matthew Hat-lead-ex, cited in Crosby, *Up and Down,* 132-3.

6   Records of Our Lady of Good Hope Catholic Church, Fort St. James, 1876-1947, in BCA, reel 22A; marriage certificate, 1876-09-173035, BCA, DVS, GR2962.

7   On the family, see Archie Binns, *Peter Skene Ogden: Fur Trader* (Portland: Binfords and Mort, 1967); and see Ogden family tree, BCA, vertical files.

8   A. Carman, May 14, 1896, cited in Crosby, *Up and Down*, 60.

9   Thomas Crosby, Fort Simpson, September 21, 1877, in *Missionary Notices*, February 1878, 273.

10   Thomas Crosby to W.H. Withrow, Victoria, October 1, 1897, reproduced in Crosby, *Up and Down*, 402.

11   Alexander Sutherland, *Methodism in Canada: Its Work and Its Story* (Toronto: Methodist Mission Rooms, 1904), 305. A similar version appears in Jackson, *Alaska, and Missions on the North Pacific Coast*, 312, based on what Crosby told him during a visit to Fort Simpson in the fall of 1879.

12   Records of Wesleyan Mission, Fort Simpson, 1874-1912, BCA, reel 31A.

13   Agnes (Hubbs) Russ and her daughter Grace (Russ) Stevens, interview with Imbert Orchard, Skidegate, 1962, BCA, tape 2442: 1-2.

14   "Colorful Indian Character Called to His Forefathers," *Western Recorder*, December 1934.

15   Crosby, *Up and Down*, 89.

16   Russ and Stevens, interview with Orchard, 1962.

17   "Local Lady's Great-Aunt Is 'Grand Old Lady of Q.C.I.'"

18   Crosby, *Up and Down*, 264.

19   Russ and Stevens, interview with Orchard, 1962.

20   "Well-Known Coast Indian Dies," *Province*, November 1934, in BCA, vertical files under Russ.

21   Morison, "A Recollection."

22   Boss, "A Tale of Northern B.C.," 90.

23   Census of Canada, 1891, 2 NW (Coast b), household 82.

24   Boss, "A Tale of Northern B.C.," 90.

25   Emma Crosby, "Happy Death of 'Clah' an Indian Covert and Preacher," in *Missionary Notices*, February 1878, 298.

26   "Colorful Indian Character."

27   Pierce, *From Potlatch to Pulpit*, 13-14.

28   Elizabeth Anderson Varley, *Kitimaat My Valley* (Terrace: Northern Times Press, 1981), 15.

29   According to Crosby, "during our trip, on the way to the Naas, we had to sleep out all night, after our canoe had been partly upset and all our goods and chattels wet." Crosby, *Up and Down*, 327.

30   Amos E. Russ and his family moved back to Ontario in 1878, where he continued to support Crosby's efforts at Fort Simpson. See Runnalls, *It's God's Country*, 63.

31   Sarah Hart, Port Simpson, November 2, 1892, "From Miss Hart," *Missionary Outlook* 13 (January 1893): 11.

32   Numerous editions were published in London by Hatchard and by the Religious Tract Society, in New York City by the American Tract Society, and in other places as well.

33   Crosby, *Up and Down*, 75-6.

34   Bolt, *Thomas Crosby*, 65.

35   Neylan, *The Heavens Are Changing*, 257. Neylan posed the argument that destroying, particularly burning, material items was a way for the Tsimshian to transfer those objects to the spirit world.

36   Crosby, *Up and Down*, 66.

37   Marriage certificate, 78-89-001150, BCA, DVS, GR2962.

CHAPTER 6: ADVERSITY

1 Crosby, *Up and Down*, 87.
2 Gagan, *A Sensitive Independence*, 16. The timing was similar to what occurred in other countries. In *Missionary Women: Gender, Professionalism and the Victorian Idea of Christian Mission* (Woodbridge, GB: Boydell Press, 2003), Rhonda Anne Semple describes the formation of comparable bodies in Britain at about the same time (esp. pp. 20-5), as does Jane Hunter in the United States in *The Gospel of Gentility: American Women Missionaries in Turn-of-the-Century China* (New Haven: Yale University Press, 1984).
3 "Prayer Card Leaflet," *Missionary Leaflet* 7, 4 (April 1891): 8.
4 Cornish, *Cyclopaedia of Methodism in Canada*, 620, 622.
5 The engraving is in Jackson, *Alaska, and Missions on the North Pacific Coast*, 309, the exploits on 302-27.
6 Marriage certificate, 1879-09-003-2820, BCA, DVS, GR 2962.
7 Thomas Crosby, "Fort Simpson," Methodist Church, *Annual Report*, 1879-80, xiv-xv.
8 Ibid., xiv.
9 Emma Crosby, "A Missionary Heroine," *Missionary Outlook* 19, 4 (April 1899): 91.
10 Death registration, Innissfel District, Simcoe County, p. 156, 01837, OPA.
11 Thomas Crosby to Ebenezer Robson, Port Simpson, May 8 and June 8, 1881, BCA, H/D/R57/C88.
12 Gagan, *A Sensitive Independence,* 17.
13 Mrs. E.S. Strachan, "Early Days of the Woman's Missionary Society," quoted in H.L. Platt, *The Story of the Years: A History of the Woman's Missionary Society of the Methodist Church, Canada, from 1881 to 1906*, vol. 1 (Toronto: Methodist Church, 1908), 15.
14 Cited in "Open Letter to the Members of the W.M.S. of the Methodist Church," 76.
15 Read at annual meeting of the Methodist Church of Canada, 1881, and printed in *Missionary Outlook* 1, 11-12 (November-December 1881): 139-41.
16 Thomas Crosby to Ebenezer Robson, Nanaimo, August 27, Port Simpson, September 17, and Nanaimo, October 11, 1881, BCA, H/D/R57/C88.
17 Crosby, *Up and Down,* 327; also Ebenezer Robson, "Port Simpson Mission Boat," *Missionary Outlook* 5, 1 (January 1885): 3.
18 Alexander Sutherland in *Missionary Outlook,* 1, 11-12 (November-December 1881): 139, 141.
19 November 8, 1881, 1st annual meeting, minute book, WMS, UCA.
20 *Missionary Outlook* 2, 2 (February 1882): 24.
21 Platt, *The Story of the Years*, 22.
22 November 8, 1881, 1st annual meeting, minute book, WMS, UCA.
23 May 1882, board of management, minute book, WMS, UCA.
24 *Missionary Outlook* 2, 11 (November 1882): 173.
25 Kate Hendry to her sister and niece, Victoria, July 14, 1882, BCA, ECH/38.
26 *Missionary Outlook* 2, 11 (November 1882): 174.
27 Kate Hendry to her sister and niece, Port Simpson, July 2, 1882, BCA, ECH/38.
28 Note in *Missionary Outlook* 2, 11 (November 1882): 174.
29 Crosby, *Up and Down*, 86.

CHAPTER 7: CHANGING TIMES

1 September 7, 1882, annual general meeting, minute book, WMS, UCA.
2 Hendry to her sister and niece, July 2, 1882.
3 Kate Hendry to her sister, Port Simpson, July 25, 1882, BCA, ECH/38.

4   Newton H. Chittenden, *Travels in British Columbia* (Vancouver: Gordon Soules, 1984 [1882]), 76.
5   Post Office Inspector to Postmaster General, Victoria, December 13, 1883, LAC, Post Office Inspectors Reports, RG3, file 1883-890, reel C-7226.
6   Post Office Petition signed by seventeen Fort Simpson residents, n.d., LAC, Post Office Inspectors Reports, RG3, file 1889-216, reel C-7228.
7   Thomas Crosby, "Fort Simpson," Methodist Church, *Annual Report*, 1880-81, xiv.
8   Federal postal service was established to and from Fort Simpson in 1885, the name being officially changed to Port Simpson at the beginning of 1900. George H. Melvin, *The Post Offices of British Columbia, 1858-1970* (Vernon: the author, 1972), 41, 97.
9   Dennis Jennings in "Along the Line," *Missionary Outlook* 2, 12 (December 1882): 190.
10 Chittenden, *Travels*, 75.
11 Jennings in "Along the Line," 191.
12 Report from 1890, cited in Crosby, *Up and Down,* 57-9; also 76-7.
13 Crosby, *Up and Down,* 86.
14 Printed as "The Crosby 'Home,'" *Missionary Outlook* 2, 11 (November 1882): 167-8.
15 Annie D. (Mrs. Frederick C.) Stephenson, *One Hundred Years of Canadian Methodist Missions, 1824-1924,* vol. 1 (Toronto: Missionary Society of the Methodist Church and Young People's Forward Movement, 1925), 179-80; WMS, *Annual Report,* 1882, 9; 1883, 6; 1885, 8; WMS petition to Superintendent General of Indian Affairs, April 13, 1891, DIA, Black Series, RG 10, vol. 3853, file 77,025; September 27, 1882, board of management, minute book, WMS, UCA.
16 Jennings in "Along the Line," 191.
17 I.W. Powell, report in DIA, *Annual Report,* 1879, 121.
18 "Statement of Rev. T. Crosby," in *Letter from the Methodist Missionary Society to the Superintendent-General of Indian Affairs respecting British Columbia Troubles* (Toronto: Methodist Church Missionary Society, 1889), 2.
19 "Letter of Protest of Indian Chiefs and Others at Port Simpson," Port Simpson, October 5, 1881, in *Letter from the Methodist Missionary Society,* 13.
20 Crosby to Robson, June 8, 1881.
21 Thomas Crosby to D.V. Lucas, Alert Bay, November 20, 1882, UBCCC.
22 Crosby, *Up and Down,* 255.
23 Russ and Stevens, interview with Orchard, 1962.
24 Dalzell, *Queen Charlotte Islands,* 98.
25 Russ and Stevens, interview with Orchard, 1962.
26 February 28, 1883, central board, minute book, WMS, UCA.
27 Printed as "The Crosby 'Home,'" *Missionary Outlook* 3, 6 (June 1883): 91-2.
28 *Missionary Outlook: A Monthly Advocate, Record, and Review,* which began publishing in January 1881, printed Emma's letters about the girls' home
29 Kate Hendry to Maggie, Port Simpson, February 22, 1883, BCA, EC/H38.
30 Kate Hendry to family, Port Simpson, June 11, 1883, BVS, EC/H38.
31 Hendry to Maggie, February 22, 1883.
32 Hendry to family, June 11, 1883.
33 May 12, 1883, central board, minute book, WMS, UCA.
34 Hendry to unnamed, June 11, 1883.
35 Hendry to friends, January 21, 1884.
36 Ibid.
37 Ibid.

38 Ibid.
39 Printed as "Women's Work," *Missionary Outlook* 4, 4 (April 1884): 59. It was described as "excerpts of a letter."
40 Alfred and Kate Dudoward worked for a time at Kitimaat, following the departure of George Edgar and his family. Crosby, *Up and Down*, 255.
41 The story is told in L. Morice, "Rev. George Edgar," typescript in UCAVST, Vertical file for George Edgar.
42 Kate Hendry to her sisters, Port Simpson, August 6, 1884, BCA, EC/H38.
43 WMS, *Annual Report*, 1884, 23.
44 October 22, 1884, annual meeting, WMS, UCA.
45 Platt, *The Story of the Years*, 35-6.
46 See Robert C. Scott, *My Captain Oliver: A Story of Two Missionaries on the British Columbia Coast* (Toronto: United Church of Canada, 1947).
47 Ebenezer Robson, "Fort Simpson Missionary Boat," *Missionary Outlook* 5, 1 (January 1885): 3.
48 See Bolt, *Thomas Crosby*, 75-6.
49 William Smithe, British Columbia Commissioner of Lands and Works, at meeting with the Tsimshian held in Victoria, February 1887, cited in Bolt, *Thomas Crosby*. 79.
50 Thomas Crosby to Ebenezer Robson, Aberdeen, July 14, 1885, BCA, H/D/R57/C88.
51 Note in *Missionary Outlook* 5, 8 (August 1885): 114.
52 Emma Crosby, "A Missionary Heroine," *Missionary Outlook* 19, 4 (April 1899): 91.
53 Alexander Sutherland, "Special Report," Missionary Society of the Methodist Church, *Annual Report of the Auxiliary Missionary Society of the Toronto Conference*, 1885, xi-xii.
54 Alexander Sutherland, "Notes of a Tour among the Missions of British Columbia," *Missionary Outlook* 5, 10 (October 1885): 150.
55 Sutherland, "Special Report," xii.
56 David Swanson, cited in Alexander Sutherland, "Notes of a Tour among the Missions of British Columbia, IV," *Missionary Outlook* 6, 1 (January 1886): 2.
57 Thomas Wright, cited in Sutherland, "Notes of a Tour," 6, 1: 2.
58 Matthew Shepherd, cited in Sutherland, "Notes of a Tour," 6, 1: 2.
59 Charles Price, cited in Sutherland, "Notes of a Tour," 6, 1: 2.
60 James Wright, cited in Sutherland, "Notes of a Tour," 6, 1: 2.
61 Sutherland, "Special Report," xiii.
62 Sutherland, "Notes of a Tour," 6, 1: 2. To Crosby's credit, even if to no effect, he had written and would write numerous letters asserting the Tsimshian position on land. See correspondence in UBCCC.
63 Alexander Sutherland, "Notes of a Tour among the Missions of British Columbia, IV," *Missionary Outlook* 6, 2 (February 1886): 31.
64 Ibid., 32.
65 Marriage registration, 85-09-092432, BCA, DVS, GR2962.
66 Chief Albert Nelson (Neeshot), cited in Sutherland, "Notes of a Tour," 6, 2: 32-3.
67 Chief Paul cited in Sutherland, "Notes of a Tour," 6, 2: 33.
68 Thomas Crosby to Ebenezer Robson, Bella Bella, October 12, and Port Simpson, November 13, 1885, BCA, H/D/R57/C88.
69 WMS, *Annual Report*, 1885, 15.
70 Marriage certificate, 1885-09-003127, BCA, DVS, GR 2962.
71 Hendry to unnamed, June 11, 1883.
72 Hendry to her sisters, August 6, 1884.

73 "Woman's Missionary Society – Annual Meeting," *Missionary Outlook* 6, 1 (January 1886): 5.
74 Marriage registration, 90-09-004697, BCA, DVS, GR2962.
75 See Runnalls, *It's God's Country*, 111.
76 The typical, two-week preaching trip is described at length in Crosby's letter of April 15, 1886, in "Port Simpson District," *Missionary Outlook* 6, 5 (May 1886): 107-09.
77 Death registration, Toronto Division, York County, p. 571, 11182, OPA.
78 Thomas Crosby, September 18, 1886, "Port Simpson," *Missionary Outlook* 6, 11 (November 1886): 174.
79 "Great Missionary of Methodists Is Dead."
80 Crosby, *Up and Down*, 340.
81 Sarah Hart, Port Simpson, January 5, 1891, *Missionary Leaflet* 7, 3 (March 1891): 2.
82 December 10, 1886, entry in Agnes Knight, journal, BCA, F/7/W15.

CHAPTER 8: GOOD INTENTIONS GONE AWRY
1 Hendry to unnamed, June 11, 1883, and to friends, January 21, 1884.
2 Kate Hendry to Maggie, Port Simpson, December 26, 1882, BCA, ECH/38.
3 Agnes Knight, January 1886, cited in Platt, *The Story of the Years*, 34.
4 Agnes Knight Walker, "Reminiscences of Miss Agnes Knight (later Mrs. R.J. Walker), Bella Bella, Port Simpson and Cape Mudge," BCA, F7/W15r/A1.
5 WMS, *Annual Report*, 1895, 19.
6 Agnes Knight, Port Simpson, January 27, 1886, "The Crosby Home," *Missionary Outlook* 6, 5 (May 1886): 74-5.
7 Agnes Knight Walker, On board B. *Boscowitz*, July 16, 1890, *Missionary Leaflet* 6, 9 (September 1890): 6.
8 Sara Hart, Port Simpson, *Missionary Leaflet* 7, 6 (June 1891): 6.
9 Walker, "Reminiscences."
10 H.L. Platt, *Story of the Years*, 38-9.
11 Sara Hart, FS, 31 March 1892, *Missionary Leaflet* 8, 6 (June 1892): 6.
12 Hendry to Maggie, December 26, 1882.
13 Mrs. Redner, Port Simpson, June 21, 1893, *Missionary Leaflet* 9, 8 (August 1893): 5-6.
14 Sarah Hart, Port Simpson, January 5, 1891, *Missionary Leaflet* 7, 3 (March 1891): 3.
15 Emma Crosby, unpublished letter sent to WMS annual meeting, November 1885, quoted in WMS, *Annual Report*, 1885, 17; and "Woman's Missionary Society – Annual Meeting," *Missionary Outlook* 6, 1 (January 1886): 5.
16 WMS, *Annual Report*, 1889, 48.
17 Cornish, *Cyclopaedia of Methodism in Canada*, 553-4.
18 WMS, *Annual Report*, 1885, 43.
19 WMS, *Annual Report*, 1886, 8; 21 October 1896, 5th annual meeting, WMS minute book.
20 Mrs. R.J. Walker (Agnes Knight), "Narrative of Indian Missionary Adventuring on Quadra Island," 1, BCA, E7/W15/1A.
21 "Report of the General Board of Missions of the Methodist Church, for the Quadriennial Period Ending June 30th, 1880 [sic]," *Missionary Outlook* 10, 10 (October 1890): 148.
22 WMS, *Annual Report*, 1884, 27.
23 October 17-18, 1888, 7th annual meeting, WMS minute book; WMS, *Annual Report*, 1888, 9.
24 See "The Troubles on the Skeena," *Missionary Outlook* 8, 9 (September 1888): 130-1; Methodist Church, Missionary Society, *Letter from the Missionary Society*.
25 "Notes from the North-West," *Missionary Outlook* 8, 12 (December 1888): 179.
26 "'Glad Tidings' Mission," *Missionary Outlook* 9, 9 (September 1889): 132.

27 Methodist Church, *Annual Report*, 1890-91, xxxi.

28 Alfred E. Green, Port Simpson, February 19, 1890, *Missionary Outlook* 10, 6 (June 1890): 93.

29 June 10, 1890, and August 14, 1891, entries, Nellie Bolton, diary, BCA, E/C/B631, reel 472A.

30 Septima M. Collis, *A Woman's Trip to Alaska* (New York: Cassell, 1890), 181-3.

31 Henry Browne to Emma Crosby, January 23, 1914.

32 Boss, "A Tale of Northern B.C.," 23, typescript in BCA, Ms. 771, 183-4; death certificate, 89655, BCA, Division of Vital Statistics, GR2951. Alexander's daughter Maggie, by his first wife, had, like the Crosby children, been sent away to get an education (in her case to Vancouver); see Jean Barman, *Constance Lindsay Skinner: Writing on the Frontier* (Toronto: University of Toronto Press, 2002), 30-4.

33 Alfred E. Green, Port Simpson, September 20, 1889, *Missionary Outlook* 9, 11 (November 1889): 175; marriage certificate, 90-09-004697, BCA, Division of Vital Statistics, GR2962.

34 Boss, "A Tale of Northern B.C.," 195.

35 Wesleyan Mission, Fort Simpson, 1874-1912.

36 Boss, "A Tale of Northern B.C.," 195.

37 Alfred E. Green, Port Simpson, February 19, 1890, "The Indian Work," *Missionary Outlook* 10, 6 (June 1890): 94.

38 March 12, 1890, entry in Bolton.

39 Agnes Knight in WMS, *Annual Report*, 1887, 66.

40 Walker, "Reminiscences."

41 Sarah Hart, Port Simpson, January 5, 1891, *Missionary Leaflet* 7, 3 (March 1891): 3.

42 Walker, July 16, 1890.

43 Mrs. Redner, Port Simpson, September 3, 1894, *Monthly Letter* 11, 10 (November 1894): 5.

44 WMS, *Annual Report*, 1890, 5.

45 M.J. Cartmell to Emma Crosby, Hamilton, February 15, 1914, UBCCC.

46 Martha Cartmell, Sunnyside, North Pacific Cannery, Skeena River, September 11, 1890, *Missionary Leaflet* 6, 11 (November 1890): 3.

47 September 15-16, 1890 entries in Bolton.

48 Cartmell, September 11, 1890: 3.

49 September 17, 1890, entry in Bolton.

50 Printed in "Correspondence," *Missionary Outlook* 11, 4 (April 1891): 55-6.

51 For one of these quarterly letters, see Sarah Hart, Port Simpson, November 2, 1892, "From Miss Hart," *Missionary Outlook* 13, 1 (January 1893): 11-12.

52 WMS, *Annual Report*, 1890, 18.

53 Designs and WMS petition to Superintendent General of Indian Affairs, April 13, 1891, DIA, Black Series, RG 10, vol 3853, file 77,025.

54 "Prayer Card Leaflet," *Missionary Leaflet* 7, 4 (April 1891): 8; March 17, 1891, motion passed by executive committee, WMS minute book.

55 WMS statement, n.d., and Deputy Superintendent General of Indian Affairs to Superintendent General of Indian Affairs, Ottawa, February 24, 1893, DIA, Black Series, RG 10, vol 3853, file 77,025; October 17, 1893, 11th annual meeting, minute book, WMS, UCA.

56 Writing on the reformatory and disciplinary ethos of industrial and residential schools, Jamie S. Scott describes how the penitentiary model of industrial and residential schools was part of a larger Canadian ideal for schooling based on a "congregate system," which was designed to school juvenile delinquents in a secured space. See Jamie S. Scott, "Penitential and Penitentiary: Native Canadians and Colonial Mission Education," in Scott and Griffiths, eds., *Mixed Messages*, 111-33.

57 Cartmell, September 11, 1890: 3.

58 Katie O'Neill Boss, interview with Imbert Orchard, September 9, 1966, BCA, tape 1231.
59 Sarah Hart, Port Simpson, October 23, 1891, *Missionary Leaflet* 8, 1 (January 1892): 3.
60 Boss, "A Tale of Northern B.C.," 24, 53.
61 Ibid., 53-4.
62 Ibid., 23-4.
63 "A Trip on the 'Glad Tidings,'" *Missionary Outlook* 9, 3 (March 1889): 46.
64 See Bolt, *Thomas Crosby*, 114; and *Minutes of the Proceedings of the First [Second etc] Session of the British Columbia Conference of the Methodist Church* (Toronto: William Briggs), published annually from the time the conference held its first annual meeting in 1887.
65 October 18, 1897, entry in Ebenezer Robson, diary, BCA, H/D/R57, R57.24.
66 See Bolt, *Thomas Crosby*, 92-3.
67 Information comes from Greenaway, "The Challenge of Port Simpson," 60, 75, 77; and "Port Simpson Church Register, 1874-96," in UCTVSA. In 1899 the Methodists would form the Epworth League, complete with street evangelism and marching band, to compete with the Salvation Army. According to local historian R.G. Large, all written records of the Salvation Army in northern British Columbia were lost during the Second World War, making it difficult to ascertain its history. R. Geddes Large, *The Skeena: River of Destiny*, 103.
68 Large, *Skeena: River of Destiny*, 92.
69 Marriage registration, 87-09-003071, BCA, DVS, GR2962.
70 W.H. Withrow, *Our Own Country Canada* (Toronto: William Briggs, 1889), 572.
71 Boss, "A Tale of Northern B.C.," 56.
72 Neylan, *The Heavens Are Changing*, 241, 236. Neylan examined the transformation of physical space in Tsimshian villages, suggesting that missionization challenged, redefined, and realigned boundaries for many Tsimshian cultural containers, such as houses. She traced how the physical features of Tsimshian homes had transformed as a result of mission and economic influences. See 234-65.
73 February 28, 1891, entry in Bolton.
74 Marriage registration, 86-09-173045, BCA, DVS, GR1962.
75 May 4, 1891, entry in Bolton.
76 Boss, "A Tale of Northern B.C.," 56, 90-91.
77 "Chief of Tsimpsean Indian Tribe Dead," *Province*, November 12, 1935.
78 Boss, "A Tale of Northern B.C.," 55-6.
79 August 30, 1891, entry in Bolton.
80 Boss, "A Tale of Northern B.C.," 80-1, 89, 91; British Columbia, Department of Education, *Annual Reports*.
81 Wiggs O'Neill, "Like the RCMP, Teacher Got Her Man," *Kitimaat Northern Sentinel*, August 13, 1864.
82 Boss, "A Tale of Northern B.C.," 80-1, 91; British Columbia, Department of Education, *Annual Reports*.
83 Marriage registration, 88-09-173926, BCA, DVS, GR2962.
84 "C.W.D. Clifford (1842-1916)," *Smithers Interior News,* September 19, 1979.
85 Pre-Confederation marriage records, 1859-1872, BCA, GR3044; also Sylvia Van Kirk, "Tracing the Fortunes of Five Founding Families of Victoria," *BC Studies* 115/16 (1997/98): 148-79.
86 Boss, "A Tale of Northern B.C.," 74, 101.
87 E.S. Rupert, "The Relative Claims of Domestic and Foreign Missions on the Liberality of the Church," *Missionary Outlook* 12, 5 (May 1892): 69.
88 "Prayer Card Leaflet," *Missionary Leaflet* 8, 3 (March 1892): 6-7.

89   Alfred E. Green in Runnalls, 114.
90   Henry Browne to Emma Crosby, January 23, 1914.
91   Miss Paul, Port Simpson, *Monthly Letter* 12, 12 (December 1895): 2.
92   Miss Beavis, Port Simpson, February 4, 1896, *Monthly Letter* 13, 6 (June 1896): 3.
93   See J.C. [Jessie Crosby], "Missionary Work in British Columbia" [c1893], UBCCC; WMS, *Annual Report*, 1893, 51; 1894, xxiii.
94   March 22-23, 1895, special executive committee meeting, WMS meeting book.
95   WMS, *Annual Report*, 1894, 123; "District Doings," *Missionary Outlook* 14, 8 (August 1894): 122.
96   "The Indian Work," *Missionary Outlook* 12, 4 (April 1892): 54.
97   Thomas Crosby to Ebenezer Robson, December 15, 1897, BCA, H/D/R57/C88.
98   Annie D. (Mrs. Frederick C.) Stephenson, *One Hundred Years of Canadian Methodist Missions, 1824-1924*, vol. 1 (Toronto: Missionary Society of the Methodist Church and Young People's Forward Movement, 1925), 212-13.
99   June 30, 1897, entry in Robson diary.
100 Crosby to Withrow, Victoria, October 1, 1897.
101 Stephenson, *One Hundred Years*, 213.
102 WMS, *Annual Report*, 1897, 150, 161.
103 October 20, 1898, 16th annual meeting, WMS minutes.
104 *Monthly Letter* 15, 11 (December 1898): n.p. The earlier pamphlets in the "Our Work" series, each measuring 8 x 6 cm, or 6 1/8 x 4 3/4 inches, in size, included no. 2: *Our Chinese Rescue Home*, no. 4: *Medical Work among the Indians of B.C.*, and no. 5: *Manners and Customs of the Indians of Simpson District, B.C.*
105 H.L. Platt, *Story of the Years*, 36.
106 A.E. Roberts to Thomas Crosby, Chilliwack, September 25, 1911, UBCCC.
107 Thomas Crosby to Ebenezer Robson, Sardis, August 28, 1901, BCA, H/D/R57/C88.
108 Death certificate, 1991-32280, BCA, DVS, GR 2951.
109 Marshall, *Secularizing the Faith*.
110 Thomas Crosby, letter written on 40th anniversary of Methodist missionaries to British Columbia, Toronto, January 18, 1899, BCA, H/D/R57/C88r.
111 Note in *Methodist Recorder* 1 (1899): 4.
112 "Nanaimo Indian Mission," typescript in UCA, John Douse fonds.
113 Death certificate, 1914-44299, BCA, DVS, GR 2951.
114 Cole, *Captured Heritage*, 218, 224.
115 Copy located in William Lashley Hall, Correspondence, BCA, H/D/H14.2.
116 "Dates in the Life of Rev. Thomas Crosby"; death certificate, 1914-44299, BCA, DVS, GR 2951. Among contemporaries critiquing Thomas Crosby during his lifetime was Constance Lindsay Skinner in her play *Birthright*, copyrighted in 1906 in the United States. Having spent her teenage years with Maggie Alexander (see Chapter 8, note 32), whose uncle headed the HBC post at Fort Simpson much of the time the Crosbys were there, Constance was well aware of their perspectives and used them to devastating effect in her portraits of missionary Robert Maclean and his family. *Birthright* is innovative for juxtaposing missionary attitudes with those of the Aboriginal and mixed race people they were there to convert, who comprise half of the play's characters. While *Birthright* was performed in the United States in the early twentieth century, it would not be so in Canada until 2003, and then published two years later. See Constance Lindsay Skinner, *Birthright*, adapted by Joan Bryans (Toronto: Playwrights Canada Press, 2005).
117 "The Late Dr. Crosby," *Daily News-Advertiser*, January 15, 1914.

118 "Death of Mrs. T. Crosby," *Western Recorder* 2, 2 (August 1926): 13. Thomas Harold Crosby became head of the British Columbia division of Canadian Westinghouse and chaired the BC Power Commission, 1954-59. "Retired B.C. Power Head Dies," *Province*, July 17, 1965.
119 Emma Crosby to Jessie Harris, Vancouver, July 26, 1926, UBCCC.
120 Conversation between H. Hager, L. Hagar, Hare, and Barman, October 30, 2000.
121 Strachan and Ross, *Story of the Years,* 20.
122 Emma Crosby to Grace Crosby, Vancouver, August 3, 1920, UBCCC.
123 Emma Crosby to Jessie Harris, Vancouver, July 26, 1926, UBCCC.
124 Emma Crosby to Jessie Harris, June 26, 1926.
125 Grace Crosby, handwritten notes, UBCCC.
126 Emma Crosby to Jessie Harris, July 26, 1926.

CHAPTER 9: REPATRIATION
 1 Conversation between Louise Hager, quoting her mother, and Jan Hare, June 2004.
 2 Conversation between L. Hager, H. Hagar, Hare, and Barman, October 30, 2000.
 3 Henry Browne to Emma Crosby, January 23, 1914.
 4 Mary Taylor Huber and Nancy C. Lutkehaus, "Introduction: Gendered Missions at Home and Abroad," in their edited *Gendered Missions*, 13.
 5 Bolt, *Thomas Crosby*, 98.
 6 Carey, "Companions in the Wilderness," 239.
 7 Robert, *American Women in Mission*, 35.
 8 Title of C.L. Higham, *Noble, Wretched, and Redeemable: Protestant Missionaries to the Indians in Canada and the United States, 1820-1900* (Calgary, AB: University of Calgary Press, 2000), which compares nineteenth-century Protestant missionaries' views of Aboriginal peoples in the United States and Canada.
 9 Susan Neylan, "Longhouses, Schoolrooms, and Workers' Cottages: Nineteenth-Century Protestant Missions to the Tsimsian and the Transformation of Class through Religion," *Journal of the Canadian Historical Association*, n.s. 11 (2000): 51.
10 Caroline Dudoward, "The Dudowards of Fort Simpson," paper presented at the Beyond Hope Conference. Kamloops, May 11, 2001, courtesy of Caroline Dudoward.
11 On the complexities and significance of indigenous peoples' responses to missionaries, see, among other studies, Steven Kaplan, ed., *Indigenous Responses to Western Christianity* (New York: New York University Press, 1995); John C. Hawley, ed., *Historicizing Christian Encounters with the Other* (London: Macmillan, 1998); Robert L. Montgomery, *Introduction to the Sociology of Missions* (Westport, CT: Praeger, 1999).
12 Craig, *Missionary Lives*, 56.
13 "Great Missionary of Methodists Is Dead," *Province*, January 15, 1914.
14 Sara Hart, Port Simpson, September 29, 1890, *Missionary Leaflet* 6, 12 (December 1890): 6.
15 Dennis Jennings in "Along the Line," *Missionary Outlook* 2, 12 (December 1882): 189.
16 Letters of January 5, 1875, and February 8, 1876.
17 Jennings in "Along the Line," 189-90.
18 Letter from Alfred E. Green, cited in Crosby, *Up and Down*, 236.
19 Crosby, *Up and Down*, 233.
20 Alfred Dudoward and others to editor, Port Simpson, April 27, 1885, UBCCC.
21 Unsigned draft to unsigned, Ottawa, July 6, 1886, UBCCC.
22 Agnes Knight in WMS, *Annual Report*, 1886, 57.
23 Thomas Crosby to D.V. Lucas, November 20, 1882.
24 Agnes Knight in WMS, *Annual Report*, 1886, 58.

25 Emma Douse to her mother, Hamilton, February 18, 1874, in this volume.
26 Peter Williams points to a fear, within the English Anglican hierarchy, "that their women missionaries would use the new opportunities to forge marriage relationships which they had not been able to make at home." See Peter Williams, "'The Missing Link': The Recruitment of Women Missionaries in Some English Evangelical Missionary Societies in the Nineteenth Century," in Bowie, Kirkwood, and Ardener, *Women and Missionaries*, 43-84, esp. 62.
27 Hendry to unnamed, June 11, 1883.
28 Hendry to her sisters, August 6, 1884.
29 Mrs. Cox, "Pierce, the Halfbreed Missionary," (1914?), in Barbeau Northwest Coast Files, Canadian Centre for Folk Culture Studies, Museum of Civilization, Ottawa, B-F-321-8. We are grateful to Carol Cooper for making this source available to us.
30 Boss, "A Tale of Northern B.C.," 194-5.
31 Susanna Laurence, Nanaimo, May 2, 1890, "British Columbia," *Missionary Outlook* 10, 9 (September 1890): 144.
32 WMS, *Annual Report*, 1901, lxxxvi.
33 Crosby, *Up and Down*, 83.

Bibliography

Manuscript Sources

Barbeau, Marius. Northwest Coast Files. Canadian Centre for Folk Culture Studies, Museum of Civilization, Ottawa.

Bolton, Nellie. Diary. British Columbia Archives, E/C/B631, reel 472A

Boss, Katie O'Neill. Interview with Imbert Orchard, September 9, 1966. British Columbia Archives, tape 1231.

Boss, Martha Washington (O'Neill), "A Tale of Northern B.C. from Cariboo to Cassiar." Typescript. British Columbia Archives, Victoria. Ms. 771.

Canada. Census, 1891. On microfilm.

Canada. Department of Indian Affairs. Correspondence. Department of Indian Affairs, Black Series, RG 10 series on microfilm.

Canada. Post Office. Records. Library and Archives Canada, Ottawa, Post Office Inspectors Reports, RG3, on microfilm.

Crosby, Emma. Correspondence. University of British Columbia, Special Collections, Vancouver, Crosby Collection.

Crosby, Grace. Papers. University of British Columbia, Special Collections, Vancouver, Crosby Collection.

Crosby, Jessie. "Missionary Work in British Columbia" (c. 1893). University of British Columbia, Special Collections, Vancouver, Crosby Collection.

Crosby, Thomas. Correspondence. British Columbia Archives, H/D/R57/C88.

—. Correspondence and Papers. University of British Columbia, Special Collections, Vancouver, Crosby Collection.

Crosby family. Bible. University of British Columbia, Special Collections, Vancouver, Crosby Collection.

Douse, John. Fonds. United Church Archives, Emmanuel College, Victoria University, University of Toronto, Toronto.

—. Miscellaneous correspondence. Library and Archives Canada, Ottawa. MG19-F18.

Dudoward, Caroline. "The Dudowards of Fort Simpson." Paper presented at the Beyond Hope Conference. Kamloops, May 11, 2001.

Dufferin family. Correspondence. Library and Archives Canada, Ottawa, FA127, reel A-420.

Duncan, William. Correspondence and Papers. UBC Library, Duncan Papers on microfilm.

Fort Simpson. School. Register, 1857-60. Duncan Papers, UBC Library, Microfilm #2547, reel 16.

Hendry, Kate. Correspondence. British Columbia Archives, ECH/38.

Methodist Church. Woman's Missionary Society. Records. United Church Archives, Emmanuel College, Victoria University, University of Toronto, Toronto.

Morice, L. "Rev. George Edgar." Typescript. United Church Archives, Vancouver School of Theology, Vancouver, vertical file.

Morison, Charles F. "A Recollection of the Early Days in Northern British Columbia" (1919). Typescript. University of British Columbia, Special Collections, Vancouver, Imbert Orchard Papers, box 2, file 9.

Ogden family. Family tree. British Columbia Archives, vertical files.

Orchard, Robert. Diary. http://members.home.net/billwarnica.

Our Lady of Good Hope Catholic Church, Fort St. James. Records, 1876-1947. British Columbia Archives, reel 22A.

Port Simpson Church. Register, 1874-96. United Church Archives, Vancouver School of Theology, Vancouver.

Pre-confederation marriage records, 1859-1872. British Columbia Archives, GR3044.

Robson, Ebenezer. Diary. British Columbia Archives, H/D/R57, R57.24.

Russ, Agnes (Hubbs) and Grace (Russ) Stevens. Interview with Imbert Orchard, Skidegate, 1962. British Columbia Archives, tape 2442.

St. Andrew's Catholic Church, Victoria. Records, 1849-1934. British Columbia Archives, Add. Ms. 1.

St. Ann's Academy, Victoria, B.C. Pupil Registration, 1858-1923. St. Ann's Archives, Victoria.

Tate, Charles M. "Autosketch of My Life." Typescript. United Church Archives, Vancouver School of Theology, Vancouver.

Vital statistics. British Columbia Archives, Victoria.

Vital statistics. Ontario Provincial Archives, Toronto.

Walker, Agnes Knight. "Narrative of Indian Missionary Adventuring on Quadra Island." Typescript. British Columbia Archives, E7/W15/r A.

–. "Reminiscences of Miss Agnes Knight (later Mrs. R.J. Walker), Bella Bella, Port Simpson and Cape Mudge." Typescript. British Columbia Archives, F7/W15r/A1.

Wesleyan Mission, Fort Simpson. Records, 1874-1912. British Columbia Archives, Reel 31A.

PRINTED SOURCES

Andrews, Charles Leroy. *Wrangell and the Gold of the Cassiar.* Seattle: L. Tinker, 1937.

Arctander, J.W. *The Apostle of Alaska.* New York: Revell, 1909.

Barman, Jean. *Constance Lindsay Skinner: Writing on the Frontier.* Toronto: University of Toronto Press, 2002.

–. *Sojourning Sisters: The Lives and Letters of Jessie and Annie McQueen.* Toronto: University of Toronto Press, 2003.

Beynon, William. "The Tsimshian of Metlakatla, Alaska." *American Anthropologist* 43 (1941): 83-88.

Binns, Archie. *Peter Skene Ogden: Fur Trader.* Portland: Binfords and Mort, 1967.

Bolt, Clarence. *Thomas Crosby and the Tsimshian: Small Shoes for Feet Too Large.* Vancouver: UBC Press, 1992.

Bowie, Fiona, Deborah Kirkwood, and Shirley Ardener, eds. *Women and Missionaries: Past and Present.* Providence, RI: Berg, 1993.

British Columbia, Department of Education. *Annual Report.*

Brock, Peggy. "Building Bridges: Politics and Religion in a First Nations Community." *Canadian Historical Review* 81 (2000): 67-96.

Brouwer, Ruth Compton. *New Women for God: Canadian Presbyterian Women and India Missions, 1876-1914.* Toronto: University of Toronto Press, 1990.

"C.W.D. Clifford (1842-1916)." *Smithers Interior News,* September 19, 1979.

Carey, Hilary M. "Companions in the Wilderness? Missionary Wives in Colonial Australia, 1788-1900." *Journal of Religious History* 19, 2 (1995): 227-48.

"Chief of Tsimpsean Indian Tribe Dead." *Province,* November 12, 1935.

Chittendon, Newton H. *Travels in British Columbia.* Vancouver: Gordon Soules, 1984 [1882].

Cole, Douglas. *Captured Heritage: The Scramble for Northwest Coast Artifacts.* Vancouver: UBC Press, 1995.

Collis, Septima M. *A Woman's Trip to Alaska.* New York: Cassell, 1890.

Collison, William Henry. *In the Wake of the War Canoe.* Charles Lillard, ed. Victoria: Sono Nis, 1981.

"Colorful Indian Character Called to His Forefathers." *Western Recorder,* December 1934.

Cornish, George H. *Cyclopaedia of Methodism in Canada.* Toronto: Methodist Book and Publishing House, 1881.

Craig, Terrence L. *The Missionary Lives: A Study of Canadian Missionary Biography and Autobiography.* Leiden: Brill, 1997.

Crosby, Thomas. *Among the An-ko-me-nums or Flathead Tribes of Indians of the Pacific Coast.* Toronto: William Briggs, 1907.

–. *Up and Down the North Pacific Coast by Canoe and Mission Ship.* Toronto: Missionary Society of the Methodist Church, 1914.

Dalzell, Kathleen E. *The Queen Charlotte Islands, 1774-1966.* Terrace: C.M. Adam, 1968.

Davis, E.A. "The Philosophy of Methodism." In E.A. Davis, ed., *Commemorative Review of the Methodist, Presbyterian and Congregational Churches in British Columbia,* 38-9. Vancouver: Wrigley, 1925.

"Death of Father Douse." *Christian Guardian,* May 12, 1886.

"Death of Mrs. T. Crosby." *Western Recorder* 2, 2 (August 1926).

Dictionary of Hamilton Biography 1. Hamilton: Dictionary of Hamilton Biography, n.d.

Douse, John. *A Register or Alphabetical Arrangement of the Wesleyan Methodist Ministers and Preachers, in connection with the Canada Conference.* Toronto: Guardian, 1853.

Dufferin and Ava, Marchioness of. *My Canadian Journal 1872-78.* London: John Murray, 1891.

Dufferin and Ava, Marquis of. *Journal of the Journey of His Excellency the Governor-General of Canada from Government House, Ottawa, to British Columbia and Back.* London: Webster and Larkin, 1877.

Edwards, Gail. "Creating Textual Communities: Anglican and Methodist Missionaries and Print Culture in British Columbia, 1858, 1914." PhD diss., University of British Columbia, 2001.

Edwards, Gail. "'The Picturesqueness of His Accent and Speech': Methodist Missionary Narratives and William Henry Pierce's Autobiography." In Alvyn Austin and Jamie S. Scott, eds., *Canadian Missions, Indigenous Peoples: Representing Religion at Home and Abroad,* 67-87. Toronto: University of Toronto Press, 2005.

Flemming, Leslie A. *Women's Work for Women: Missionaries and Social Change in Asia.* Boulder: Westview, 1989.

"Founders of B.C." *Victoria Times,* April 22, 1967.

Furtwangler, Albert. *Bringing Indians to the Book.* Seattle: University of Washington Press, 2005.

Gagan, Rosemary R. *A Sensitive Independence: Canadian Methodist Women Missionaries in Canada and the Orient, 1881-1925.* Montreal and Kingston: McGill-Queen's University Press, 1992.

Galois, Robert. "Colonial Encounters: The Worlds of Arthur Wellington Clah, 1855-1881." *BC Studies* 115/116 (1997/98): 105-47.

"Great Missionary of Methodists Is Dead." *Province*, January 15, 1914.

Greenaway, Archibald McDonald. "The Challenge of Port Simpson." B.Div. thesis, Vancouver School of Theology, 1955.

Grimshaw, Patricia. *Paths of Duty: American Missionary Wives in Nineteenth-Century Hawaii*. Honolulu: University of Hawaii Press, 1989.

Hawley, John C., ed. *Historicizing Christian Encounters with the Other*. London: Macmillan, 1998.

Higham, C. L. *Noble, Wretched, and Redeemable: Protestant Missionaries to the Indians in Canada and the United States, 1820-1900*. Calgary: University of Calgary Press, 2000.

Hill, Patricia R. *The World Their Household: The American Woman's Foreign Mission Movement and Cultural Transformation, 1870-1920*. Ann Arbor: University of Michigan Press, 1985.

Hosmer, Brian C. *American Indians in the Marketplace: Persistence and Innovation among the Menominees and Metlakatlans, 1870-1920*. Lawrence: University Press of Kansas, 1999.

Huber, Mary Taylor, and Nancy C. Lutkehaus, eds. *Gendered Missions: Women and Men in Missionary Discourse and Practice*. Ann Arbor: University of Michigan Press, 1999.

Hunter, Andrew. *A History of Simcoe County*. Vol. 1. Barrie, ON: County Council, 1909.

Hunter, Jane. *The Gospel of Gentility: American Women Missionaries in Turn-of-the-Century China*. New Haven: Yale University Press, 1984.

Jackson, Sheldon. *Alaska, and Missions on the North Pacific Coast*. New York: Dodd, Mead & Co., 1880.

Kaplan, Steven, ed. *Indigenous Responses to Western Christianity*. New York: New York University Press, 1995.

Katz, Michael B. *The People of Hamilton, Canada West: Family and Class in a Mid-Nineteenth-Century City*. Cambridge: Harvard University Press, 1975.

Katz, Michael B., Michael J. Doucet, and Mark J. Stern. *The Social Organization of Early Industrial Capitalism*. Cambridge: Harvard University Press, 1982.

Keenleyside, Vi. *They Also Came*. Duncan, BC: Vibook Committee, 1987.

Kirkwood, Deborah. "Protestant Missionary Women: Wives and Spinsters." In Fiona Bowie, Deborah Kirkwood, and Shirley Ardener, eds., *Women and Missionaries: Past and Present*, 23-42. Providence, RI: Berg, 1993.

Large, R. Geddes. *The Skeena: River of Destiny*. Vancouver: Mitchell Press, 1957.

"The Late Dr. Crosby." *Daily News-Advertiser* (Vancouver). January 15, 1914.

Letter from the Methodist Missionary Society to the Superintendent-General of Indian Affairs respecting British Columbia Troubles. Toronto: Methodist Church Missionary Society, 1889.

"Local Lady's Great-Aunt Is 'Grand Old Lady of Q.C.I.'" *Omineca Herald*, July 25, 1952.

Lodwick, Kathleen L. *Educating the Women of Hainan: The Career of Margaret Moninger in China, 1915-1942*. Lexington: University Press of Kentucky, 1995.

Macdonald, Lesley A. Orr. *A Unique and Glorious Mission: Women and Presbyterianism in Scotland, 1830-1930*. Edinburgh: John Donald, 2000.

Marshall, David B. *Secularizing the Faith: Canadian Protestant Clergy and the Crisis of Belief, 1850-1940*. Toronto: University of Toronto Press, 1992.

Mayne, R.C. *Four Years in British Columbia and Vancouver Island*. London: John Murray, 1862, repr. 1969.

Melvin, George H. *The Post Offices of British Columbia, 1858-1970*. Vernon: the author, 1972.

Methodist Church of Canada. *Annual Report.*
–. British Columbia Conference. *Minutes of the Proceedings.* Toronto: William Briggs.
–. Woman's Missionary Society. *Annual Report.*
Methodist General Conference. *Centennial of Canadian Methodism.* Toronto: William Briggs, 1891.
Miller, Jay. *Tsimshian Culture: A Light through the Ages.* Lincoln: University of Nebraska Press, 1997.
Missionary Leaflet. Toronto: Women's Missionary Society.
Missionary Outlook: A Monthly Advocate, Record, and Review. Toronto: Methodist Missionary Society.
Montgomery, Robert L. *Introduction to the Sociology of Missions.* Westport, CT: Praeger, 1999.
Monthly Letter. Toronto: Women's Missionary Society.
Neylan, Susan. "'Eating the Angels' Food': Arthur Wellington Clah – An Aboriginal Perspective on Being Christian, 1857-1909." In Alvyn Austin and Jamie S. Scott, eds., *Canadian Missions, Indigenous Peoples. Representing Religion at Home and Abroad,* 88-108. Toronto: University of Toronto Press, 2005.
–. *The Heavens Are Changing: Nineteenth-Century Protestant Missions and Tsimshian Christianity.* Montreal and Kingston: McGill-Queen's University Press, 2003.
–. "Longhouses, Schoolrooms, and Workers' Cottages: Nineteenth-Century Protestant Missions to the Tsimshian and the Transformation of Class through Religion." *Journal of the Canadian Historical Association* n.s. 11 (2000): 51-86.
O'Neill, Wiggs. "Like the RCMP, Teacher Got Her Man." *Kitimaat Northern Sentinel,* August 13, 1964.
Patterson II, E. Palmer. *Mission on the Nass.* Waterloo: Eulachon Press, 1982.
Perry, Adele. "The Autocracy of Love and the Legitimacy of Empire: Intimacy, Power and Scandal in Nineteenth-Century Metlakahtlah." *Gender and History* 16, 2 (2004): 261-88.
Pierce, William Henry. *From Potlatch to Pulpit.* Vancouver: Vancouver Bindery, 1933.
"Pioneer Missionary to Pacific Dead." *Mail & Empire,* January 15, 1914.
Platt, H.L. *The Story of the Years: A History of the Woman's Missionary Society of the Methodist Church, Canada, from 1881 to 1906.* Vol. 1. Toronto: Methodist Church, 1908.
Porterfield, Amanda. *Mary Lyon and the Mount Holyoke Missionaries.* New York: Oxford University Press, 1997.
Prang, Margaret. *A Heart at Leisure from Itself: Caroline Macdonald of Japan.* Vancouver: UBC Press, 1995.
"Retired B.C. Power Head Dies." *Province,* July 17, 1965.
Robert, Dana L. *American Women in Mission: A Social History of Their Thought and Practice.* Macon GA: Mercer University Press, 1996.
Runnalls, F.E. *It's God's Country: A Review of the United Church and Its Founding Partners, the Congregational, Methodist, and Presbyterian Churches in British Columbia.* Ocean Park, BC: n.p., 1974.
Rutherdale, Myra. "'I Wish the Men Were Half as Good': Gender Constructions in the Canadian North-Western Mission Field, 1860-1940." In Catherine A. Cavanaugh and Randi R. Warne, eds., *Telling Tales: Essays in Western Women's History,* 32-59. Vancouver: UBC Press, 2000.
–. "Mothers of the Empire: Maternal Metaphors in the Northern Canadian Mission Field." In Alvyn Austin and Jamie S. Scott, eds., *Canadian Missions, Indigenous Peoples. Representing Religion at Home and Abroad,* 46-66. Toronto: University of Toronto Press, 2005.

–. "Revisiting Colonization through Gender: Anglican Missionary Women in the Pacific Northwest and the Arctic, 1860-1945." *BC Studies* 104 (1994-95): 3-23.

–. *Women and the White Man's God: Gender and Race in the Canadian Mission Field.* Vancouver: UBC Press, 2002.

Scholefield, E.O.S., and F.W. Howay. *British Columbia from the Earliest Times to the Present.* Vol. 3. Vancouver: S.J. Clarke, 1914.

Scott, Jamie, S. "Penitential and Penitentiary: Native Canadians and Colonial Mission Education." In Jamie S. Scott and Gareth Griffith, eds., *Mixed Messages: Materiality, Textuality, Missions,* 111-33. New York: Palgrave Macmillan, 2005.

–, and Gareth Griffiths. *Mixed Messages: Materiality, Textuality, Missions.* New York: Palgrave Macmillan, 2005.

Scott, Robert C. *My Captain Oliver: A Story of Two Missionaries on the British Columbia Coast.* Toronto: United Church of Canada, 1947.

Seguin, Margaret (Anderson), ed. *The Tsimshian: Images of the Past – Views for the Present.* Vancouver: UBC Press, 1983.

Selles, Johanna M. *Methodists and Women's Education in Ontario, 1836-1925.* Montreal and Kingston: McGill-Queen's University Press, 1996.

Semple, Neil. *The Lord's Dominion: The History of Canadian Methodism.* Montreal and Kingston: McGill-Queen's University Press, 1996.

Semple, Rhonda Anne. *Missionary Women: Gender, Professionalism and the Victorian Idea of Christian Mission.* Woodbridge, GB: Boydell Press, 2003.

Skinner, Constance Lindsay. *Birthright.* Adapted by Joan Bryans. Toronto: Playwrights Canada Press, 2005.

Stephenson, Annie D. (Mrs. Frederick C.). *One Hundred Years of Canadian Methodist Missions, 1824-1924.* Vol. 1. Toronto: Missionary Society of the Methodist Church and Young People's Forward Movement, 1925.

Strachan, E., and W.E. Ross. *The Story of the Years: A History of the Woman's Missionary Society of the Methodist Church, Canada, 1906-1916.* Vol. 3. Toronto: Woman's Missionary Society, Methodist Church, 1917.

Sutherland, Alexander. *Methodism in Canada: Its Work and Its Story.* Toronto: Methodist Mission Rooms, 1904.

Tate, C.M. "Fifty Years with the Methodist Church in British Columbia." In E.A. Davis, ed., *Commemorative Review of the Methodist, Presbyterian and Congregational Churches in British Columbia.* Vancouver: Wrigley, 1925.

Van Kirk, Sylvia. "Tracing the Fortunes of Five Founding Families of Victoria." *BC Studies* 115/16 (1997/98): 148-79.

Varley, Elizabeth Anderson. *Kitimaat My Valley.* Terrace: Northern Times Press, 1981.

Verney, Edmund. *Vancouver Island Letters.* Allan Pritchard, ed. Vancouver: UBC Press, 1996.

Weaver, John C. *Crimes, Constables, and Courts: Order and Transgression in a Canadian City, 1816-1970.* Montreal and Kingston: McGill-Queen's University Press, 1995.

Welter, Barbara. "She Hath Done What She Could: Protestant Women's Missionary Careers in Nineteenth-Century America." In Janet Wilson James, ed., *Women in American Religion,* 111-25. Philadelphia: University of Pennsylvania Press, 1980.

Wesleyan Female College. *Annual Catalogue.* Hamilton: Spectator. Available from Canadian Institute for Historical Microreproductions.

Westfall, William. *Two Worlds: The Protestant Culture of Nineteenth-Century Ontario.* Kingston: McGill-Queen's University Press, 1989.

Whitehead, Margaret. "'Let the Women Keep Silence': Women Missionary Preaching in British Columbia, 1860s-1940s." In Elizabeth Gillan Muir and Marilyn Färdig Whiteley, eds., *Changing Roles of Women within the Christian Church in Canada*, 117-35. Toronto: University of Toronto Press, 1995.

–. "Women Were Made for Such Things: Women Missionaries in British Columbia, 1850s-1940s." *Atlantis* 14, 1 (1988): 141-50.

Williams, Peter. "'The Missing Link': The Recruitment of Women Missionaries in Some English Evangelical Missionary Societies in the Nineteenth Century." In Fiona Bowie, Deborah Kirkwood, and Shirley Ardener, eds., *Women and Missionaries: Past and Present*, 43-84. Providence, RI: Berg, 1993.

Withrow, W.H. *Our Own Country Canada*. Toronto: William Briggs, 1889.

Wright, E.W., ed. *Lewis and Dryden's Marine History of the Pacific Northwest*. New York: Antiquarian Press, 1961.

Yohn, Susan M. *A Contest of Faiths: Missionary Women and Pluralism in the American Southwest*. Ithaca: Cornell University Press, 1995.

Index

Printed and bound in Canada by Friesens

Set in Garamond Pro by Artegraphica Design Co. Ltd.

Text design: Irma Rodriguez

Copy editor: Joanne Richardson

Proofreader and indexer: Dianne Tiefensee

Cartographer: Eric Leinberger